Pleasure and Panic

Pleasure and Panic

New Essays on the History of Alcohol and Drugs

EDITED BY DAN MALLECK AND
CHERYL KRASNICK WARSH

UBCPress · Vancouver · Toronto

31 30 29 28 27 26 25 24 23 22   5 4 3 2 1

Printed in Canada on FSC-certified ancient-forest-free paper (100% post-consumer recycled) that is processed chlorine- and acid-free.

Library and Archives Canada Cataloguing in Publication

Title: Pleasure and panic : new essays on the history of alcohol and drugs / edited by Dan Malleck and Cheryl Krasnick Warsh.
Names: Malleck, Dan, 1968– editor. | Warsh, Cheryl Krasnick, 1957– editor.
Description: Includes bibliographical references and index.
Identifiers: Canadiana (print) 20220213216 | Canadiana (ebook) 20220213305 | ISBN 9780774867511 (hardcover) | ISBN 9780774867528 (paperback) | ISBN 9780774867535 (PDF) | ISBN 9780774867542 (EPUB)
Subjects: LCSH: Drugs of abuse—Canada—History. | LCSH: Drugs of abuse—United States—History.
Classification: LCC RM316 .P54 2022 | DDC 616.86—dc23

Canadä   ·

UBC Press gratefully acknowledges the financial support for our publishing program of the Government of Canada (through the Canada Book Fund), the Canada Council for the Arts, and the British Columbia Arts Council.

Printed and bound in Canada by Friesens
Set in Minion Pro and Helvetica Condensed by Apex CoVantage, LLC
Copy editor: Frank Chow
Indexer: Matthew MacLellan
Cover designer: Alexa Love

UBC Press
The University of British Columbia
2029 West Mall
Vancouver, BC V6T 1Z2
www.ubcpress.ca

Contents

Acknowledgments

This book began as an invited symposium on the history of drugs and alcohol in Canada, held at Vancouver Island University (VIU) in November 2015. We would like to thank all the participants in that symposium, many of whose works are included here. We would also like to thank VIU president emeritus Ralph Nilson for his encouragement, Nicole Vaugeois and the VIU Scholarly Research and Creative Activity office for their financial and conference preparation support, Tim Lewis for History Department support, and the Social Sciences and Humanities Research Council of Canada (SSHRC) for a Connections Grant.

Dan: My thanks to Bonnie (along with Zeeba, Taz, and Moo Moo, as if they care) for much-needed distraction, patience, and compassion. Most especially, my thanks to Cheryl, who has invited me on two collections to share the joys and pains, as it were, of the process. Perhaps by the time this book is in print we will yet again be able to sit in a pub somewhere and toast our work.

Cheryl: My thanks to Michael and Sarah for everything, including showing up to eat at the conference dinners, along with Dylan (as he then was) and Orion (since we are thanking pets). We started this journey before cannabis was legal and completed it when Canadians couldn't enter churches unless they were going to AA meetings in the basement. Thanks to Dan, my collections partner and friend.

Both editors thank the various contributors to this volume for their patience as the complicated process unfolded, and the readers, even the one who didn't understand what we were doing, because they helped strengthen the collection. As ever, we thank the amazing team of editors at UBC Press, whose attention to detail makes us look good.

Pleasure and Panic

Introduction

Problems with Pleasures

Dan Malleck

Mind-altering, mood-changing substances permeate our culture and absorb our attention. We talk about booze, dope, smokes, and weed. There are intoxicants, hallucinogens, psychotropics. You can have a habit, addiction, vice, or dependency. These terms are threaded through our lives, sometimes surreptitiously, often blatantly in mass and social media, weekend parties, and at the local watering hole. Politicians debate cannabis legalization; public health officials scrutinize safe injection sites; police bust illegal drug rings; government officials contemplate broadening tobacco restrictions; community organizations try to address street-level drug use; media wring their hands about dangerous new party drugs; public health officials condemn e-cigarettes and vaping; physicians wrestle with protocols for prescribing addictive opioids. It is an understatement to say that drugs, alcohol, and tobacco modify modern life.

Each of the above narratives draws upon established meanings and values, while forging new ones. Legal or illegal, recreational or medicinal, personal or social, these substances have implications that supersede their chemical or biological effects and that make sense only when we consider historical precedents. Restrictions on non-medical drug use, for example, although they may have occurred in distinct moments in time (when the legislation passed, when regulations were enacted), were the end result of broad change. They were not merely about politicians or officials deciding that the non-medical use of certain drugs should be restricted, but rather the outcome of a combination of factors, including the gradual development of ideas about what it meant to use a substance exclusively for pleasure, the growing medical authority over psychoactive chemicals, and expansive social movements against recreational substance consumption.[1] Moreover, possibly the best-known legislative curtailment of substance use, the liquor prohibition in Canada and the United States in the first part of the twentieth century, was not a moment of cultural madness but the result of the convergence of historical dynamics driven by social movements, industrialization, policy modification, and legal innovations in attempt to contain the effects of drinking and drunkenness on society.[2]

Such stories illustrate how many factors influenced the shift both in popular understanding of drugs and alcohol and in the way governments dealt with them. Ideas about why addiction is considered a problematic state, questions about why governments are interested in regulating or prohibiting substances that simply give pleasure, and the phenomenon of intense social opprobrium directed towards people who consume things for fun: these issues can be informed by looking at the long history of drugs and alcohol. In this way, even so-called designer drugs, however new they are, draw upon earlier understandings of what it means to consume a mind-altering substance. The idea of enjoyment, as philosopher Richard Klein notes, seems illegitimate when it comes to both policy formation and the cultural interpretation of substance consumption.[3] Indeed, the emphasis upon harm reduction to deal with criminalized drug use is based in historical understandings of drug prohibition, informed by sociological theories of deviance, restriction, and criminalization.[4] Such panic-oriented analyses must be paralleled with the understanding of substance use as a pursuit of pleasure, and the production and sale as actual businesses, whether legal or otherwise. This volume examines the different ways that ideas of drink and drugs affected and were affected by the culture in which they were being discussed and observed, and the people who had the power to define fact and value.[5]

Historians normally trace the modern concern with recreational substance use to the rise of temperance sentiment at the beginning of the nineteenth century. The overconsumption of alcoholic beverages had been the focus of periodic moments of panic prior to that time – such as the "Gin

Craze" of the first part of the eighteenth century, which was caused and eased by government regulation and taxation – but the nineteenth century ushered in a sustained push against drink and drunkenness in general.[6] Some historians have linked this with industrialization and the growth of automation in factories, some have seen the temperance movement as a manifestation of status anxiety among a middle-class population that saw its place in society as tenuous. This early temperance movement was literally so: it encouraged moderation, and provided a hierarchy of drinks of varying value or dangers. Benjamin Rush placed beer, porter, cider, and light wines among the valuable beverages, whereas spirits would lead to ruin.[7] American military surgeon Edward Cutbush understood that water was the best beverage for soldiers to drink, but knowing they would not confine themselves to that rather unexciting tipple, listed the benefits of beer, cider, wine, and other beverages, leaving aside, as had Rush, spirits as singularly problematic.[8]

As the movement grew, temperance drew a wide range of adherents. North American evangelicals, inspired by episodic Great Awakenings, saw their role in society as one of actively reforming and elevating their fellow citizens. In the United Kingdom, the teetotal movement was led by liberal reformers who sought to lift their working-class compatriots from the degradation caused by drink. Workers saw a temperate approach to drinking as a pathway to financial stability, and bound together in proto-self-help organizations such as the Washingtonians, to support the weaker of their fellow citizens.[9] Regardless of the origins, by the middle of the century the acceptability of consuming a substance for simple recreational purposes had become suspect. These movements grew and expanded, drawing new participants to a campaign that saw drink as one of the worst dangers and outcomes of industrial society. Places like Manchester, a rapidly growing industrial town, became an epicentre for innovative approaches to temperance. Moreover, women, often sidelined in the early years of the temperance movement, became more socially and politically active, with their socially proscribed role as stewards and protectors of the home serving as justification for their movement into the public realm to protect all homes from liquor. Such efforts were manifested most notably in the creation of the Woman's Christian Temperance Union (WCTU) in North America, which spread around the world (and was affiliated with the British Women's Temperance Association).[10]

Yet alcoholic beverages were not driven from the world, no matter how hard some reformers pushed, and the reason lay in the complicated nature of the substance itself. Many people rejected the "capital-T-total-temperance" view of temperance leaders like Joseph Livesey, and later evangelical groups like the WCTU, the UK Alliance, the Dominion Alliance, and the Anti-Saloon League.[11] Many viewed moderation as a more reasonable approach. So as temperance became equated with abstinence, views hardened. Indeed, alcohol was not viewed as entirely without its virtues. For much of the century, medicinal alcohol was ubiquitous; its many often contradictory physical and neurological effects (it could both stimulate and relax while also warming and giving energy) meant that it remained a valuable component of the *materia medica*.[12] Although they recognized concerns with overdrinking, many physicians saw the benefits of alcohol in precise application, and general usefulness. Even as the century came to an end, and various forms of legislative restriction limited the reach of the liquor industry, medical use was an excepted, and accepted, form of alcohol consumption.[13] This exception caused problems for pharmacists, who were given the authority to sell drink as medicine but did not always colour inside the lines of the law.

The rising temperance movement drove several key changes in the way people viewed substance use for personal recreation. First, pleasurable drinking became constrained. Some argued that there was no good limit of drink, while others, like Dr. Francis Anstie, used research to argue that in fact there was a precise limit of absolute alcohol that could be consumed before it became dangerous.[14] Nevertheless, such measurements were developed in a period when drinking had ceased to be a social norm for many people. Such attitudes leaked into ideas of other substance use. Opium was long known to have habit-forming properties, and many reformers vilified the account of Thomas De Quincey, the "English opium-eater," as encouraging rather than cautioning against recreational opium use. De Quincey's *Confessions of an English Opium-Eater* caused a stir when it was first published in a serialized form in the 1820s. The image of the problematic laudanum drinker, whose drug use began as a combination of therapeutic and recreational application but became pathologized as he was unable to escape the bondage of his habit, provided a trope for pathologized substance use.[15] Combine this with the sense of responsibility that individuals were expected to have for their physical selves, and the rise of a rational recreation movement that encouraged people (especially the working class) to use their leisure time in a productive manner, and the casual use of such substances – opium, brandy, spirits, even beer – became even more problematic.[16]

Nevertheless, it persisted. Brewers and distillers, however much they were in competition with each other, often banded together to resist the pressures of temperance. This was especially the case in the United Kingdom, as the "drinks question" took on a partisan character, with the Tories representing the drinks industry (the wets) and the Liberals supporting temperance (the dries).[17] In North America, such divisions were not so stark, and numerous political parties attempted to play both sides of the field.[18] Nevertheless, it is worth noting that histories of the politics of the drinks industry are much less robust than those of the temperance movement, a phenomenon that may be the result of limited availability of primary sources rather than a lack of activity by the wets. Indeed, the constant failures, or at least limited success, of many prohibition campaigns illustrate how powerful, albeit subtle, the drinks industry's political and social influence could be.

By the end of the nineteenth century, the organizations advocating temperance and lobbying for prohibition had grown into a remarkably robust international movement. Drinking was being constrained, new regulatory approaches were being investigated, and medical organizations to research inebriety and develop ways to treat it had begun to unite the concerns over drinking and those over drug habits. Combined with these movements, new drugs that held tremendous therapeutic promise quickly transmogrified into social menace of their own. First cocaine, lauded as a valuable stimulant and potential treatment for opium and alcohol habits, and later heroin, an opioid that was originally believed to be a non-addictive replacement for morphine and a treatment for the habit, joined opium and alcohol as problematic substances.[19] Many laws that restricted drug use, and also laws that placed restrictions on the expansion of the proprietary medicine industry, focused on opiates (including morphine and heroin), cocaine, and alcohol as the three worst problems in a generally unregulated industry.[20]

These issues of predominantly domestic drug use were intricately connected to a broad international concern about opium smoking in Asia. First discussed by evangelical missionaries in Asia and then exacerbated by the British imposition of opium trade in China, the opium traffic inspired a large anti-opium movement first in Great Britain and later across the globe.[21] With Chinese people immigrating around the world, often as low-paid labour in dangerous workplaces like mines and railways and as sailors in port cities, concern about the introduction of opium smoking to "white" populations intensified concern about the recreational use of drugs. As several historians have explained, western observers did not accept the possibility that Chinese people smoked opium for therapeutic purposes, and instead saw opium smoking as an indication of the degraded state of the Chinese as a race.[22] Thus, numerous early anti-opium laws began as bans on opium used for smoking laws. In Australia, this had a further racial component since the first anti-opium law was a prohibition on selling to indigenous people. By the end of the first decade of the twentieth century, laws banning opium smoking were in place in Australia (1905), Canada (1908), the United States (1909), and elsewhere.[23]

Heavy restrictions on opium for non-medical use were part of a pattern of increased restriction on recreational substance use in general. Local option laws allowed municipalities to prohibit the sale of alcoholic beverages, and also placed restrictions on the sale of medicinal alcohol. In the United States, some states implemented prohibition through constitutional amendments.[24] During the First World War, the United Kingdom instituted as tight state management of liquor sales, something unheard of before the war and quickly dismantled when it ended.[25] Canada passed prohibition legislation in 1917, although many provinces had already enacted prohibitory laws of their own.[26] This prohibition persisted in many provinces after the war. Canadian prohibition was limited, however, allowing liquor to be manufactured as long as it was sold in large quantities or shipped outside the province. American prohibition came in the form of a constitutional amendment, so manufacture was also prohibited. When prohibition ended in Canada, provincial governments introduced government-run distribution systems (not unlike the one that the United Kingdom had put in place during the war).[27] In the United States, the end of prohibition resulted, in many states, in a much more liberal system.[28]

By this time, there was no longer a question in the minds of most legislators that the recreational use of drugs was not to be sanctioned, and that the recreational use of liquor was acceptable but within specific and narrowing parameters. In Canada, provincial licensing boards created regulations about how, when, and by whom liquor could be sold, but were dedicated to instilling a responsible relationship with drink in the citizenry. At the same time, the beverage industry doubled down on its self-image as responsible, moderation-minded corporate citizens, with campaigns such as Seagram's "Pay Your Bills First" advertisements reinforcing this message.[29] Industry representing respectable drinking, individuals encouraged to drink less and more responsibly, public health reminding us of the apparent dangers of drinking: Michel Foucault would call the process "biopolitics," which actively encouraged people to represent good citizenship through the way they used and treated their bodies. Here drinking and using drugs, even personal consumption and in private, was a statement about one's citizenship.[30]

As the century progressed, drug and alcohol use, although treated differently, continued to share elements of constraint based upon the views of regulatory officials. In the case of new drugs, such as lysergic acid diethylamide (LSD) and the re-emergence of older drugs such as cannabis, governments identified indulgence as problematic without considered investigation, and attempted to restrain their use. Nevertheless, these drugs and their consumers were part of a broader cultural shift, a movement away from older ways of viewing the self and the management of the individual within society. The use of such drugs was therefore seen as a necessary manifestation of countercultural identity. In a world where many people saw authority as overbearing and illiberal, the use of drugs to "free the mind" was both a cultural marker of individualism and a break from earlier regulated constraints.[31] Governments hoping to address this phenomenon needed to place it in its cultural box, and often saw drug use, regardless of the effect of the drugs, as deeply problematic. Such ideas were based in earlier notions of the dangers of opium and cocaine, and the movement to curtail the damage caused by drunkenness.

As this historical overview has illustrated, the negative connotations of drugs and counterculture have deep roots in social movements concerned with the consumption of mind-altering substances, especially by young people, as endangering society. One of the fears generated by opium dens was over the potential for young westerners to become corrupted: it was a key conceit in fiction such as Oscar Wilde's *The Picture of Dorian Gray* and other, less elegant and more alarmist propaganda and yellow journalism through the nineteenth century and into the twentieth.[32] By the 1960s, drug users represented, either through criminalization and labelling or the appeal of escapism in a politically troubled decade, an alternative way of viewing the world. Although the sixties are often remembered fondly as a quirky time of change, counterculture was a manifestation of anti-authoritarian critiques of power and authority. To the hegemon, such critiques were likely more threatening than the drug use itself. Yet here drug use represented the same kinds of decline and moral catastrophe that the temperance movement saw in drunkenness a century earlier and · reformers implied in the opium dens. The connection of drunkenness with economic and moral decline from the 1820s onward were not casual observations; to many people they were genuine and imminent dangers to society. In this way, we see continuity across time and substance. Thus, when authorities observed the drug use at music festivals, or when an artsy hippie community manifested itself in New York City's Greenwich Village or Toronto's Yorkville, or officials interviewed John Lennon and Yoko Ono during their pot-scented "Bed-ins for Peace," they saw genuine threats to the social order on brazen display.

Much of the history of drugs and alcohol has focused on these substances as problems, rather than as commodities people have enjoyed for centuries. Whether it was nineteenth-century concerns over drunkenness, iatrogenic opium use, Chinese opium smoking, or patent medicines; or twentieth-century concerns over cannabis, LSD, and counterculture itself, histories of drugs and alcohol have tended to reiterate the problem framework in which these substances were widely discussed. Less prominent have been the academic histories of production. Outside of official histories of pharmaceutical companies and pharmacies, the business side of opium and other drugs is difficult to uncover given the illicit nature of these substances from the beginning of the twentieth century, and thus the tendency of producers not to leave a paper trail. There has been more work on the history of alcohol, however. Much of it has been written by amateur historians with an eye to hagiography or celebratory studies of brewers and distillers, but some more nuanced research on the alcoholic beverage industry has emerged. More recently, scholars have begun engaging in detailed and sophisticated examinations of several key beverage industries, both as businesses themselves and as they reacted against the predations of temperance.[33] In the United Kingdom, this was an especially potent field, since the temperance movement and the drinks industry coalesced around different political parties and solutions to the drink question normally involved market-based strategies to reduce consumption rather than prohibition.[34] The drinks industry in the United Kingdom was more openly allied against temperance than the industries in Canada and the United States, although this apparent phenomenon may also be the result of a dearth of evidence for North American jurisdictions rather than actually different historical patterns. The wets, be they individuals with an economic interest in the continued sale of liquor or individuals who simply saw prohibition as antithetical to liberty and liberal governance, were able at times to unite and actively repel prohibitionist campaigns, especially against local option (the process whereby electors in individual municipalities voted their communities dry).[35]

In the last decades of the twentieth century and into the twenty-first, new legal approaches to drugs and alcohol have begun to reconsider strict prohibition and overly stringent criminal regimes. Some of this is the result of public health advocates' efforts to push for harm reduction, an approach that recognizes that most of the worst harms of illegal drug use are the product of prohibition rather than characteristics of the drugs themselves. Needle exchanges and safe injection sites, begun by activists and supported at times by the courts, changed understandings of drug use and, more crucially, affected a perception of criminalization as more harmful than helpful. Moreover, activists for cannabis decriminalization contrasted their drug of choice with legal intoxicants (usually alcohol and tobacco) and argued that "Mary Jane" was a friend, had numerous medical applications, and moreover could treat conditions that were eluding contemporary pharmacology. As a result, both harm reduction and cannabis activism began to change public perceptions of these drugs and led to concerted discussion about the problems of criminalization. In Canada, as early as the 1970s the Royal Commission on the Non-medical Use of Drugs (the Le Dain Commission) argued that cannabis criminalization made no sense and that it would be better to decriminalize.[36] Subsequent Conservative governments have tended to roll back discussion on drugs, pushing it further into the problem framework. Thus Prime Minister Stephen Harper's argument that harm reduction was meaningless because taking drugs was harmful and you couldn't reduce harm while allowing people to do harmful things was part of an attempt to dismantle the InSite safe injection clinic by deploying discourses rooted in established moral categories of drug use shaped by prohibition.[37] These attempts failed because the advocates for InSite argued successfully before the Supreme Court of Canada that InSite was vital to the protection of "life and the security of the person" provisions of the Canadian Charter of Rights and Freedoms. In a 9–0 decision, the justices ruled that the government needed to pay attention to "the balance between achieving public health and public safety."[38] Health was a key consideration in rewriting national drug laws.

Ironically, the public health arguments that so heavily influenced the change in attitudes about drug criminalization have often been used to restrict and heavily curtail access to a range of intoxicants. Bolstered by the success in banning smoking in public places, health campaigners have turned their eyes to restrictions on alcohol. The smoking bans came about when public health advocates were able to recast arguments about the freedom to smoke into arguments about the freedom to be smoke-free. Liberty was involved in both, but the freedom to smoke in public was presented as imposing upon the same sorts of freedom for "life and the security of the person" because of the demonstrated carcinogenic effects of second-hand smoke (also called passive smoking).[39] Yet as British libertarian economist Christopher Snowden has argued, the success of the campaign against second-hand smoke has emboldened reformers to reach further into the lives of individuals. Fat, sugar, salt, and alcohol were placed into the same type of problem framework that succeeded for tobacco.[40] Various states and provinces have contemplated or enacted various labelling restrictions on alcohol, including warning labels similar to those on cigarette packages, and signs in bars warning women that drinking will harm your child, notwithstanding the more nuanced understanding provided by research on drinking while pregnant suggesting that heavy and persistent drinking was the real problem.[41]

Such mission creep by an increasingly activist public health industry also infected discourse around cannabis legalization in Canada. Advocacy for legalizing the medical use of cannabis, enabling people with conditions ranging from glaucoma to cancer to post-traumatic stress disorder to use it for therapeutic purposes with a doctor's approval, further softened opposition to its continued criminalization. If something could do that much good, the argument went, how could it be so bad? This health-focused impetus persisted in the Liberal Party of Canada's support for full legalization of non-medical cannabis. The two main justifications reiterated that balance of public safety and public health, with the prime minister, the health minister, and the public safety minister all explaining that it would undercut criminal gangs and keep cannabis out of the hands of children, while following "public health principles." Consequently, policy briefs from various sectors across the country emphasized the potential health harms of cannabis consumption. That fine line seemed impossible to tread.

In many ways, the stories of tobacco restriction, cannabis legalization, and the harm reduction strategies of safe injection sites harken back to Victorian-era temperance. None too subtly, the temperance movement argued that pleasure for pleasure's sake was antithetical to realizing the moral nation. This was especially an argument of evangelical Protestant temperance advocates (in Canada, the temperance movement was dominated by Methodists), who were at the centre of the push for legislated prohibition. Nevertheless, with an eye towards personal temperance, establishment churches (Anglican and Roman Catholic) also urged their members to practise moderation in all things.[42] Controlling human passions was central to Christian theology, and pleasure for pleasure's sake was a distraction from good self-discipline and restraint. Such condemnation of pleasure seeking through substance consumption remains, but morality is replaced by health, and responsible citizens are expected to protect and nurture their health, thus embodying the ideals of the state as law-abiding moderate consumers of such substances. As long as drugs and alcohol are framed as undermining that bodily integrity, they will continue to be looked at askance.

Connecting the Essays

This collection assembles new work by emerging and established scholars studying drugs and alcohol in history, to explore some of the connections and disconnections between the stories. It emerged from a symposium held at Vancouver Island University in which each researcher's work was discussed in detail. In the process of discussion and reflection, valuable interconnections and patterns emerged. Current arguments over medical and recreational cannabis are reflected in stories of advocacy for medical heroin in hospice care and in debates among pharmacists over how to deal with restrictions on medical liquor. The nuances in contemporary debates about the role of government in regulating and managing individual substance use appear in stories of nineteenth-century brewery adulteration cases and the twentieth-century Le Dain Commission inquiry into recreational drug use. What on the surface seem to be disparate topics, then, emerge in connections previously unforeseen. Such thematic convergences are essential components of historical and, we contend, contemporary understanding of the complex issue of substance misuse, abuse, regulation, and restriction in our society.

Although a variety of mind-altering substances have been part of human society for millennia, alcohol has been arguably the most contested in the Anglo-American world for the past few centuries. Essays by Jonathan Reinarz and Matthew Bellamy consider how the brewing industry dealt with competition and regulation. Reinarz looks at a seemingly odd case of challenges to the British brewery Flowers when rumours circulated that the brewery used horse meat in the brewing process. He expertly teases out the way that such charges can gain traction, and how the brewery reacted to the suspicions of what can only be considered distasteful and problematic modification to its beer. The story connects to issues of adulteration, both industry and government regulation over the process of brewing, and the cultural meaning of horses in British society. Bellamy looks at the brewing industry in Canada roughly a century later. Whereas Reinarz considers the travails of a single brewery in the face of challenges in a highly competitive market, Bellamy looks at how the brewing industry itself reacted to and collaborated to help shape government regulation of its businesses. In the decades after liquor prohibition in Canada, brewers, more than distillers and vintners, used their considerable clout to ensure that Canadians could have easy and unfettered access to their products, and that government regulations stayed out of the way.

Government regulation can reveal any number of cultural and social idiosyncrasies, and Sarah Hamill's study of liquor regulation and race in post-prohibition Alberta demonstrates the complexity of social assumptions in the face of community realities. Liquor regulations forbad Chinese Canadians from holding a liquor licence, yet Hamill's work explores an exception to that rule, and how it reveals both ongoing racial tensions between Chinese and non-Chinese residents and also the bureaucratic machinations that often led to adjustments in the rules according to local community needs and demands. Connections between race and drink in Canada usually involve discussions of Indigenous people and alcohol use, which was heavily restricted prior to the 1950s. But racial restrictions were fluid. Indigenous soldiers who entered Ontario beverage rooms were sometimes permitted to drink despite legal prohibitions, because their race was considered by staff and regulators to be eclipsed by their status as soldiers (itself a problematic category of drinker, as Renée Lafferty-Salhany notes in her chapter).[43] Similarly, in Hamill's work the Chinese hotelkeeper should not have been granted a licence to sell liquor, but he was a well-respected member of the community and considered such an excellent licensee that authorities made an exception. His racial difference was not as important as his ability to conform to expectations of the state. Nevertheless, when he attempted to expand his business, his outsider status trumped his respectable comportment.

The challenge of liquor regulation stemmed from the embedded ideas about the dangers of liquor. Many of these were shaped by the temperance movements of the nineteenth and early twentieth centuries. Yet just as the complexity of brewing and regulation reveals the story to be more nuanced than popular notions might suggest, so the story of the temperance movement has many facets. Cynthia Belaskie's chapter on the activities of the Manchester branch of the British Women's Christian Temperance Association (WCTA) explores how the members of this organization sought to affect the politics of the community to facilitate more temperance-oriented public policies. The women of the WCTA undertook a broad array of activities, some of which, such as working with the families of drunks, were well within the accepted work of active community-minded middle-class women. Other activities, however, such as lobbying and organizing around local politics, took the women into less traditional areas, in which some felt comfortable whereas others were unsure of their proper role.

Women and drink have been an oft-analyzed topic, and the images of the fallen woman, the pathetic wife of a drinker, and the noble rescuer of the downtrodden are three tropes that have appeared constantly in literature against drinking. Building upon her classic examination of the perceptions of women drinkers in Victorian and Edwardian Canada, Cheryl Krasnick Warsh explores the way that women who were "under the influence" have been viewed from the middle of the nineteenth century up to the present. She explodes the simplified tropes of women who embodied virtue, victim, or vixen. Most notably, she explores how medicinal alcohol complicated the issue of women and drink, and how medicine legitimized certain forms of drinking as well as drug consumption, but also how such substance use could lead to other forms of illness and deviance. Warsh's original 1993 essay inspired extensive discussion for a generation of students, and its expansion here should engender ongoing discussion of society's complicated understanding of women, drink, and drugs.

Women drinkers were considered to be a problem because drinking was anathema to womanhood, but when looking at soldiers and drink, issues of gender and respectability have a different meaning. In Lafferty-Salhany's examination of ideas of drink in the armies of the War of 1812, issues of physiology of drink, respectable manhood, proper soldiering, and military camaraderie all intersect in a complex appreciation of the meaning of drink in a military context. Much of the medical knowledge of alcohol discussed by US military physician James Mann was based upon observation of the use of alcohol in the military setting, extant physiological and philosophical understandings of the body and its processes, and the physician's distaste for liquor as anything but a medicine. This in turn shaped his ideas on how to reform the army, both with regard to the drinking practices of officers and enlisted men and in the authority granted to medical personnel to effect change.

The medicinal quality of liquor discussed by James Mann featured in many discussions of drink in culture, and Dan Malleck's essay on the way pharmacists dealt with restrictions on liquor sales demonstrates that regulation of liquor was often accompanied by intensely fraught discussions of its medical usefulness. In Ontario from the 1870s, government regulation of liquor reached into medical chests and pharmacy storerooms, restricting sales, limiting access, and, in the views of pharmacists, challenging their professional autonomy. At the heart of the issue was who determined the proper medical use of liquor, who could sell it, and when such medical use transmogrified into deviant consumption. It would have been a much less problematic issue if all pharmacists fit the idealized notion of a professional gentleman that the pharmacy leadership envisioned, but many pharmacists were interested in maintaining profitable businesses first, and following some idealized notion of a noble profession second, or third, or fourth. So inside and outside the pharmacy profession, the issue of medicinal liquor sales challenged both the professional identity and sometimes the financial viability of neighbourhood pharmacists.

Purchased at the pharmacy, alcohol was a medicine, in effect a drug dispensed to treat illness. Indeed, the twentieth-century drug laws restricting access to psychotropic substances were rooted in the pharmacy laws of the nineteenth century. Yet these medicinal roots often disappeared as the century progressed. In the last half of that century, and into the twenty-first, the easy, often simplistic, and clearly socially framed distinction between legal and illegal, medicinal and recreational, and legitimate and illegitimate substance use came under increasing scrutiny. In Canada in the late 1960s and early 1970s, official investigations of non-medical drug use revealed many of the challenges to government action. The association between drug use and people considered part of a deviant subclass was challenged by examinations of casual usage and the power of celebrity. Eric Fillion's chapter on surveillance of drug use in youth counterculture explores how some governmental and non-governmental agencies sought to define youth counterculture and its drug use. Fillion considers the formation of knowledge through such agencies as the print media and police, and how this knowledge was structured by the authority of the observers. This in turn drove certain ways of viewing and challenging youth drug use. These authoritative voices then attempted to drive the narrative of the Le Dain Commission, with a certain degree of success.

But the Le Dain Commission was not singular in its investigation, and other voices, whose authority was rooted in popular culture, also held sway. As Greg Marquis's chapter demonstrates, the commissioners were not immune to the power of celebrity. Their interviews with John Lennon and Yoko Ono during their iconic Bed-in at the Queen Elizabeth Hotel in Montreal helped provide additional perspectives on the use of recreational drugs, and the ways that such drugs are framed by various agencies, voices, and ideals. Marquis demonstrates the intersection of popular culture, drug use, and government regulation, and the importance of understanding this remarkable cultural shift. Lennon and Ono were symbolic of this cultural moment, and it was not the cult of personality but rather cultural personification that encouraged the commissioners to seek the input of international superstars.

Discussions of drug use and the cultures of drugs can often be romanticized along with the popular culture in which it often takes place, but drug use was neither a throwaway behaviour nor one of marginal importance. Counterculture activists may have used drugs, but the drugs they used, as with alcohol a century earlier, were often also medicines. LSD is a good example of this, emerging as it did from pharmaceutical attempts to address psychotropic illnesses such a schizophrenia, and only then gaining the attention of the counterculture as a way of "expanding the mind."[44] This tension between medicine and recreation was exacerbated when activists attempted to treat the problems created by psychotropic drug use. Christian Elcock's examination of the Chicago LSD Rescue Service and its founder, George Peters, is a study of the challenges that groups who attempted to mitigate some of the harms of drug use faced in the early years of harm reduction. Peters's efforts involved skating on the margins of legality, often acting illegally, and all in the interest of the welfare of individuals whose drug use led them into dangers. Peters's work involved both myth debunking and political activities to help those whose experience with drugs was not the romanticized experience of mind expansion touted by people like Timothy Leary. It was an important struggle to reframe drug use as something that should not just be ignored or demonized, but may even require help and thoughtful strategies to avoid the worst excesses of drug use.

Complicating Themes

In assembling this collection, we had numerous debates about how best to arrange the essays, debates rooted in the social and cultural complexity of drugs and alcohol. A careful reader of this introduction will see how other connections could be made, other groupings formed, and other themes explored. On a broad level, many of these essays illustrate the perpetual tension between things that are legal but unsavoury or culturally marginal, and those that are illegal but culturally appropriate. For example, drinking alcohol might be legal, but when, if ever, was excessive consumption considered appropriate? Consuming certain drugs might be illegal, but within certain subcultures it might be entirely appropriate or expected. In some jurisdictions, cannabis might be legal when administered under a physician's professional scrutiny, but not when self-administered, even if it is for the same neurological experience. John Burnham captured this tension in *Bad Habits,* exploring how the "vice constellation" connects a variety of activities (smoking, drinking, swearing, gambling, drug taking, and sexual impropriety) with overlapping notions of legality and propriety.[45] Illegal gambling was connected to drinking and smoking, drinking to illegal prostitution, and all activities to swearing, which was not illegal but was socially distasteful (and, depending upon the words used, possibly even illegal, or at least immoral). David Courtwright has recently examined these activities as forms of "limbic capitalism," with big business harnessing the reward systems in the human brain for profit: to drugs, alcohol, sugar, and tobacco he adds gambling, pornography, Internet gaming, and numerous other apparently addictive activities.[46] Whenever we consider substances that have some accepted application but can be also used for pleasure, we encounter such complicated considerations. It is beyond the scope of this introduction to cover all such connections, but we encourage readers to think about how both the context of and reason for an individual's use of a substance informs and drives the meaning of that use. Medical versus non-medical, public versus private, therapeutic versus recreational, amateur versus professional – these are some of the many interconnections and thematic overlaps that inform the structure and inclusion of essays in this collection. Given how the histories of substances are often histories of this tension between proper and improper use and misuse, and the meaning of that use, whether it is drinking soldiers or drinking women, pot-smoking rock stars or pot-smoking hippies or an LSD-using subclass, liquor-vending pharmacists or liquor-selling Albertans of Chinese origin, these substances, sought for recreation, medication, socialization, and palliation, remain problematic pleasures.

Notes

1 Virginia Berridge, *Opium and the People: Opiate Use and Drug Control Policy in Nineteenth and Early Twentieth Century England* (London: Free Association Books,

1999); David Musto, *The American Disease: Origins of Narcotic Control,* 3rd ed. (New York: Oxford University Press, 1999); Dan Malleck, *When Good Drugs Go Bad: Opium, Medicine, and the Origins of Canada's Drug Laws* (Vancouver: UBC Press, 2015); Desmond Manderson, *From Mr. Sin to Mr. Big: A History of Australian Drug Laws* (Oxford and Melbourne: Oxford University Press, 1993).

2 Craig Heron, *Booze: A Distilled History* (Toronto: Between the Lines, 2003); Ann-Marie E. Szymanski, *Pathways to Prohibition: Radicals, Moderates, and Social Movement Outcomes* (Durham: Duke University Press, 2003).

3 Richard Klein, *Cigarettes Are Sublime* (Durham, NC: Duke University Press: 1993); Richard Klein, "What Is Health and How Do You Get It?" in *Against Health: How Health Became the New Morality,* ed. Jonathan Metzl and Anna Kirkland (New York: NYU Press, 2010), 15–25.

4 A good amount of this came about through the work of people like Robin Room and his colleagues at the Addiction Research Foundation.

5 Paul Starr uses the term "define fact and value" in explaining Max Weber's notion of cultural authority. Starr applies it in his analysis of the rise of the US medical profession but suggests that this authority was limited. Paul Starr, *The Social Transformation of American Medicine: The Rise of a Sovereign Profession and the Making of a Vast Industry* (New York: Basic Books, 1982).

6 Patrick Dillon, *Gin: The Much-Lamented Death of Madam Geneva* (Boston: Justin Charles and Company, 2002); Jessica Warner, *Craze: Gin and Debauchery in an Age of Reason* (New York: Basic Books, 2002). On the push for regulation, see Dan Malleck, "Regulation and Prohibition," in *A Cultural History of Alcohol in the Age of Industry, Empire and War, 1850–1950,* ed. Deborah Toner (London: Bloomsbury Academic Press, 2021): 65–86.

7 Harry G. Levine, "The Discovery of Addiction: Changing Conceptions of Habitual Drunkenness in America," *Journal of Studies on Alcohol* 15 (1978): 493–506. On debates about the primacy of Rush, see Roy Porter, "The Drinking Man's Disease: The 'Pre-History' of Alcoholism in Georgian Britain," *British Journal of Addiction* 80 (1985): 385–96; Jessica Warner, "'Resolv'd to Drink No More': Addiction as a Preindustrial Construct," *Journal of Studies on Alcoholism* 55 (November 1994): 685–90; Peter Ferentzy, "From Sin to Disease: Differences and Similarities between Past and Current Conceptions of Chronic Drunkenness," *Contemporary Drug Problems* 28 (Fall 2001): 363–90; James Nicholls, "Vinum Britannicum: The 'Drink Question' in Early Modern England," *Social History of Alcohol and Drugs* 22 (Spring 2008): 6–25.

8 Edward Cutbush, *Observations on the Means of Preserving the Health of Soldiers and Sailors* (Philadelphia: Thomas Dobson, 1808).

9 William White, *Slaying the Dragon: The History of Addiction Treatment and Recovery in America* (Bloomington IL: Chestnut Health Systems, 1998) 8–14; Katherine Chauvigny, "Reforming Drunkards in Nineteenth Century America: Religion, Medicine, Therapy," in *Altering American Consciousness: The History of Alcohol and Drug Use*

in the United States, 1800–2000, ed. Sarah Tracey and Caroline Jean Acker (Amherst and Boston: University of Massachusetts Press, 2004), 108–23; Crowley and White, *Drunkard's Refuge: The Lessons of the New York State Inebriate Asylum* (Amherst: University of Massachusetts Press, 2004), 8–10. For a hagiographic examination of the Washingtonians, see Christopher M. Finan, *Drunks: An American History* (Boston: Beacon Press, 2017): 25–53.

10 Ruth Bordin, *Women and Temperance: The Quest for Power and Liberty, 1873–1900* (Philadelphia: Temple University Press, 1981); Jack S. Blocker Jr., *American Temperance Movements: Cycles of Reform* (Boston: Twayne Press, 1987); Barbara Epstein, *The Politics of Domesticity: Women, Evangelism, and Temperance in Nineteenth-Century America* (Middletown, CT: Wesleyan University Press, 1981); Carol Mattingly, *Well Tempered Women: Nineteenth Century Temperance Rhetoric* (Carbondale: Southern Illinois University Press, 1998); Jack S. Blocker Jr., *Give to the Winds Thy Fears: The Women's Temperance Crusade, 1873–1874* (Westport, CT: Greenwood Press, 1985); Sharon Anne Cook, *Through Sunshine and Shadow: The Woman's Christian Temperance Union, Evangelicalism, and Reform in Ontario, 1874–1930* (Montreal and Kingston: McGill-Queen's University Press, 1995); Ian Tyrrell, *Women's World/Women's Empire: The Woman's Christian Temperance Union in International Perspective, 1880–1930* (Chapel Hill, NC: University of North Carolina Press, 1991). There is some evidence that women were not as prominent in temperance politics as the historiography might indicate. See Darren Ferry, ch. 3 in *Uniting in Measures of Common Good: The Construction of Liberal Identities in Central Canada* (Montreal and Kingston: McGill-Queen's University Press, 2008); Dan Malleck "The Problem with the Problem of Alcohol in Canada's History," *Intersections* 3.3 (Fall 2020): 11–12.

11 Annemarie McAllister, *Demon Drink? Temperance and the Working Class* (Kindle edition, 2014); Brian Harrison, *Drink and the Victorians: The Temperance Question in England, 1815–1872* (London: Faber and Faber, 1971).

12 See Harry W. Paul, *Bacchic Medicine: Wine and Alcohol Therapies from Napoleon to the French Paradox* Clio Medica: Studies in the History of Medicine and Health Series (Amsterdam: Brill Rodopi, 2001).

13 Normally, liquor laws made special exemption for alcohol for medicinal, scientific, industrial, and sacramental uses.

14 Francis E. Anstie, *On the Uses of Wines in Health and Disease* (New York: J.S. Redfield, 1870); Arthur Baldwin, "Anstie's Alcohol Limit: Francis Edmund Anstie, 1833–1874," *American Journal of Public Health* 67 (July 1977): 679–81; James Kneale and Shaun French, "Moderate Drinking before the Unit: Medicine and Life Assurance in Britain and the US c.1860–1930," *Drugs: Education., Prevention and Policy,* 22 (2015): 111–17.

15 Berridge, *Opium and the People;* Alethea Hayter, *Opium and the Romantic Imagination* (London: Faber and Faber, 1968); Howard Padwa, *Social Poison: The Culture and Politics of Opiate Control in Britain and France* (Baltimore: Johns Hopkins University Press, 2012).

16 Peter Bailey, *Leisure and Class in Victorian England: Rational Recreation and the Contest for Control, 1830–1885* (New York: Methuen, 1978, 1987).

17 John Greenaway, *Drink and British Politics since 1830* (Basingstoke, UK: Palgrave Macmillan, 2003); David W. Gutzke, *Protecting the Pub: Brewers and Publicans against Temperance* (London: Royal Historical Society, 1989); James Nicholls, *Politics of Alcohol: A History of the Drink Question in England* (Manchester: University of Manchester Press, 2009).

18 Szymanski, *Pathways to Prohibition;* Blocker, *American Temperance Movements.*

19 Joseph Spillane, *Cocaine: From Medical Marvel to Modern Menace in the United States, 1884–1920* (Baltimore: Johns Hopkins University Press, 2000).

20 See Dan Malleck, "Proprietary Medicines and the Nation's Health," ch. 7 in *When Good Drugs Go Bad,* 167–93; Dan Malleck, "Regulating Proprietary Medicines," ch. 8 in *When Good Drugs Go Bad,* 194–213; Dan Malleck, "Pure Drugs and Professional Druggists: Food and Drug Laws in Canada, 1870s–1908," *Pharmacy in History* 48 (2006): 103–15; John Parascandola, "Patent Medicines in Nineteenth-Century America," *Caduceus* 1 (Spring 1985): 1–41; R.G. Guest, "The Development of Patent Medicine Legislation," *Applied Therapeutics* 8, 9 (September 1966): 786–89; Glenn F. Murray, "Cocaine Use in the Era of Social Reform: The Natural History of a Social Problem in Canada, 1880–1911," *Canadian Journal of Law and Society* 2 (1987): 29–43; Glenn F. Murray, "The Road to Regulation: Patent Medicines in Canada in Historical Perspective," in *Illicit Drugs in Canada: A Risky Business,* ed. Judith C. Blackwell and Patricia G. Erikson (Toronto: Nelson Canada, 1988), 72–87.

21 Berridge, *Opium and the People,* 173–205; David Edward Owen, *British Opium Policy in China and India* (Cambridge: Yale University Press, 1934); David Anthony Bello, *Opium and the Limits of Empire: Drug Prohibition in the Chinese Interior, 1729–1850* (Cambridge, MA: Harvard University Press, 2005); Harry G. Gelber, *Opium, Soldiers and Evangelicals: Britain's 1840–42 War with China, and Its Aftermath* (Basingstoke, UK: Palgrave Macmillan, 2004); Julia Lovell, *The Opium War: Drugs, Dreams and the Making of China* (London: Picador, 2011).

22 This perspective has been scrutinized in some detail by Yangwen Zheng, *The Social Life of Opium in China* (Cambridge: Cambridge University Press, 2005); Frank Dikötter, Lars Laamann, and Zhou Xun, *Narcotic Culture: A History of Drugs in China* (Hong Kong: Hong Kong University Press, 2004); Richard Newman, "Opium Smoking in Late Imperial China: A Reconsideration," *Modern Asian Studies* 29 (1995): 765–94.

23 The US law was a weak approach to legislation; the more significant law was the Harrison Act of 1914. Musto, *The American Disease,* 24–48.

24 See Szymanski, *Pathways to Prohibition;* Blocker, *Retreat from Reform: The Prohibition Movement in the United States, 1890–1913* (Westport CT: Greenwood Press, 1976).

25 Robert Duncan, *Pubs and Patriots: The Drink Crisis in Britain during World War One* (Liverpool: University of Liverpool Press, 2013).

26 Heron, *Booze,* 235–66.

27 Ibid., 269–96.

28 Twiley Wendell Barker Jr., *State Liquor Monopolies in the United States* (PhD diss., University of Illinois, 1965).

29 Lisa Jacobson, "Navigating the Boundaries of Respectability and Desire: Seagram's Advertising and the Meaning of Moderation after Repeal," *Social History of Alcohol and Drugs* 26 (Summer 2012): 122–46.

30 On liquor control and biopolitics, see Dan Malleck, *Try to Control Yourself: The Regulation of Public Drinking in Post-Prohibition Ontario* (Vancouver: UBC Press, 2012), especially the introduction.

31 Marcel Martel, *Not This Time: Canadians, Public Policy, and the Marijuana Question, 1961–1975* (Toronto: University of Toronto Press, 2006); Erika Dyck, *Psychedelic Psychiatry: LSD from Clinic to Campus* (Baltimore: Johns Hopkins University Press, 2008).

32 For three examples, see Allen S. Williams, *Demon of the Orient and His Satellite Fiends of the Joints: Our Opium Smokers as They Are in Tartar Hells and American Paradises* (New York: printed by the author, 1883); H.G. Cole, *Confessions of an American Opium Eater: From Bondage to Freedom* (Boston: James H. Earle, 1895); and Frederick J. Masters, "The Opium Traffic in California," *Chautauquan* 24 (1896): 54–61.

33 Amy Mittelman, *Brewing Battles: A History of American Beer* (New York: Algora Publishing, 2008); Maureen Ogle, *Ambitious Brew: The Story of American Beer* (New York: Harcourt, 2006); James Sumner, *Brewing Science, Technology and Print, 1700–1880* (Pittsburgh: University of Pittsburgh, 2013); Matthew Bellamy, *Brewed in the North: A History of Labatt's* (Montreal and Kingston: McGill-Queens University Press, 2019). Scholarly treatment of distilling is still limited, but try Karl Raitz, *Making Bourbon: A Geographical History of Distilling in Nineteenth-Century Kentucky* (Lexington: University Press of Kentucky, 2020); Ronald Weir, *The History of the Distillers Company, 1877–1939: Diversification and Growth in Whisky and Chemicals* (Oxford: Clarendon Press, 1999).

34 Gutzke, *Protecting the Pub;* Nicholls, *Politics of Alcohol;* Greenaway, *Drink and British Politics since 1830.*

35 Syzmanski, *Pathways to Prohibition;* Gutzke, *Protecting the Pub.*

36 Martel, *Not This Time.*

37 Gloria Galloway, "Harper Takes Aim at Drug Culture," *Globe and Mail,* October 5, 2007.

38 *Canada (Attorney General) v PHS Community Services Society,* 2011 SCC 44, [2011] 3 SCR 134, https://scc-csc.lexum.com/scc-csc/scc-csc/en/item/7960/index.do. See also Kirk Makin, Sunny Dhillon, and Ingrid Peritz, "Supreme Court Ruling Opens Doors to Drug Injection Clinics across Canada," *Globe and Mail,* September 30, 2011.

39 Jarrett Rudy, *The Freedom to Smoke: Tobacco, Consumption and Identity* (Montreal and Kingston: McGill-Queen's University Press, 2005).

40 Christopher Snowden, *Kill Joys: A Critique of Paternalism* (London: Institute of Economic Affairs, 2017).

41 Janet Golden, *Message in a Bottle: The Making of Fetal Alcohol Syndrome* (Boston: Harvard University Press, 2006); Elizabeth M. Armstrong, *Conceiving Risk, Bearing Responsibility: Fetal Alcohol Syndrome and the Diagnosis of Moral Disorder* (Baltimore: Johns-Hopkins University Press, 2008).

42 Although there were some strong and passionate Catholic opponents of drink, most notably Father Charles Chinquy in Canada and Father Theobold Matthew in Ireland, the dry city on the hill remained an Evangelical Protestant dream. Jan Noel, *Canada Dry: Temperance Crusades before Confederation* (Toronto: University of Toronto Press, 1995); Elizabeth Malcolm, *"Ireland Sober, Ireland Free": Drink and Temperance in Nineteenth-Century Ireland* (Syracuse, NY: University of Syracuse Press, 1986).

43 See Malleck, *Try to Control Yourself.*

44 Dyck, *Psychedelic Psychiatry.*

45 John C. Burnham, *Bad Habits: Drinking, Smoking, Taking Drugs, Gambling, Sexual Misbehavior and Swearing in American History* (New York: NYU Press, 1994).

46 David T. Courtwright, *The Age of Addiction: How Bad Habits Became Big Business* (Cambridge, MA: Belknap Press of Harvard University Press, 2019).

PART 1

Popular Pleasure and Panic

The Transgressive Woman

Gender, Class, Alcohol, and Drugs in Canada from 1850

Cheryl Krasnick Warsh

During the late nineteenth century, the temperance movement was a platform for the reformist energies of educated middle-class, evangelical English Canadian women.[1] The movement's critique of the male subculture of saloons and brothels, which were targeted as breeding grounds for pauperism, disease, crime, and corruption, expanded into a generalized attack upon male privilege and male public spaces.[2] Temperance agitation produced short-term victories in the form of provincial and federal prohibition legislation, but it never completely eliminated alcohol consumption, although it did curb the worst excesses of public drinking. Furthermore, the inroads made by women into male public spaces as a consequence of transformational social forces such as urbanization, industrialization, coeducation, immigration, and mass culture did not eliminate public drinking; rather, they opened new venues and reconfigured traditional ones to accommodate middle- and upper-class female drinkers along with the working-class women who had always had some limited space in public drinking establishments.

In all cultures that comprised Canada's drinking population, the imbibing woman was acceptable so long as she was a light drinker. The drunken woman and certainly the alcoholic woman were not. This attitude predated temperance by millennia and has persisted well beyond prohibition's repeal. Female drug addicts face similar, if not harsher, judgments. Women's "special roles" as mothers and sexual beings requiring containment led to the archetypes of the bad mother and the fallen woman, and their association with substance abuse. Despite women's expanded roles in the twentieth century, and the more permissive values of a society heavily influenced by mass culture, these archetypes have had remarkable longevity.

This chapter is a longitudinal overview of attitudes, practices, and consequences of female use of alcohol and recreational drugs in the later nineteenth and twentieth centuries. The temperance movements introduced many middle-class Anglophone Canadian women to male activities such as political organization, lobbying, and campaigning, which laid the foundation for the suffrage movement. At the same time, these reformers sought to save their working-class sisters from the saloons many of the latter enjoyed as respite from their hardscrabble lives. Middle-class women themselves were at risk of substance abuse, through the overuse of either fortified tonics or narcotics prescribed by physicians or pharmacists. By the twentieth century, temperance rhetoric was drowned out by the seductive calls of advertisers, films, and magazines that associated alcohol use with gaiety, modernity, and romance. The encouragement of drug use was more muted but also associated with modernity. The triumph of scientific medicine was accompanied by a growing reliance on medications to stifle all pain – physical and emotional – and the marketing of opiates, barbiturates, anti-depressants, and other narcotics was primarily geared towards the female patient market.

Yet the growing acceptability of female substance use did not necessarily lead to a growing acceptance of its casualties. Indeed, the nineteenth-century tropes of the female drinker and drug addict as degraded women and bad mothers echoed in the pronouncements and actions of twentieth-century magistrates who incarcerated alcoholics and drug addicts as vagrants and prostitutes, and social workers who cut off their mothers' allowances and took away their children. More freedoms led to more mixed messages. Women were essential workers during the two world wars, but too much fun in the canteen after the factory whistle blew could lead to the reckless endangerment of the Dominion's fighting forces through the transmission of venereal diseases. In the postwar era, alcohol use was domesticated, but female addiction reflected poorly on husbands, was grounds for divorce, and therefore laid the groundwork for secret drinking. Class and ethnicity, as in the nineteenth century, figured into the treatment (judicial, medical, and social) of the female addict. Middle-class white women could be quietly treated in office or residential programs. Working-class or indigent women, particularly Aboriginal women and other women of colour, who lacked resources and were often homeless, could not be secret addicts, and faced similar calumny to their sisters in the Victorian period. The twentieth-century cross-messages of the fun-loving girl and the mother on a pedestal reveal how deeply and persistently gendered messages about substance use and abuse have resonated.

Protestant evangelicalism in early nineteenth-century North America appealed to many women because its tenets contradicted earlier concep-tualizations of the female sex as disorderly daughters of Eve. The ideology of True Womanhood, which provided the justification for female reform activ-ities, ascribed an inherent superiority to middle-class women based upon the characteristics of purity, piety, and submissiveness – characteristics that appeared incompatible with the drinking woman.[3] True Womanhood, however, was a construct of the 1830s and 1840s. By the late nineteenth-century, many veteran female reformers found, to their consternation, that drinking among middle-class women seemed to be on the increase, or at least was more public. Alcohol was associated with hospitality in all classes from the nineteenth century onward, with only a brief interlude during prohibition and temperance years. Cookbooks, etiquette books, and store catalogues instructed elegant hostesses on the proper pairings of wines with courses, and sold crystal glasses and decanters sized for various beverages. Respectable women's preferences for cordials and light wines indicated that even as they drank, they were attempting to avoid intoxication. In the nineteenth century, public drinking was available to propertied women in hotel dining rooms and restaurants, while German immigrants established beer gardens as family entertainment.[4]

For working-class women, the urban male saloon was never exclusively male. Working and neighbourhood women were able to save their pen-nies by stopping by for the "free lunch." They would enter by the "ladies' entrance" side door, which enabled them to avoid the gauntlet of the main barroom. The ladies' entrance also provided quick access for carry-out alcohol, known as "rushing the growler," purchased by either women or their children for consumption at home with family members and friends.[5]

Organized labour was not immune to the middle-class fears of the drinking woman; one labour leader fretted about working-class women who went "into grocery stores on the pretense of purchasing groceries and buy liquors at the same time, and the men will know nothing about it until their wives are to such an extent controlled by the use of liquor that they are past redemption."[6] In 1884, Toronto temperance bodies petitioned city council to abolish the sale of liquor in grocery stores, claiming that such sales in England had resulted in a thirteen-fold increase in intemperance in women. Grocers would secretly deliver the liquor and charge the purchases as tea and sugar.[7]

The entry of single women into the paid workforce in cities around the turn of the twentieth century, beyond the guidance and control of their parents, was a focus for the generalized anxieties of the pious middle class, who feared the moral consequences of rapid social change. Recreational activities in which working women were engaged, such as dancing and skating, led to a conservative backlash that tarred all amusements with the brush of sexual immorality.[8] The upholders of public virtue worked to close the dance halls, enforce curfews, and support alternative and respectable entertainments such as the YWCAs and organized sports.[9]

The conservative forces were supported by members of the medical profession, who in the late nineteenth century developed biological models describing the evils attendant upon rapid social change, including the status of women.[10] Nowhere was the "unnatural" aspect of social change more apparent to conservative physicians than in the prospect of women engaging in the male occupation of public drinking and falling into the male vice of drunkenness. The male drunkard was the brute, the physical aggressor, the wastrel. A female drunkard therefore risked being regarded as brutish and as possessing traits that were at once negative and masculine. Since in the Manichean world of late Victorian biology, woman was body, and particularly a vessel for reproduction, the prevalent view of the female alcoholic was expressed in sexual terms.

Medical discourse concerning the female alcoholic tended to focus on gender-specific stereotypes: the fallen woman and the bad mother, who together represented the ultimate forms of female degradation. These stereotypes were especially compelling because they crossed class lines. The factory worker and the shop clerk, the slum mother and the society matron could all, through weakness of will and the snare of alcohol, be thrown into the abyss of degradation. By the turn of the twentieth century, respectable women felt compelled to conceal their drinking, a consequence of decades of temperance rhetoric. The temperance movement vilified the saloon as a den of iniquity that sent forth drunkards to impoverish, injure, and perhaps murder their families, and drinking establishments of any type were portrayed as the enemies of all women. Women who frequented such places were assumed to be prostitutes or gin-shop derelicts. Yet alcohol did not always have negative connotations for women.

In its many forms, liquor was an integral part of women's daily lives for much of the nineteenth century. In an era of unpasteurized milk and uncertain water supply, liquor was considered a pure and safe beverage. With increasing availability of alternative beverages, notably tea and coffee, and with the rise of temperance agitation in the 1830s and 1840s, alcohol's position as drink of choice diminished; as a medicine, however, it retained its popularity for many succeeding decades. Liquor was believed to stimulate and support the system, prevent fevers and infectious diseases, facilitate breastfeeding, and provide the stamina necessary for hard physical labour.[11]

The middle to late decades of the nineteenth century were the heyday of the therapeutic use of alcohol. The perceived stimulating effects of brandies, wine, and whisky were indicated for debilitating disorders and fevers, while clarets and sherries were highly regarded for their ability to aid in digestion. Liquor therapies were most in vogue during the years when the temperance movement was gaining strength, and many physicians were placed in the embarrassing position of defending their medicines to a public over whom they expected to possess moral superiority as their professional due. They therefore attempted, unsuccessfully, to classify liquor as a dangerous drug, like opium or chloral hydrate, over which they should have control.

By the beginning of the twentieth century, decades of temperance propaganda had instilled in the Canadian public the idea that alcohol consumption could be a health risk, although the persistence of alcohol therapy kept stores of fortified wines and distilled spirits in kitchen pantries and physicians' medical stores. During the Spanish influenza epidemics in 1918–19, there was great demand for the release of alcoholic beverages for medicinal purposes in jurisdictions throughout North America. Tonic wines such as Vin Mariani and St. Augustine Tonic Wine were advertised as family tonics used to cure tired brains and fortify blood and nerves. The copy for Wincarnis, a widely advertised British tonic with 14 percent wine, advised the female reader to drink it daily with soda water. In the French-language Quebec newspaper *La Presse* in 1914, Wincarnis was prescribed for young mothers to conserve their strength. After Canadian prohibition expired in 1919, Vin St. Michel was available in Quebec for nursing mothers to consume at the recommended dosage of three glasses a day.

The nineteenth-century temperance movement had used the tools of popular culture, such as broadsheets, popular music, parades, and games to advance its message. By the twentieth century, a mass culture had emerged that drowned out its message of abstinence. John Burnham has argued that consumer culture subverted traditional Judeo-Christian values, with the judgment of good and evil minor vices being replaced with activities that were deemed cool or uncool.[12] The fact that mass culture emanated from the large cities, with their teeming immigrant and working-class subcultures, accelerated this preoccupation with the new, the daring, and the countercultural. Gender played a critical role in the process, as middle-class women remade their places in liberal democracies and even in modernizing autocracies. In North America, one generation defied their mothers and engaged in suffrage and reform activities for the rights of coeducation and professional employment, with the avowed goals of eliminating the excesses of industrial capitalism, including drunkenness. This generation was in turn challenged by their daughters, who wanted to join their confreres in the clubs for a drink or a smoke after university classes or a day's work. The Great War accelerated changes already in the making, and by the interwar period, women found their way, in increasing numbers, into formerly male-only spaces, such as drinking establishments.[13] Mass media, particularly films and magazines, shaped the performance of these activities while providing justification for the view that any backlash from elders and traditional community leaders was simply fustiness. These transformations in gendered behaviours occurred across the industrializing world – from Europe to South America and beyond.[14]

By 1924, prohibition was abandoned in New York and other urban centres, with police collecting fines in a perfunctory way rather than closing down the nightclubs and speakeasies that were hidden from the street. By eliminating the worst excesses of public drunkenness and degenerate saloons, and increasing the price of beverages, prohibition became glamorized. Events in US cities, and particularly in New York, were important for Canadians because most of the American periodicals with a large readership north of the border were produced in that city, and the features, pictorials, and advertisements familiarized Canadians with American perspectives. Magazines such as *Vogue* printed monthly columns on the trendy clubs where the smart set drank and danced, and by the end of the twenties, American cinema was awash in alcohol as the wealthy and sophisticated drank bootlegged liquor in champagne glasses at lively house parties. Their audience likewise could host home-based cocktail parties. As drinking became domesticated and consumption directed by the hostess, the need and support for prohibition were eliminated.[15] But with domestic consumption came easy accessibility to alcohol, and the heightened risk of excessive secret drinking.

According to the marketing, however, alcohol was part of a healthy, fun lifestyle. During the 1920s, Quebec had the most liberal liquor laws in North America, and many Canadian newspapers and magazines originated in the province. In both French- and English-language ads, beer was characterized as a health drink, through the healthful action of "enzymes" on digestion, and alcohol advertisements became increasingly lifestyle-oriented. They included high-status sports such as tennis, golf, and yachting, as well as fishing and relaxing at the cottage. While these ads did not depict women engaged in these activities and drinking, they were not depicting men in saloons or other male-only venues. Women could play tennis and golf, and cottages were family-oriented. This marketing also helped domesticate liquor consumption and, with its emphasis upon outdoor activities and sports, still found in alcohol and tobacco ads to this day, minimized any association with health risks.[16] In reality, few young women were likely to be finishing off a round of golf with a beer. In big cities like Toronto and Montreal, youth of all classes imbibed liquor at parties and dance clubs, and young girls were "frequently ... brought home in carriages intoxicated, to the distress and heart-breaking trouble of the parents."[17]

The devil-may-care, immediate-gratification lifestyle of the consumer-oriented New Woman, promoted in movies and advertisements, had its limits, as many aspiring flappers learned. In the interwar period, the tremendous losses of the Great War, along with fear of immigrants and communism, led to a reframing of Victorian pure womanhood into concerns for "race suicide."[18] Young white women who were controlling their childbearing and participating actively in male public spaces such as universities, offices, and streets in ever greater numbers faced conservative backlash. Contemporary crises such as juvenile delinquency, labour unrest, and the aspiration of immigrants and people of colour to the privileges of the native-born, white elite could in some conservative minds be traced back to middle-class women's shirking of their traditional domestic responsibilities. Particular targets were women who engaged in public drinking. While social mores were shifting and becoming more permissive, women, particularly of the working and lower classes, felt the limit of that shift when confronted by authorities. In the late 1920s, single mothers who applied for an Ontario Mothers' Allowance, for instance, would be subjected to home visits to guarantee that there was "no car, no radio, no liquor permit" in the home. In 1927, one mother, a part-time waitress, had her allowance cut off because the investigator considered waitresses to be "the lowest types of girls that walked," and had received a letter stating that the mother had been "running around with men and had been brought home intoxicated in a taxicab." Even though her union official spoke up in her defence, the allowance was not reinstated.[19]

For most Canadian working-class and middle-class women who were not dependent upon government assistance for survival, the replacement of prohibition laws with provincial regulation regimes facilitated the normalization of female drinking. One unintended result of the opening of government liquor stores, before public drinking establishments were reintroduced, was that drinking took place in the home, and in many households became a shared activity between spouses and among family members.[20] Women were slowly admitted into beer parlours through the late 1920s and 1930s, although full acceptance of women's public drinking was not apparent until the 1960s.[21]

Given the fears of physicians and reformers over the rise of the female public drinker, was there actually an increase in female drunkenness from the late nineteenth century that would continue into the more permissive years of the twentieth century? In Ontario from the 1880s to 1920s, 16 percent of admissions for alcoholism to Guelph's Homewood Retreat, a large private asylum, were female. In the same period, 16 percent of those sentenced for drunk and disorderly conduct in the province were also female. Both women of the propertied classes and those among the most indigent experienced identical levels of alcoholism.[22]

Female alcohol consumption in Canada did increase after the expiration of national prohibition in 1919. Between 1922 and 1930, the official per capita consumption rate increased over 60 percent. Of those deaths attributed to alcoholism and cirrhosis of the liver occurring between 1921 and 1949, 29 percent were women in the 1920s, increasing to 31 percent in the 1930s, and 34 percent in the 1940s. Three percent of convictions for drunkenness involved women in the 1920s, 4.7 percent in the 1930s, 6.6 percent in the 1940s, and 6.8 percent between 1950 and 1955. Clearly, the majority of drinking women were not imbibing in public, or at least were less likely to be charged with liquor offences. In 1973, the Addiction Research Foundation of Ontario determined that "15.7 percent ... of our estimated 400,000 problem drinkers [were] female," which was consistent with the pre-1920 rates. By the 1990s, female alcohol consumption, while consistently less than male, had risen significantly. In a 1992 national survey, 83.8 percent of Canadian men were self-reported drinkers, and 71.8 percent of women were as well. The men drank 5.3 drinks per week, compared with 2 drinks for women.[23] Heavier drinking by women was taking a toll, however: in 1995, of the estimated 6,503 Canadians who died from alcohol consumption, 1,823, or 28 percent, were women. In the same year, of the 80,946 Canadians hospitalized for alcohol-related disorders, 29,181, or 36 percent, were women.[24]

Yet the medical, reform, and legal concerns over female alcoholism were most intense at the turn of the twentieth century, when the rates of the disorder remained fairly consistent. It may well have been concern over female drinking habits, rather than excessive use of alcohol, that was increasing. Even in a contemporary context, "it is possible that the exaggerated claims of deviant drinking among women actually reflect a societal reaction to any drinking among women. While light or moderate drinking has been quite normative for men, it may be that light or moderate drinking for women is still to some extent not culturally acceptable."[25] As a consequence, family members were often accomplices in maintaining a cloak of secrecy around female alcoholics, who became "skeletons in the households ... Associated with the use of spirits is an increasing dread of exposure and a shrinking from society, and even from relatives and friends," concluded American asylum superintendent Thomas Crothers.[26] Medical experts theorized about the reasons, ranging from the physical to the psychological, for excessive drinking among women. The "painful performance of her special function" – that is, the pain associated with menstruation and childbirth – was cited as a cause for alcohol abuse.[27]

The material bases for alcoholism among women were accompanied by what female drinking represented in symbolic terms. Intemperance was a problem of all classes, but it was associated with filth, disease, immorality, and ignorance – all stereotypical of the "dangerous" lower classes. It was also associated with men; consequently, the female drunkard was a particularly degraded creature. For a woman to be drunk was for her to engage in unseemly, unwomanly behaviour. This was an ancient construct. In the *Talmud*, the primary source of Jewish philosophy and practice, it is instructed that "a cup of wine is good for a woman; two are degrading; three induce her to act like an immoral woman; and four cause her to lose all self-respect and sense of shame."[28] Yet this spoke to the woman's behaviour, not to the essence of her womanhood. As late as the first half of the nineteenth century, Canadian women were censured not for consuming alcohol but for over-imbibing and losing self-control. For instance, a Baptist Church member from Dundas, Ontario, was disciplined by her church in 1847 for being "under the influence of too much liquor," and other women "also appear to have had trouble defining the point at which one had drunk too much liquor."[29]

By the second half of the nineteenth century, the growth of congested cities with immigrant and other indigent populations crammed into filthy slums, and the experience of waves of deadly epidemics of typhoid, typhus, and smallpox blamed upon the slum dwellers, led to hardening attitudes of rich against poor, native-born against immigrant. The temperance campaigns crystallized much of those attitudes into the temperate elite versus the drunken masses, and actions by the state targeted and labelled the degraded. Vagrancy laws were used to sweep the undeserving off the streets. Vagrant women were considered loose, inebriated, idle, insane, and aggressive. The elites in Montreal demanded that vagrant women be segregated while incarcerated, so that they do not "contaminate" the other, presumably less degraded, criminal women.[30]

Alcoholic women of higher social status could be equally disgraceful and carried a potential for contamination. Because the respectable woman was forced to drink in secret, she learned "the art of lying and dissimulation."[31] Louise C.'s husband, a Toronto businessman, committed her to the Homewood Retreat not so much for her ten-year-long drinking problem as for her public displays: "We have told her time and time again, if she feels these spells coming on, to go into her room [and drink] all she wants but to remain there so as to keep it private, but no, just as soon as she starts drinking, downtown she goes and you can't keep her out of public places where she makes a show of herself.[32] Louise's case showed that female alcoholism was even more unacceptable when its victims engaged in unfeminine public activities that embarrassed.

Mendacious, disruptive, and shameless, these alcoholic women had fallen far from the pedestal of True Womanhood, were embarrassments to their families, and, even worse, could be investing their progeny with a hereditary taint. Parents who scrupulously kept their children away from intoxicants could nonetheless be endangering their offspring and their race by continuing to drink themselves. The degeneration theories of Cesare Lombroso and Bénédict Augustin Morel posited that drunkenness in one generation would produce idiocy, insanity, and criminality in future generations. Lombrosian principles of degeneration found favour in Canadian circles of power and influence. Restricting the immigration of the feeble-minded, insane, and other undesirables was a core feature of immigration policy from the mid-nineteenth century, and the pseudo-science of eugenics was spearheaded by the Canadian National Committee for Mental Hygiene, directed by C.K. Clarke, former superintendent of the Asylum for the Insane, Toronto. Even Tommy Douglas, socialist premier of Saskatchewan and lauded as the father of Canadian Medicare, wrote his Master of Social Work thesis at McMaster University on the need to control "sub-human" families.[33] "Depravity is stamped, like the mark of Cain, upon the foreheads of the posterity of drunken parents, especially when the mother has been a victim to the habit, or has been in the habit of using alcoholics," wrote Canadian physician William Bessey.[34]

That deviance in behaviour paralleled deviance in gender was evident in Lombroso's influential study *The Female Offender*, which described a literal mark of Cain. Through his detailed measurements of skull sizes, distances between eyes and ears, and abundance of hair, Lombroso created an archetype of the criminal half-woman that found resonance in criminology for decades. The criminal women were "singularly virile ... having the bodies of women, but all the air of brutal men, whom they resemble sometimes, even in their dress."[35] Lombrosian typologies survived well into the twentieth century. Sadie K., by 1949, was a career institutionalized individual when she was committed on a government warrant for the criminally insane to the Provincial Mental Hospital, Essondale, in Coquitlam, British Columbia. Her psychopathy was described by physicians and social workers in terms of her "gender transgressions": "The patient ... affects masculine mannerisms, smokes incessantly and is fond of liquor and men. She has a loud voice and swears frequently. She has always been extremely aggressive. She left home at 15 because she could not stand the brutal treatment she received at the hands of her father ... The patient's first child [was cared] for in a Children's Aid Society foster home ... The mother has shown no interest in her."[36]

Sadie's degeneracy was proven, in part, by her failure as a mother. From the moral reformers of the Victorian period to modern government social workers, the consensus was that the drinking mother could not be a good mother, and the damage began with the unborn child. That heavy drinking by pregnant women can cause damage to fetuses has been recognized for millennia. In ancient Carthage, for instance, there were proscriptions against drinking on wedding nights to protect the unborn.[37] Race and class impinged upon how a female addict would be represented. Aboriginal women who drank were consistently singled out as bad mothers. Nineteenth-century fur traders wrote of the plight of Homeguard women (i.e., Aboriginal women who lived near the fur-trading posts) who became alcoholic, rendering them "prone to jealous acts of violence and the neglect of their children [as well as] debauching their morals."[38]

Bad women could also be drug users, and responses to female drug addiction have been both consistent with and distinguished from the liquor campaigns. In the nineteenth century, attitudes towards narcotics use and overuse among women were more complex than towards alcohol, in no small part because narcotics use was invariably initiated by physicians. Opium, termed "God's Own Medicine" by eighteenth-century American expert on inebriation Dr. Benjamin Rush, was (and is) a superb painkiller. In an age when physicians treated symptoms, not diseases, efficacious anaesthetics, analgesics, sedatives, and hypnotics were widely used. Along with opium and its derivatives (morphine, heroin, paregoric, and laudanum), other narcotics, including paraldehyde, cocaine, and chloral hydrate, were widely available from physicians and pharmacists, and by mail order. By the later nineteenth-century, opium "habits" began to present themselves, and physicians in private practice and asylums attempted to cure them. The imperfect state of medical knowledge led physicians to use other substances to wean their patients from their addiction. Whisky was used to break opium habits, cocaine for morphine, and paraldehyde for chloral hydrate – invariably leading to multiple addictions.[39] Mood-altering drugs, first introduced by physicians and druggists for physical complaints, became habits for women in need of emotional release, especially in a culture where saloons and alcohol were male preserves. Women who "never knowingly would touch liquor would drink it and opiates as 'medicine.'"[40]

At the turn of the twentieth century, the disease model of addiction emerged parallel to a recognition of addiction as a social problem. Opponents of the disease model argued that diseases were not voluntarily contracted or voluntarily cured through abstinence. On the other hand, the imperfect disease model also absolved the failures of practitioners to produce permanent cures, since relapses were considered the fault of the addict.[41] Since addiction was both a medical and a social problem, its only solution appeared to be to legislate the temptation out of the reach of the morally weak. The first move to limit the availability of opiates in Ontario was The Ontario Pharmacy Act of 1875, which, however, still permitted over-the-counter sale of opium by registered pharmacists. It was not until 1908 that opium and cocaine were banned from patent medicines by the Proprietary or Patent Medicine Act. The ban did not necessarily result in instant compliance, given spotty surveillance and limited government resources. For instance, ads for nineteenth-century patent medicines such as Lydia Pinkham's Vegetable Compound, Gin Pills, Dodd's or Red Pills, and Lambert & Fellows' Syrup were published in French-language popular magazines in Quebec well into the 1930s. While some narcotics may have been removed, these nostrums certainly included alcohol, and compounds such as Gin Pills included strychnine and arsenic.[42]

Nevertheless, the passage of the Proprietary and Patent Medicine Act was simultaneous with the criminalization of opiate use and was due at least as much to racism as to a public health problem. In 1908, following his investigation of the Vancouver riot of 1907, Deputy Minister of Labour Mackenzie King undertook a private study of the opium trade in Canada. His report depicted "the ruin of white women" and other "moral calamities" "caused" by the Chinese opium trade.[43] The Opium Act of 1908 and the Opium and Drug Act of 1911, which banned the sale of opiates for non-medical purposes, and their possession and use, respectively, were aimed at the Chinese Canadian community. The fact that opiate use was associated with the alien indicated that by 1908 opium was no longer an integral part of the popular culture. Most of its uses had been rendered obsolete by chloral hydrate, the bromides, and eventually the new synthetic drugs, such as aspirin. Improvements in sanitation, and pure food and milk legislation, substantially decreased the incidence of gastrointestinal disorders for which opium was a specific remedy. The older generation of respectable middle-aged addicts had largely died out, leaving only a residue of younger users "hooked" (through recreational rather than iatrogenic use) on the expensive and outlawed opiate derivatives: morphine and heroin. By the 1920s, the furtive dope fiend was entrenched in the public imagination. For many women in a culture that valued the nurturing qualities of womanhood, with the consequent calumny associated with the failure to provide such nurture, denial of addictions was a common reaction. Furthermore, many medical professionals shared that attitude by failing to diagnose substance abuse in women. This resulted in delays in seeking treatment and in problems becoming very severe by the time they were confronted. Hence, these individuals were perceived as particularly bad women and mothers.[44]

The other stereotype associated with female drunkenness and drug addiction was the belief that its victims tended to be prostitutes, although there was much debate over which was cause and which effect. The Victorian city was a bustling place, but much of its public spaces were considered off limits for respectable women, particularly after sundown. Prostitution flourished in a culture with a sexual double standard and few employment or relief options for poor women. In cities like Montreal, many of the streetwalkers were alcoholics who resorted to prostitution to pay for food, rooms, and alcohol.[45] Women arrested for drunk and disorderly behaviour in Canadian cities in the mid-to-late nineteenth century often were impoverished Irish immigrants, many of whom worked as domestics and a few as prostitutes. The two roles were often interchangeable, since domestics were vulnerable to sexual abuse in Victorian households, and if they should become pregnant and/or discharged, they lost not only their wages but also their homes. These women often turned to prostitution to survive, while others pragmatically concluded that they might as well get paid for the sexual exploitation they had experienced while "respectably" employed.[46] When Irish immigrant women were arrested or institutionalized for alcohol consumption, this was represented in the literature of moral reform as well as in police reports as evidence of a degraded, backward culture.

By the turn of the century, the temperance crusades had virtually eliminated the presence of respectable women in the "working man's club" (i.e., saloons and taverns). Barmaids, wives, and other women stopping by for a quiet drink through a side entrance were either banned by provincial legislation or made unwelcome by tavern keepers or male patrons, who would assume they were prostitutes or "loose" women, and sexually harass or abuse them.[47] Like the indigent Irish, Aboriginal women were subjected to calumny, sexual abuse, and incarceration by virtue of their ethnicity as well as class and gender. From the earliest years of settlement in the town of Victoria, the ban on liquor sales to Indigenous peoples was due in large part to attitudes towards the women. When an African-Canadian man was arrested in 1861 for beating up an Indigenous woman on Kanaka Road," the report noted that every night on the waterfront, "a number of whites and blacks, who consider themselves civilized beings [delighted] in getting [such women] drunk," and act disreputably. A watchmaker in Victoria was discovered one night with an Indigenous woman in his apartment, "en dishabille, giving [her] a drink of liquor."[48] In these cases, the men were portrayed as degrading themselves by consorting with and taking advantage of degraded alcoholic women.

And what happened to the trope of the drinking woman as the fallen woman in the twentieth century, with the acceleration of the processes of modernization? The new consumer culture in the interwar period included magazines, radio shows, and especially the cinema, which portrayed drinking as a glamorous activity for young moderns and an essential component of courting rituals, and de-gendered habits of consumption. The popularity of the cinema affected drinking patterns in paradoxical ways. On the one hand, the movie theatre replaced the saloon for many working-class men, a development applauded by social workers. On the other hand, the images portrayed in movies were not necessarily positive. Although from the 1920s, women had been depicted on the screen, in press releases, and in advertisements as drinkers, the image of the female alcoholic retained its Victorian overtones; women were still portrayed as sexually promiscuous and morally degraded, and alcoholic women in feature films were "social obscenities, more humiliated, somehow harder to watch than alcoholic men."[49]

Thus, there remained limits upon this new freedom, as laws and customs were slow to adapt to the emergent popular culture. Through the interwar period, women who entered Canadian beer parlours, especially alone, were still liable to be labelled as prostitutes or disreputable women.[50] While many women saw nothing wrong with having a quiet glass of beer with friends, either female or male, beer parlour and hotel owners were reluctant to allow them entry. As these drinking places now operated under the new regime of provincial liquor control, both tavern keepers and liquor control board administrators were wary of any activities that echoed the prewar, disreputable saloon, and disreputable women were considered a major component of that. Under the early Liquor Control Board of Ontario, even the venerable barmaid was not permitted to return to duty.[51] When these conservative strictures came up against the permissive modern era, however, they could not eliminate female drinking – only drive it underground. An American reporter described female drinking in postwar Montreal, where it was illegal for women to drink in taverns:

> Between midnight and morning, in a cabaret and in a half-dozen bootlegging clubs and joints I saw hundreds of women drinking; many of them were mere girls, and fully one third of them were drunk. A newspaper woman I met that night in a "blind pig" club where three hundred men and women were drinking, told me she had seen a thousand women drunk in such places in Montreal.[52]

Beginning in the late 1920s, women slowly began to legally enter public drinking establishments in Canada. British Columbia was the first jurisdiction to allow women to drink in a separate section of beer parlours. A continuation of the nineteenth-century ladies' entrances, the "Women with Escorts" area was so delineated to reduce the "risk" of prostitutes plying their trades in bars.[53] These areas were also favoured by women who wanted to have a drink with their friends without being harassed by bar patrons. British Columbia's earlier experiences with prostitution likely shaped this regulation. The demographic and labour realities of western Canadian cities and towns meant that alcohol and prostitution fulfilled social needs in these resource-based economies. Vancouver's vice industry was considered as economically essential as sawmills, railways, and grain elevators.[54] In the 1919 memoir of a Canadian prostitute, "Madeline" asserted that "the sale of liquor was just as important as the sale of sex in the profitability of a brothel."[55]

Despite (or because of) more permissive attitudes, conservative opinion makers and agents of the state continued to equate drinking with loose morals and deviant behaviour, as those women confronted by these social arbiters would find out. By the 1930s, according to advice columnist Dorothy Dix, the independent flapper era was dead. Dix quoted a university campus survey, which found that "80 percent of the men questioned declared that girls who smoke and drink and overdo the use of rouge and lipstick made no hit with them."[56] Women who recounted their first experiences of moving to the city for work in the 1930s knew that "it was no good to 'run around' with a crowd that was believed to indulge in the 'evil' delights of the city: alcohol, drugs or prostitution."[57]

Magistrates, social workers, police, and other agents of the state "knew" the differences between good and bad girls. As in the Victorian era, the economic exigencies of the Great Depression rendered many young working-class women vulnerable to vice. While paying lip service to victims of poverty, the adherents of the eugenics movement, which flowered in the 1920s and '30s, were motivated to hunt out carriers of the "hereditary taint." Margaret Patterson, Toronto's first female magistrate, described the girls who came before her court in a *Chatelaine* article from 1935. Few of the girls were "truly bad," she commented, "in the sense that they were lacking good qualities, and were wicked, unprincipled, immoral, pernicious, unwholesome, corrupting, and noxious." But it took little for them to descend into vicious conduct, like Leta, a good-time girl who "threw parties at her apartment with liquor and cigarettes" and was up on robbery charges,[58] or Nancy, "a reformed harlot," who had been convicted for drunkenness and seduced by a "smart laddie in a grey felt hat" who was a procurer in Ontario's white-slave traffic.[59]

Charlotte Whitton, a eugenicist in Ottawa's child welfare system in the 1930s, and later the first woman mayor of the city, described fallen women (unwed mothers) as "delinquent, immoral and inferior mentally." Ottawa's Children's Aid Society, like others around the country, questioned unwed, young pregnant women not only on their sexual histories but also on their other "bad habits," such as "smoking, drinking, and attending dance halls and movies."[60] Superintendents in nursing schools in the 1930s disciplined students for smoking, because "smoking leads to alcohol and progresses to promiscuity."[61]

By definition, and in line with the realities of a patriarchal social structure, a "furtive dope fiend" would be a fallen woman. Feminine "weakness and guile" were employed by desperate middle-class addicts to secure drugs from physicians and pharmacists by inventing and exaggerating illnesses such as kidney problems. Registered nurses fed their addictions by forging prescriptions and siphoning off patient supplies. The 1920s "flaming youth" generation included young women who experimented with drugs along with their male counterparts. According to Vancouver police reports in 1921, downtown opium joints and "snow sheds" catered to "young girls and boys of the white race." One young woman testified that she went "partly for the cocaine, and partly because other young folks went there."[62]

Working-class women often resorted to prostitution to support drug habits, or resorted to drugs to cope with the physical and socio-emotional hardships of prostitution. In the 1930s, drug use among Montreal's prostitutes was "endemic," and cocaine and heroin was present in the city's brothels. Contemporary social reformers said that prostitutes "shot up to keep up their pep and snap," and some had a morphine habit of "ten grams a day" and concealed their "decks of cocaine in their high heels."[63] According to police reports, one Vancouver addict in the 1920s displayed the hallmarks of Lombrosian degeneration. The child of a Russian-born bootlegger and a prostitute stepmother, "B" had been a prostitute and drug addict since her teens, and was described by police as a "resentful, rebellious ... sullen, foul-mouthed girl, mentally dull and utterly lacking in any moral sense."[64]

Over the next few decades, the proportion of female drug users convicted under Canada's Opium and Narcotic Drug Act grew steadily. While less than 10 percent of drug offenders were women before 1937, the proportion increased to 21 percent by 1946 and 37 percent by 1961. Women who became addicted to legal drugs tended to be, as in decades past, associated with the health professions – as nurses, doctors, or wives of doctors. Another outcast subgroup who experienced higher levels of drug use in the post-war era were members of lesbian communities.[65] While rates of drug use were increasing, attitudes towards the female addict were consistent with those in earlier generations. Besides being a fallen woman, the addict was a priori a bad mother. The criminalization of drug use meant that addicts would experience a "cycle of arrest and imprisonment," and regulation by government social services, rendering it virtually impossible for drug offenders to retain custody of their children, who were placed in the care of family members or government agencies, or put up for adoption.[66] In the interwar era, social service workers strongly encouraged addicts to give up their children.

With full mobilization in Canada during the Second World War, women's economic participation was essential and encouraged. Consorting with His Majesty's soldiers, however, was not, and as the cases of venereal disease became numerous enough to threaten the fighting force, loose women on the home front and overseas were blamed. Public health pamphlets were printed for Canada's soldiers and the public, warning women that they might engage in immoral activity while drunk, and warning men that liquor might lower "their standards of female companionship." Graphic posters underlined the threat that "liquor plus loose women equals Syphilis and Gonorrhea," which not only weakened Canada's fighting capacity but also threatened the future and stability of its families when the soldiers returned.[67]

Degeneration theory was alive and well in the female branches of the Canadian Armed Forces. Recruits to the Canadian Women's Army Corps were routinely subjected to intimately personal interviews and physical examinations, since every woman was "potentially an embodiment of all that was held to threaten the social order. So-called illegitimate pregnancy, venereal disease, poverty, drinking, dancing, and sex topped [the recruiter's] list of social and individual pathologies."[68] Nor did these attitudes disappear after the war. Unwed mothers who took the putative fathers to court for child support in the 1950s were treated with contempt and humiliation by the men's lawyers, who cited histories of drinking, going out unchaperoned, and "necking" as evidence of promiscuity and general degradation. Children's Aid Society intake interviews continued to solicit "information about smoking, drinking and attendance at dance halls and moving picture houses," and used this information to deny women financial support.[69]

Yet women continued to receive cross-messages with respect to drinking. After repeal of American prohibition in 1933, brewers targeted women in beer advertising, creating beer-based cookbooks to encourage the domestic integration of a beverage long associated with the saloon. Wartime beer ads promoted women's war work and portrayed husbands contentedly drinking in happy homes.[70] Canadian wartime liquor ads, known as institutional ads since corporations could not overtly sell products during wartime restrictions, occasionally portrayed female shoppers, although they were not shown in the act of purchasing alcoholic beverages. When provincial liquor laws concerning advertising were loosened enough in the late fifties to depict women, they were shown as shoppers and hostesses of lively or intimate house parties. Ontario's Brights Wines created ads that aggressively pursued the female market. In "I've Got a Reputation Now!" the double entendre was illustrated with a picture of a housewife looking coy and brazen at the same time. According to the text, her reputation was made by introducing Brights 74 Sherry to her women's club. Brights followed this with another ad recommending "For Bridge, Meeting or Tea – 74 for Me!" If women followed this advice, they would be drinking alcohol at every woman-centred social event.[71] In 1954, upscale women's fashion magazine *Vogue* presented the "Deuces Wild" diet to help its readership fit into haute couture (or its facsimiles). The sparse 950-calorie daily plan included reduced sugar recipes for "long cool drinks with alcohol." Wine cobblers, mint juleps, and frozen daiquiris need not have been eliminated from the elegant woman's activities, which included card parties.[72]

In the postwar era, Edith Lisansky Gomberg was a leader in social research on alcohol, and introduced general and professional audiences to the special concerns of the woman drinker. Gomberg encountered more formerly secret drinkers seeking treatment. She stressed that public drunkenness did not constitute alcoholism, although such displays were much scorned where women were concerned. Gomberg made the point, which seems self-evident yet was rarely spelled out, that the changes in the status of women, and the greater acceptability of drinking among women, exposed more of them to the possibility of becoming alcoholics. She noted that the postwar stereotype of the woman alcoholic, which was partly framed in the popular media, was either that of the bored socialite or the broken, "end-of-the-road woman who appears in court." Gomberg also denied the association of female alcoholism and sexual promiscuity, arguing that drug addiction was "more frequently a concomitant of prostitution than is alcoholism."[73]

After a generation of more liberalized views on women's drinking, and the rebirth of the women's movement in the 1960s, female alcoholism became a recognized area of public concern. Recovering alcoholic Marty Mann, through her work with the National Council on Alcoholism in the United States, spearheaded public education about female alcoholism, estimated to afflict almost a million Americans, and its special stigma. A flurry of articles and studies were presented over the next fifteen years as medical practitioners, sociologists, and other specialists rediscovered the drunken woman, and rehashed the Victorian narratives. Dr. Laurence Senseman, who ran a private addictions clinic in the 1960s, reminded physicians that

> the patient herself often does not know that she is an alcoholic, so that she can scarcely be expected to reveal this fact to her physician. It is all too easy for the physician to regard as utterly preposterous the notion that the gray-haired, pleasant lady in his office, perhaps the staid town librarian or the minister's wife, is an alcoholic.[74]

By 1972, so many studies had been published that Vera Lindberg compiled a review of the literature. She noted that inebriation was still not accepted in women and that alcoholism, even if labelled a disease, was treated as a "disgrace," leading to secret drinking and denial by spouses, friends, and health care professionals. Women continued to cite gynecological issues, marital problems, grief, boredom, and demands of small children as the reasons for their excessive drinking. Lindberg concluded that many of the "identified precipitants" related to women's adjustment to and acceptance of their femininity, and feelings of inadequacy and "social ineptness." The a priori nature of this reasoning is evident. Housewives who had drinking problems and cited aspects of their life experiences as women and housewives as the cause of their alcoholism displayed maladjusted femininity. Should they have been citing their too-frequent liquid business lunches, the demands of their executive positions, or hanging out at the pub after work? No, those would be the reasons for male alcoholism in the 1970s. What is evident is that alcoholism could have been triggered by any life event or circumstance; how it was interpreted was heavily based upon gender, class, and ethnicity.[75]

In terms of therapies, there was recognition by the 1970s that treatment options developed for men, notably the fraternally based Alcoholics Anonymous, did not answer the needs of female alcoholics. This problem was highlighted when former US First Lady Betty Ford courageously made public her own secret drinking. Yet woman-centred studies elided into stereotypical recommendations. In a small 1971 study of alcoholic patients, fourteen of twenty-one subjects related their drinking to their menstrual cycle, with premenstrual tensions triggering excessive drinking. The proposed solution, however, was fraught with dangers that had already been recognized in the 1870s. Three of the women purportedly maintained their sobriety for over a year by being administered the anti-anxiety drugs chlordiazepoxide or diazepam for ten days every month. Were these women cured of alcoholism or did their physicians replace one addictive substance with another?[76] This point was made in the late 1980s, when testimony before the US Senate Subcommittee on Alcohol Abuse in Women noted that sedatives and tranquilizers, used in combination with alcohol, compounded the toxic and lethal effects of both substances. Physicians were more likely to prescribe drugs for women than for men with alcohol problems, and the women would suffer more from "devastating" cross-addiction.[77] Because there were fewer treatment options for women, and women and their families were more likely to try to hide the addiction from the community, women tended to consult their family physicians more often than men, which was the case for all ailments. The physicians, for their part, had few treatment options other than medication.

By the last decades of the twentieth century, mass media reflected the cross-messages women received concerning alcohol consumption. Drinking was prominent in American television programming, which was popular in Canada. By the 1970s, the portrayal of or discussions about drinking became increasingly frequent, with both female and male characters equally likely to drink. Drinking itself was presented as social, as associated with business, or as a means of dealing with "crisis situations."[78] Drinkers were more likely to be involved in romance than non-drinkers. When female alcoholics were depicted, they were more likely to be married, and/or to be killed in crime shows.[79]

A 1980s study of daytime and prime-time soap operas, dramas with a primarily female audience, found that these programs normalized drinking in that drinking scenes, background drinking, and verbal references to drinking were common. These references were equally divided between positive portrayals (at restaurants, parties, ceremonies, or relaxation) and negative portrayals, which usually involved heavy drinking caused by family problems or depression, leading to more serious problems. The normalizing behaviour included routines such as taking a drink immediately upon getting home from work from decanters that were in clear view.[80] On television shows in general, heroes, villains, and comic characters all drank. While there was disapproval of drunkenness, drinking was mostly taken for granted. In the early 1980s, drugs were invariably portrayed negatively in police dramas, which focused on pushers and criminals victimizing youth. A notable exception was marijuana, which was portrayed as a "kind of humorous plaything," with characters in situation comedies unwittingly eating hash brownies and then acting out foolish behaviours for comedic effect.[81]

In television, of course, commercial advertising was at least as influential as the programming itself, and drug and alcohol advertisements comprised 12 percent of American commercial content by the end of the twentieth century. The ads were gendered in terms of placement. Alcohol ads, overwhelmingly for beer, were concentrated in sports broadcasts. Over-the-counter medications, ranging from weight-loss products and vitamins to pain relievers, were concentrated in the afternoons, when the demographic audience consisted of housewives watching soap operas. The medications advertised reflected women's sex roles in American culture related to sexual attractiveness and their role as caretakers of family health. This pattern of medication promotion was generational. Persistent administration of medicine by parents to their children – i.e., those children who had parents who medicated them as children at the first sign of a cold or any illness – correlated with university students who smoked tobacco, consumed alcohol or any illegal substance, or took pills for euphoric effects.[82]

Despite decades of "enlightened" social research, alcoholism and addiction continue to be viewed through the lens of not only gender but also race and class. In contemporary Canadian society, Aboriginal women experience entrenched racism, poverty, and marginalization, resulting in high levels of substance abuse.[83] Because their essential role is that of family and community caretaker, it was particularly painful when they were labelled or when they self-identified as bad mothers due to alcoholism or addiction.[84] By the end of the twentieth century, addiction researchers had codified the damage to fetuses from heavy alcohol consumption by the mother into Fetal Alcohol Syndrome (FAS), Fetal Alcohol Effects (FAE), and presently Fetal Alcohol Spectrum Disorder (FASD). FAS is a preventable disorder with devastating birth defects, including stunted growth, central nervous system and intellectual impairment, and impulsive, destructive behaviours that often lead to incarceration.[85] About 100 children in Canada are born with FAS every year. FAE children, estimated at 300 born each year, present milder symptoms, such as hyperactivity and learning disabilities, which are often undiagnosed.[86]

FASD cases are not evenly distributed in Canada; they are more prevalent in remote rural communities and in some Aboriginal populations.[87] An estimated 30 percent of children (mostly Aboriginal) with physical or learning disabilities in Northern British Columbia and the Yukon Territory could be suffering from FASD. Although recognized as a serious public health issue among First Nations organizations – most of whom have embraced informational campaigns to warn women against drinking during pregnancy – there is little follow-up or referral for medical treatment (if available), even when pregnant women report heavy drinking.[88] That is, FASD becomes part of the constellation of poor living conditions experienced in First Nations communities, and remains the fault of the individual drinking mother.

While the damage from FASD is apparent, its etiology remains clouded in mystery. Other contributing factors may be smoking, poor eating habits and general ill-health, and genetic predisposition; faulty transfer of nutrients across the placenta may also be at work. Furthermore, heavy drinking at different critical stages of fetal development can lead to different birth defects. Because of the uncertainty regarding "safe limits" for drinking while pregnant, Canadian public health officials advise women to abstain from alcohol completely as soon as they are aware that they are pregnant, or when they are trying or are likely to become pregnant – that is, one drink indeed may be too many. Thus, the association of female drinking with genetic battery and murder made by Victorian commentators is echoed in contemporary concern over FASD. This emphasis still obscures the much greater incidence of male domestic violence and psychological abuse that often arise from alcoholism, and has negative consequences for women (pregnant and otherwise) and children in households. Except where automobiles are concerned, male drinking patterns have rarely been addressed or modified in the past few decades.

Although less common than alcohol-related congenital problems, the effects on the fetus of maternal drug use can be very deleterious. Street drugs have been associated with "low birth weight, preterm birth and childhood developmental and behavioural problems."[89] In 1995, 254 pregnant women in Canada were treated for drug addiction, and the "most frequently detected infant morbidity related to substance abuse involves the effects of drugs on mothers and their unborn infants." Between 1977 and 1997, an additional 105 children died after contracting AIDS through perinatal transmission of HIV from infected, drug-using mothers.[90] These cases, though tragic, did not seem to warrant the moral panic that developed in relation to drug use in pregnancy at the end of the twentieth century.

This moral panic originated in the "war on drugs" waged by a succession of US administrations, and highlighted in the international media through the trope of the "crack mother" and pregnant women involved with methamphetamine labs.[91] Infants born addicted to crack cocaine are particularly heartbreaking; they cry constantly, cannot be comforted, and must be swaddled and held in dark, quiet rooms to find any relief.

The mothers of such infants were stereotyped as poor, unmarried African American drug addicts who were the most degraded and undeserving of women and mothers. The lack of treatment options, support networks, housing, and employment for these women was absent from the discourse, which focused, like the temperance literature of a century earlier, upon the personal failings of the fetus vessel. The continued preoccupation with the trope of the bad mother was apparent in US senator Brock Adams's 1990 speech: "No example more fully demonstrates the slavery of drug addiction than the pregnant addict. To learn that the craving for drugs can override even essential maternal concern for the well-being of an unborn child is a frightening and tragic phenomenon."[92]

The calumny directed at the bad mother, particularly the pregnant addict, continues to limit harm reduction options. In the rare instances where pregnant women are able to access methadone treatment for their addictions, it has been determined that their infants, although initially experiencing methadone withdrawal, can be medically managed and do not develop congenital malformations or exhibit notable neuro-behavioural consequences as they mature. More importantly, their mothers experience general improvement in health, nutrition, and infant care preparation, all to the "enormous benefit" of their babies.[93]

Within the Canadian context, the mother/addict who was the archetypal figure of calumny was the Aboriginal woman. In the 1950s, "Kitty H.," an Aboriginal runaway, became a drug user in Vancouver and "gave birth to a premature baby that lived for only four days. Her husband blamed her for the child's death, as she was using drugs at the time. Overwhelmed with guilt and remorse, she broke down and received shock treatment."[94] Up to the present, women like Kitty have been considered "expected offenders" rather than "ideal (less blameworthy) offenders."[95] Despite, or perhaps due to, Aboriginal women's histories of generational trauma, victimization, and endemic poverty, state and public responses to their addictions are less sympathetic than for middle-class, white Canadians. Aboriginal female drug users are more likely to experience incarceration, often in maximum security. They are also more likely to lose their children. In 2007, 1 out of every 10 First Nations children in Canada was placed in care, compared with a rate of 1 out of 200 non-Aboriginal children. Consequently, many Aboriginal women will conceal their drug use and avoid treatment to stay under the radar of social services.[96]

The intersection of race, class, and gender in the state's treatment of the Aboriginal pregnant addict found full expression in a case that was ultimately decided in the Supreme Court of Canada. *Winnipeg Child and Family Services (Northwest Area) v G. (D.F.)*[97] involved a young Aboriginal woman who was addicted to glue sniffing and was five months pregnant with her fourth child when she was apprehended by Winnipeg Child and Family Services. Because of her addiction, two of her children had been born severely disabled and were permanent wards of the state. A Superior Court judge had ordered her detention for treatment in a health centre until the birth of her child. One of the grounds for this ruling was the court's *parens patriae* jurisdiction, or ability to intervene for the protection of a child, but this power had never been used for a fetus. The Supreme Court overturned the lower court decision on the basis that there was no *parens patriae* legislation in Canada that extended to the fetus, that a pregnant woman and her fetus were one, and that to intervene was to radically impinge upon the fundamental liberties of the mother.

Because of the wider ramifications of this case, there were a number of interveners (interested parties who make representations to the court), including a variety of pro-life, pro-choice, Métis, and civil liberties groups, and the case became a spectacle of competing religious, social, and political organizations fighting over the body of an Aboriginal addict. Even more telling, the original order had been for compulsory treatment only for the course of the pregnancy, i.e., to provide the best conditions for the birth of a healthy child who would not, at least in the short term, become an expense for the state, and not for treatment leading to a cure for the addicted mother.

In 2010, "Mrs. G." spoke out about her experiences. Surrendered to Child and Family Services with her seven siblings by her father after her mother's death, she found refuge on the streets, sniffing glue and eventually working in the sex trade: "I thought I was going to die. I wanted to die." During the legal battle over her involuntary commitment, she voluntarily entered treatment, which she called "a miracle ... I prayed, I fell asleep ... I woke up [with] no cravings. I was changed overnight." Mrs. G. credits her baby boy with "saving her life."[98] Her story of degradation and redemption was reminiscent of many a temperance tale, but in this instance she had the support of many powerful organizations and individuals who aided her recovery while pursuing their own agendas.

Over the span of almost 150 years, the medical and temperance discourse contributed to the oppression of the majority of female drug addicts and alcoholics. Greater participation in public life and public spaces, including drinking establishments, did not eliminate the Victorian tropes of the bad mother and the fallen woman. At the same time, women received cross-messages from mass media, experts, and figures of authority, telling them that they were liberated enough to drink but risked their femininity if they got drunk. Their use of recreational drugs could endanger their children, but prescription and over-the-counter medication were theirs for the taking. These cross-messages resulted in a continued reluctance, on the part of women who were victims of substance abuse, to emerge from the shadows of shame and seek the help they needed.

Notes

1 Twenty-five years ago, I examined attitudes towards the female alcoholic in "Oh, Lord, Pour a Cordial in Her Wounded Heart: The Drinking Woman in Victorian and Edwardian Canada," in *Drink in Canada: Historical Essays,* ed. Cheryl Krasnick Warsh (Montreal and Kingston: McGill-Queen's University Press, 1993), 70–91. This chapter revisits and updates the subject, as I take advantage of the flowering of gender and alcohol history since the 1990s.

2 For more on the temperance movement, social reform, and Canadian women, see Carol Bacchi, *Liberation Deferred? The Ideas of the English-Canadian Suffragists, 1877–1918* (Toronto: University of Toronto Press, 1983); Mariana Valverde, *The Age of Light, Soap and Water: Moral Reform in English Canada, 1885–1925* (Toronto: McClelland and Stewart, 1991); and Sharon Anne Cook, *Through Sunshine and Shadow: The Woman's Christian Temperance Union, Evangelicalism, and Reform in Ontario, 1874–1930* (Montreal and Kingston: McGill-Queen's University Press, 1995).

3 See Barbara Welter's classic essay, "The Cult of True Womanhood, 1800–1860," *American Quarterly* 18 (Summer 1966): 151–74.

4 Catherine Gilbert Murdock, *Domesticating Drink: Women, Men and Alcohol in America 1870–1940* (PhD diss., University of Pennsylvania, 1995), 164–78, 195–200.

5 Madelon Powers, *Faces along the Bar: Lore and Order in the Workingman's Saloon, 1870–1920* (Chicago: University of Chicago Press, 1998).

6 Craig Heron, *Booze: A Distilled History* (Toronto: Between the Lines, 2003), 126–27. The evils of the grocer's licence in Britain, and the growing acceptance of women

purchasing liquor for the home, is discussed in Wm. Wynn Westcott, "Inebriety in Women and the Overlaying of Infants," *Journal of Inebriety* 1, 2 (1903): 66.

7   T.H. George, "Letter to the Editor: Grocers Liquor Licenses," *The Toronto Mail*, February 18, 1884.

8   Heron, *Booze,* 209.

9   See Carolyn Strange, "From Modern Babylon to a City upon a Hill: The Toronto Social Survey Commission of 1915 and the Search for Sexual Order in the City," in *Patterns of the Past: Interpreting Ontario's History,* ed. Roger Hall, William Westfall, and Laurel Sefton MacDowell (Toronto: Dundurn Press, 1988), 255–77.

10   Carroll Smith-Rosenberg, "The New Woman as Androgyne," in *Disorderly Conduct: Visions of Gender in Victorian America* (New York: Oxford University Press, 1985), 261.

11   Sarah E. Williams, "The Use of Beverage Alcohol as Medicine 1790–1860," *Journal of Studies on Alcohol* 41, 5 (1980): 546–49.

12   John Burnham, *Bad Habits: Drinking, Smoking, Taking Drugs, Gambling, Sexual Misbehavior and Swearing in American History,* rev. ed. (New York: NYU Press, 1994), 1–22.

13   Cheryl Krasnick Warsh, "Smoke and Mirrors: Gender Representation in North American Tobacco and Alcohol Advertisements before 1950," *Histoire sociale/Social History* 31, 62 (November 1998): 183–222.

14   Cheryl Krasnick Warsh and Dan Malleck, *Consuming Modernity: Gendered Behaviour and Consumerism before the Baby Boom* (Vancouver: UBC Press, 2013).

15   Murdock, *Domesticating Drink,* 164–78, 195–200, 241–44.

16   Greg Marquis, "Alcohol Is Good for You: Health Messages in Canadian Newspaper Advertisements, 1890–1930" (unpublished manuscript, 2011), typescript, 5–6, 19–21.

17   Heron, *Booze,* 210.

18   Jane Nicholas, *The Modern Girl: Feminine Modernities, the Body and Commodities in the 1920s* (Toronto: University of Toronto Press, 2015), 97.

19   Margaret Little, "Ontario Mothers' Allowance Case Files as a Site of Contestation," in *On the Case: Explorations in Social History,* ed. France Iacovetta and Wendy Mitchinson (Toronto: University of Toronto Press, 1998), 237.

20   Heron, *Booze,* 288. Because of strict advertising codes, it was not until the early 1960s that women were portrayed as drinking in liquor ads. See Cheryl Krasnick Warsh and Greg Marquis, "Gender, Spirits and Beer: Representing Female and Male Bodies in Canadian Alcohol Ads, 1930s–1970s," in *Contesting Bodies and Nation in Canadian History,* ed. Patrizia Gentile and Jane Nicholas (Toronto: University of Toronto Press, 2013).

21   Heron, *Booze,* 289, 331; see Robert A. Campbell, *Demon Rum or Easy Money: Government Control of Liquor in British Columbia from Prohibition to Privatization* (Ottawa: Carleton University Press, 1991).

22   See Warsh, "Oh, Lord," Table 1: Drunk and Disorderly Commitments: Ontario," 77–79.

23 Reginald G. Smart and Alan C. Ogborne, *Northern Spirits: A Social History of Alcohol in Canada* (Toronto: Addiction Research Foundation, 1996), 66.

24 Eric Single, Minh Van Truong, Edward M. Adalf, and Anca Lalomiteanu, comps. *Canadian Profile: Alcohol, Tobacco and Other Drugs* (Toronto: Addiction Research Foundation, 1999): 17. See https://tinyurl.com/y3zbne25.

25 Kaye Fillmore, "When Angels Fall: Women's Drinking as Cultural Preoccupation and as Reality," in *Alcohol Problems in Women,* ed. Sharon Wilsnack and Linda Beckman (New York: Guilford Press, 1984), 22.

26 Thomas D. Crothers, "Is Alcoholism Increasing among American Women?" *North American Review* 155 (1892): 734.

27 Dr. Agnes Sparks, "Alcoholism in Women – Its Cause, Consequences and Cure," *Medical Record* 52 (November 13, 1897): 699.

28 This passage was cited by Edith Lisansky Gomberg, "Historical and Political Perspective: Women and Drug Use," Journal of Social Issues 38, 2 (1982): 16.

29 Lynne Marks, "No Double Standard? Leisure, Sex, and Sin in Upper Canadian Church Discipline Records, 1800–1860," in eds. Nancy Forestell, Kathryn McPerson and Cecilia Morgan, *Gendered Pasts: Historical Essays in Masculinity and Femininity in Canada* (Toronto: University of Toronto Press, 2014): 53–54.

30 Mary Anne Poutanen, "The Homeless, the Whore, the Drunkard, and the Disorderly: Contours of Female Vagrancy in the Montreal Courts, 1810–1842," in McPherson et al., *Gendered Pasts,* 30, 33–34.

31 Elizabeth Chesser, "Inebriety among Women," *British Journal of Inebriety* 6 (1909): 188.

32 Cheryl Krasnick Warsh, *Moments of Unreason: The Practice of Canadian Psychiatry and the Homewood Retreat, 1883–1923* (Montreal and Kingston: McGill-Queen's University Press, 1989), 81.

33 Angus McLaren, *Our Own Master Race: Eugenics in Canada, 1885–1945* (Toronto: University of Toronto Press, 1990, 2014), 166. See also Robert Vineberg, "Healthy Enough to Get In: The Evolution of Canadian Immigration Policy Related to Immigrant Health," *International Migration and Integration* 16 (2015): 286–89.

34 William E. Bessey, "On the Use of Alcoholic Stimulants by Nursing Mothers," *Canada Medical Record* 1 (1872–73): 197.

35 Cesare Lombroso and William Ferraro, *The Female Offender* (1894; repr. London: Peter Owen, 1959), 95, 129, 152–53.

36 Robert Menzies and Dorothy Chunn, "The Gender Politics of Criminal Insanity: 'Order-in-Council' Women in British Columbia, 1888–1950," *Histoire sociale/Social History* 31, 62 (November 1998): 274.

37 Smart and Ogborne, *Northern Spirits,* 119.

38 James B. Waldram, D. Ann Herring, and T. Kule Young, *Aboriginal Health in Canada: Historical, Cultural and Epidemiological Perspectives* (Toronto: University of Toronto Press, 1995), 139.

39 Warsh, *Moments of Unreason,* 162.

40 Sarah Stage, *Female Complaints: Lydia Pinkham and the Business of Women's Medicine* (N.Y.: Norton, 1979): 167.

41 Ibid., 168–70.

42 Denyse Baillargeon, "Medicine Advertising, Women's Work, and Women's Bodies in Montreal Newspapers, 1919–39," in *Consuming Modernity: Gendered Behaviour and Consumerism before the Baby Boom,* ed. Cheryl Krasnick Warsh and Dan Malleck (Vancouver: UBC Press, 2013), 79.

43 Catherine Carstairs, *Illegal Drug Use, Regulation, and Power in Canada, 1920–1961* (Toronto: University of Toronto Press, 2006), 17.

44 Manuella Adrian and Florence Kellner, "Introduction: The Need for a Woman-Centred Approach to Substance Abuse Issues," in *Women's Use of Alcohol, Tobacco and Other Drugs in Canada,* ed. Manuella Adrian, Colleen Lundy, and Marc Eliany (Toronto: Addiction Research Foundation, 1996), xii.

45 Poutanen, "The Homeless, the Whore," 40.

46 See Warsh, "Oh, Lord," Tables 1–3, 77–79.

47 Heron, *Booze,* 112–13.

48 Jean Barman, "Aboriginal Women on the Streets of Victoria: Rethinking Transgressive Sexuality during the Colonial Encounter," in *Contact Zones: Aboriginal and Settler Women in Canada's Colonial Past,* ed. Katie Pickles and Myra Rutherdale (Vancouver: UBC Press, 2005), 209.

49 Melinda Kanner, "That's Why the Lady Is a Drunk: Women, Alcoholism and Popular Culture," in *Sexual Politics and Popular Culture,* ed. Diane Raymond (Bowling Green, OH: Bowling Green University Press, 1990), 183, 186. See also Lori Rotskoff, *Love on the Rocks: Men, Women and Alcohol in Post–World War II America* (Chapel Hill: University of North Carolina Press, 2002).

50 Robert A. Campbell, "Ladies and Escorts: Gender Segregation and Public Policy in British Columbia Beer Parlors, 1925–1945," *BC Studies* 105–6 (Spring/Summer 1995): 120–21.

51 Heron, *Booze,* 289.

52 Ibid., 289.

53 Marcel Martel, *Canada the Good: A Short History of Vice since 1500* (Waterloo, ON: Wilfrid Laurier University Press, 2014), 119. See also Campbell, "Ladies and Escorts."

54 Greg Marquis, "Vancouver Vice: The Police and the Negotiation of Morality, 1904–1935," in *Essays in the History of Canadian Law IV: British Columbia and the Yukon,* ed. Hamar Foster and John McLaren (Toronto: University of Toronto Press, 1995), 243.

55 Lindsey McMaster, *Working Girls in the West: Representations of Wage-Earning Women* (Vancouver: UBC Press, 2007), 106.

56 Katrina Srigley, *Breadwinning Daughters: Young Working Women in a Depression-Era City, 1929–1939* (Toronto: University of Toronto Press, 2010), 28.

57 Ibid., 83.

58 Ibid., 83–85.

59 Ibid., 89.

60 Nicholas, *Modern Girl*, 107. During the late 1930s, Charlotte Whitton was instrumental in refusing the entry of Jewish child refugees from Nazi Germany. See Joanne Chianello, "Whitton's Controversial Past under Microscope Again," *Ottawa Citizen*, May 3, 2011, C8.

61 Kathryn McPherson, "The Case of the Kissing Nurse: Femininity, Sexuality, and Canadian Nursing, 1900–1970," in Forestell et al, eds. *Gendered Pasts*, 185.

62 Carstairs, *Illegal Drug Use*, 14, 50, 56–57.

63 Andrée Levesque, *Making and Breaking the Rules: Women in Quebec, 1919–1939* (Toronto: McClelland and Stewart, 1994), 123.

64 Carstairs, *Illegal Drug Use*, 63.

65 Ibid., 66–67, 71, 80.

66 Ibid., 80.

67 Ruth Roach Pierson, *They're Still Women After All: The Second World War and Canadian Womanhood* (Toronto: McClelland and Stewart, 1986), 206.

68 Jennifer Stephen, *Pick One Intelligent Girl: Employability, Domesticity, and the Gendering of Canada's Welfare State, 1939–1947* (Toronto: University of Toronto Press, 2007), 86.

69 Lori Chambers, *Misconceptions: Unmarried Motherhood and the Ontario Children of Unmarried Parents Act, 1921–1969* (Toronto: University of Toronto Press, 2007), 38, 51.

70 Nathan Michael Corzine, "Right at Home: Freedom and Domesticity in the Language and Imagery of Beer Advertising 1933–1960," *Journal of Social History* 43, 4 (Summer 2010): 843–46.

71 "I've Got a Reputation Now!" (Brights Wines advertisement), *Maclean's*, June 7, 1958, 62; "For Bridge, Meeting or Tea – 74 for Me!" (Brights Wines advertisement), *Maclean's*, April 9, 1960, 34. Warsh and Marquis, "Gender, Spirits and Beer," 214.

72 "New Diet: 'Deuces Wild,'" *Vogue*, May 15, 1954, 52–54.

73 Edith Lisansky [Gomberg], "The Woman Alcoholic," *Annals of the American Academy* 315 (1958): 73–76.

74 Laurence A. Senseman, "The Housewife's Secret Illness: How to Recognize the Female Alcoholic," *Rhode Island Medical Journal* 49 (1966): 40–42.

75 Vera Lindbeck, "The Woman Alcoholic: A Review of the Literature," *International Journal of the Addictions* 7, 3 (1972): 568–70, 575.

76 Myron Belfer, Richard Shader, Mary Carroll, and Jerold Harmatz, "Alcoholism in Women," *Archives of General Psychiatry*, 25 (December 1971): 540–44.

77 Florence Ridlon, *A Fallen Angel: The Status Insularity of the Female Alcoholic* (Lewisburg, PA: Bucknell University Press, 1988), 32–33.

78 D.T. Lowry, "Alcohol Consumption Patterns and Consequences in Prime-Time Network TV," *Journalism Quarterly* 58, 1 (1981): 2–8.

79 Nancy Signorielli, "Drinking, Sex and Violence on Television: The Cultural Indicators Perspective," *Journal of Drug Education* 17, 3 (1987): 246, 248, 255.

80 Lawrence Wallack, Warren Breed, and James De Foe, "Alcohol and Soap Operas: Drinking in the Light of Day," *Journal of Drug Education* 15, 4 (1985): 368–69.

81 Warren Breed and James De Foe, "Mass Media, Alcohol and Drugs: A New Trend," *Journal of Drug Education* 10, 2 (1980): 136–37.

82 James Rooney, "An Analysis of Drug Advertisements on Network Television in the United States" (paper presented to the Kettil Bruun Society for Social and Epidemiological Research on Alcohol, Edinburgh, Scotland, June 1996), 7–10, 12.

83 Colleen Dell and Jennifer Kilty, "The Creation of the *Expected* Aboriginal Woman Drug Offender in Canada: Exploring Relations between Victimization, Punishment, and Cultural Identity," *International Review of Victimology* 19, 1 (June 14, 2012): 4.

84 Ibid., 12.

85 The characteristics of lack of inhibition and impulsive behaviour among some children of inebriate mothers were recognized by fin-de-siècle physicians. See Dr. W.C. Sullivan, "The Causes of Inebriety in the Female and the Effects of Alcoholism on Racial Degeneration," *Journal of Inebriety* 1, 2 (1903): 64.

86 Smart and Ogborne, *Northern Spirits,* 119.

87 Single et al, *Canadian Profile,* 177.

88 Smart and Ogborne, *Northern Spirits,* 120.

89 Pertice M. Moffitt, "In the Dark: Uncovering Influences on Pregnant Women's Health in the Northwest Territories," in Beverly Leipert, Belinda Leach and Wilfreda Thurston, eds. *Rural Women's Health* (Toronto: University of Toronto Press, 2012): 330–31.

90 Single et al, *Canadian Profile,* 169, 193.

91 Dell and Kilty, "Creation," 4, 6.

92 Nancy Campbell, "Regulating 'Maternal Instinct': Governing Mentalities of Late 20th Century U.S. Illicit Drug Policy," *Signs: Journal of Women in Culture and Society* 24, 4 (1999): 895–96, 898–99, 902.

93 Stephen Kandall, *Substance and Shadow: Women and Addiction in the United States* (Cambridge, MA: Harvard University Press, 1996), 285, 288–90.

94 Carstairs, *Illegal Drug Use,* 5.

95 Dell and Kilty, "Creation," 1.

96 Ibid., 3, 2, 6.

97 [1997] 3 SCR 925.

98 "Woman in Fetus Rights Case Speaks Out," *CBC News,* December 15, 2010.

"To Find Out the Best Men and to Try to Get Them In"

2

Women, Temperance, and Politics in Manchester, 1873–1919

Cynthia Belaskie

October Meeting "Manchester Women's Christian Temperance Association and Police Court Mission."– A meeting of this Association held yesterday at the rooms of the YMCA was largely attended. Hughes presided, and the meeting was addressed by Mrs H Dodds and Miss Thomson on municipal work amongst women. The former said that *the conscience of women was being aroused, and now many would only vote for men who had the best interests of the city at heart.* There were three things women could do. *They could use their votes, canvass for good men, and work in many ways for the welfare of the city in which they lived.* Thomson spoke on the responsibility of the vote, and entreated the women present to *use their influence for temperance, purity, and righteousness.* The municipal franchise was after all, she said, more important than the Parliamentary, for it influenced home life.[1]

The newspaper clipping above was probably from October 1898, and probably from the *Manchester Guardian,* but it could have come from any point between 1895 and 1908, when Flora Dodds and Helen Thomson were constant champions of women's role in politics and were mentioned regularly in all the local papers. Although these thirteen years were Dodds and Thomson's heyday, the sentiments expressed about the importance of women's involvement in politics and their responsibilities for the public good have roots that run deep into the 1870s, when the Manchester Women's Christian Temperance Association (MWCTA) was formed, and branches that stretch into the 1920s as these women's rights and temperance activists persisted in their mission.

Long before they had the parliamentary franchise, the Manchester Women wielded political power and influence. They were strategic and effective political actors. They had time, money, power, and influence on their side. They were critical in their evaluation of candidates and worked hard to "find out the best men and to try to get them in."[2] They did not just use the temperance movement as a training ground to gain political acumen that they could use in the cause of suffrage, although it may have served this dual purpose. They were authentic in their political support, with true conviction that the temperance candidate would bring about positive social and political change. Their energetic engagement in politics was just one way they strove to achieve their elusive goal of a dry and prosperous Manchester.

This chapter explores the ways the Manchester Women engaged in politics. At the local level, we find them organizing city-wide, long-term boycotts. They were on the streets canvassing for particular candidates, and in drawing rooms encouraging women to do everything in their power to vote. They stood in front of large crowds and won supporters, both men and women, in their drive for women's enfranchisement. They also tried to exert their power and influence beyond the local level, and sent countless memorials to elected officials in support of temperance bills. They made their opinions known on other issues of national and international importance, throwing their collective weight against injustice whenever they could. The Manchester Women gained particular expertise in the legal system as they navigated the liquor-licensing sessions, and they used this official mechanism of the state to enact very local change. Ultimately, however, this is a story of a rise and fall, since just as they became experts in navigating the system, they system changed and they were knocked back to being minor actors on a large stage.

The Manchester Women's Christian Temperance Association

The Manchester Women's Christian Temperance Association (MWCTA) was formed in 1875 by Rebekha Hind Smith, a long-time temperance innovator and activist. In the late 1860s, she and her husband recognized the importance of class-based temperance societies and founded the first British Workman's Public-Houses.[3] The Workman's Pubs offered the same conviviality and service as traditional public houses, with two major differences. They sold no intoxicating drink and offered free education in the form of regular lectures and debates.[4] The same logic the Hind Smiths applied to class would also be applied to sex, and it was in this vein that Rebekha started the MWCTA in 1875. She wrote and spoke widely about her temperance accomplishments, and was a well-known figure in the temperance world. Even after moving to London in 1881, she remained president of the MWCTA until 1888.[5] Like other charities, the association was unwilling to sever its affiliation with this temperance pioneer because of the trustworthiness and integrity her name bestowed on it.

Like many other Victorian women's philanthropic organizations, the MWCTA had a sophisticated power structure. An elected executive committee of influential wealthy women sat at the helm. Over the years, they employed a number of women to work in various secretarial and organizing positions. Smaller committees handled specific duties, such as the book stall or mission to working women. Smaller local branches in Manchester's neighbourhoods reported to the central group. They also paid dues. The particular flavour of each local branch derived from the characteristics of the neighbourhood. Some had drawing room meetings. Others had large mixed-sex socials. All encouraged visitors to their meetings to sign the pledge and take up the temperance cause.

The MWCTA was the largest women's temperance association in England and affiliated with the British Women's Temperance Association (BWTA) in 1886.[6]

Flora Dodds and Helen Thomson

It is not surprising that Flora J. Dodds and Helen Bishop Thomson drew a large crowd to the meeting described in the clipping at the outset of this chapter. They were a dynamic pair of temperance workers who spent decades on political work. They did more than give speeches (although Thomson was a much sought after speaker and addressed dozens of meetings a month). They devoted an enormous amount of energy to effect change in Manchester's political landscape. They campaigned for "dry" candidates at the municipal and parliamentary levels. They spoke to women one-on-one, trying to convince them to vote or at least be interested in political affairs. Apathy was their enemy, and both displayed agitation when women voters were uninterested or uninformed.

It is important to get a picture of the kind of political organizers that Dodds and Thomson were. They differed from the famous suffragettes, the Pankhursts, in not being especially well bred or wealthy, but neither were they among the working-class Manchester suffragists that Jill Liddington and Jill Norris write about in *"One Hand Tied behind Us."*[7]

Flora Dodds was married to a master butcher, Henry.[8] Although they had only one surviving child, Herbert, her home often had two or three young men apprenticing under her husband. At times, other family members also lived with the Doddses; for example, the 1901 census showed her sister and niece sharing her already bustling home.[9] The Doddses were well enough off, which is to be expected as her husband was a successful skilled tradesman. She always had a domestic servant, which likely made managing motherhood, her philanthropic duties, and a busy household easier. In the census, her sister's profession was listed as "Housekeeper." She was likely managing the Dodds home since both Henry and Flora were at the peak of their careers and probably unable to pay much attention to the details of home life. Flora joined the MWCTA in 1893, when she was about forty-eight years old.[10] By 1901, she was working as a Poor Law guardian. The census painted a picture of a busy and vibrant household. Flora probably did not need temperance activism simply to fill her days, which suggests an authentic desire to bring about genuine change in her community and a family that supported her activism.

Helen Bishop Thomson, on the other hand, was a professional temperance worker. She was hired by the MWCTA in 1895 at age forty-two, and immediately began political organizing.[11] She earned a good wage from the association, and was its highest-paid employee at £75 annually, significantly more than what other employees were taking home.

Although she was the association's organizing secretary, the great bulk of her work was not strictly for temperance advocacy but for political activities. Thomson came to the MWCTA from Edinburgh, and her work in Manchester was a natural extension of the informal apprenticeship she would have done at home and in her paid employment. Her father was a Baptist minister, and her mother was listed in the census rolls as a Baptist minister's wife.[12] In the 1881 census, her brother was shown as the head of the household and was listed as a teacher at Edinburgh University.[13] Thomson attended school until she was at least eighteen, in 1871. Both she and her younger sister, Isabella, listed themselves as private teachers once their studies were over, whereas her eldest sister, Catherine, stated that she lived by private means.[14] From this family history, we may infer that Helen Thomson was a well-educated, articulate activist who trained in ministerial work at the feet of her religious parents and lived in a home that encouraged learning.

Much of the literature on the connection between British women's temperance and political activism focuses on temperance women's agitation for the parliamentary vote. As the work of Lilian Lewis Shiman and Olwen Niessen demonstrates, the temperance movement had formidable leaders, such as Julia B. Wightman and Lady Henry Somerset, who fought for temperance, suffrage, purity, and many other social justice causes.[15] Although Wightman and Somerset did an enormous amount of work at the local level, that work has been analyzed from a national perspective: What did their leadership mean to English women? How did their local work have a national impact? It has also been explained as a training camp for national-scale projects, or as a bit of a hobby on the side. The value of local work for its own sake is missing from these studies. Ian Tyrrell's seminal *Woman's World/Woman's Empire* demonstrates the transnational reach of temperance women's political discourse. Tyrrell reveals an intricate web of sometimes contradictory or at least competing reasons why temperance women campaigned for the vote. Some sought fairness or gender equality, others were motivated by what they saw as women's higher morality, and still others simply wanted to facilitate the passage of temperance legislation. Mostly, however, "temperance women," Tyrrell argues, "tended to combine arguments of natural rights indiscriminately with those of expediency and to see both as necessary to justice, in much the same way as other suffragists did between 1900 and 1920."[16] And while temperance women may have made strong arguments for the franchise, he contends that they lacked the ability to actually effect political change. They could "attempt to shame men into action on moral issues ... [but] the reality was that women lacked political power."[17]

More recently, though, historians have begun delving into how politics operated on the local level, and, as this chapter contends, by turning our gaze to the municipality, we see that women had far more political power than the literature has previously revealed. When we add to this discussion the role of women's political work at the local level, we begin to see that women were rather powerful. In her work on philanthropy and women's citizenship, Andrea Geddes Poole finds that even without the parliamentary franchise, women were "active elements" in Victorian political life.[18]

Steven King's study of women Poor Law guardians in Bolton and Lancashire demonstrates how important it is for historians to turn their gaze towards the local and away from what he claims are overemphasized national movements. He finds that the focus on the national downplays the "individual and collective achievements of local female guardians."[19] The case of women and temperance in Britain is similar to what King finds in studies of the Poor Law. After the British Women's Temperance Association became a unifying national organization in 1876, historians tended to leave out the local woman thumping for temperance. Who can blame them? The BWTA had fantastically public schisms, groups splitting from their leadership over ideology, wildly wealthy and beautiful presidents, and an international profile.[20] Although the dramatic story of the BWTA in the last quarter of the nineteenth century certainly cannot be generalized to the experience of the local temperance worker, what it does do is help contextualize the work that was being done locally. The women of the Manchester Women's Christian Temperance Association were part of this large collective action. They had voting rights within the BWTA and reported back on the friction in those powder keg meetings. This, however, was not the sum of their experience as temperance workers, but more of a footnote. The Manchester Women were influential actors in their own city and in their own right, and because of this they were invited to participate in guiding the national agenda.

Engagement with Local, National, and International Politics

Boycotts

At only thirteen pages long, the Manchester Women's fourth annual report was a modest document but played an important part in legitimizing this venture of philanthropic women. The report outlined the "Basis" for the group and gave an account of its activities for the year 1879, a list of all its donors and the amounts contributed, and a list of some of the "Grocers, Greengrocers and Confectioners" in the city who were not licensed to sell alcohol. The latter list was part of a "Special Appeal to Lady Housekeepers" to stop frequenting establishments that sold alcoholic beverages. The appeal's goals were twofold. First, the Manchester Women argued that women of a certain stature, who would never drink in public houses, were becoming drunkards in their own homes because they could purchase alcohol along with their groceries and imbibe later at home in secret. Frequenting unlicensed grocers would prevent this from happening. Second, the Manchester Women wanted to encourage people to "no longer give their silent but powerful encouragement to the *wrong side*."[21] The Manchester Women were encouraging their contemporaries to vote with their pocketbooks.

Although the Manchester Women would all have been too young to remember the slave sugar boycotts of 1825–29, their mothers and grandmothers could have participated in this important domestic act and its powerful effects. Clare Midgely argues that the sugar boycotts provided "the domestic roots of popular support for abolition."[22] In the early years of the MWCTA, its members focused their campaigns for change on the home, yet, by initiating boycotts of particular vendors, they were making the home a decidedly political space.

There is a sense in the annual report that the boycott met with resistance. Housekeepers were not necessarily flocking to the Manchester Women's grand scheme. As the report states, some simply did not want to change from the grocer they liked or was nearby, to which the Manchester Women countered that drink was such a vicious homewrecker that it was worth the discomfort of change. Other women claimed they simply did not know which grocers were unlicensed, so the Manchester Women took up the lengthy and labour-intensive process of compiling and publishing a list. This list of unlicensed grocers became a mainstay of the MWCTA's annual reports, taking up the back pages for decades. The Manchester Women were under no illusion that the boycott would provide a quick fix to the liquor problem, but it was part of a larger political campaign that they were engaged in for the long haul.

Memorials and Resolutions

Memorials and resolutions were used by the Manchester Women to disseminate their positions on different issues to all levels of government. Typically, the women would hold meetings on particular topics, such as liquor licensing laws or prostitution. After a rousing talk by an expert on the subject, they would vote on a memorial or resolution – relatively short, elegant prepared statements that outlined the women's collective perspective on a given issue. The memorials were always signed by the most prestigious officers of the organization, and if possible by other official delegates at the meetings. They were intended for specific local or national politicians or magistrates. Sometimes they were directed to the Queen. They were usually mailed, but sometimes deputations of Manchester Women would present memorials in person at public functions, and they were also sent to the local papers for publication. Resolutions were similar to memorials in their design but were less grand. Many more resolutions were published than memorials. Sometimes many resolutions were adopted in a single public meeting. They often made it into the local papers but without the names of particular officers attached to them, being attributed to the entire meeting instead. Memorials and resolutions demonstrated a solid understanding of often complex domestic and foreign legal and political matters, and they urged readers to take specific actions. The Manchester Women's opinions got attention, and they received notes of thanks for their memorials. They were often called on to sign memorials in collaboration with other philanthropic organizations, which suggests that their power and prestige were recognized more broadly, including by their peers in the temperance movement, not just women's groups.

The MWCTA wrote countless memorials and passed resolutions on temperance issues. For example, in the late 1890s, it urged Parliament to enact the Sunday Closing Bill. "That this meeting of the Manchester and Salford Women's Christian Temperance Association records its adherence to the principles of the Sunday Closing (England) Bill, and earnestly enjoins its members to urge their representatives in Parliament to support the second reading of the measure on February 10," read one resolution published in the local papers on February 7, 1897.[23] As part of this campaign, the association also had its organizing secretary, Mrs. Franks, send letters to every branch secretary "asking her to take action with reference to the second reading of the Sunday Closing Bill," at the same time urging them to work for women's suffrage and urge their MPs to pass the women's enfranchisement bill.[24] Franks also wrote to each local MP herself in support of these two bills. It may have been a coincidence that both a women's suffrage bill and a temperance bill would come before Parliament within days of each other, but this situation beautifully demonstrates just how entwined the issues of suffrage and temperance were, not only for these women but for broader English society as well.

At the same time, the Manchester Women were using memorials and resolutions to express their anger and frustration over the continued application in India of the Contagious Diseases Acts, which had been enacted to deal with prostitution in army towns and naval ports. The unequal treatment of men and women was a constant theme in the Manchester Women's work, and things came to a head in 1897. It is fascinating that the memorials and resolutions sent to the most powerful statesmen were not about drink or even suffrage but about prostitution in India. One resolution declared the association's "undying opposition to State sanction of, and provision for vice," and urged "each member of the M&SWCTA [Manchester and Salford Women's Christian Temperance Association] both to show her detestation of, and to do all in her power to prevent anything being done officially to facilitate indulgence in immorality either at home or by the British troops in India."[25] The Manchester Women sent this resolution to the prime minister, Lord Salisbury; the secretary of state for India, Lord George Hamilton; and all the branches of the British Women's Temperance Association.

It was especially gutsy of the Manchester Women to send the resolution to their fellow BWTA members since Lady Henry Somerset, their much-loved president, was on record as arguing that the cantonments were necessary since, if soldiers could not be prevented from visiting prostitutes while in the field, they should at least be protected from disease by institutionalizing or detaining women working as prostitutes.[26] The MWCTA constituted the largest union affiliated with the BWTA and although the resolution may have laid bare some cracks in the organization, it also demonstrated the Manchester Women's power to act autonomously. Far from simply toeing the party line, they were passionate, determined, and unafraid of upsetting the status quo to push forward in the right direction.

Taking this very public stance on the one-sided regulations on prostitution in India was a courageous move. In 1893, when the topic first came up as a possibility for a public meeting, the Manchester Women initially wanted to hold separate meetings for women and men. When their guest speakers refused to address single-sex meetings, all but one of the Executive Committee members agreed to speak publicly about prostitution, sex, and inequality.[27] Four years later, they stood firm against their own national leader, publishing their opinions about sex in reports sent to specific politicians. This notable shift speaks to their commitment to having a political voice. Much was in jeopardy – their respectability and the support of the national BWTA, for example – yet they stood by their convictions.

Politics in the Streets and in Drawing Rooms

Manchester is well documented as the birthplace of a variety of women's political activism. Women were especially active in Manchester's Anti-Corn Law League in the 1830s and 1840s.[28] The Pankhursts started their political life in Manchester.[29] The working-class suffragists in the guilds and trade unions were well organized and active too.[30] It was in this environment that the Manchester Women were making their claim on political power and encouraging other women to follow suit. During elections, they could be found in the streets campaigning for the best men and women and in drawing rooms trying to convince otherwise indifferent women voters to get involved in the political process, and teaching them how to do it.

Politically minded women canvassing for votes in elections where they themselves could not cast a ballot was nothing new. It was a popular and sometimes even effective tactic. Particularly noteworthy was Barbara Bodichon's passionate campaigning for John Stuart Mill in 1865.[31] Like Bodichon, the Manchester Women had money, time, influence, and big ideas. Enthusiastic canvassers, they did not depend solely on volunteers to lead the charge; instead, in 1895 they hired an organizing secretary,

Helen Thomson (whom we met earlier), to dedicate her working hours to campaigning whenever necessary.[32] In the same year, they also took political and municipal work out of the general work of the organization and made it the focus of a special subcommittee.

Thomson was immediately put to work canvassing women and negotiating to get more of them women inspired to vote, or at least interested enough in politics to get their husbands to vote the right way. Within her first weeks of work in the summer of 1895, she was tasked with finding out which candidates for the general election in August were the best temperance men, and holding meetings to encourage women to political action. She devised a list of questions for the various MWCTA branch secretaries to pass on to their local candidates, whose answers would determine whether or not they would get the Manchester Women's support. Branches were also encouraged, wherever and whenever possible, to send a deputation of officers to deliver these questions to the candidates in person. From their records, it seems that it was possible to meet with only one Liberal candidate, who turned out to be worthy of their support.[33] The reports do not mention who won the general election. In biweekly meeting minutes and the annual report, the outcome of the election is remarkably absent from an otherwise detailed account of the MWCTA's political organizing tactics. From the way they approached the next election, it appears that this first attempt to have Thomson canvass for votes may have been too ambitious, and she may have been spread too thin trying to ascertain every single candidate's stance on temperance and women's enfranchisement.

On the heels of the August general election came a municipal election that autumn, so Thomson's canvassing continued. The Manchester Women distributed 5,000 handbills to women voters in Manchester and Salford, but their real efforts were on the ground in All Saints Ward. This time, they decided to focus on wards where a true temperance candidate was being challenged by someone aligned with the drink trade. In All Saints Ward, a temperance man, Mr. Arrandale, was opposed by a hotelkeeper, Mr. Fulton. The Manchester Women were charged with canvassing for women's votes, and Arrandale's success – he won by fifty-eight votes – could very well have been due to their efforts. He thanked the Manchester Women "heartily" for their work. The tactic of concentrating efforts on a particular candidate worked again a few weeks later in the race for alderman in the same ward. The Manchester Women appeared to have found a way to successfully navigate the political system. Within a year, they were getting requests from political candidates asking for their help in canvassing for votes[34] – more requests, in fact, than Thomson could handle on her own, so volunteer members from the Political and Municipal Committee took the lead in canvassing in some races. The Manchester Women worked like this for years, sometimes winning, sometimes not, but always devoting enormous resources to support the driest candidates.

When the time finally came for women to vote, the Manchester Women's efforts to win over women voters were were not as successful as their early electoral victories. Year after year Helen Thomson and Flora Dodds, who were superintendents of the Municipal and Political Departments, respectively, bemoaned women voters' lack of interest. "The Municipal field is one to which women should pay earnest attention. Women have a vote in these elections, and they should bring the weight of their influence and the power of their vote to make life sweeter, clearer, purer," they declared in MWCTA's 1904 annual report, but lamented that "the amount of indifference is appalling, and it needs to be pressed on all women that here, at any rate, this influence is most potent for good."[35] Since 1875, the Manchester Women had been trying to effect change, not only regarding alcohol but also in the way women engaged in politics. They were very strategic in maximizing the effectiveness of their own municipal votes, ensuring, for example, that a Manchester Woman who would not normally meet the property requirement to vote in municipal elections was put on the lease for their offices so that they could guarantee one more active temperance voter at the polls.[36] For women who were so enthusiastic in fulfilling their civic duties, it must have been frustrating and disheartening to see other women with the power to vote not bothering to cast a ballot. Political apathy was their foe as much as the bottle.

Brewster Sessions: A Case Study of the Rise and Fall of the Manchester Women's Political Power

In 1893, the Manchester Women began experimenting with attempts to influence the outcomes of the Brewster Sessions, the local board of magistrates that decided whether or not establishments could obtain or renew licences to sell liquor.[37] That year, they sent a memorial to the magistrates asking for the number of licences to be reduced and for new ones not to be granted. They never knew whether the memorial was read, but were satisfied with the outcome of that session. On the heels of this success, they sent letters to all of their branches encouraging them to get involved in agitating at the Brewster Sessions. At the Chorlton-cum-Hardy branch, Mrs. Meade, a Manchester Woman appeared before her local session and opposed an off-beer licence wherein one could sell beer for consumption off the premises. The application was refused.[38] Whether this was due to Meade's testimony is unknown, but the thrill of winning must have been energizing, and the Manchester Women recommended in their annual report for 1893 that women attend the sessions whenever possible in order to learn the rules and the kinds of evidence needed to persuade the magistrates to deny licence applications.

Clara Swallow, a long-time executive member, consistently attended the Brewster Sessions at the Minshull Street Police Court.[39] While it is difficult to get a sense of who she was simply from meeting minutes and annual reports, we do know that she was unmarried and did not shy away from political engagement. Since she lived with her parents, she did not have a municipal vote, but readily took the opportunity to get one in 1899, when the Manchester Women put her name on their lease. Her mother also sat on the Executive Committee of the MWCTA.

Swallow became the association's expert on the Brewster Sessions and was elected superintendent of its Brewster Committee. She knew the rules and challenged the magistrates when they were not followed. She often gathered evidence against new licence applications on her own, but when she took on a legal issue, she worked in tandem with the Manchester Women's lawyer, a Mr. Batty. For instance, in 1899 a licence to sell beer was granted to a restaurant owner, John Robinson. Batty and Swallow discovered that Robinson did not live on site, which was a requirement for a beer licence. They appealed the licence at a higher court and won.[40]

Perhaps due to such legal successes, interest in the Brewster Sessions grew quickly among the MWCTA membership. In her 1899 annual report, Swallow lamented that more women were not going to court to try to block the granting of licences.[41] Only a year later, though, she reported that almost every branch was doing work in the Brewster Sessions.[42] The well-publicized fight to keep the new Palace of Varieties from securing a

licence may have helped raise support for this type of work. In his successful case against the Palace, Batty argued on "behalf of the *girlhood* of this
great city – that in the hours of excitement and entertainment their brain
might be kept clear of the blight of drink."[43] While not all of her campaigns
were successful, for about a decade Swallow honed her skills in court and
built momentum for this type of hands-on work, where women, with or
without the franchise, could be part of real legal change that impacted
people's lives in the Manchester and Salford communities.

The Brewster Sessions changed in 1904, however. They were moved out
of the municipalities and to the County Quarter Sessions. Those making
the rulings were not necessarily part of the communities they were making decisions for. They were not elected representatives, but appointed.
The Manchester Women were concerned as they could see the influence
and expertise they had worked for so long to secure start to slip away.[44]

For the next two years, the sessions seemed to run almost as they
always had. Swallow was able to continue her work in the courts and was
buoyed by her successes. In fact, under the new rules, new licences had
to be given six public notices. When these notices were published in the
newspaper, Swallow mobilized the local branches to secure witnesses
against the licences. Some of her recruits testified in court; others attended
as spectators.[45] It seemed that in this new system the Manchester Women
had greater opportunity to mobilize their membership and magnify their
impact in the courts.

By 1909, though, it became impossible for Swallow to gather enough
information and present it herself in the courts. Batty's expertise was
needed for all cases, and he was hired to contest all licences.[46] The effects of
the centralization of the sessions were finally felt: Swallow's court experience was no longer sufficient to wage a competitive fight against the liquor
interests. There were now only three sessions, each covering a very large
area and a good number of licences. The sessions were held on consecutive
days or on the same day, so even though notices were published, it was
impossible for Swallow to gather evidence against licences and present it
herself. Although she still canvassed, gathered signatures on petitions,
and found witnesses to testify against the licences, Batty took care of the
professional legal work. It was no longer good enough for a Manchester
woman to represent the Manchester Women's interests.

What is notable about the case of Clara Swallow and the Brewster Sessions is that her experience demonstrates that the movement towards political power was not a linear one. While in 1903 she was a skilled political actor effecting real change, by 1904 her position was more precarious as a woman philanthropist thrust into a new legal system and having to start her apprenticeship and rebuild her networks of influence. There was no consistent path towards increasing prestige and responsibility. This trajectory is also interesting when compared with Swallow's own life course. When her Brewster Sessions work began, she was thirty-eight or thirty-nine years old.[47] When the system changed in 1904, she was fifty, and by the time Batty really took over the work in court, she was fifty-five years old. One can well imagine Swallow's frustration at having to start over and facing increasingly alienating procedures at the Brewster Sessions when she should have been a well-seasoned expert at ease with the duties of her work.

Conclusion

Temperance women interacted with politics on a number of fronts. The case of the Manchester Women exemplifies this because their records were extensive and their political work robust, though not unusually so. Looking at how they worked for political change paints a nuanced picture of their lived experience as political actors without parliamentary franchise. Not having the vote did not restrict their influence in public life. They considered their disenfranchisement a gross injustice and rallied for the vote whenever possible, but they also seized every opportunity to engage with a political system that in some cases did not want them, while in other cases very much welcomed their energy, influence, and enthusiasm – and probably their money too.

Notes

1   Unattributed newspaper clipping pasted in 1895–99 Manchester Women's Christian Temperance Association (MWCTA) Minute Book (M286/1/1-2), Manchester Archives and Local Studies (MALS), Manchester, UK.

2   Executive Committee Meeting Minutes, September 20, 1893, MWCTA Minute Book (M286/1/1-2), MALS.

3   Robert Rae, ed., *The National Temperance League's Annual for 1881* (London: National Temperance Publication Depot, 1881), 121.

4   Raymond Caulkins, *Substitutes for the Saloon* (London: Houghton, Mifflin, 1901), 245.

5 Executive Committee Meeting Minutes, May 4, 1881, and February 1, 1888.

6 Ibid., June 2, 1886.

7 Jill Liddington and Jill Norris, *"One Hand Tied behind Us": The Rise of the Women's Suffrage Movement* (London: Virago, 1979).

8 Ancestry.com and The Church of Jesus Christ of Latter-Day Saints, 1891 England Census [online database] (Provo, UT, Ancestry.com Operations, 2004), RG12/3197.

9 Ancestry.com and The Church of Jesus Christ of Latter-Day Saints, 1901 England Census [online database]. (Provo, UT: Ancestry.com Operations, 2004), RG13/3666.

10 Executive and General Committee Meeting Minutes, December 3, 1893.

11 Executive Committee Meeting Minutes, April 3, 1895; FreeBMD, England and Wales, Civil Registration Death Index, 1837–1915 [online database] (Provo, UT: Ancestry.com Operations, 2006), "Deaths Registered in October, November and December 1909," 302.

12 Parish: Edinburgh Buccleuch; ED: 72; Page: 11; Line: 3; Roll: CSSCT1861_128 [online database] (Provo, UT: Ancestry.com Operations, 2006).

13 Parish: Edinburgh St Cuthberts; ED: 16; Page: 5; Line: 3; Roll: cssct1881_280.

14 Parish: Edinburgh St Cuthberts; ED: 76; Page: 12; Line: 19; Roll: CSSCT1871_164.

15 Lilian Lewis Shiman, *Women and Leadership in Nineteenth-Century England* (New York: St. Martin's Press, 1992); Olwen Niessen, *Aristocracy, Temperance and Social Reform: The Life of Lady Henry Somerset* (London: I.B. Tauris, 2007).

16 Ian Tyrrell, *Woman's World/Woman's Empire: The Woman's Christian Temperance Union in International Perspective, 1880–1930* (Chapel Hill: University of North Carolina Press, 1991), 223.

17 Ibid., 221.

18 Andrea Geddes Poole, *Philanthropy and the Construction of Victorian Women's Citizenship* (Toronto: University of Toronto Press), 10.

19 Steven King, *Women, Welfare and Local Politics 1880–1920* (Sussex, UK: Sussex Academic Press), 19.

20 See Shiman, *Women and Leadership.*

21 MWCTA, Fourth Annual Report, 1879, 11–12. MALS emphasis in original.

22 Clare Midgely, "Sugar Slave Boycotts, Female Activism and the Domestic Base of British Anti-Slavery Culture," *Slavery and Abolition* 17, 3 (December 1996): 137.

23 Unattributed newspaper clipping pasted in 1895–99 MWCTA Minute Book (M286/1/1-2).

24 Executive Committee Meeting Minutes, February 17, 1897.

25 MWCTA, 1896 Annual Report, 1897, 57–58. MALS.

26 Jane Jordan and Ingrid Sharpe, eds., *Josephine Butler and the Prostitution Campaigns: Diseases of the Body Politic,* vol. 5 (London: Routledge, 2003), 553–55.

27 Cynthia Belaskie, "Tying White Ribbons around the World: Manchester's Temperance Women in Late-Nineteenth Century Transnational Feminism," *Women: A Cultural Review* 23:1 (January 2012): 46–61.

28 F.K. Prochaska, *Women and Philanthropy in Nineteenth-Century England* (Oxford: Oxford University Press, 1980), 63.

29 June Purvis, *Emmeline Pankhurst: A Biography* (London: Routledge, 2002), 40.

30 Liddington and Norris, *"One Hand Tied behind Us."*

31 Constance Rover, *Women's Suffrage and Party Politics in Britain 1866–1914* (London: Routledge, 1967), 11.

32 Executive Committee Meeting Minutes, July 17, 1895.

33 Ibid.

34 Ibid., October 21, 1896.

35 MWCTA, Twenty-Eighth Annual Report, 1904, 40. MALS.

36 Executive Committee Meeting Minutes, May 3, 1899.

37 MWCTA, Eighteenth Annual Report, 1893, 29. MALS.

38 Ibid.

39 MWCTA, Twenty-Fourth Annual Report, 1899, 68. MALS.

40 Ibid.

41 Ibid.

42 MWCTA, Twenty-Fifth Annual Report, 1900, 17. MALS.

43 Ibid.

44 MWCTA, Twenty-Eighth Annual Report, 1904, 34–35.

45 MWCTA, Thirty-Second Annual Report, 1908, 26–27. MALS.

46 MWCTA, Thirty-Third Annual Report, 1909, 23. MALS.

47 Clara Louisa Swallow, Birth Record, http://www.freebmd.org.uk/cgi/information. pl?cite=9y2SQKa%2FdO%2BoynWKy8jq0w&scan=1.

Youth, Drugs, and Surveillance at Manseau's Woodstock Pop Festival

3

Eric Fillion

In the summer of 1970, the town of Manseau found itself in the headlines of Quebec's major newspapers after announcing that it would host the province's first outdoor rock music festival. Held on a farm located 200 kilometres northeast of Montreal, on the south side of the St. Lawrence River, the Woodstock Pop Festival promised to honour the legacy of its New York namesake of the previous year.[1] Woods Productions, the company responsible for the event, showed that it meant business when it hired Michael Lang, co-founder of the Woodstock Music and Art Fair, as its technical adviser. The organizers had such high hopes that they contemplated shooting a "rockumentary" in the vein of Michael Wadleigh's *Woodstock*, which had premiered earlier that year.[2] They estimated that 150,000 people would flock to the Quebec countryside the weekend of July 31 to see a stellar cast of performers: Jimi Hendrix, Little Richard, Dr. John the Night Tripper, and Canned Heat were some of the names leaked to the press. Whether the organizers were optimistic or delusional (many claimed that they were blatantly dishonest) is still up for debate.[3]

Be that as it may, the festival was doomed from the start, with Woods Productions struggling to meet the requirements of various government ministries, delays in the issuing of proper permits, claims that the local Mafia was financing the operations, and rumours that none of the artists billed for the festival had signed contracts. In the end, between 10,000 and

15,000 people showed up instead of the expected 150,000. It rained on opening night, and those who stayed and battled the weather were treated to recorded music instead of the promised acts. Only Dr. John the Night Tripper made the trip to Manseau, sharing the stage with mostly mediocre bands, Hare Krishna devotees, and various impromptu performers. Disillusioned, festivalgoers drank alcohol, took drugs, shed their shirts and trousers, or simply hitchhiked home while hordes of onlookers, spurred by the news that entrance fees had been abolished, streamed through the gates to observe hippies in action.[4]

Not everyone returned home disenchanted when the festival ended. Reporters dispatched by various newspapers, officers of the Sûreté du Québec (SQ), and experts from Quebec's Office de la prévention et du traitement de l'alcoolisme et des autres toxicomanies (OPTAT) all welcomed this unprecedented opportunity to study, from up close, the counterculture youth.[5] This was timely, considering that the Canadian government had just launched a commission of inquiry into the non-medical use of drugs. The Le Dain Commission's mandate was to report on the state of knowledge regarding the phenomenon in Canada, to inquire into the cultural and socio-economic factors that explained it, and to make policy recommendations.[6] Through its investigative work and multiple reports, it prompted public debates around the country. "It both catalyzed discussion and served as an institutional site through which the Canadian drugs discourse could operate," explains Kyle Grayson.[7] Manseau's Woodstock Pop Festival provided the framework for such discourse in Quebec during the summer of 1970. It gave reporters, the SQ, and OPTAT a chance to gain knowledge and develop expertise within the clearly demarcated perimeter of a remote festival site. Thus, the festival served as an open-sky laboratory for gathering both hard and soft data regarding the non-medical use of drugs.

This case study focuses on the interplay between various figures of authority and their relationship with the youth of Quebec. It complements a growing literature on the counterculture in Canada by uncovering some of the voices that sought to ascribe meanings to the phenomenon and its sites.[8] Stuart Henderson, in his study of Toronto's Yorkville (i.e., Canada's Haight-Ashbury, which was the epicentre of the counterculture in California), contends that a nexus of performative and discursive practices involving a variety of historical actors – hippies, greasers, bikers, and weekenders, as well as police officers, local politicians, reporters, and various social experts – influenced the shape that centres of youth culture took during the 1960s and 1970s. "Yorkville was a contested territory," he concludes.[9] Marcel Martel revisits some of the same actors in his study of social control and the marijuana question. His discussion of the widespread public debates that accompanied the Le Dain Commission reveals a constellation of interest groups – the medical community, social scientists, the pharmaceutical industry, and the Royal Canadian Mounted Police (RCMP), among others – that competed for influence and authority as the youth of Canada asserted their freedom to smoke.[10] Manseau's Woodstock Pop Festival was one such contested site where the print media, the SQ, and OPTAT sought to acquire legitimacy as authoritative voices on the counterculture youth and its presumed predisposition towards recreational drugs.

In the summer of 1970, youth surveillance in Quebec was the means by which the print media, the SQ, and OPTAT produced what Michel Foucault calls "power/knowledge."[11] It was the channel through which they manifested and legitimized their authority, accumulating "ostensible truths" and framing the object of their surveillance in ways meant to amplify their respective contributions to the Canadian drugs discourse.[12] Foucault writes:

> In any society, there are manifold relations of power which permeate, characterise and constitute the social body, and these relations of power cannot themselves be established, consolidated nor implemented without the production, accumulation, circulation and functioning of a discourse. There can be no possible exercise of power without a certain economy of discourses of truth which operates through and on the basis of this association. We are subjected to the production of truth through power and we cannot exercise power except through the production of truth.[13]

The Woodstock Pop Festival was a spectacle that required decoding. By casting their gaze upon festivalgoers, reporters, police officers, and OPTAT's medical experts and sociologists mobilized the power of discourse to define, contain, protect, reform, and assert authority over the counterculture youth of Quebec while also positioning themselves vis-à-vis competing governmental and non-governmental actors.[14]

The paternalistic undertone found in the approaches and narratives put forth by these various actors echoed the "legal paternalism" that informed the work of the Le Dain Commission – that is, the belief that "the State, in addition to being the guardian of public order, has a *paternalistic function that allows it to use certain forms of legal constraints to prevent non-autonomous persons from harming themselves.*"[15] This undertone was also consistent with the intergenerational power dynamics at play in Manseau. That the event served to contain (and enable the study of) disruptive youth cultures should not have come as a surprise. Festivals are rarely strictly about liminal exuberance and buoyant, collective self-affirmation. They are also "internal political devices" that allow authorities to exert power and "develop the new forms of regulation required to maintain social control."[16] Hence the pervasive surveillance experienced by festivalgoers in the past as well as today.[17]

This chapter is thus informed, in part, by recent scholarship on surveillance in Canada. The historiography of surveillance brings into focus a decades-long history of political policing that reveals how unusual the Canadian state is "in so insistently focussing its surveillance activities inwards."[18] With respect to the youth of Canada, scholars make extensive use of declassified RCMP files to shed light on "paternalistic mounted police attitudes" towards youngsters who were perceived to be vulnerable to the "dangerous intellectual virus" of subversive leftist groups.[19] Focusing on the Red Scare and the Cold War, their discussion of the societal anxieties generated by youth cultures deals only peripherally with the phenomenon of non-medical drug use.[20] Paying close attention to the particularities of the Quebec landscape, the following pages explore the topic of youth surveillance within the broader context of the drugs discourse – looking at the interplay between the print media, the SQ, and OPTAT – while decentring somewhat the RCMP by using recently declassified SQ files preserved at the Bibliothèque et Archives nationales du Québec (BAnQ).[21]

Prelude

Canadians learned that their government was launching a commission of inquiry into the non-medical use of drugs on May 1, 1969. The initiative came from John Munro, minister of national health and welfare, who believed that a public policy solution could be found to the problem of drug use in Canada.[22] The latter part of the 1960s had seen a surge in the consumption of illicit substances: from lysergic acid diethylamide (LSD) to amphetamines and cannabis. Prohibited under the Narcotic Control Act of 1961, cannabis was especially popular among teenagers and young adults, alerting authorities to the fact that the phenomenon of non-medical drug use could no longer be reduced to a matter of deviancy.[23] Users were increasingly from middle-class settings and they shared neither the criminal profile nor the so-called outcast status of hard drug offenders. Still, the long-term association of drug use with immorality and depravity, which was often combined with the fear of "others," was sufficient cause for alarm.[24] Many Canadians thus believed that drug consumption constituted a pressing moral, health, and public security issue at the end of the 1960s. The Le Dain Commission proposed to investigate the phenomenon and make comprehensive policy recommendations. It was "an exercise in state knowledge gathering, as well as a justification for the expansion of the expert-guided therapeutic state," explains Greg Marquis.[25] Tabled in the House of Commons, on June 19, 1970, its interim report fell short of advocating the legalization of cannabis, but it voiced concerns regarding police repression and the imposition of harsh criminal punishments for what many considered minor offences. Most importantly, the report stressed that additional research on the short- and long-term effects of non-medical drug use was needed before a consensus could be reached.[26]

The widening generational divide that accompanied the counterculture movement fuelled the sense of urgency with which adults responded to the rising phenomenon of non-medical drug use. As Doug Owram points out, the baby boomers' rebellions of the 1960s had been fermenting for a decade as postwar "prosperity sustained and extended the power of youth culture."[27] He adds that prosperity "also created an optimism and enthusiasm for experimentation with alternative lifestyles, free of the hang-ups of materialism, that could make sense only to a generation that took material comfort as given."[28] Generational tensions ensued, contends Martel, and "in this context drug use was perceived either as a threat to social values or as part of a new value system."[29] This passage towards a new value system occurred wherever baby boomers could claim the space needed to act out their youthful rebellious identities. Chief among these sites were large-scale outdoor pop festivals.

These gatherings of rock music aficionados began to dot the North American landscape during the 1967 "Summer of Love," spreading north and east from California, where the counterculture movement was in full swing. The Fantasy Fair and Magic Mountain Music Festival and the Monterey International Pop Music Festival, both held near San Francisco in June 1967, paved the way for similar events the following year: Washington's Sky River Rock Festival (August 31 to September 2) and Florida's Miami Pop Festival (December 28–30), among others. The August 1969 Woodstock Music and Art Fair marked the apex of the phenomenon as more than 400,000 people spilled over and beyond the 600-acre upstate New York dairy farm where performers such as Jefferson Airplane, the Grateful Dead, Janis Joplin, and Jimi Hendrix made history. Canadian promoters flirted with pop festivals at the turn of the 1970s, but they showed little inclination to venture into the precarious territory of large-scale events held in unconventional settings, opting instead for stadiums, where unknowns were fewer. The Vancouver Pop Festival of August 1969 was one of a few rare exceptions, but a group of entrepreneurs in Quebec were determined to eclipse that and other efforts by staging an outdoor event that would rival, albeit on a smaller scale, the already mythical Woodstock Music and Art Fair.[30]

The Manseau festival was the brainchild of entrepreneurs Roger Vandal, president of Woods Productions, Réal Le Roy, and the Filiatrault brothers: Raymond, Fernand, Pierre, and Réal. They hired Michael Lang to provide input on the project, but the bulk of contractual and day-to-day media relations were the responsibility of Richard "Ziggy" Wiseman. After securing a site for the event, a sixty-acre farm on the outskirts of Manseau, the group obtained the necessary authorizations from municipal and provincial authorities. During a special town meeting on June 16, 1970, the mayor and council voted not to oppose the project as long as Woods Productions agreed to a series of conditions outlined in a promptly written contract.[31] The organizers agreed to assume full responsibility for the planning and execution of the event, to maintain peace and order in the areas surrounding the farm where the festival would be held, to purchase liability insurance, to remit 1 percent of the value of all ticket sales to the municipality, and to ensure the health and safety of festivalgoers. The contract also stipulated that Woods Productions needed to coordinate with the SQ and obtain the proper permits from the Quebec government before going ahead. Confident in the viability of the project, Vandal affixed his signature to the bottom of the contract.[32]

Elected officials had already been discussing whether or not Quebec should host pop festivals when they received the news that Woods Productions had signed a contract permitting it to stage a large-scale outdoor concert in Manseau. Pressed to clarify the government's position, Jérôme Choquette, the minister of justice, explained that efforts had been undertaken to educate municipalities about the health and security issues that accompanied this novel social phenomenon. In the case of Manseau, he added that Woods Productions would have to meet a list of conditions prior to receiving a permit to hold the event.[33] Vandal and his associates had to spend large sums of money on infrastructure to address concerns regarding access to food and water, hygiene, medical care, transportation, and public safety. Work progressed slowly, however, leading to speculation that the entire affair was a fraudulent scheme and that the promoters planned to disappear with the money collected through ticket sales.[34] Woods Productions carried on nonetheless, and finally obtained its permit on July 22, less than two weeks before the event.

First Act: The Print Media

Quebec dailies and weeklies wasted no time disseminating the news that Manseau would host the province's first large-scale outdoor rock festival. *La Presse, Le Journal de Montréal, The Gazette, Photo-police, Le Nouvelliste,* and *L'Union,* among others, took an interest in the event, from its planning stages to its aftermath.[35] *La Presse*'s Claude Gravel predicted that reporters would disagree on the meaning of the spectacle that was about to unfold, but in the end the media coverage formed a relatively coherent whole.[36] Indeed, Quebec newspapers presented, for the most part, a common front in their efforts to cast themselves as the most legitimate and comprehensive source of information on the counterculture youth and the non-medical use of drugs.[37] To achieve this, they channelled as many resources as possible towards Manseau. For Trois-Rivières's *Le Nouvelliste* (the festival was to take place in its backyard), this meant dispatching seven reporters and one photographer as well as securing the services of a helicopter pilot.[38] More than 250 media representatives planned to visit Manseau on the weekend of July 31. What did they expect to see? Would they witness an authentic performance by the rebellious youth of Quebec? "Sera-ce plutôt une fausse jeunesse, qui acceptera ... de jouer un grand jeu ... sans se soucier à qui le grand jeu profite?" asked Gravel.[39]

The weeks leading up to the event set the tone. The newspapers straddled the fence between nurturing anxiety among their readership and keeping a lid on moral panic with regular updates about the health and public safety precautions taken by both the Quebec government and Woods Productions. Reporters also highlighted the strategies employed by medical experts and police officers to ensure the safety of the festivalgoers converging on Manseau.[40] The publication of a map of the festival site depicting the location of OPTAT's drug treatment tents was meant to reassure parents, and to warn youngsters who had already purchased tickets to be safe.[41] Discussions of the SQ's expected imposing presence in Manseau served similar purposes. Woods Productions had hired a private security firm to ensure safety within the perimeter of the festival site, but the provincial police force had a mandate to supervise operations from the outside, keeping track of suspicious individuals going in and out while monitoring traffic and ensuring public safety in and around Manseau. Newspapers – perhaps inadvertently – sent mixed messages by vacillating between reassuring and alarming reports.

There was unease in the air, with a significant portion of the coverage questioning the ethics, honesty, and competence of the organizers. The recent publication of the Le Dain Commission's interim report also informed some of the other reservations expressed in the press. On July 15, *Le Nouvelliste* published a summary of the document, emphasizing claims made during the public inquiries that soft drugs led to hard drugs and criminal behaviour.[42] "Les festivals pop sont-ils propices au trafic de la drogue?" asked the same newspaper the following day.[43] Manseau residents were told to lock their doors, load their firearms, and herd livestock into pens or barns.[44] The town's bank emptied its coffers and announced that it would be closed during the festival.[45] Reporters added fuel to the fire by telling their readers that similar events held elsewhere had either degenerated into chaos or been cancelled by local authorities.[46] *Photo-police*'s Yvon Dupuis did his part by publishing the following note:

[Dans une telle manifestation d'hystérie collective], les jeunes garçons et filles (de 7–8–9 ans) se mêlent à une foule d'adultes en délire ... la drogue circule à profusion, les pieds piétinent les corps, la bestialité la plus répugnante prend libre cours, les aliments manquent, les salops pullulent, tout est saleté, inconscience, luxure et bêtise ... Avis aux intéressés : NOUS SURVEILLONS![47]

Not all reporters succumbed to this sense of panic, but most headed towards Manseau with a strange mixture of both excitement and trepidation.

One thing is certain: reporters quickly established the fact that the festival was a spectacle whose protagonists lacked both authenticity and maturity. They bombarded their adult readership with sensationalist images of nudity and drug use, validating in the process the fears that had been growing during the weeks leading up to the event.[48] Reporters were concerned with youngsters, not marginal hippies who numbered at most 500, according to *L'Union*.[49] The rest were poseurs who practised "du hippisme de fin de semaine," nothing more.[50] *Le Journal de Montréal* referred to the youth of Quebec in ways that caricatured and belittled acts of youthful rebellion such as bathing and walking in the nude, smoking cannabis, building a shelter using wooden debris, and hitchhiking home.[51] "Youngsters seek elusive spirit," insisted *The Gazette*'s George Radwanski.[52] He explained:

They journeyed to Manseau to build their own temporary world of the young, and they have wound up being treated more like animals in a compound – tough-looking men from Montreal's East End, maintaining "security" on the site, and riot-equipped Provincial Police on the road are their keepers. In their strangely middle-class New Suburbia ... the young act out the rites of the Woodstock ritual. The girls shed their bras. The boys doff their trousers. And they do their best to pomp together in the shallow, stagnant brown waters of a nearby creek. But most of all, they turn to drugs ... They kill the boredom, they kill the passing hours. Heavy-lidded, they sprawl under the leaden sky side-by-side – alone, staring blankly at secrets only they can see. And they wait for the music.[53]

Less than twelve hours into the event, reporters reached the consensus that festivalgoers were the unsuspecting victims of entrepreneurs eager to make a profit on a counterculture that had gone mainstream. In other words, the young idealists had paid between $12 and $15 to take part in a spectacle and play the parts expected of them.

The picture that emerged by the end of the weekend was that excessive drug use had been at the heart of this so-called ritual. Although rock celebrities occupied centre stage within the counterculture movement – some of them even acting as star witnesses for the Le Dain Commission – they were not part of the experience at Manseau.[54] *Le Nouvelliste* declared that in the absence of prominent headliners, drugs had been the real stars of the festival.[55] Reporters did not hold back in documenting the sale and consumption of illicit substances. Images of festivalgoers rolling and smoking joints, traffickers advertising their products using makeshift displays, and distressed drug users lying on stretchers abounded. *La Presse* went a step further, by featuring a close-up of a young man injecting "speed" into his veins.[56] Quebec's newfound tolerance for the non-medical use of drugs was perhaps a means of defusing the revolutionary fervour of the 1960s, speculated Louis-Bernard Robitaille.[57] If that was the case, such laxity came at a cost, as signalled by reports that hundreds of overdoses and a thousand bad trips had plagued the festivities.[58]

Once the event was over, Quebec's dailies and weeklies tackled the question that preoccupied the various parties interested in the Le Dain Commission's public debates. Leon Harris, writing for *The Gazette*, asked: "Leniency is fine, but can the kids cope?"[59] Not on their own, he answered.[60] Reporters noted that the lack of live music, boredom, and the realization that Manseau's Woodstock Pop Festival had been both an illusion and a fraud led youngsters to indulge in drugs, but such a response was also an indication of their immaturity and their vulnerability vis-à-vis potentially dishonest promoters, traffickers, and countless "pervers ... aux instincts dénaturés."[61] The paternalistic tone of the newspapers' discussion of non-medical drug use was dismissive of the festivalgoers' agency. It also echoed parental concerns that teenagers needed both physical and moral protection.[62] Reporters failed to take this opportunity to articulate clearly their views on the decriminalization of substances such as cannabis. Instead, they stressed that youngsters, parents, and government authorities had much to learn from the experience. In the context of the drug debate, the print media helped steer public opinion on the side of caution with its barrage of evocative headlines and explicit photos, both of which spoke to the media's authority as a source of information.

Patting themselves on the back, reporters contended that their abundant coverage explained why the vast majority of Quebec youth were not duped. The teenagers and young adults who decided to stay home that weekend helped defeat what appeared to be an attempt to exploit youthful idealism. *La Presse* wrote that "la jeunesse actuelle n'est pas assimilée ... et quand on veut l'intéresser, elle exige des preuves."[63] *Bien public* corroborated: "Notre jeunesse québécoise a démontré une fois de plus, que sous les dehors désinvoltes, elle était capable de sens critique et de refus quand on prétend l'abuser d'aussi canaille façon."[64] These responsible and sensible youngsters had benefited, of course, from the support of parents who kept themselves informed about pop festivals, remained clear-headed, and dialogued with their children in a genuine spirit of openness. "Le fiasco de Manseau est une grande victoire. C'est la victoire des parents et des jeunes," affirmed *L'Action nationale.*[65] Surrogate parents also deserved praise, as one concerned citizen put it in a letter published by *The Gazette*. Referring to the Quebec government's decision to suspend the issuing of permits for future pop festivals, the writer insisted that Premier Robert Bourassa be given an award for "Parent of the Year."[66] The letter continued: "Here at last is a father who is not afraid to say no to his children and that enough is enough when he feels that they have gone too far."[67] The SQ was also singled out for accolades, thanks in great part to the visibility accorded to it by the print media, which had kept its gaze directed towards Manseau throughout the summer of 1970.

Second Act: The SQ

The Sûreté du Québec traces its origins to the creation in 1870 of the Police provinciale du Québec (PPQ). At the turn of the twentieth century, it was the only provincial force and its mandate expanded from protecting parliamentary buildings to crime prevention and law enforcement as Quebec industrialized and became further integrated into the North American economy, both official and underground. Renamed the Sûreté provinciale (SP), the force worked closely with the Service de surveillance (later renamed Police des liqueurs), the Police des circulations, and a corps of detectives based in Montreal. These various bodies merged under the name

Sûreté provinciale du Québec (SPQ) on the eve of the Second World War as the province prepared to clamp down on leftist agitators. The Quiet Revolution brought further changes: the force adopted its new colours and had a final name change, to the Sûreté du Québec. By the end of the 1960s, the SQ had centralized its administration, established state-of-the-art recruit training facilities in Montreal, created an Unité d'urgence in response to growing civil unrest, and founded the Centre de renseignements policiers du Québec (CRPQ), the province's first centralized intelligence database, completing in the process what Jean-François Leclerc describes as a technocratic revolution.[68] The force was now prepared to assume its role as a policing and intelligence agency.

Yet the SQ was not quite ready to submit a brief to the Le Dain Commission when it was invited to do so in the autumn of 1969. As Martel points out, it "lack[ed] expertise in the field of drug enforcement," and therefore had no objection to letting the RCMP speak for its officers during the public inquiry.[69] However, Maurice Saint-Pierre, director general of the SQ, noted that the phenomenon of non-medical drug use among teenagers and young adults was a growing concern in Quebec, and that his force had the responsibility of becoming increasingly proficient in this field.[70] The SQ had relied on the expertise of its federal and Montreal counterparts in the past, but it now wished to accumulate the knowledge necessary to speak with authority on the topic. Hence, Saint-Pierre's decision to encourage officers to take university courses and attend conferences dealing with hallucinogens and other illicit substances. He stated to the Le Dain Commission: "Pour le moment, nous allons concentrer notre attention à l'éducation de nos membres. Cette formation comprendra des notions de base, sur l'origine des drogues, les conséquences psychiques et physiques, les effets bénéfiques en médecine et la loi."[71] Manseau's Woodstock Pop Festival thus came at an opportune time, considering the SQ's renewed thirst for knowledge.

Eager to find out more about the links between recreational drugs and the counterculture youth, the SQ expected front-row seats during the festival since Manseau did not have a municipal police force. In the National Assembly of Quebec, Minister of Justice Choquette reassured the members in attendance that the SQ was actively engaged in assessing the situation and devising plans to ensure public safety. He then invited them to a special screening of a film shot the previous year during the Woodstock Music and Art Fair, which the SQ had obtained from New York law enforcement agencies.[72] Following the screening, investigators Richard Masson and Yvan Aubin, accompanied by Corporal R. Gosselin, visited the site of the upcoming festival to validate the information they had read in the press and to get a better sense of what to expect. They concluded that the SQ would have to do more than direct traffic: it would have to enforce peace and order around the farm while the security agency hired by Woods Productions handled the situation within the site itself.[73] Growing increasingly worried, the people of Manseau concurred and urged the SQ to do what it could "pour faire assurer dans les limites de la municipalité le bon ordre, la paix et la sécurité des citoyens."[74] On the eve of the festival, the SQ moved into a local school, which had been transformed into a temporary operational base for the occasion.

"Opération Manseau" lasted five days (from July 30 to August 3), mobilized 203 members of the force, and cost the government $120,000.[75] There was one officer per seventy festivalgoers at the peak of the event; the ratio was one to fifteen at the lowest point of the weekend.[76] The SQ's primary role was to ensure the security of Manseau's residents and to police both the roads and fields adjacent to the farm where the event was taking place. In accordance with government recommendations, the SQ adopted a policy of non-intervention within the perimeter of the festival site. Its only official presence inside the gates was a team from the morality brigade, which remained confined to a small tent.[77] On the surface, the weekend was uneventful, with only fifteen arrests, two of which led to charges: one concerned a stabbing and the other a case of nudity on a public beach near Manseau. The SQ kept busy by providing care to unconscious or heavily intoxicated festivalgoers who had wandered beyond the farm. It also seized small quantities of cannabis but let the culprits go as it prepared for the arrival of hundreds of bikers suspected of drug trafficking. The tip, which came from a biker, was apparently unsubstantiated.[78]

Despite the restrictions imposed on it, the SQ managed to conduct a number of undercover surveillance operations throughout the weekend. Indeed, several officers circulated incognito among festivalgoers, taking photos and filming both petty pushers and suspected members of the drug underworld, including representatives of the Mafia supposedly disguised as hippies.[79] The SQ sent this material and drugs acquired on site to the RCMP for processing and identification purposes.[80] Not all suspects could be identified, but enough evidence was accumulated to suggest that Woods Productions – or individuals attached to the organization – had connections to organized crime.[81] The SQ's collaboration with its federal counterpart suggests that the two shared similar views with respect to drug policing. In its briefs to the Le Dain Commission, the RCMP advocated against reclassifying cannabis from the Narcotic Control Act to the Food and Drugs Act, insisting that soft drugs posed serious health risks and led to the consumption of hard drugs and growing criminality.[82] The RCMP seemed intent on holding drug users responsible for their actions. It also seemed disinclined to accept criticisms of its officers' use of force during police interventions.[83] It is fair to assume that the SQ was receptive to the RCMP's views, particularly since the provincial force had yet to acquire enough experience and knowledge to articulate its own response to the so-called drug problem.

Their powers heavily circumscribed in Manseau, Corporal Jean-Luc Paquin and agent Roger Hovington worked as undercover agents during the festival. Their mandate was twofold: to track the movement of traffickers, and to study, from up close, the behaviour of drug users. In their surveillance report, they distinguished between so-called authentic hippies and the rest of the festivalgoers, noting that the former numbered fewer than 500.[84] Paquin and Hovington did not explain the criteria upon which they based their estimate, but their report leaves no doubt that they were primarily concerned with the impressionable teenagers and young adults who had travelled to the event. The two men were especially appalled by the abundance of, and ease of access to, drugs, as well as by the exhibitionist inclinations of festivalgoers who publicly swallowed, injected, or smoked substances (marijuana, hashish, mescaline, and LSD) fully aware of the illegality of their actions.[85] The widespread consumption of recreational drugs made infiltration somewhat difficult for undercover agents, including Paquin and Hovington, who were nearly exposed after refusing a joint offered to them by a group of young adults.[86]

In the context of the Le Dain Commission, Paquin and Hovington were concerned first and foremost with the harmful effects of recreational drugs on innocent youngsters – first-time users who presumably came to Manseau to perform the part, fit in, and assuage their need to belong. They were especially critical of reporters who disseminated the news that police officers, having been denied access to the festival site, would not enforce the Narcotic Control Act. The issue was not so much that it encouraged the non-medical use of drugs but that it sent traffickers the message that this would be a lucrative weekend. As a result, the best Paquin and Hovington could do was to sympathize with the young users they encountered. According to them, those who turned to drugs were youthful victims struggling to deal with the fact that they had been deceived by dishonest promoters, exploited by drug traffickers, and abandoned by rock groups who failed to perform. The youngsters' immaturity and their naive adolescent sociability explained the excessive consumption of drugs. Paquin and Hovington were struck by the sadness and melancholy they saw on the faces of festivalgoers.[87] They noted, with an infantilizing empathy, that they regretted being unable to prevent innocent boys and girls from initiating themselves to recreational drug use. They felt powerless and deplored this "dévalorisation du travail policier causée par de telles relâches."[88]

The two undercover officers were not alone in their dismay. Captain Robert Trupin corroborated his colleagues' observations following an incognito tour of the festival site. Like them, he felt disempowered by the fact that he could not prevent youngsters from being exploited by deceptive individuals who, under the cover of "Peace & Love," associated themselves with members of criminal organizations.[89] Trupin noted that "cet ensemble de faits créa une situation extrêmement déplaisante et moralement inacceptable pour tout homme bien pensant, surtout un policier."[90] Echoing Paquin and Hovington, he resented the fact that he could not be a father figure of authority for the young people trapped in the bad trip that Manseau represented to him. In their reports, the three men depicted users as unsuspecting, and often immature, victims. In denying the youth their agency, they shifted the responsibility for this fiasco onto the shoulders of the organizers while stating firmly that, if similar festivals were to be held in the future, traffickers would have to be prevented from conducting their illegal business. Thus, the experience strengthened their resolve to oppose decriminalization and to continue supporting the RCMP in its war on drugs.

Third Act: OPTAT

Trupin, Paquin, and Hovington did not suffer in vain. As *Le Journal de Montréal* explained, there were some "gagnants dans la débâcle" since Manseau's Woodstock Pop Festival offered government-mandated medical and social experts an unprecedented opportunity to acquire further expertise on the topic of non-medical drug use.[91] André Boudreau, director general of OPTAT, noted that the quantity of marijuana absorbed on Saturday evening alone surpassed that consumed in one month across the province.[92] The absence of police repression on the site meant that the counterculture youth felt free to experiment without fear of punishment, thereby making the festival an open-sky laboratory, in the eyes of OPTAT's experts. Raymond Gendron, speaking for the Ministry of Health, stated:

> Personnellement, je crois que l'expérience que nous avons vécu[e] ici, et les leçons que nous pourrons en tirer surtout au sujet des problèmes de la drogue, vaut beaucoup plus que tout l'argent que le gouvernement du Québec a dépensé pour les activités para-festival. Pour les psychiatres, psychologues, sociologues, travailleurs sociaux et autres, qui ont œuvré ici et qui ont fait des études ... c'est une expérience inestimable. En dehors de telle manifestation elle aurait pu coûter près d'un million![93]

At the end of the day, the experiment cost the government a mere $20,000.

OPTAT came into being in 1966 with the merger of four government organizations concerned with the prevention and treatment of alcoholism. Bill 292, to which OPTAT owed its existence, did not become law until two years later, at which point the organization became an integral component of Quebec's Ministry of Health. Under the directorship of Boudreau, it published a bimonthly publication titled *Informations sur l'alcoolisme et les autres toxicomanies (IAAT)* and a scientific journal titled *Toxicomanies*. It also printed and distributed educational pamphlets, organized conferences and lectures, managed a documentation centre, helped facilitate research projects, and coordinated the efforts of several clinics and consultation centres.[94] In 1969, OPTAT conducted a vast study of substance abuse in Montreal high schools. It found that more than 20 percent of graduating students had tried at least one type of drug, and that differences with respect to gender, religion, and language were marginal. Not surprisingly, researchers found that student support for the counterculture and protest movements was a key factor in the non-medical use of drugs.[95]

OPTAT was therefore well prepared to participate in the drug debate engendered by the Le Dain Commission. In its November 1969 brief, the organization placed emphasis on its threefold mandate: prevention, research, and treatment. It discussed at length its findings regarding the social and economic factors that influenced the non-medical use of drugs among teenagers and young adults in Quebec. OPTAT joined its Ontario counterpart, the Addiction Research Foundation, in calling for the reclassification of cannabis from the Narcotic Control Act to the Food and Drugs Act, noting, however, that it was too early to legalize the psychotropic since additional research was needed.[96] Boudreau then waited impatiently for the Le Dain Commission's interim report in the summer of 1970.[97] When it finally arrived, he and his team promptly reviewed the document. They were pleased that the commissioners were receptive to the idea of reclassifying cannabis, but remained concerned that the final recommendations would encourage the federal government to encroach on provincial areas of jurisdiction, namely, health and education. OPTAT had raised the issue months earlier at a federal-provincial conference of health ministers in Ottawa. On July 24, Boudreau and his colleagues raised it again with their superiors at the Ministry of Health, insisting that OPTAT was best equipped to educate the public, provide therapeutic care, conduct research, and assert provincial prerogatives in the drug debate.[98] The Quebec government had just issued the permit allowing Woods Productions to proceed with its festival, and OPTAT intended to be there.

Discussions about sending a delegation of medical and social experts to Manseau had begun earlier that summer. One did not become an expert on drug abuse by studying the counterculture youth from a distance; one needed to be where the action was.[99] OPTAT's position was that the festival would be "un terrain d'expérience tout désigné pour ses thérapeutes pas encore tellement habitués aux problèmes de toxicomanies et d'autre part un excellent moyen de publicité pour son action dans notre société."[100] The organization sent fourteen doctors, fifteen medical students, and twenty-five nurses on the road.[101] Accompanying them were three sociologists – Jean-Marc Bernard,

Léandre Bilodeau, and André Jacob – whose mandate was to prepare a comprehensive report on the event.[102]

The delegation worked around the clock throughout the weekend. It counted on the help of Ambulance Saint-Jean, which handled the transport of injured or intoxicated festivalgoers, and Drug-Aid, a small team of health professionals who offered assistance to a few dozen individuals. OPTAT's Centre avancé de traitement oversaw the bulk of the work, treating 174 cases of drug intoxication (from severe bad trips to mild dizziness), 212 cases of injuries (burns, cuts, twisted ankles, etc.), and 142 cases of problems ranging from sore throats to allergic reactions, and diarrhea. The vast majority of those treated were men between the ages of seventeen and twenty-one.[103] LSD was the culprit in most of the cases that required medical attention, which led OPTAT's experts to voice concerns that drug dealers, in their quest for large profits, had mixed the drug with cheap chemicals, thereby endangering the life and health of inexperienced users, who were most susceptible to overdose.[104] Marijuana and hashish, on the other hand, were involved in only 10 percent of the cases. The picture that emerged from OPTAT's observations thus differed considerably from that found in newspapers.

Like reporters and SQ officers, OPTAT's sociologists refused to believe in the spectacle that the youth of Quebec put on in Manseau. According to them, there were few authentic hippies at the festival and most of them had left by Saturday afternoon, when "pseudo-hippies" and various onlookers stormed the site.[105] Bernard, Bilodeau, and Jacob wrote that the audience was composed mostly of youngsters, between the ages of fifteen and twenty-five, who embraced aspects of the hippie culture without necessarily adopting its reclusive, oppositional posture.[106] The three experts then forcefully denounced the alarmist and sensationalist tone with which reporters discussed the event, because it caused unnecessary panic among parents while fuelling the curiosity and defiant spirit of festivalgoers. OPTAT's criticism of the media reflected its members' belief that only they could speak objectively as informed and responsible adults on the topic of youth cultures and the non-medical use of drugs:

> On peut résumer l'évènement de Manseau en disant que ce festival a été une tentative ratée d'exploitation organisée de notre jeunesse, que malgré cela les jeunes ont démontré à la population qu'ils savent se

conduire et ce contrairement à ce qu'ont pu laisser croire les journaux à sensation qui ont exploité à fond les quelques rares scènes de nudité et la consommation de drogue supposément orgiaque.[107]

Bernard and his colleagues opted to sympathize with their youthful subjects in their efforts to make OPTAT the primary vehicle for the articulation and deployment of policies dealing with research, prevention, and treatment. They concluded their report by stressing that one should not take positions hastily in the drug debate on the basis of the media's coverage of the festival.[108]

As for Boudreau, he published his own observations in the September-October 1970 edition of *IAAT,* echoing his colleagues' claim that as a stratagem designed to exploit the youth, the Manseau festival had failed, in part because youngsters proved more lucid than expected, particularly those who saw the event for what it was and chose to boycott it. Boudreau then enumerated six lessons learned during the summer: (1) there is nothing authentic about pop festivals since the original Woodstock cannot be restaged; (2) future events of that nature must be organized for and by the youth of Quebec with the support of the province's Ministry of Cultural Affairs; (3) single-day events must be prioritized over multi-day ones; (4) legislation should be enacted to prevent other Manseau-like gatherings from springing up; (5) if some of the laws associated with the Narcotic Control Act are unenforceable, they should be changed; and (6) the state must commit to supporting research on the short- and long-term effects of non-medical drug use. The last two points were prods that Boudreau directed at the government for the purpose of advancing OPTAT's agenda.[109]

With the "power/knowledge" it accumulated, OPTAT reaffirmed its belief that the government needed to amend existing legislation regarding drugs such as marijuana. Conditions within the perimeter of the festival site had certainly differed from those normally encountered in urban settings, but the experience sufficed to make the case that less police repression and more government-funded research were needed to better understand the phenomenon of non-medical drug use. In making that argument, OPTAT situated itself vis-à-vis the media, but also the SQ and the Le Dain Commission. Shortly after the festival, Boudreau published a summary of OPTAT's position regarding the commission's interim report. He stated once again that organizations such as his were – and had to remain – at the forefront of drug use prevention, research, and treatment since education and health were provincial areas of jurisdiction. He repeated his colleagues' criticisms of the media, called for less drug policing and more police community outreach, dismissed as unscientific the studies conducted by organizations that did not carry the official seal of the state, and noted that the ongoing criminalization of drugs such as cannabis inhibited OPTAT's ability to fulfill its mission.[110] Through its presence in Manseau, the organization further consolidated its status as the primary interlocutor for all matters relating to the non-medical use of drugs in Quebec.[111]

Conclusion

For one long weekend in the summer of 1970, the print media, the SQ, and OPTAT cast a persistent gaze upon the festivalgoers who had assembled in Manseau to stage a new, albeit elusive, Woodstock. From the outset, all three refused to believe in the spectacle unfolding before their eyes, determined as they were to find a niche for themselves in the public debate engendered by the Le Dain Commission. Resolutely, they asserted their authority through the production of "truths" about the youth of Quebec. It was a process that involved more empathy than discipline, but it was no less pervasive. "Surveillance is only ever a means to other ends, of governance, which may include both care and protection," writes David Lyon.[112] The journalists, police officers, and experts who travelled to Manseau adopted a paternalistic attitude towards festivalgoers, who were presumed to lack both agency and autonomy. Their contribution to the drugs discourse ineluctably aligned with the "legal paternalism" that underlay parts of the Le Dain Commission's work.[113] It spoke more about their self-perception and aspirations than about the object of their surveillance. Manseau's Woodstock Pop Festival provided the print media, the SQ, and OPTAT with the unprecedented opportunity to both construct and project the "power/knowledge" that was expected of participants in the drug debate of the late 1960s and early 1970s. It was an opportunity not to be missed.

Notes

1 The event would soon be renamed "Festival flop de Manseau" by disgruntled participants and observers. See René Homier-Roy, "Dans un climat de découragement

on s'amuse avec ce qu'on peut," *La Presse,* August 1, 1970, 6; and "Le Festival pop de Manseau: la farce de l'année au Québec," *L'Union,* August 4, 1970, 6.

2 Michael Brendan Baker writes that the word "rockumentary" is a "portmanteau" used to describe "documentary films about rock music and related idioms," which "usually feature some combination of performance footage, interviews, and undirected material." Michael Brendan Baker, *Rockumentary: Style, Performance and Sound in a Documentary Genre* (PhD diss., McGill University, 2011), 2. See also Eric Fillion, "Le rock québécois débarque en France. *À soir on fait peur au monde, Tabarnac,* ou: le retour par le rockumentaire," *Nouvelles Vues* 16 (Winter-Spring 2015), http://www.nouvellesvues.ulaval.ca/index.php?id=2719; as well as Gunnar Iversen and Scott MacKenzie, eds., *Mapping the Rockumentary: Images of Sound and Fury* (Edinburgh: Edinburgh University Press, 2021).

3 For a discussion of the festival's origins, its organizers, its music (or lack thereof), and the factors that led to its failure, see Dominic Houde, *De Woodstock à Manseau: manifestations musicales et contre-culture aux États-Unis et au Québec (1967–1970)* (MA thesis, Université de Sherbrooke, 2014); and Jacques Crochetière, *Le Woodstock Pop Festival de Manseau, 1970* (Quebec City: Éditions GID, 2020).

4 "Tranquillité déconcertante," *L'Union,* August 4, 1970, 8.

5 The Office de la prévention et du traitement de l'alcoolisme et des autres toxicomanies (OPTAT) was known in English-speaking circles as the Office for the Prevention and Treatment of Alcoholism and Other Toxicomanias.

6 Canada, *House of Commons Debates,* 28th Parliament, 1st session, vol. 8 (1969): 8203.

7 Kyle Grayson, *Chasing Dragons: Security, Identity, and Illicit Drugs in Canada* (Toronto: University of Toronto Press, 2008), 152. Grayson further explains that the term "drugs discourse" describes "the constellation of discourses that construct knowledge of illicit and licit drugs and those involved in their production, distribution, and consumption." Ibid., 6.

8 The political scientist Gaétan Rochon explained in 1979 that the counterculture in Quebec was unique because it occasionally served as a point of convergence for three groups: nationalists, leftists, and the apolitical youth of Quebec. Sean Mills's study of political activism in 1960s Montreal deals with the first two groups. The festival-goers who assembled in Manseau belonged for the most part to the third. See Gaétan Rochon, *Politique et contre-culture: essai d'analyse interprétative* (Montreal: Cahiers du Québec/Hurtubise, 1979), 19; Sean Mills, *The Empire Within: Postcolonial Thought and Political Activism in Sixties Montreal* (Montreal and Kingston: McGill-Queen's University Press, 2010); Jean-Philippe Warren and Andrée Fortin, *Pratiques et discours de la contreculture au Québec* (Montreal: Septentrion, 2015); as well as Karim Larose and Frédéric Rondeau, eds., *La contre-culture au Québec* (Montreal: Les Presses de l'Université de Montréal, 2016). See also Colin Coates, ed., *Canadian Countercultures and the Environment* (Calgary: University of Calgary Press, 2015); and Bryan D. Palmer, *Canada's 1960s: The Ironies of Identity in a Rebellious Era* (Toronto: University of Toronto Press, 2009).

9   Stuart Henderson, *Making the Scene: Yorkville and Hip Toronto in the 1960s* (Toronto: University of Toronto Press, 2011), 272.

10   Marcel Martel, *Not This Time: Canadians, Public Policy, and the Marijuana Question, 1961–1975* (Toronto: University of Toronto Press, 2006).

11   Michel Foucault, *Discipline and Punish*, trans. Alan Sheridan (New York: Vintage Books, 1995), 27.

12   Michel Foucault writes that governmentality rests on the "development of a whole complex of *savoirs*" (i.e., ostensible truths): Michel Foucault, "Governmentality," in *The Foucault Effect: Studies in Governmentality*, ed. Graham Burchell, Colin Gordon, and Peter Miller (Chicago: University of Chicago Press, 1991), 103.

13   Michel Foucault, "Two Lectures," in *Power/Knowledge: Selected Interviews and Other Writings*, trans. Alessandro Fontana and Pasquale Pasquino, ed. Colin Gordon (New York: Vintage Books, 1980), 93.

14   Kyle Grayson contends that the power of discourse lies "in its ability to shape interpretative dispositions and frame descriptions that make action possible." He adds: "Discourse, then, is not mere rhetoric; it imbues subjects, objects, and the relationships among them with meaning." Grayson, *Chasing Dragons*, 14. For other references to Foucault and the place occupied by interest groups in the Canadian drugs discourse, see Dan Malleck, *When Good Drugs Go Bad: Opium, Medicine, and the Origins of Canada's Drug Laws* (Vancouver: UBC Press, 2015); and Catherine Carstairs, *Jailed for Possession: Illegal Drug Use, Regulation, and Power in Canada, 1920–1961* (Toronto: University of Toronto Press, 2006).

15   Line Beauchesne, "Setting Public Policy on Drugs: A Choice of Social Values," in *The Real Dope: Social, Legal, and Historical Perspectives on the Regulation of Drugs in Canada*, ed. Edgar-André Montigny (Toronto: University of Toronto Press, 2011), 29 (emphasis in original).

16   Neil Ravenscroft and Xavier Matteucci, "The Festival as Carnivalesque: Social Governance and Control at Pamplona's San Fermin Fiesta," *Tourism, Culture and Communication* 4 (2003): 1–2. See also Jean-Louis Fabiani, "Festivals, Local and Global: Critical Interventions and the Cultural Public Sphere," in *Festivals and the Cultural Public Sphere*, ed. Liana Giorgi, Monica Sassatelli, and Gerard Delanty (New York: Routledge, 2011), 96; and Jonathan R. Wynn, *Music/City: American Festivals and Placemaking in Austin, Nashville, and Newport* (Chicago: University of Chicago Press, 2015), 4.

17   Although surveillance at contemporary festivals is a growing concern, the topic remains for the most part understudied. See Kara C. Hoover et al., "Surveillance, Trust, and Policing at Music Festivals," *The Canadian Geographer* (2021): 1–18; John Wäfler, "The Surveillance of Film Festivals in Switzerland: The Case of Locarno International Film Festival," in *Cultural Transfer and Political Conflicts: Film Festivals in the Cold War*, ed. Andreas Kotzing, Caroline Moine, and Bill Martin (Gottingen: V&R Unipress, 2017), 141–52; Gianluca Mezzofiore, "Big Festival Brother? What Summer Music Festivals Are Doing with Your Personal Data," *Mashable*, May 14, 2016, https://mashable.

com/2016/05/14/music-festivals-personal-data-privacy/#SI2WkflKlgqC; and Delilah Friedler, "Music Festivals Are the Corporate Dystopia We Deserve: Coachella Allows Us to Purchase Tickets to Our Own Subjugation," *The Outline*, April 19, 2018, https://theoutline.com/post/4215/music-festivals-dystopia-coachella?zd=1&zi=cvbsbwem.

18 Reg Whitaker, Gregory S. Kealey, and Andrew Parnaby, *Secret Service: Political Policing in Canada from the Fenians to Fortress America* (Toronto: University of Toronto Press, 2012), 7.

19 Steve Hewitt, "Information Believed True: RCMP Security Intelligence Activities on Campuses and the Controversy Surrounding Them, 1961–71," *Canadian Historical Review* 81, 2 (June 2000): 196–97. See also Steve Hewitt, "Spying 101: The RCMP's Secret Activities at the University of Saskatchewan, 1920–1971," in *Whose National Security? Canadian State Surveillance and the Creation of Enemies*, ed. Gary Kinsman, Dieter K. Buse, and Mercedes Steedman (Toronto: Between the Lines, 2000), 91–109; Steve Hewitt, *Spying 101: The RCMP's Secret Activities at Canadian Universities, 1917–1997* (Toronto: University of Toronto Press, 2002); Steve Hewitt and Christabelle Sethna, "Sex Spying: The RCMP and Women's Liberation Groups," in *Debating Dissent: Canada and the Sixties*, ed. Gregory S. Kealey, Lara Campbell, and Dominique Clément (Toronto: University of Toronto Press, 2012), 135–51; Christabelle Sethna, "High-School Confidential: RCMP Surveillance of Secondary School Student Activists," in Kinsman, Buse, and Steedman, *Whose National Security?* 121–28; Paul Axelrod, "Spying on the Young in Depression and War: Students, Youth Groups, and the RCMP, 1935–1942," *Labour/Le Travail* 35 (Spring 1995): 43–63; David Austin, *Fear of a Black Nation: Race, Sex, and Security in Sixties Montreal* (Toronto: Between the Lines, 2013); Christabelle Sethna and Steve Hewitt, *Just Watch Us: RCMP Surveillance of the Women's Liberation Movement in Cold War Canada* (Montreal and Kingston: McGill-Queen's University Press, 2018); and Reg Whitaker, *Spying on Canadians: The Royal Canadian Mounted Police Security Service and the Origins of the Long Cold War* (Toronto: University of Toronto Press, 2017).

20 Two notable exceptions: Marcel Martel, "They Smell Bad, Have Diseases, and are Lazy: RCMP Officers' Reporting on Hippies in the Late Sixties," in *The Sixties in Canada: A Turbulent and Creative Decade*, ed. M. Ethena Palaeologu (Montreal: Black Rose Books, 2009), 165–92; and Steve Hewitt, "'While Unpleasant It Is a Service to Humanity': The RCMP's War on Drugs in the Interwar Period," *Journal of Canadian Studies* 38, 2 (Spring 2004): 80–104. The former deals with the RCMP and its targeting of hippies as an identifiable – albeit marginal – group, while the latter brings into focus the RCMP's persecution of Asian Canadians and the racist discourse employed by the force to legitimize its importance during the 1920s and 1930s. For the pre-1960s period, see also Carstairs, *Jailed for Possession;* and Catherine Carstairs, "Becoming a 'Hype': Drug Laws, Subculture Formation, and Resistance in Canada, 1945–61," in Montigny, *The Real Dope*, 248–68.

21 Only two books have been written on the SQ: Nicole Jobin, *La Sûreté du Québec de 1870 à 1995* (Montreal: Comité du 125ᵉ anniversaire de la Sûreté du Québec, 1995);

and J. Raymond Proulx, *La Sûreté du Québec depuis 1870* (Montreal: Sûreté du Québec, 1987). The two non-scholarly surveys fail to engage critically with the history of provincial policing in Quebec as they both carry the official seal of the SQ. Bibliothèque et Archives nationales du Québec (BAnQ) currently holds the Fonds Sûreté du Québec (FSQ), parts of which remain restricted under Section 28 of Quebec's *Loi sur l'accès aux documents des organismes publics et sur la protection des renseignements personnels*. It should be noted that the findings of the Commission d'enquête sur des opérations policières en territoire québécois inspired a handful of scholars to write the SQ into the history of RCMP illegal activities in Quebec. Likewise, the report of the Commission d'enquête chargée de faire enquête sur la Sûreté du Québec encouraged studies on corruption within the provincial police force. See Commission d'enquête sur des opérations policières en territoire québécois, *Rapport de la Commission d'enquête sur des opérations policières en territoire québécois* (Quebec City: Gouvernement du Québec, Ministère de la Justice, 1981); Commission d'enquête chargée de faire enquête sur la Sûreté du Québec, *Rapport de la Commission d'enquête chargée de faire enquête sur la Sûreté du Québec: pour une police au service de l'intégrité et de la justice,* vol. 1 (Sainte-Foy: Publications du Québec, 1998); Whitaker, Kealey, and Parnaby, *Secret Service;* Jacques Bourgault and James Iain Gow, "Le difficile contrôle des activités et comportements de la police: le cas de la Sûreté du Québec," *Revue canadienne de science politique* 35, 4 (December 2002): 747–70; and Louis Fournier et al., *La police secrète au Québec: la tyrannie occulte de la police* (Montreal: Éditions Québec/Amérique, 1978).

22 Canada, *House of Commons Debates,* 28th Parliament, 1st session, vol. 8 (1969): 8202–203.

23 Charges related to cannabis rose from 78 to 37,668 between 1964 and 1973. During this period, the number of convictions increased by over 700 percent (from 28 to 19,929). Susan Boyd, Connie I. Carter, and Donald Macpherson, *More Harm than Good: Drug Policy in Canada* (Halifax and Winnipeg: Fernwood Publishing, 2016), 21.

24 For a discussion of how race and nation informed the Canadian drugs discourse in the late nineteenth century and early twentieth century, see Carstairs, *Jailed for Possession;* Malleck, *When Good Drugs Go Bad;* and Grayson, *Chasing Dragons.*

25 Greg Marquis, "Constructing an Urban Drug Ecology in 1970s Canada," *Urban History Review* 42, 1 (2013): 37.

26 Canada, *House of Commons Debates,* 28th Parliament, 2nd session, vol. 8 (1970): 8329. The Le Dain Commission's other reports were published in 1972 (*Final Report on Cannabis* and *Treatment*) and 1973 (*Final Report*).

27 Doug Owram, *Born at the Right Time: A History of the Baby Boom Generation* (Toronto: University of Toronto Press, 1996), 174.

28 Ibid.

29 Martel, *Not This Time,* 13.

30 They were not alone in planning such an event in Canada, as the case of Ontario's Strawberry Fields Festival indicates. For more information on this other Woodstock-inspired

event, consult Chapter 4. See also Greg Marquis, *John Lennon, Yoko Ono, and the Year Canada Was Cool* (Toronto: James Lorimer & Company Ltd., 2020).

31 Assemblée spéciale – procès-verbal, June 16, 1970, Archives municipales de Manseau (AMM).

32 Contrat entre la Corporation municipale de la paroisse de Saint-Joseph de Blandford et Woods Productions, June 16, 1970, BAnQ, FSQ, E100, Dossier Opération Festival Pop de Manseau (DOFPM).

33 Quebec, *National Assembly Debates,* 29th Legislature, 1st session (1970): 610. See also Quebec, *National Assembly Debates,* 29th Legislature, 1st session (1970): 13–14.

34 Rapport d'enquête – dossier no. 029020770001, July 9, 1970, BAnQ, FSQ, E100, DOFPM.

35 These various newspapers scrutinized all aspects of the festival throughout the summer of 1970, providing sustained coverage for their French- and English-speaking urban readers as well as for others who lived near Manseau.

36 Claude Gravel, "À une journée de Manseau," *La Presse,* July 30, 1970, 4.

37 The newspapers discussed here constitute a representative cross-section of Quebec's journalistic landscape in 1970. Only *Le Devoir* (its key reporter, Jean Basile, was about to launch the countercultural publication *Mainmise*) and the left-leaning *Québec-Presse* took a more sympathetic approach to youth cultures, focusing more on the co-opting of the counterculture than on the phenomenon of non-medical drug use that so preoccupied the other dailies and weeklies.

38 "*Le Nouvelliste* au Festival," *Le Nouvelliste,* July 31, 1970, 1.

39 All French quotations in this chapter have been translated in the notes. "Will it instead be a false youth who will agree ... to play an elaborate game ... without worrying who is set to benefit from that game?" Gravel, "À une journée de Manseau," 4.

40 See "Au cas où ça pète, il y aura un véritable centre médical à Manseau," *Le Journal de Montréal,* July 27, 1970, 5; Claude Jodoin, "Manseau, 48 heures avant le jour 'P' ... 150 'privés' assureront la sécurité des fêtards au festival pop," *Le Journal de Montréal,* July 30, 1970, 2; "Choquette: le festival pop correspond au mouvement d'émancipation de la jeunesse," *La Presse,* July 24, 1970, 1; and Pierre-A Champoux, "Toutes les mesures d'hygiène et de sécurité prises," *Le Nouvelliste,* June 27, 1970, 10.

41 Pierre-A Champoux, "À Manseau en toute sécurité," *Le Nouvelliste,* July 24, 1970, 11; and "Au cas où ça pète, il y aura un véritable centre médical à Manseau," 5.

42 Jean-Marc Beaudoin, "Le rapport de la Commission d'enquête sur l'usage des drogues à des fins non médicales," *Le Nouvelliste,* July 15, 1970, 40.

43 In English: "Are pop festivals conducive to drug trafficking?" Pierre-A Champoux, "Les festivals pop sont-ils propices au trafic de la drogue?" *Le Nouvelliste,* July 16, 1970, 10.

44 "Le curé de Manseau: surveillez vos poules," *Photo-police,* August 8, 1970, 5; "Résidants et vacanciers sont armés," *Le Journal de Montréal,* August 1, 1970, 2; and Ingrid Saumart, "Manseau attend fébrilement l'heure décisive du Festival," *La Presse,* July 29, 1970, 14.

45   "La banque se vide," *Le Journal de Montréal,* July 28, 1970, 3.

46   See "Un festival pop interdit aux É.-U.," *Le Journal de Montréal,* July 28, 1970, 3; "Woodstock in France a connu le même sort que celui de Manseau," *Le Journal de Montréal,* August 3, 1970, 2; "Woodstock, le pionnier des festivals pop au siècle des défoulements massifs," *La Presse,* July 29, 1970, 14; "Un week-end néfaste pour les festivals," *La Presse,* August 3, 1970, 9; and "Un festival pop cause de graves ennuis à Toronto," *Le Nouvelliste,* June 29, 1970, 1.

47   In English: "[In such a display of collective hysteria], young boys and girls (7–8–9 years old) mingle with a crowd of delirious adults ... drugs circulate profusely, feet trample bodies, bestiality in its most disgusting form manifests itself, food is lacking, bastards abound, everything is dirt, recklessness, lust and stupidity ... Take note: WE ARE WATCHING." Yvon Dupuis, "Les festivals 'pop,'" *Photo-police,* June 20, 1970, 30.

48   The August 1, August 3, and August 8 editions of *Le Journal de Montréal, La Presse,* and *Photo-police,* respectively, are a case in point.

49   "Le Festival pop de Manseau: la farce de l'année au Québec," *L'Union,* August 4, 1970, 6.

50   In English: "weekend hippy posturing." Ibid.

51   "Les à-côtés de Manseau," *Le Journal de Montréal,* August 1, 1970, 5; "Palmarès de 10,000 jeunes ... jusqu'ici," *Le Journal de Montréal,* August 1, 1970, 2; and "On a 'tripé' de toutes les façons, mais pas sur le pouce," *Le Journal de Montréal,* August 3, 1970, 2.

52   George Radwanski, "Youngsters Seek Elusive Spirit," *The Gazette,* August 1, 1970, 3.

53   Ibid.

54   On the topic of celebrities, see Chapter 4.

55   Jean-Marc Beaudoin, "La vedette du festival pop: LA DROGUE," *Le Nouvelliste,* August 3, 1970, 1.

56   Louis-Bernard Robitaille, "Le Québec est entré dans l'ère de la tolérance," *La Presse,* August 3, 1970, 8.

57   Ibid.

58   Leon Harris, "1,000 Bad Trips as Drugs Flow Free," *The Gazette,* August 3, 1970, 3; and Jean-Marc Beaudoin, "600 jeunes ont dû être soignés après s'être adonnés à la drogue," *Le Nouvelliste,* August 3, 1970, 1.

59   Leon Harris, "Drugs: Leniency Is Fine, but Can the Kids Cope," *The Gazette,* August 8, 1970, 7.

60   Ibid.

61   In English: "perverts ... with deviant instincts." "Plusieurs profitent d'occasions semblables pour satisfaire leurs penchants," *Le Nouvelliste,* August 3, 1970, 2.

62   Sylvio St. Amant, "Pop Festivals," *The Gazette,* August 18, 1970, 12.

63   In English: "The youth of today are not assimilated ... and they demand proofs when we solicit their attention." Ingrid Saumart, "Les organisateurs du festival rejettent sur tout le monde la responsabilité de l'échec," *La Presse,* August 3, 1970, 6.

64   In English: "Despite an appearance of nonchalance, the youth of Quebec demonstrated once again that they are capable of critical thinking and opposition when we try to

take advantage of them in such dishonest ways." Clément Marchand, "Épilogue à un fiasco," *Le Bien public,* August 7, 1970, 3.

65 In English: "The Manseau fiasco is a great victory. It's the victory of parents and youngsters." "Le fiasco de Manseau n'est pas un fiasco," *L'Action nationale,* October 7, 1970, 160.

66 F.M. Kidd, "Pop Festival Ban," *The Gazette,* August 21, 1970, 6.

67 Ibid.

68 Jean-François Leclerc, "La Sûreté du Québec des origines à nos jours: quelques repères historiques," *Criminologie* 22, 2 (1989): 124.

69 Martel, *Not This Time,* 51.

70 Maurice Saint-Pierre to Gérald Le Dain, October 29, 1969, Library and Archives Canada (LAC), Commission of Inquiry into the Non-Medical Use of Drugs Fonds (CINMUDF), RG33-101, vol. 21, file Quebec Legal.

71 In English: "For now, we will focus our attention on educating our members. This training will include basic notions about the origins of drugs, their psychological and physical effects, their beneficial aspects from a medical point of view, and the law." Ibid.

72 Quebec, *National Assembly Debates,* 29th Legislature, 1st session (1970): 14, 435.

73 Richard Masson to L. Descent, July 3, 1970, BAnQ, FSQ, E100, DOFPM.

74 In English: "to ensure order, peace, and the security of citizens within the boundaries of the municipality." Assemblée régulière – procès-verbal, July 6, 1970, AMM.

75 Festival pop de Manseau – coût approximatif de l'opération policière, [August 1970], BAnQ, FSQ, E100, DOFPM.

76 "Un policier par 20 spectateurs ... un journaliste sur 16 personnes," *Photo-police,* August 8, 1970, 7.

77 "Palmarès de 10,000 jeunes ... jusqu'ici," 2.

78 For a detailed list of police interventions in Manseau, see Bilans des activités policières à Manseau 'Pop' Festival, August 3, 1970, BAnQ, FSQ, E100, DOFPM; and Registre des évènements, July 30 to August 2, 1970, BAnQ, FSQ, E100, DOFPM.

79 The author tried to obtain a copy of the film shot during the festival, but SQ analysts in charge of archival records could not locate the document.

80 Rapport de l'agent Georges Raymond, September 14, 1970, BAnQ, FSQ, E100, DOFPM; and Rapport de l'agent Claude Plouffe, September 22, 1970, BAnQ, FSQ, E100, DOFPM.

81 J.L. Gendron to Maurice Saint-Pierre, September 23, 1970, BAnQ, FSQ, E100, DOFPM; and H. Patenaude to Maurice Saint-Pierre, August 12, 1970, BAnQ, FSQ, E100, DOFPM.

82 Martel, *Not This Time,* 137–38.

83 Ibid., 151.

84 Rapport du caporal Jean-Luc Paquin, [August 1970], BAnQ, FSQ, E100, DOFPM.

85 Ibid.

86 Ibid. and Rapport d'enquête – dossier no. 029020770001, August 4, 1970, BAnQ, FSQ, E100, DOFPM.

87   Rapport du caporal Jean-Luc Paquin, [August 1970], BAnQ, FSQ, E100, DOFPM.

88   In English: "devaluation of police work caused by such laxity." Ibid.

89   Rapport du capitaine Robert Trupin, August 17, 1970, BAnQ, FSQ, E100, DOFPM.

90   In English: "this set of facts created an extremely unpleasant and morally unacceptable situation for any principled man, especially a policeman." Ibid.

91   In English: "winners in the debacle." "Seuls gagnants dans la débâcle: les 60 experts du gouvernement," *Le Journal de Montréal,* August 3, 1970, 3.

92   Cited in "L'expérience de Manseau ne peut que nous amener à réfléchir," *La Tribune,* August 3, 1970, 12.

93   In English: "Personally, I believe that the experience we have had here, and the lessons we can learn from it, especially with regards to drug-related problems, is worth much more than all the money that the Government of Quebec has spent on activities peripheral to the festival. For the psychiatrists, psychologists, sociologists, social workers and others who have worked and studied here ... it is an invaluable experience. In another context, the experience could have cost nearly a million dollars!" Cited in "Seuls gagnants dans la débâcle," 3.

94   For a comparative analysis of OPTAT and Ontario's Addiction Research Foundation, see Marcel Martel, "'The Age of Aquarius': Medical Expertise and the Prevention and Control of Drug Use Undertaken by the Quebec and Ontario Governments," in *The Sixties: Passion, Politics, and Style,* ed. Dimitry Anastakis (Montreal and Kingston: McGill-Queen's University Press, 2008), 99–115.

95   Lucien Laforest, *La consommation de drogues chez les étudiants du secondaire et du collégial de l'île de Montréal: une enquête auprès de 4,500 étudiants (avril 1969)* (Quebec City: OPTAT, 1969).

96   Rapport à la Commission d'enquête sur l'usage des drogues à des fins non médicales, November 1969, BAnQ, Fonds Ministère de la Santé et des Services sociaux (FMSSS), E8, 1984-05-001\4, OPTAT.

97   André Boudreau to Gérald Le Dain, July 3, 1970, LAC, CINMUDF, RG33-101, vol. 21, file Quebec Educational.

98   André Boudreau to Jacques Brunet, July 24, 1970, BAnQ, FMSSS, E8, 1984-05-001\4, OPTAT; and Quelques commentaires concernant le rapport provisoire de la Commission d'enquête sur l'usage des drogues à des fins non médicales, n.d., BAnQ, FMSSS, E8, 1984-05-001\4, OPTAT.

99   Claude Benoit to P.A. Marquis, June 30, 1970, BAnQ, FMSSS, E8, 1984-05-001\8, OPTAT.

100 In English: "a convenient terrain of experience for its therapists who may not yet be entirely familiar with addiction problems and, on the other hand, an excellent means of publicity for its work in our society." Rapport sur le Festival pop de Manseau, August 28, 1970, BAnQ, FMSSS, E8, 1984-05-001\8, OPTAT.

101 Festival Manseau – liste du personnel, n.d., BAnQ, FMSSS, E8, 1984-05-001\8, OPTAT.

102 Rapport sur le Festival pop de Manseau, August 28, 1970, BAnQ, FMSSS, E8, 1984-05-001\8, OPTAT.

103 Ibid.

104 "Seuls gagnants dans la débâcle: les 60 experts du gouvernement," 3; and Robitaille, "Le Québec est entré dans l'ère de la tolérance," 8.

105 Rapport sur le Festival pop de Manseau, August 28, 1970, BAnQ, FMSSS, E8, 1984-05-001\8, OPTAT.

106 Ibid.

107 In English: "We can sum up the events of Manseau by noting that it was a failed, organized attempt at exploiting our youth, that in spite of that youngsters have shown to the broader population that they know how to behave in contrast with the image conveyed by newspapers who sought to exploit the few rare scenes of nudity and the supposedly orgiastic use of drugs." Ibid.

108 Ibid.

109 André Boudreau, "Réflexions sur Manseau et l'avenir des festivals pop," *Informations sur l'alcoolisme et les autres toxicomanies* 6/5 (September-October 1970): 3–4. See also Rapport sur le Festival pop de Manseau, August 28, 1970, BAnQ, FMSSS, E8, 1984-05-001\8, OPTAT.

110 André Boudreau, "Quelques commentaires sur le rapport Ledain," *Informations sur l'alcoolisme et les autres toxicomanies* 6/6 (November–December 1970): 3–4.

111 Thus, André Boudreau would have objected to lay initiatives such as those of George Peters's LSD Rescue Service, which is the focus of Chapter 7. In addition to insisting on the professionalization of medical knowledge, OPTAT's director general perceived non-medical drug use as a problem that required going beyond harm reduction to treatment and recovery. Still, Boudreau shared with Peters the belief that criminalization had as one of its adverse effects the inhibition of research (at least with respect to softer drugs such as cannabis).

112 David Lyon, *Surveillance Studies: An Overview* (Cambridge: Polity, 2007), 67.

113 Beauchesne, "Setting Public Policy on Drugs," 29.

John Lennon, the Le Dain Commission, **4** and the Rise of the Celebrity Activist

Greg Marquis

On the surface, having John Lennon in 1969 advise a Canadian government inquiry on the non-medical use of drugs made as much sense as consulting with Elvis Presley on prescription drug use or, for a more recent analogy, with Ted Nugent on gun control. After all, the most famous member of the Beatles, the world's first super pop group, had created some of his most innovative music while under the influence of LSD, began using cocaine in 1968, was still possibly a heroin addict, was a heavy consumer of marijuana, and would continue to use various drugs into the 1970s. In 1969, he had been denied admission to the United States on the grounds of being an "undesirable alien" because of a recent marijuana conviction in Britain. He was also known to drink excessively to the point of becoming abusive and violent, although this was not widely reported in the media. According to biographers, the former Beatle settled down to a life of domesticity and relatively healthy living following the birth of his second son, when he was in his mid-thirties.[1]

This essay examines a little known chapter in Canada's reaction to the "drug problem" in the late 1960s: a secret meeting in Montreal between John Lennon and his wife, Yoko Ono, and members of the Commission of Inquiry into the Non-Medical Use of Drugs, commonly known as the Le Dain Commission. The informal meeting took place on December 22, 1969, in a private railway car in Montreal's Central Station as the two celebrities prepared to head to Ottawa to meet Prime Minister Pierre Elliot Trudeau.[2] Lennon's transcribed testimony was released to an Ottawa researcher by Library and Archives Canada in 2003 and is available on the Ottawa Beatles Site (https://beatles.ncf.ca/). Ono's testimony was redacted as she was still living.[3]

Why was Lennon, a known anti-establishment figure,[4] deemed a credible voice by members of the Le Dain Commission? There are five main reasons: (1) Lennon was one of the most visible and vocal spokespersons for youth and the counterculture, and for a number of years the media had fixated on his public statements and even his song lyrics; (2) Le Dain commissioners, staff, and researchers were interested in hearing multiple views on the subject of drug use; (3) Lennon had gained prestige as a new type of celebrity activist as a result of his peace initiative, which attempted to reassure so-called squares by calling on youth to protest non-violently; (4) his message of liberalization made a distinction between harmful and benign drugs, reflecting themes in medical and social science literature and law reform discourses popular with liberal intellectuals, journalists, public health officials, and politicians;[5] and (5) Lennon's three visits to Canada in 1969 and his positive statements on the country were flattering to its anti-American nationalism, which was then running near high tide.

Celebrity Activists: An Overview

Lennon's support of progressive causes – a number of them controversial at the time – and his message of peace and humanity, reinforced by songs such as "Give Peace a Chance," "Imagine," and "Happy Xmas (War Is Over)," combined with his untimely death at the hands of an obsessive fan elevated him to the status of a secular saint, despite revelations of his less-than-saintly behaviour in his twenties and thirties.[6] His music also remained popular and influential despite the breakup of the Beatles shortly after his visits to Canada. By the late 1960s, celebrities speaking out, endorsing, and funding social and political causes was not a new phenomenon. Some authors point to the nineteenth-century roots of celebrity activism. By the 1930s and 1940s, a number of prominent singers and actors were associated with left-wing causes. In the 1960s, Hollywood actors and pop stars were speaking on behalf of, and attending events and raising funds for, causes such as civil rights and the anti-war movement. In the late 1960s and early 1970s, entertainment celebrities were enlisting the support of other entertainers for Democratic presidential candidates in their battle against Richard Nixon. In subsequent decades, singers such as Bob Geldof, Bono, Sting, and Madonna were associated with campaigns against war, famine, environmental degradation, and poverty in the developing world. Lennon, with his mass appeal and constant media presence, was "credited with capacities superior to those of other people."[7]

During the 1960s, the most closely watched celebrities were those who could influence youth. The power of pop stars over the young was recognized in the case of the first major drug bust of rock musicians in Britain, the arrest of two members of the Rolling Stones, Keith Richards and Mick Jagger, in 1967. Jagger was sentenced to three months in prison for possessing amphetamine pills, Richards to one year for permitting his home to be used for marijuana smoking, and an associate to six months for heroin possession. Bandmate Brian Jones was busted in a separate raid that year. Chief Justice Parker, who quashed the sentences of Richards and Jagger at appeal, admonished Jagger that as a celebrity he had to be held to a higher standard. As "the idol of a large number of the young in the country," he had "very grave responsibilities."[8] Although the Stones, the "bad boys" of rock, would later be identified with humanitarian causes, it was Lennon, through his promotion of peace, who was an early contributor to a global civil society based on pop star activism.

Activist celebrities would not exist without a fan base and media interest, and the Beatles and their management were masters of developing both. By 1964, the group appeared to be blazing new ground as cultural ambassadors for Britain and as a voice for youth. Lennon biographer Philip Norman describes the arrival of the Beatles in New York on February 7, 1964, as "the moment that the Sixties got going in earnest."[9] Their appearance on the *Ed Sullivan Show,* viewed by 73 million in the United States, made "Beatlemania" a mainstream phenomenon. Canadian journalist Allan Fotheringham, who attended a pre-show press conference in Vancouver in 1964, wrote in *Maclean's:* "The Beatles press conference has become as memorable an institution as President Roosevelt's fireside chats; and at the Vancouver session, Paul, John, George and Ringo were at their flippant best. Eighty-nine newsmen crowded into a room designed for forty ... After the long buildup, the performance itself was no anti-climax."[10] A large part of the excitement of a Beatles press conference was the irreverent humour of the young musicians, especially Lennon, who has been credited by one biographer with "inventing the sound bite." Critics were not always appreciative of popular responses to the group and were especially patronizing towards "hysterical" teenage female fans. The press was also attracted to the group because of the literary and artistic interests of its members – Lennon as an author, for example, and the entire group in movies such as *A Hard Day's Night*.[11]

Lennon left his wife, Cynthia, in 1968 and married Japanese artist Yoko Ono the following year. With their every move closely watched by the press, they decided to exploit media interest by staging a "demonstration" for peace from their bed in the Amsterdam Hilton. The couple had released the experimental album *Two Virgins* in 1968, provoking controversy by posing nude for the cover, and were pushing the boundaries of Ono's performance art by appearing onstage in bags. Lennon explained that "if everyone stayed in bed for a week, there'd be no killing." This event, like the follow-up in Montreal, mimicked the eighteenth-century vogue of genteel hosts receiving guests in their bedchambers. The media-savvy couple, who were collaborating on music, art, and film projects, made sure a film crew was on hand to record the "bed-in."[12] By this time Lennon was reflecting many of the views of Britain's left, which was critical of the Labour government's support of American policy in Southeast Asia and arms sales to Rhodesia. Yet in his statements and music (especially the song "Revolution," released on the B side of "Hey Jude" in 1968), Lennon supported progressive causes but questioned support for a violent path to social change evident in much of the rhetoric of the left. In other words, he rejected the direct action rhetoric of 1968 and held on to much of the utopianism and pacifism of 1967.[13]

John Lennon, the Beatles, and Drugs

All members of the Beatles were associated with drug use or problems at various stages in their careers. Paul McCartney, Ringo Starr, and George Harrison all struggled with alcohol in the 1970s after the breakup of the group, and the former two with cocaine. In 1980, McCartney was arrested for carrying marijuana in his luggage when entering Japan; a few years later, Starr was treated for alcoholism. But in the 1960s the big issue was the degree to which the lyrics of their bestselling songs, such as "Day Tripper" and "Lucy in the Sky with Diamonds," were legitimizing drug use among youth. As their music became more original and innovative, the Beatles were one of a large number of rock groups feared by the forces of the status quo for corrupting youthful attitudes towards drugs, sexuality, and authority. Given the intense media and intellectual interest in the group by the late 1960s, probing their views on drugs and society was not necessarily controversial in all establishment circles. But Lennon and Ono visited Canada in late 1969 not to promote drug legalization but world peace. The Le Dain Commission took advantage of their presence to include them among the more than 600 groups or individuals it consulted. And the visiting celebrities, although there was little public knowledge of their involvement, utilized the occasion to promote decriminalization of marijuana as a step towards a more peaceful and humane society.

Lennon's earliest drug was nicotine, hardly a surprise in a nation where by the time of his eighth birthday in 1948 over 80 percent of men and 40 percent of women were regular smokers. By the mid-1960s, as the Beatles were becoming famous globally, the rate for men was still 70 percent. As a youth, art student, budding rock musician, and seasoned recording artist, Lennon found himself in milieus where heavy smoking was the norm, including club gigs and recording sessions. As a student, he smoked British cigarettes, and when on tour in the United States, the band sported brands such as Marlboros. Later in his life, French Gitaines, known for their strong and aromatic tobacco, were Lennon's favourite brand. He was never able to give up smoking, unlike colleague George Harrison, who quit in 1997 when he was being treated for lung cancer, an affliction that killed him four years later, at age fifty-eight.[14]

The second psychoactive substance Lennon encountered as an adolescent was alcohol. Like many of his fellow art college students in Liverpool, he spent time in local pubs. When the Beatles began to perform as a professional act, especially in Hamburg, Germany, the use of alcohol was pervasive as the venues were bars or strip clubs. Unknown to fans during the heyday of the "Fab Four," Lennon, according to a number of accounts, was a belligerent and aggressive drunk, known to insult and even assault people, including friends such as bandmate Stu Sutcliffe. These antics continued into the 1970s, when he knocked Native American guitarist Jesse Ed Davis unconscious with a bottle. As noted above, all members of the Beatles at various times in their lives consumed unhealthy amounts of alcohol, which was an occupational hazard of show business.[15]

Throughout their early performing and recording careers, members of the Beatles relied on "pep" pills for extra energy in order to complete long gigs, deal with life on the road, and endure arduous studio sessions. The drug used to enhance their performance in their gruelling Hamburg club dates in the early 1960s was Preludin (phenmetrazine), then sold as a diet pill. It was supposedly introduced to the group by British singer Tony Sheridan. Uppers were also readily available from waiters and other contacts in the German club scene. According to Philip Norman, who has documented the Hamburg years, John was a heavy user of "prellies."[16] Another account suggests that the Beatles relied on prellies during early recording sessions. Joe Goodden argues that the group could have not weathered the intense schedule of the classic Beatlemania period (750 concerts in two years) without stimulants.[17] Reports of undisclosed "pills" (presumably uppers) would be linked to Lennon in later years. Yoko Ono later revealed that when she first met her future spouse, he had copious supplies of LSD, Mandrax (the sedative methaqualone, marketed as Quaaludes in the United States), and various pills ("ludes" became a popular club drug in the 1970s).[18]

According to one account, Lennon and his bandmates were introduced to marijuana in 1964 by Bob Dylan, whom they met at their New York hotel on their first American tour. Other sources suggest that the drug would have been known to musicians in Hamburg, Liverpool, and London in the early 1960s. The Beatles became recreational users and regularly carried pot with them on tour. Marijuana also supposedly enhanced the songwriting and recording processes. *Rubber Soul* (released in December 1965) was regarded by fans and the Beatles themselves as the "pot" album. Lennon later disclosed that they had smoked marijuana in Buckingham Palace in 1965 while waiting to be invested with the Order of the British Empire by Queen Elizabeth II. In 1967, a "legalize pot" rally was held in London's Hyde Park, and a full-page ad in the London *Times* cited reasons why cannabis should be decriminalized. The Beatles and their manager helped pay for the advertisement, and their names were soon leaked to the public by a newspaper columnist. The ad described the law against cannabis as "immoral in principle and unworkable in practice." According to

Mark Donnelly, this was an attempt to influence the work of the Wooton Committee, which was investigating the medical evidence surrounding marijuana use.[19] Unlike Canada's Le Dain Commission, the committee sought advice from a small number of experts and a handful of intellectuals, mainly writers. No pop stars or representatives of youth were consulted. In 1969, the committee's report, although warning that opiates were harmful, endorsed liberalization. It was rejected by the Labour government, but in 1971 Parliament passed the Misuse of Drugs Act, which reduced criminal penalties for cannabis use.[20]

The Beatles were never caught with marijuana when on tour but, as noted above, the British police took an aggressive stance towards drug use by pop stars. In late 1968, John and Yoko were temporarily staying in an apartment in London's Montagu Square. The flat had previously housed the American rock guitarist Jimi Hendrix, a heavy user of drugs, and according to Norman, Lennon "carefully swept" the residence for drugs before moving in. Unfortunately he missed some hashish (cannabis resin), which was the basis of the charge. In order to save Yoko (who was not a British citizen) from deportation, he agreed to plead guilty to the possession charge and paid a fine. A number of authors have suspected that the pop star was framed by the police. The guilty plea would later complicate Lennon's plan to move to the United States.[21]

In 1965, John and Cynthia Lennon were unknowingly introduced to LSD at a London party hosted by John's dentist. The substance was placed in sugar cubes in after-dinner coffee.[22] Music critics and journalists have argued that the group's experimentation with "acid" inspired the mystical lyrics of many of their compositions in the near future. In 1972, Lennon described the innovative album *Revolver* (1966) as "the acid album," and one song in particular, Lennon's "Tomorrow Never Knows," was viewed as an example of the emerging genre of LSD-inspired psychedelic rock. In 1967, McCartney became the first Beatle to publically admit to using the drug, which was banned in Britain in 1966 and in the United States two years later. One of the causes of the Beatles's falling out with the Maharishi Mahesh Yogi, the Indian guru whom they followed in 1967 and 1968, was his opposition to LSD. In fact, as part of his program of transcendental meditation, he made them sign a pledge, soon violated, against drug use. More than two decades later, Lennon bragged, "I took millions of trips in the Sixties," and still regarded acid as having furthered his individual growth. In his opinion, the CIA and "the Army" introduced LSD "to control people and what they did was give us freedom."[23]

There is evidence that the Beatles became familiar with cocaine in 1967 and that Lennon, together with Ringo Starr, used it into the 1970s. But the more serious problem was heroin. Lennon supposedly had a fear of injecting drugs and looked down on heroin addicts as weak "junkies." Yet in 1968, during the recording of the *White Album,* both John and Yoko became addicted to the substance, which they inhaled. In his 1971 interview with *Rolling Stone* magazine, he spoke of heroin use as a past problem: "It just was not too much fun." The couple supposedly decided to quit on their own because they planned to have a child. The harrowing experience prompted Lennon to write "Cold Turkey" (discussed below), which was released as a Plastic Ono Band single in 1969. Lennon later admitted that he was still addicted when he gave his first public performance without the Beatles in Canada that fall: "We were full of junk ... I could hardly sing any of them [songs in the set]. I was full of shit."[24]

As noted in the interim report of the Le Dain Commission in 1970, Lennon, the other Beatles, and other rock musicians such Frank Zappa of the Mothers of Invention, Grace Slick of Jefferson Airplane, the singer Donovan, and even LSD guru Dr. Timothy Leary condemned "speed," amphetamines injected under the skin. "Speed freaks" were both pitied and despised by the counterculture.[25] The first major counterculture figure to speak out against speed was the poet Allen Ginsberg in 1965. The phrase "speed kills" gained popularity in the North American media following the murder of Linda Fitzpatrick in 1967. Voices within the counterculture worried that speed was "a deadly threat to the utopia that young cultural pioneers were trying to bring to America."[26] Research indicated that the chances of dying from a methamphetamine overdose in the 1960s and 1970s were remote, but heavy speed use did undermine an individual's health.[27]

John and Yoko and Canada: "Just about Getting Groovy"

In 1969, John Lennon was full of praise for Canada's society, media, and political leaders.[28] He had last been in the country in the summer of 1966, when the Beatles were winding up what turned out to be their last world tour. Riding the wave of Beatlemania, they had played in Vancouver,

Toronto, and Montreal in 1964 and returned to Toronto for two concerts in 1965. A few days after their two performances in Maple Leaf Gardens in 1966, the Beatles, with minor exceptions, never performed again in a concert setting. By this time, the group had ceased to be a charming boy band singing songs of heterosexual romance and were incorporating social issues into their music and statements. At the time, *Revolver* was the top-selling album in Canada, and at a press conference reporters fielded questions about humanitarian causes, Christianity, the generation gap, and the meaning of song lyrics. The press conference took place just as a conservative backlash was starting to brew in the United States over Lennon's statement to a British reporter that the Beatles, and rock and roll, were "more important than Jesus Christ." Like many pop performers, the Beatles were under pressure to take a stand on the morality of American military involvement in Vietnam. When asked about the war, Lennon replied: "I mean, we all just don't agree with war for any reason whatsoever. There's no reason on earth why anybody should kill anybody else." Lennon, McCartney, and Harrison also spoke in favour of young Americans resisting the draft and seeking refuge in Canada.[29]

On May 25, 1969, Lennon and Ono flew from the Bahamas to Toronto with Ono's daughter. They were briefly detained by immigration officials because of Lennon's recent conviction for marijuana possession. The conviction had kept them out of the United States. Lennon explained that they chose Canada because it was close to the United States. Their media campaign for peace was obviously aimed at America. Lennon planned to travel to Montreal to stage a second bed-in and to meet Pierre Trudeau. He explained that they hoped to take their message of peace to the prime minister and eventually to President Nixon. This would be symbolized by a gift of acorns, which would be planted for peace. They also wanted to inspire "kids" in America to be non-violent in their protests.[30] Lennon expressed surprise that he would be denied entry to Canada: "We all thought that it was sort of like home. Sort of like popping into Ireland only a bit further."[31] Immigration officials granted several days' grace for an appeal of the decision, and the couple flew to Montreal.

During most of their remaining time in Canada, Lennon and Ono spent seven days staging their famous bed-in at Montreal which, together with the Amsterdam event, was much maligned by critics. At this time "The

Ballad of John and Yoko," which was inspired by the Amsterdam bed-in, was climbing the charts on both sides of the Atlantic. The single was banned by CHUM-AM in Toronto because of the line "Christ, you know it isn't easy."[32] The bed-in was a media event, "a commercial for peace," in Lennon's words. He told the press: "We can't lead a parade or a march." Their goal was "to interest young people in doing something for peace." Hopefully "the hippest ones" (youth) would help get the message out to "the squares." During the event, the couple was kept busy with interviews. Conscious of the role of the media and especially television in making the Beatles the first super group, Apple press agent Derek Taylor granted easy access to journalists and television crews. The event also attracted a number of celebrities, such as LSD advocate Timothy Leary, entertainers Tommy Smothers and Petula Clark, comedian/activist Dick Gregory, and even right-wing cartoonist Al Capp. Many of these celebrities sang on the recording of "Give Peace a Chance," which was written and recorded during the bed-in.[33]

On June 3, the couple took part in a seminar on world peace at the University of Ottawa, where their student handlers were Hugh Segal and Allan Rock. Accompanied by Derek Taylor, they visited 24 Sussex Drive; finding that Prime Minister Trudeau was not home, they left flowers with a lone Mountie on guard duty as a token of peace.[34] On June 4, they arrived by train in Toronto, checked into the Windsor Arms Hotel, then drove to Niagara Falls for a film shoot. Taylor told reporters that despite being banned by many North American radio stations, "The Ballad of John and Yoko" was selling well (it was not banned by the BBC). In Montreal, Lennon told *Globe and Mail* pop music journalist Ritchie Yorke that such bans were "insane" and that "they" (presumably squares) "hate what Christ stood for" and "can only hear His name in church."[35]

After the bed-in, the celebrity couple was interviewed on the CBC television program *Weekend* by Lloyd Robertson. With them to discuss their campaign and a plan for a peace festival in Canada was progressive Rabbi Abraham Feinberg of Toronto's Holy Blossom Temple. Lennon continued to praise Canada, claiming that its press treated them "as human beings."[36] Their visit to Canada generated controversy but also goodwill. During the show, producers surprised the guests with a video link from Winnipeg with Russell Doern, the deputy speaker of the Manitoba legislature. The province was preparing for its centennial celebrations in 1970, and Premier Ed Schreyer, who wanted his government and province to appear young and modern, had tasked Doern with asking the celebrities to visit the province to promote peace. In a letter to Lennon, the NDP premier stated: "Through news media accounts of your statements and actions with respect to world peace I believe I have gained some understanding of your philosophy and find myself substantially in accord with it."[37] Although vague on the details, Lennon promised that they would visit Manitoba. This set off a conservative backlash in Winnipeg and beyond, spearheaded by a controversial talk radio host. Anti-Lennon telephone calls, letters, and petitions reflected fear of hippies, drugs, the new morality, and a youthful peace movement that seemed to lionize communism. Seizing upon media coverage of militant student protest, the letter writers also linked hippies with violence. Even more shocking to conservative, middle-aged Manitobans, Lennon would have been on the same celebrity guest list as Queen Elizabeth. In the end, the formal invitation to Lennon was never sent.[38]

Later in June, after Lennon had been forced to leave Canada, Toronto hosted a pop festival that would help create a chain of events that would bring him back to Canada. The Toronto Pop Festival was a financial success, with at least 50,000 attendees, thousands of them from out of town, including the United States. The lineup featured The Band, Al Kooper, Johnny Winter, Sly and the Family Stone, Procul Harum, Jose Feliciano, Edwin Starr, Chuck Berry, Tiny Tim, Ronnie Hawkins, Blood, Sweat and Tears, the Velvet Underground, Steppenwolf, and Alice Cooper, as well as lesser-known Canadian acts such as Motherlode and Robert Charlebois. One poster, attempting to put a political gloss on the two-day event, billed it as "Liberation Days." Despite the counterculture marketing angle, most accounts suggest that the festival, held at Varsity Stadium, was orderly.[39]

In September 1969, the city hosted a second major concert, the Toronto Rock and Roll Revival, which featured the world debut of Lennon and Ono's Plastic Ono Band. This was credited with being the first major "rock nostalgia" concert in North America, inspired by the performance of the American neo–doo-wop group Sha Na Na at Woodstock the previous month. Promoted by locals Kenny Walker and John Brower, the event included Chuck Berry, Little Richard, Bo Diddley, and Jerry Lee Lewis. Somewhat out of place was the controversial American group The Doors, headed by Jim Morrison. The organizers contacted Lennon with the idea that he and Ono could attend the event as guests. Encouraged by Ritchie Yorke, Lennon was invited to perform at the event with Ono. They brought with them guitarist Eric Clapton. Before taking the stage, Lennon requested cocaine; the substance that was provided was possibly cocaine or some mysterious street drug.[40] The performance was a major coup for the promoters as Lennon had not played before a live audience in four years. One of the songs featured in their set of eight was the new composition "Cold Turkey," which documented the couple's addiction to heroin, which they were attempting to break. Although it was actually an anti-drug song, its controversial subject matter meant that it was banned on many radio stations. It was released as a single the following month and reached number 30 in Canada. Most star-struck fans at Varsity Stadium were apparently unfazed by Ono's experimental onstage antics and her growing reputation as the woman who was causing tensions among the Beatles. Although still suffering from heroin addiction, Lennon was thrilled to meet the rock and roll giants of his youth and happy to be performing before a live audience. The songs recorded in Toronto were mastered for a new album called *The Plastic Ono Band – Live Peace in Toronto 1969*. Such was Lennon's star power that this live album charted at number 10 in the United States.[41]

Following the Toronto appearance, Lennon worked with John Brower to plan a "peace festival" someplace in Ontario. Rumours circulated that it would be bigger than Woodstock and involve the other Beatles and even Elvis (the latter was highly unlikely given Presley's views on communists, drug liberalizers, and British rockers, shared at his 1970 meeting with President Nixon). Lennon and Brower were assisted by Ritchie Yorke. Inspired by the large and relatively peaceful festival crowds at Woodstock and on Britain's Isle of Wight, Lennon expressed optimism to reporters about the transformative power of mass events. He lent his name to the Woodstock-inspired event to be held in Canada in 1970, but ended up parting with Brower and the other backers as he wanted a free concert. By 1970, Lennon would finally be granted entry to the United States and was becoming interested in other projects. First planned for near Moncton, New Brunswick, but blocked by the provincial government, the Strawberry Fields Festival (its name aimed at exploiting the popularity of the Beatles) was held at Mosport Park in Bowmanville, Ontario in the summer of 1970.

The promoters obtained a court injunction to overcome opposition from municipal officials and the Ontario Provincial Police.[42] Strawberry Fields was marketed as festival of "peace and freedom" but it was a profit-making venture with no involvement by Lennon. As revealed in 2007, that did not stop the RCMP Security Service from monitoring Lennon's political activities during his Canadian visit, and sharing information with the FBI on the planned peace festival.[43]

Lennon continued to generate international headlines. In late November, he returned his Order of the British Empire award to the Queen with the following note: "Our Majesty, I am returning this M.B.E. in protest against Britain's involvement in the Nigeria-Biafra thing, against our support of America in Vietnam and against Cold Turkey slipping down the charts. With love, John Lennon." On December 15, he and Ono visited Canada for the third time that year, arriving in Toronto to launch a "peace offensive" during the Christmas season. Their host was transplanted American rocker Ronnie Hawkins. The campaign involved a series of billboards in twelve cities around the world, one of them Toronto, with the message "War is Over." Posters and handbills were also distributed. Three days later, they were interviewed by communications theorist Marshall McLuhan at the University of Toronto. The initial forty-five-minute meeting and a shorter interview were filmed by the CBC.[44] The celebrities explained to McLuhan that their peace mission was much broader than attempting to influence attitudes towards the conflicts in Vietnam and Biafra: "We really believe that those wars are manifestations of the whole world's violence."[45] Lennon understood drug problems in terms of the pressures of modern society on the individual: "All the adults are on alcohol, sleeping pills and barbiturates, all the kids are on pot and methadrine or whatever it is. The problem isn't what they take or the drug problem. The problem is the society which makes us have to smoke cigarettes, drink, take drugs or whatever." During a debate with the Canadian academic, Lennon condemned speed, supported legalization of marijuana, and expressed support for banning other recreational drugs.[46]

On December 23, Lennon and Ono met with Pierre Trudeau in Ottawa for fifty minutes. Lennon was positive about the encounter: "He is beautiful. He is the first head of a country that I have spoken to. Just beautiful."[47] The audience with Trudeau, who was described as the youngest and hippest of the leaders of the Western industrial nations, and who had been the focus of his own media-fuelled "mania" in 1968, flattered Canadian nationalists. It confirmed that the nation was not only a peaceful "honest broker" with a reputation for humanity and social justice but also "cool." Years later, Yorke described Lennon's meeting with the prime minister as an example of "political pop." Following their chat with Trudeau, the couple met with health minister John Munro, whom they described as "hip" and open minded. Munro had met Lennon on his previous visit to Ottawa and was impressed with his politeness and seriousness. In remarks to the media, Lennon explained that they were offering Canada their help on the drug problem. The gist of their message was the need for balanced information on and responses to drug use, the legalization of marijuana, and warning of the dangers of hard drugs.[48] Munro, who was already on record as questioning the alleged dangers of cannabis use, viewed LSD as a dangerous drug.[49]

The Private Testimony of John Lennon

On the previous day, in their private railway car in Montreal, Lennon and Ono met two members of the Le Dain Commission for a private hearing.[50] Two members of the commission's staff – Ralph Miller and Charles Farmilo – were also present, as was a tape recorder. Miller, the commission's research director, was a young American recruited from McMaster University. Farmilo, a senior research associate, had a background in chemical toxicology. Earlier in the day, Lennon and Ono had staged a press conference at the Château Champlain Hotel in support of their "War is Over" campaign. At the time, both celebrities were still recovering from heroin addiction (a reason they became converts in 1970 to Arthur Janov's "primal scream" therapy). Lennon and Ono were not the only rock musicians contacted by members of the inquiry. Commissioner Ian Campbell recalled meeting with (but not recording conversations with) the Grateful Dead, Grace Slick, and Led Zeppelin. It was part of an approach that involved meeting informally with small groups of people, including drug dealers, to discuss modern drug issues. Campbell, born in 1927, was a political scientist and the new dean of Arts at Montreal's Sir George Williams University (site of a well-publicized protest in 1970). His colleague, born in Germany in 1911, was Dr. Heinz E. Lehmann, a psychiatrist who was a

McGill University professor and a hospital clinical director and director of research. In the late 1950s, he had pioneered the use of chlorpromazine to treat schizophrenia. He was the only commissioner to publicly admit to having smoked cannabis.[51] Yorke, who had joined Lennon's entourage, later claimed that Gerald Le Dain and an unidentified colleague were encouraged by Lennon to try marijuana and did do in the privacy of the celebrities' sleeping car, but other sources, including Yorke's February 7, 1970, *Rolling Stone* piece, suggest that the commission's chairperson was not present.[52]

Lennon's remarks were somewhat disjointed and the narrative is disrupted by the absence in the transcript of Ono's contribution (she spoke more than sixty times during the meeting). As expected, Lennon supported the decriminalization of cannabis, which he admitted to using in order to relax, and the provision of realistic information on drugs and more humane treatment services. But in keeping with previous, more public statements, his views on the proper role of drugs were complex. He was really interested in the broader issue of peace and believed that drugs ultimately were not the answer. Drug abuse, like war, famine, and other types of human suffering, was, in his view, a product of frustration born out of a modern, dehumanized society ("repressed automatons"). At times, the commissioners appeared to share this view or at least appreciate the argument. Lennon was impressed by Canada's "sane" discussion of drug issues, claiming that "Canada looks like the only hope" and could lead the world by example through more humane drug policies: "You are the new country ... let us envy Canada." America was "too paranoiac to do anything" in terms of drug reform. The conversation was full of sociological analysis, philosophical statements, and references to international relations, the generation gap, and popular culture. Lennon's intense interest in television is apparent in the discussion. One senses that the two middle-aged commissioners, both academics, were trying to be "hip" with the young celebrities. Campbell, a university dean, explained that one of the goals of the commission was to "plan greater communication between one generation or one part of the population to another."[53]

Lennon argued that the hard-line prohibitionist approach to marijuana despite its relatively benign properties was creating cynicism and distrust among youth towards warnings about genuine threats as such heroin and amphetamines. He mentioned the negative impacts of alcohol and prescription drugs several times. His take on LSD was somewhat confusing. At one point, he claimed that it had not caused him harm, but later he condemned "the free use of it" and said that "it probably does burn your head off." He associated marijuana with "the non-violent movement" and defended users from criticisms that they lacked drive and energy by pointing out that at least they were not going to war and were contributing to music and art. As in other interviews, he was optimistic about the communal nature of mass rock festivals and regarded their negative portrayals in the media as attempts by the "Establishment" to instill fear of youth.[54] As for the Establishment, he was optimistic that much of it could be won over by changes in social mores and fashion (such as "Beatle haircuts" and mod clothes); at any rate the future belonged to the young. On this basis, he optimistically referred to 1970 as "Year One" in the evolution of a more humane world and hoped that the "War is Over" campaign and planned peace festival would empower people to act. On the other hand, Lennon sympathized with the older generation (the parents of youth) who had in effect been brainwashed into "straight" thinking. In addition to mass music gatherings, he pointed to the "back to the land" and environmental movements as positive signs that thoughtful youth envisioned a society "without competitive drives and restrictions."[55]

The commissioners asked Lennon and Ono for suggestions on concrete actions. One way to "sell pot to the Government" was to stress the economic benefits of legalized marijuana sales. The "machine" (the Establishment, capitalism, government) could benefit from legalization through taxation, profits, and other spinoffs. Lennon mentioned more than once the end of capital punishment in Britain in the 1960s despite polls suggesting public opposition to abolition, and he hoped that political leadership in the future would be equally visionary. Campbell's comments and questions were fairly non-judgmental but at times foreshadowed the cautious views expressed in his minority report in the Le Dain Commission report on cannabis. Lennon rejected any notion that marijuana was a gateway to harder drugs, and argued that addiction or abuse of speed, heroin, or alcohol was rooted in the individual, not the substance. The meeting ended with the commissioners explaining their schedule and suggesting that they seek further feedback from the celebrities in the near future, and with one or more unidentified staffers explaining the power of police agencies in influencing drug control policies. Finally, Lennon promised to give the officials the couple's "hot line" (the private telephone number they made available to various progressive causes).[56]

Conclusion

John Lennon's meeting with two of the Le Dain commissioners was reported in brief to the world by Ritchie Yorke in *Rolling Stone* in early 1970.[57] Even before the Beatles formally broke up later that year, Lennon appeared to be adjusting well to life as a solo artist and activist. *Rolling Stone* named him Man of the Year for 1969 and Britain's ATV television network declared him one of three Men of the Decade (along with Ho Chi Minh and John F. Kennedy). Lennon's post-Beatles activism was complex – he continued to identify with progressive causes, including gender equality, regretting his earlier treatment of women. In interviews, he portrayed himself as resisting pressures to conform, whether from teachers to be a model student or from fans to be a Beatle, and, despite his middle-class upbringing, claimed to identify with the working class ("Working Class Hero" was released as the B side of the single "Imagine" in 1970). He and Yoko Ono continued to support social justice campaigns on both sides of the Atlantic. In a 1971 interview, they theorized that the real reason behind their ongoing deportation battle in the United States was their advocacy of peace. Lennon, despite his growing international reputation as a humanitarian, did not take part in the influential Concert for Bangladesh, organized in New York by George Harrison in 1971. He was asked to perform but refused because Ono would have been excluded. Like other left-wing celebrities, he was soon targeted by the FBI and the Nixon White House, as documented in Jon Wiener's 1999 book *Gimme Some Truth: The John Lennon FBI Files*. Wiener's research, based on Access to Information Requests for FBI files, indicates that the persecution of Lennon, which ceased after Nixon won the 1972 election, was orchestrated at the highest levels and involved not only the White House and the FBI but also the Immigration and Naturalization Service, the CIA, and British intelligence. Associations with Yippie leaders Abbie Hoffman and Jerry Rubin and Black Power activists Bobby Searle and Angela Davis, as well as British Black Power leader Michael X and the Provisional IRA, seemed to clash with Lennon's 1969 pacifist message. One classified report in 1972 claimed that Lennon, whose phone was tapped, had contributed money to a New Left group dedicated to disrupting the Republican National Convention and (erroneously) that he had been appointed to the National Commission on Marihuana and Drug Abuse.[58]

Lennon continued to have a complicated and shifting relationship with psychoactive substances in the post–Canadian interlude years. He and Ono fought Nixon's attempt to have him deported and became permanent residents of New York. During a period of separation from Ono between 1973 and 1975, Lennon, in the company of friends such as singer Harry Nilsson and Who drummer Keith Moon, drank heavily and consumed pills. Somehow he remained productive, recording three albums, including *Mind Games*. Following his reconciliation with Ono, he appeared to have adopted a relatively healthy lifestyle, with the exception of his smoking habit noted above. In a *Playboy* interview released two days before his murder in 1980 by Mark Chapman, he portrayed himself as a reformed individual who, under Ono's tutelage, followed a "macrobiotic" diet of fish, rice, and whole grains, and was an involved father. Interviewer David Sheff noticed that he was a heavy user of French cigarettes. Lennon explained that "macrobiotic people don't believe in the Big C" (cancer).[59] He claimed that he had not consumed LSD "in years" but was not averse to more natural substances such as peyote or mushrooms. He denounced cocaine (then gaining popularity among entertainers, actors, and the jet set) as a "dumb drug."[60]

None of Lennon's theories or suggestions in 1969 on drug issues, the generation gap, or peace was particularly original. Their significance lay in their source. Lennon's testimony had value because he was arguably the world's most recognized counterculture entertainment figure. Yet other than a brief reference to the Beatles in the first report, none of the four major reports of the Le Dain Commission even mentioned Lennon or Ono. If the couple's testimony had been made public, a journalist theorized in 2003, perceptions of the inquiry may have been different. The example of the Manitoba backlash against Lennon is suggestive of one possible outcome, as was the contemporary opinion in much of America that supporters of drug liberalization were "traitors" and that celebrity activists were naive, shallow attention seekers.[61] John Munro could not remember why the Montreal meeting had been held in camera, but recalled that "you could only go so far" in 1969. Another former commissioner, Marie-Andrée Bertrand, speculated that it was done in order to shield Lennon from RCMP surveillance and possible arrest.[62] In June 1970, the commission's interim report divided the Liberal cabinet by not only recommending the legalization of cannabis but also limiting fines for possession of hard drugs to $100. Health minister Munro expressed his support for transferring marijuana from the Narcotic Control Act to the less punitive Food and Drugs Act, but this never came to pass.[63] When the commission's report on cannabis came out in 1972, the two members who had met with Lennon and Ono in 1969 had divergent policy recommendations. Heinz Lehmann signed the majority report that called for decriminalizing basic possession, whereas Ian Campbell's minority report opposed decriminalization of possession and supported enhanced sanctions. A decriminalization bill was prepared for Parliament that year but no major legislative reforms were undertaken. On the practical level, previous criminal justice changes meant that the overwhelming majority of cannabis offenders would avoid jail.[64] Yet cannabis offenders would continue to be arrested in the 1970s, mostly for simple possession. As for "political pop," it failed to reduce mainstream anxieties about youth and drugs. The deaths in 1970 and 1971 of three rock superstars – Janis Joplin, Jimi Hendrix, and Jim Morrison – prolonged the association of popular music with drug abuse. Despite their Beatle haircuts and Beatle boots, the "squares" remained unconvinced of the redemptive powers of marijuana. John Lennon's views on marijuana would prevail in part in 2018, nearly a half-century after he met Pierre Trudeau, when that prime minister's son Justin partially decriminalized the growing, sale, and use of the drug.

Notes

1 Philip Norman, *John Lennon: The Life* (Toronto: Anchor Canada, 2008). Joe Goodden's *Riding So High: The Beatles and Drugs* (n.p.: Pepper and Pearl, 2017) makes no mention of Lennon and the Le Dain Commission. Goodden is a journalist and a founder of the Beatles Bible website (https://www.beatlesbible.com/).

2 As explained below, the meeting itself, reported in *Rolling Stone,* was not secret, but the details of the discussion were not widely reported.

3 Norman Provencher, "Lennon on Drugs: The Beatle's Secret Testimony on Marijuana in Canada," *Ottawa Citizen,* May 17, 2003. For the Le Dain Commission, see Marcel

Martel, *Not This Time: Canadians, Public Policy, and the Marijuana Question, 1961–1975* (Toronto: University of Toronto Press, 2006). An insider's account of the incident appears in a memoir by the late Ritchie Yorke: *Christ You Know It Ain't Easy: John and Yoko's Battle for Peace* (Middleton, DE: Ritchie Yorke Publishing, 2015), 95–99.

4 Mark Wheeler, *Celebrity Politics: Image and Identity on Contemporary Political Communication* (Malden, MA: Polity Press, 2013), 1.

5 Much like George Peters and the Chicago LSD Rescue Service, examined in Chapter 7, Lennon was not promoting hedonism but attempting to bridge the gap between alienated youth and mainstream opinion and exert a positive impact on drug policy and drug use.

6 For a particularly nasty commentary, see Simon Heffner, "Why Do People STILL Lionize Wife-Beating IRA Apologist John Lennon?" *Daily Mail,* April 7, 2015.

7 Liza Tsaliki, Christos Frangonikolopoulos, and Asteris Huliaras, eds., "Introduction," in *Transnational Celebrity Activism in Global Politics: Changing the World?* (Bristol: Intellect, 2011), 9.

8 Mark Donnelly, *Sixties Britain: Culture, Society and Politics* (Toronto: Pearson Longman, 2005), 153. See also Simon Wells, *Butterfly on a Wheel: The Great Rolling Stones Drug Bust* (London: Omnibus Press, 2011). The theme of the vulnerability of impressionable youth to messages about drug use is also discussed in Chapter 3.

9 Norman, *John Lennon,* 342.

10 Dorian Lynskey, "Beatlemania: 'The Screamers' and Other Tales of Fandom," *Guardian,* September 29, 2013; Beatles Press Conference, Vancouver, August 22, 1964, The Beatles Ultimate Experience, http://www.beatlesinterviews.org/db1964.0822.beatles.html.

11 Beatles Press Conference, Montreal, September 8, 1964, The Beatles Ultimate Experience, http://www.beatlesinterviews.org/db1964.0908.beatles.html.

12 Reuters, "Beatle and His Bride End Seven-Day Bed-In," *Globe and Mail,* April 1, 1969; Linda Bohnen, "On Way to Montreal Lie-In: Beatle Flies to Toronto, Detained at Airport," *Globe and Mail,* May 26, 1969.

13 Norman, *John Lennon,* 553–55, 567, 571. "Revolution 1," released on the album *The Beatles* (1969), had a slightly different lyric, which suggested that Lennon remained ambivalent about the link between violence and social progress: Thomas MacFarlane, *The Beatles and McLuhan: Understanding the Electric Age* (Toronto: Scarecrow Press, 2013), 79.

14 Details on the career of the Beatles, including their drug use, can be found on various fan websites, such as The Beatles Bible.

15 Norman, *John Lennon,* 132; 263–64; Goodden, *Riding So High,* 10–18; 266–71.

16 Norman, *John Lennon,* 201–2.

17 Goodden, *Riding So High,* 36.

18 Dan McQuade, "The Drug That Helped Turn the Beatles into the World's Greatest Band," *Village Voice,* August 14, 2014; Norman, *John Lennon,* 551.

19 Donnelly, *Sixties Britain,* 154; London *Times,* July 22, 1967.

20 UK, Home Office, *Cannabis, Report by the Advisory Committee on Drug Dependence* (London, 1969), app. 4; Stephen Abrams, "SOMA, the Wooten Report and Cannabis Law Reform in Britain during the 1960s and 1970s," in *A Cannabis Reader: Global Issues and Local Experiences,* EMCDDA Monographs 8, vol. 1, ed. Sharon Rööodner Sznitman, Börje Olsson, and Robin Room (Luxembourg: European Monitoring Centre for Drugs and Drug Addiction, 2008), ch. 4.

21 Norman, *John Lennon,* 573–74; 577–78; 691. Two years later, police raided Harrison's home and charged him and his wife with cannabis possession.

22 Jann S. Wenner, "John Lennon Remembers," *Rolling Stone,* January 21, 1971.

23 Norman, *John Lennon,* 500; David Sheff, "Interview with John Lennon and Yoko Ono," *Playboy,* January 22, 1981.

24 "The Beatles and Drugs," The Beatles Bible, http://www.beatlesbible.com/; Wenner, "John Lennon Remembers."

25 Commission of Inquiry into the Non-Medical Use of Drugs, *The Non-Medical Use of Drugs: Interim Report of the Canadian Government Commission of Inquiry* (Toronto: Penguin Books, 1971), 79.

26 Nicolas Rasmussen, *On Speed: The Many Lives of Amphetamines* (New York: NYU Press, 2008), 183.

27 Nicholas L. Parsons, *Meth Mania: A History of Methamphetamine* (Boulder, CO: Lynne Rienner Publishers, 2014), 79–88.

28 MacFarlane, *The Beatles and McLuhan,* app. A, "Interview with John Lennon, December 20, 1969"; app. B, "Meeting with Marshall McLuhan, December 20, 1969."

29 Beatles Press Conference, Toronto, August 17, 1966, The Beatles Ultimate Experience, http://www.beatlesinterviews.org/db1966.0817.beatles.html.

30 Bohnen, "On Way to Montreal."

31 Ibid.

32 N.A., "Lennon Urges Plugging of Peace," *Globe and Mail,* June 4, 1969; Norman, *John Lennon,* 596–97.

33 Mark Reid, "Come Together," *Canada's History* 93, 2 (April-May 2013): 20–27. A video produced for the original recording can be viewed at https://www.youtube.com/watch?v=ftE8vr0WNus.

34 N.A., "Lennon Urged Plugging of Peace."

35 Ibid.

36 The introduction to the show is available online at https://www.youtube.com/watch?v=JzqnDU4H1zM.

37 Matthew Rankin, "The Ballad of John and Yoko," *Beaver* 86, 6 (December 2006–January 2007): 45–47.

38 Ibid.

39 Ritchie Yorke, "POP SCENE: Festival Success 'Due to Police,'" *Globe and Mail,* June 23, 1969; Ritchie Yorke, "The Doors Signed for Rock Show," *Globe and Mail,* August 22, 1969.

40 Yorke, *Christ You Know It Ain't Easy,* 55.
41 N.A., "The Lennons and a Plea for Peace," *Globe and Mail,* September 15, 1969; Ritchie Yorke, "The Lennons and the Rock n' Roll Revival," *Globe and Mail,* September 20, 1969. For a film of the event, see D.A. Pennebaker, *Sweet Toronto,* video, 52:52, 1969, https://www.youtube.com/watch?v=14C0FmyFobs. With Ono pregnant, the couple attempted to break their heroin snorting habit – with no medical aid – at their English estate in the summer of 1969. Lennon wrote "Cold Turkey" before September and unsuccessfully attempted to have a visiting Bob Dylan play piano on a demo recording: Goodden, *Riding So High,* 227.
42 Greg Marquis, "Rocking Free North America: The 1970s Strawberry Fields Festival and the Youth Culture Borderlands" (paper, Canadian Historical Association conference, Victoria, BC, June 2012).
43 The information on Lennon was part of security files amassed on Rabbi Feinberg: Canadian Press, "RCMP Spies Kept Watch on John Lennon in 1969," *CTV News,* July 22, 2007.
44 MacFarlane, *The Beatles and McLuhan.*
45 John Lennon and Yoko Ono interview with Marshall McLuhan, December 19, 1969, The Beatles Ultimate Experience: http://www.beatlesinterviews.org/db1969.1219.beatles.html.
46 Ibid. Lennon made a similar point when the couple was interviewed on September 11, 1971, on *The Dick Cavett Show,* where he attributed society's reliance on alcohol and drugs to a lack of personal freedom.
47 Donald Newman, "Praise for Trudeau from the Lennons," *Globe and Mail,* December 24, 1969.
48 Citizen staff: "PM 'A Beautiful Person'," *Ottawa Citizen,* December 23, 1969; Bradley Scott, "Ritchie Yorke on Rock and Roll," *Vice,* December 2, 2013, http://www.vice.com/read/ritchie-yorke-on-rock-n-roll; Jack Batten, "Canada's Struggle for Legalization," *Rolling Stone,* March 19, 1970, 22.
49 Ritchie Yorke, "I'd Rather Be Burned in Canada," *Rolling Stone,* December 13, 1970, 10.
50 Lennon's entourage included Ritchie York and his wife, Johnny Brower, Toronto rock musician Ronnie Hawkins and his wife, assistant Anthony Fawcett, and Hawkins's "bodyguard."
51 "John Lennon's Drug Testimony: 'The Le Dain Commission of Inquiry into the Non-Medical Use of Drugs – The Private Hearing of John Lennon,' December 22, 1969, in Montreal," Ottawa Beatles Site, http://beatles.ncf.ca/lennon_inquiry.html.
52 Yorke, *Christ You Know It Ain't Easy,* 97–98.
53 "John Lennon's Drug Testimony."
54 For a discussion of media reactions to rock festivals, see Chapter 3, on the 1970 Manseau Woodstock Pop Festival.
55 "John Lennon's Drug Testimony"; MacFarlane, *The Beatles and McLuhan,* 139. A year later, in his *Rolling Stone* interview, Lennon regretted his past heavy LSD use and

blamed it in part on "the stupid book of Leary's" (*The Psychedelic Experience,* by Timothy Leary, Ralph Metzner, and Richard Alpert, 1964).

56 "John Lennon's Drug Testimony."

57 Ritchie Yorke, "John, Yoko & YEAR ONE," *Rolling Stone,* February 7, 1970, 19.

58 Norman, *John Lennon,* 694–96; Jon Wiener, *Gimme Some Truth: The John Lennon FBI Files* (Berkeley and Los Angeles: University of California Press, 1999). The National Commission on Marihuana and Drug Abuse, which issued a report on marijuana in 1972, was appointed by Nixon in 1970. Known as the Shafer Commission, it held public and private hearings, hired "youth consultants" and "student researchers," and solicited views from students. Unlike the Le Dain Commission, however, it does not appear to have interviewed rock musicians and other celebrities: National Commission on Marihuana and Drug Abuse, *Marihuana: A Signal of Misunderstanding: First Report of the National Commission on Marihuana and Drug Abuse* (Washington, DC: Government Printing Office, 1972).

59 Ottawa Beatles Site, https://beatles.ncf.ca/; Sheff, "Interview with John Lennon."

60 Sheff, "Interview with John Lennon."

61 Wheeler, *Celebrity Politics,* 58–59.

62 Provencher, "Lennon on Drugs."

63 "Le Dain Report on Drugs Divides Cabinet," radio broadcast, CBC *Sunday Magazine,* June 21, 1970, 28:05, http://www.cbc.ca/archives/entry/ledain-report-on-drugs-divides-cabinet; Martel, *Not This Time.*

64 Canada, Commission of Inquiry into the Non-Medical Use of Drugs, *Cannabis: A Report of the Commission of Inquiry into the Non-Medical Use of Drugs* (Ottawa: Information Canada, 1972).

PART 2

Medicinal Pleasure and Panic

Manhood, Drink, and the "Medical Heresy" of US Army Surgeon James Mann (1812–16)   **5**

Renée Lafferty-Salhany

The pharmaceutical arsenal deployed against disease in the late eighteenth and early nineteenth century was impressive and occasionally terrifying. Physicians and surgeons employed relatively benign and occasionally appetizing substances (like chocolate, carrots, and cloves) to more power-ful ones (ipecac, digitalis, and slippery elm bark), to downright poisonous ones (arsenic, lead, copper sulfate, and mercury). Physicians also doled out an enormous amount of alcohol in both distilled and fermented varieties. Hospital stores and supplies held by regimental surgeons in North America could be, when stocked according to their wishes, impressive competition for a small tavern. One prominent American naval surgeon, for example, described the ideal hospital store of 1805 as containing at least thirty-two gallons of brandy, sixty-four gallons of white wine, and six dozen bottles of port.[1]

While often employed in hospital settings to make bitter medicines like quinine palatable, such libations were also considered medicinal in their own right. Brandy and wine could "restore tone" to the stomach, stimulate bodies rendered weak by lengthy fevers, calm anxieties and strengthen resolve before amputation, or serve as a healthful topical application for wounds.[2] In one case reported to esteemed US army surgeon James Mann during the War of 1812, a soldier suffering a debilitating and ultimately fatal infection following a horrifically delayed (and probably botched) amputation of his leg was bathed from head to toe with imported St. Croix rum as often as three or four times a day.[3]

For Mann, alcohol – particularly distilled spirits – held a "distinguished place in the *materia medica*."[4] As far as he was concerned, however, that was where they needed to stay. Outside of a physician's or apothecary's control, spirits were an "evil," one of the most destructive influences on the health of the nation's fighting force. As outlined in this chapter, Mann's concern over the consumption of spirits was frequently tied into this broader concern for the quality of American manhood, concerns he detailed in his *Medical Sketches of the Campaigns of 1812, 13, 14*. Placed in a wider context of late eighteenth- and early nineteenth-century medical thinking and read as a version of what Thomas Laqueur describes as a "humanitarian narrative,"[5] this text offers not only a nosological explanation of illness and disease during the 1812 conflict but also a clear portrait of what Mann envisioned as the ideal soldier, the ideal republican hero, the ideal man.[6] Significantly, by mobilizing his scientific expertise and appealing to the emotional urgency of an endangered and beloved nation, Mann heightened the apparent truth of his own vision for preserving that man. It was a straightforward, powerfully simplistic vision, too. It demanded, in part, tighter controls over, even prohibitions on, spirits and, crucially, greater authority for the surgeon himself. Controlling the flow of spirits was proposed as a means of simultaneously controlling bodies, preserving health, and inspiring noble, manly sacrifice in the service of the nation, as well as promoting the professional aspirations of the members of America's (equally noble and manly) army medical corps.

On James Mann, His Education, and His *Medical Sketches*

I have chosen to examine this particular surgeon's work because, although posterity has not been kind to him, Mann was one of the more influential and well-known surgeons in the Early Republic. This exploration of his medical use of alcohol, based on his 1816 record, cannot therefore claim to present anything like a definitive or complete portrait of medical thinking in relation to drink for the first decades of the nineteenth century.[7] Wherever possible, however, I have related Mann's opinions and practice to those of his contemporaries and intellectual forebears.

Mann's *Medical Sketches* is quite obviously, in many sections, a reflective memoir: its contents are deeply coloured by the ultimate outcome of the war (one he suggests was entirely defensive and from which the United States emerged victorious), by his frustration with his professional status in the army's administrative structure, as well as his urge to protect certain officers from accusations of poor leadership, cowardice, or failure.[8] However, Mann's text also makes liberal use of his wartime notes, correspondence, and reports, as well as those of his fellow army surgeons. It is remarkably readable, providing fastidious detail on epidemic and incidental diseases, surgeries, wounds, hospital organization – not to mention sweeping, romantic descriptions of the landscapes he traversed and his rumination on the American spirit and the progress of his version of civilization.

Born in 1759 in Wrentham, Massachusetts, Mann took an Arts degree at Harvard, then began his medical training under Samuel Danforth, a prominent Boston physician.[9] While an increasing number of would-be medical men were receiving training in European medical schools by the end of the eighteenth century (with Edinburgh and Paris being among the most popular destinations), this sort of education – an apprenticeship – was quite common in the United States. Some practitioners were also self-taught. The somewhat incoherent system that resulted reflected, and was supported by, the prohibitive expense of international travel, the variations in (and occasional absence of) state licensing regulations, and the nascent state of American medical schools. The country's earliest institutions, which opened in Philadelphia in 1765 and New York in 1767, graduated only a few trained physicians and surgeons each year (only fifty-one by 1776), and the expenses of, and limited positions in, these institutions made the apprenticeship system sufficiently attractive for many.[10]

Apprenticeships varied in quality across the country but were nevertheless defended by some as being the best means of educating medical practitioners.[11] Some undoubtedly received mediocre training, being taken on as an extra pair of hands to run errands or clean up the mess resulting from treatment. Others, however, appear to have received excellent training, not all of it practical. Some novices were required to obtain broad understanding of natural history, mathematics, and languages (minimally Greek, Latin, and French), their preparation assisted by growing numbers of circulating libraries and wider access to medical journals. Mann's apprenticeship, judging by his own work and the reputation of his mentor, Danforth, was of the latter sort, and thus more closely approximated the training of what the European system would have referred to as a physician, rather than that of a surgeon.[12] His knowledge of published medical texts was extensive, he was widely read in theology, philosophy, and natural history, and he was himself a relatively successful author of medical treatises.[13] He also defended the necessity for hands-on experience, as opposed to the theory-heavy training that European schools were frequently accused of giving. He argued, for example, that "a correct method of practice" in treating catastrophic injury (in this case, the sort requiring amputation) "is founded on practical facts and observations, not on speculative opinions ... Experience directs our reason, and impresses on the mind facts, in a manner which language cannot."[14]

At least some (and perhaps the most influential) of Mann's medical experience occurred in a military setting. His earliest known involvement with army life took place in the Massachusetts State Militia. In 1779, he became surgeon to the 4th Regiment in the Revolutionary War at only twenty years of age, and served two years before being captured and confined to the notorious Long Island prisoner-of-war camp.[15] This experience, I suspect, deeply coloured his attitude towards the British. In the final pages of his *Sketches,* as a curious yet clearly intentional introduction to an otherwise technically specific discussion of the best means of setting up a military hospital, Mann writes eloquently about the evolution of civilization – hardly what might have been expected in this otherwise practical section of the book. He wrote of arts and sciences within the "human race as one family," and expounded upon the contrast between uncivilized and civilized warfare. War among the civilized was, he declared, "less dreadful" than that waged by "savages," and becoming a prisoner was "not the worst of evil." A man might expect humane treatment in which he "receives from the victor every attention which humanity dictates, and circumstances allow." However, there were situations when

> the conqueror, divesting himself of the fine feelings which characterize the human heart in civil society, has satiated his thirst for revenge, by inflicting misery and distress when the fortune of war has placed his

enemy in his possession. Crimsoned with the blood of a defenceless prisoner, the victor, although educated in civil life, is but a savage.[16]

After the American Revolution, Mann resigned from the army in ill health and worked in private practice at Wrentham. Perhaps in recognition of his patriotism and war service, he was awarded an honorary degree at Yale College in 1782 and a second at Brown in 1783, and was back in service with his militia regiment during Shay's Rebellion (1786–87). He returned to private practice in New York, but re-enlisted when war with the British erupted once more in 1812. He was appointed medical director for the Northern Army by General Henry Dearborn and served in Greenbush, near Albany, for the first nine months of the conflict. For more than a year, he was the most senior physician attached to the armed forces. Frequently relocated throughout the main theatres of conflict (from Sackets Harbor to Burlington, York and through Niagara, Lewiston and Williamsville, French Mills and Plattsburgh), Mann experienced a degree of mobility essential to confirming his medical thinking about disease causation – not to mention his thinking on what was owed to the medical corps, from both the US government and its military officers.

Mann retired in 1815 as the peacetime army was reduced (receiving in the same year an honorary MD from Brown), but was reinstated a few years later when, in 1818, the Army Medical Corps was set on a permanent footing. His experience and reputation made him a relatively attractive candidate to command this body, but the position was ultimately given to a younger surgeon, Joseph Lovell, who had served under Mann in the Northern Army with some distinction.[17] Mann continued practising medicine in Boston and New York (both in the forces and privately) until he died in 1832.[18]

Health, Disease, Drink, and Manliness in the US Army

The merging of Mann's medical practice with his extensive military experience is significant. Many surgeons and physicians, in the United States and throughout the British Empire, received essential, practical career training in army or naval settings; however, the significance is not simply related to the opportunity for education. It is also, and more importantly, related to the setting in which that education took place. As Jared Orsi has noted (and as Mann clearly reflects in his *Sketches*), the US Army was not conceived by its devotees simply as an organized fighting force, or as a means of expanding territory or even garnering a regular paycheque. It was "an institution of nationalism," a place where the true man learned the necessary virtue of sacrifice for his country. It was an environment in which the meanings and limits of manliness were tested and occasionally redefined. Physical bodies, as carriers for and expressions of masculine identity, were perpetually tested and on prominent display in a military, wartime setting.[19] Mann, as a perpetual observer and intimate examiner of these bodies, had rather specific ideas about what that the ideal soldier looked like, how his body should function, and how it might be kept in fighting form.

These opinions and ideas depended on Mann's fairly typical understanding of the cause of illness. Like many of his contemporaries, he subscribed to a miasmatic, or localist, theory, which posited that the fountainhead of most illness was the environment. He did not deny or ignore the possibility of contagion: his diligence in segregating particular patients; his understanding of syphilis, smallpox, and even some fevers, his insistence on the necessity for whitewashing hospital walls with lime; and his preference for dirt floors over timber are active testimony to this. In the majority of cases, however, he sought the source of disease in things like a man's proximity to swamps and open water, prevailing winds, and seasonal shifts and sudden changes in the weather, particularly when coupled with exposure (something all soldiers experienced with depressing regularity).[20] As most physicians did, Mann also identified exposure to filth and bad smells as the inspiration of disease; putrid gases and effluvia emanating from decomposing animal or vegetable matter, unwashed bodies (particularly those upon whom lice feasted), filthy living quarters, and poorly maintained latrines were among the most common offenders.[21] Not surprisingly, like many physicians, he thus regularly extolled the virtue of cleanliness. Describing it as "the life of an army," it was to be "enforced upon soldiers with most rigid laws," because "a man cannot be made a good soldier unless he is made to keep himself clean."[22]

Importantly, even if a man was clean, free of vermin, sheltered from noxious effluvia, and protected from damp winds blowing across a swamp as autumn shifted to winter, illness might still overtake him. That is, it might if his personal habits were not *temperate*. In the eighteenth and early nineteenth centuries, temperance did not refer to abstinence from alcohol or moderate drinking alone. It was a concept that signalled gentility, good manners, and self-discipline, particularly bodily discipline in both appearance and behaviour. Its practice might even lead to social advancement.[23] Encompassing a person's broad lifeways and habits, temperance demanded attention to the amount of exercise a man took and how much he slept, to the type of shirt he wore and how often he changed it, and, crucially, to the things he consumed. A diet heavy in meat and light in vegetables, the habitual, excessive drinking of distilled liquors, or the consumption of adulterated food were all things that might tip a body out of its delicate balance.[24]

Health was restored by accelerating, slowing down, and (for maintenance) controlling what entered and what exited a body. This was the core of medical therapeutics, whether an illness was thought to have resulted from contagion, climate, noxious effluvia in local environments, or bad and excessive food and drink. Because diagnostic tools were limited to what was physically observable, physicians relied upon relatively qualitative assessments – such as the "hardness" or "softness" of a pulse – as well as, crucially, examination of bodily excretions. Sweat, vomit, urine, and feces were essential clues for diagnoses, and inspiring them was essential for treatment. Thus, patients were "cured" through various combinations of bloodletting, blistering, artificial sweating or cooling, and drastic purges of either the stomach or bowels (sometimes both, depending on the illness). These methods – dramatic and undoubtedly uncomfortable – were believed to push an illness out the body, draw pain to the surface of the skin, and ultimately restore balance.[25]

Alcohol, when judiciously and professionally employed, could effect similar curative results. During the first year of the war, for example, Mann detailed the remarkable case of a soldier suffering from the so-called bloody flux: dysentery. The disease itself was not remarkable; noted eighteenth-century army surgeon John Pringle called it "the constant and fatal epidemic of camps" and it was frequently widespread in the 1812 conflict, as in many others.[26] While standard therapeutic measures for the illness called for liberal employment of the lancet and/or doses of powerful emetics or purgatives, Mann chose a different, less explosive route: his patient was "administered from one to two pints of wine daily, for two weeks." Although milk was added to the man's diet when he achieved "the state of convalescence," "animal nutrient, even in the form of soups, was prohibited." By this extraordinary, comparatively appealing therapy, the man was rescued "from a dying state" and "eventually restored to health."[27]

Not surprisingly, the supposed medicinal benefits of alcohol resulted in concern over its quality. Sometimes, quality referred specifically to purity, as it did when Mann excoriated sutlers who "frequently sweeten their low and sour wines, by acetate of lead."[28] Other times, it referred to whether or not a spirit had been adequately aged. Generally, the belief was that aged spirits had mellowed and were, as a result, more healthful than the un-aged. In his account of the climate and settlement of the northern and western parts of New York State, for example, Mann expressed concerns over the prevalence of bad air resulting from excessive vegetable putrefaction caused by the clearing of land for farming – not to mention the bad effects of hard labour, poor hygiene, and the coarse diets of the earliest settlers. All of these dangers were exacerbated by the regular consumption of "ardent spirits of the worst quality – *new* rum and whiskey."[29]

Mann's concern in this respect was echoed by naval surgeon Edward Cutbush. While not as obviously concerned about drinking among the men (provided it was not excessive), Cutbush *was* concerned that those men should understand the relative merits of a well-aged dram. "Were I to indulge myself in enumerating all the pernicious consequences of new rum or whiskey, on the constitutions and *morals* of soldiers," he declared, "I should enlarge this part of the subject beyond the limits I have proposed." He was similarly concerned about ciders that were "recently made and used in immoderate quantities," and while "it were to be wished, that beer was more commonly used among soldiers in garrisons" (in lieu of spirits, alas for the drinker), there were equal dangers associated with poorly made beer, or beer that was "*too new.*" Such potations were "apt to produce flatulency and colic." In fact, he claimed to have witnessed, only a few days prior to writing about the dangers of un-aged alcohol, "a case of hæmorrhagy from the intestines brought on I am confident by the free use of *new whiskey.*"[30] On the other hand, sailors sent ashore as landing parties, exposed to "fatigue, hunger and damp clothing," and thus "render[ed] ... more liable to suffer from the miasma arising from marshy situations," should always have "a small quantity of spirituous liquors" (suitably aged, one imagines) available to them – so long as officers took care that they did not "abuse the use of the latter article."[31]

Generally speaking, Cutbush's vision of the medicinal value of spirits was mediated by this concern for quality, and an unequivocal opinion that it was habitual use and *excessive* consumption (particularly of distilled alcohols) that created problems – not the mere act of taking a drink. Judicious employment of spirits was even considered acceptable by Benjamin Rush, whom many consider the father of nineteenth-century abstinence campaigns. In 1777, while Rush described the effect of spirits as being contrary to soldiers' health – to the "very principles of animal life" that sustained them – he was forced to concede that there were circumstances in which "a small quantity of rum may be useful ... if it be mixed with three or four times its quantity of water."[32] He was also not opposed to the consumption of fermented alcohols and argued the health benefits of cider, the occasional glass of beer, and even a bit of wine if it was "taken only at Meals, and in moderate Quantities."[33]

The Problem of Control: *Medical Sketches* as "Humanitarian Narrative"

Rush's understanding of the health benefits of alcoholic beverages was a common one, both in and out of the medical community. Civilians (as much as soldiers) considered them necessary for everything from fending off chills and improving digestion to easing the aches and pains of both body and spirit. Drinking was, moreover, an intensely social activity. There is pervasive evidence, indeed, that it was central to men's self-definition, in particular; drinking, sometimes to excess, was crucial to acquiring and performing manliness throughout the course of the long eighteenth century.[34] The problem was that soldiers apparently could not be trusted to control themselves. Without control, discipline degraded into unmanly chaos, and both health and honour disintegrated. Left to their own tendencies (both to avoid bathing and to drink in excess), soldiers would not only sicken, Mann asserted, but develop a dangerous "military apathy" that threatened the entire noble cause of the war.[35] With control, however, a "mystical power," as Mann's colleague James Lovell described it, even the "demon diarrhæa" might be banished from the camps.[36]

The challenge of inspiring and maintaining this control was rooted the soldier's nature. Cutbush described soldiers as being "like children in many respects." While they might bear the physical markings of manhood, they too often lacked the necessary moral discipline to ensure that they did "not abuse their constitutions by excesses," and thus render themselves "slovenly and insensible to the smallest spark of military pride."[37] This was particularly true of a recruit who had, in his civilian life, grown used to heavy drinking. Such a soldier, Mann declared, would employ "all his cunning and every artifice ... to obtain the inebriating draught. Reputation, honour, health, and even life are sacrificed to his gratification."[38] So too, apparently, were his clothes: through the Revolutionary War and into the 1812 conflict, physicians and officers complained regularly that men would sell the shirts off their backs and the blankets off their beds "for drink."[39] Mann also suggested that, given the opportunity, men would steal liquor from hospital stores to quench their thirst.[40]

Even a well-clothed, robust, and healthy specimen was in danger, however. Seldom, Mann declared, would a "laborious man, replete with health ... [believe] the observance of rules and regulations of temperance ... necessary. While he is free from pain, he views disease at a distance – with a bottle of whiskey in his hand, he bids defiance to death and its terrors."[41] The resulting portrait was not an attractive one: a man whose sacred duty was to defend his country's honour, uphold its virtues, and protect his family and property – to the point of death, if necessary – was rendered sloppy, slurring, weak, and despicable.

Mann's disgust with the drunkard is palpable in his *Sketches*. Where he could obviously handle the stench of sickrooms, the sight of battlefields strewn with corpses, or medical tents overrun with grievously wounded men, nothing evoked his descriptive distain more than someone he considered inebriate (except perhaps, on occasion, the British, or the intersex individual he encountered early in the war).[42] This contempt was likely inspired, at least partially, by the visible alteration that often appeared in a man's comportment and physical control when he was in his cups. Where good manners and control of one's body distinguished man from "savage," a drunk might be incapable of appearing or acting in this way, and thus endanger his own civility. A soldier, as a representative of his country, endangered that entire nation's reputation for civility and good manners.[43]

Mann's disgust was also inspired by what he saw as the arrogance of the drinker who claimed superior knowledge of medical truths. Following his worry that healthy men were too apt to consider themselves immune to the ravages originating from a liquor bottle, for example, he provides an "anecdote ... not a fictitious picture, but a painting from the life," about being called to the sickbed of child. The child's father was absent from the home, but upon returning he "petulantly [asked] his wife why a physician was called, said, he consulted no physician, and took no drug; that his *bottle* was his only *physician,* and *rum* his only *medicine.* Rum to him was all in all, as it cured every disease." Mann replied that rum might be a "*good god*" for this "devotee of Bacchus," and when he was called back to the house a few days later – this time to attend the father, who was suffering "violent pain in his side" (the result of hard work in the sun and too much rum) – he delivered a prompt put-down. Indeed, he appears to have taunted the sick man and withheld treatment until the latter acknowledged his own folly and the physician's wisdom. "My astonishment was expressed," Mann wrote, that

> he should call the aid of a physician, having his IDOL at hand; affecting to be unwilling to prescribe, when I had so potent a DEITY as a competitor; from whose assistance he had heretofore experienced so much benefit. The man was tantalized until confession was extorted, he had tried his favorite medicine without good effect, and in vain. This was too evident to have been mistaken. An acknowledgment of the fact only was required. As soon as he was convinced of his folly, the requisite means to mitigate distress were administered.[44]

Implicit in this anecdote is the thread that weaves itself with supreme self-confidence throughout the entirety of Mann's *Sketches,* providing a deceptively simple solution to all that plagued the US Army (and perhaps even beyond): doctors needed greater authority and control. Obviously, given the common medical understanding of the period, control was crucial to a physician's efforts to effect cures and maintain a body's balance. Mann and his colleagues needed to be able to strictly regulate what went into, and what came out of, the fighting men – including what they consumed when *not* under a doctor's care. That need for regulation demanded an expansion of their military authority.

Not surprisingly, Mann's concerns about drinking provide us with some of the clearest examples of how this claim for greater authority was constructed. While they sometimes reflect a broadly moral, Christian vision of American society – like Mann, many physicians were at least partially inclined towards evangelical passions and it was a language many Americans understood[45] – they were also carefully articulated in the language of a rational, scientific expert. The apparently unassailable logic he presented was rooted in his extensive medical knowledge, what Laqueur describes as "epistemological sovereignty over the bodies ... of others," and was validated by his often extraordinary attention to detail.[46] Its urgency was then intensified by his repeated assertions of the broad dangers unrestricted drinking invited, not just for the individual but for the entire nation. These links and assertions provided Mann with a convenient and powerful (if ineffective) springboard for requesting substantial administrative changes to the hierarchical structure and regular administrative practice of the US Army. In essence, he positioned the bodies of his drunken patients in a quietly persuasive equation: they suffered, yet they were – especially in the context of war – a source of evil and potential catastrophe; their ruined and unmanly bodies weakened American defences in dangerous ways, and sullied its reputation. Indeed, Mann claimed that the British – their sworn enemies and a scourge on their nation (and probably the entire world) – possessed bodies more robust and powerful than the "pallid and emaciated" Americans. He ascribed their prowess to the (utterly false) fact that they had no access to spirituous liquor and received no spirit ration.[47] Mann and his colleagues, however, had the solution to America's flagging strength and manliness: given the opportunity, they could remedy this evil and thus protect the nation from calamity. Mann described, as Laqueur writes, "ameliorative action" as being "possible, effective, and therefore morally imperative."[48]

The nature of that action emerges, in the most obvious sense, through Mann's confident, expert warnings about the dangers of strong liquor. Throughout the *Sketches*, the inability to "restrain ... [patients] from ardent spirits" was regularly linked to a worsening of the symptoms of illness and disease.[49] Whether a man was suffering from pneumonia, jaundice, dysentery, syphilis, unremitting (or remitting) fever, even pain from a gunshot wound or an amputation, alcohol that was *not* prescribed was dangerous and occasionally fatal. Mann thus decried – as did many others – the smuggling of liquor into hospitals by well-meaning friends and attendants, or by "officious" (female) nurses who were too free with the prescriptions.[50] He also frequently condemned the apparently indiscriminate social drinking that went on outside the bounds of a hospital, and regularly excoriated the popular, false belief that a draught of spirits could ward off illness or inspire strength, particularly in cold weather.[51] Whatever the season, he repeatedly stressed that drinking was often at the root of serious illness: no other "species of irregularity, predisposes the body to disease, in so high degrees." Sickness "which might have been mild, generated only by unavoidable causes, [would become] severe, by alcoholic excitement."[52]

Mann also described how these "immoderate potations" could effect such a rapid intensification of disease. They might act both as "predisponent" and exciting causes – in the first case "by weakening the sensorial powers, and inducing general debility," and in the second by inspiring "excess of stimulation" in the stomach, or even "brain engorgement."[53] He then detailed what the liver of an inebriate looked like,[54] and how it malfunctioned. It "becomes torpid," he wrote, and "having lost its secreting powers, the blood sometimes pours in torrents, through the *ductus communis choledocus* into the duodenum; thence, evacuated *per anum*." Luckily for at least *some* of the unfortunates who experienced these symptoms, Mann declared that massive anal hemorrhaging "may prove salutary," because it would quickly remove the "spiritous excitement on the brain" and thus prevent "a more formidable disease – apoplexy."[55] Certainly, these *Sketches* are not reading for the faint of heart.

Mann frequently punctuated these kinds of medical facts and diagnoses with case study proof – humanizing the science and inspiring compassion, if not for the drinker then certainly for his struggling physician. For example, he described the sad end of a convalescent soldier in the hospital at Greenbush – one who did not respect his surgeon's authority. In "a convalescent state from the epidemic of the winter" – an epidemic of pneumonia that, it would seem, the soldier was lucky to have survived, and through which Mann and his colleagues toiled incessantly – the soldier nevertheless "left the hospital without permission, and returned to his quarters, where he drank half a pint of whiskey. A recurrence of fever was excited, with the most formidable symptoms. He was sent back to the hospital, where in twelve hours he died – a victim to folly and imprudence."[56]

Mann later reminded his readers that the "first gift of heaven" had been reason, and that men needed to exercise this gift (i.e., they needed, in part, to listen and follow medical advice) in order to maintain their health. This could not occur while a man "erroneously believed that occult agents are the sole causes of disease," and while he continued, in ignorance, to swallow large amounts of "exciting liquors" in an effort to ward off those illnesses caused by "sudden transitions of weather." "Natural evil is so intimately connected with moral," he stated, and "to obviate the *first*, man should shun the *last*." Instead of getting drunk, in other words, chilly Americans needed to dress in warm clothing (preferably wool or flannel). The result, he predicted, would be that "when they settle their annual accounts, [they would] find themselves not only richer in the means to render themselves happy, but abounding in health; the greatest blessing which man can possess on earth."[57]

Mann's knowledge of the intimate, interior effects of distilled liquor on the human body, not to mention his deceptively simple (and thus powerfully accessible) knowledge of the best means for securing happiness, were the soil from which a most radical, two-part proposal sprouted. First, he wished to eliminate altogether the long-standing tradition of doling out a spirit ration to soldiers. "Ardent spirits," he declared, "should not be used as a common beverage, diluted or not," and they were "an unnecessary part" of a soldier's diet. His opinion, he noted, "may be esteemed medical heresy by some," but temperance was "one of the precepts inculcated by our divine master ... [and] preached by his disciples." Yet, he worried, despite "all the heavy denunciations of heaven against the sin of inebriation ... few reform." Soldiers were far too willing to "render their lives wretched" in the pursuit of comfort, and as a consequence, "this vice is a growing evil." To achieve this lofty goal, he advocated, secondly, that the products of the still be completely "confined to the store-houses of druggists, and the dispensaries of physicians, [where] the sphere of their utility would be vastly enlarged." He claimed that this idea was not without historical precedent either: "The time was when ardent spirits were not known. Then the salubrious fountains of water were resorted to by the healthy and athletic to satiate their thirst."[58]

These were not Mann's only recommendations for reform. He also claimed for his profession superior abilities in identifying who could join the army in the first place. Highly critical of the army's recruiting tactics – they were far too concerned with quantity rather than quality – and deeply worried that the meagre pay offered was a disincentive to the successful, robust, and intelligent young men who would make the best soldiers, he made a number of recommendations. The most straightforward was that the government raise the bounties offered and the salaries paid to potential fighters.[59] The federal government might be forgiven for being confused about Mann's advice on this point, however, given that, in this same text, he also made a case that withholding pay improved the health of an army because it restricted soldiers' access to liquor. During the Revolutionary War, "when the army received no pay for their services, and possessed not the means to procure spirits, it was healthy." During the more recent conflict, a similar inability to meet payroll, an "embarrassment, which was considered a national calamity," was actually "a fortunate circumstance to the army" and a "blessing" for the individual soldier. "When he is found poor in money," Mann opined, "it is always the case that he abounds in health. A fact worth recording!"[60]

At the outset, however, to build an effective army, the government needed to offer better incentives to attract the naturally courageous and patriotic yeomanry of the countryside, those who fit the physical characteristics of a warrior (notably, the correct physical countenance usually signalled a correct moral one). While Mann did not provide too much detail on what these physical characteristics might have been, his naval counterpart, Edward Cutbush, did. "The figure for the profession of arms," he advised, "ought not to be defective." Such defects included "swelled legs," which "show a disposition to disease," a "compressed breast," bow legs, or a "constrained gait." He also warned against those "whose abdomen is very large" or whose "noble parts" were somehow mutilated, or those who stuttered. Habitual coughs, missing fingers or toes, scrofula scars, ulcers, watery or "fistulous" eyes, hunched backs or hernias, and other "obstructions," he argued, were "all imperfections, which render a man incapable of serving." Less obviously, implying something similar to Mann's reference to the "yeomanry" of the salubrious American countryside, Cutbush also advised that potential soldiers "should likewise be active and manifest a natural courage." They required a steady and noble character and temperament, and "if they be lively, quick and hardy, we may hope to see the germ of that heroism, which ought to animate a soldier, developed."[61]

As Mann described such men, they had the body and the character to

> cheerfully endure fatigues, colds, and expose themselves to the most threatening dangers ... The love of country, honour, the pride of conquest, incite [them] to acts of heroism. When duty calls to confront the enemy, [they] obey ... the summons with the same alacrity, as when invited by the alluring voice of pleasure to [their] amusements.[62]

This character was inspired, he concluded, by two principles: first, rigorous military discipline, doubtless supported by the temperate and sober habits advocated throughout his *Sketches*, which would help a man overcome any fear of danger. And, second, the knowledge "that he possesses a native property – liberty, independence, and a right of soil" that he would "support and defend without compulsion." Indeed, the love of these things meant that American soldiers would never be, like their European counterparts, "but machines" whose courage was "wholly artificial." They could endure the worst kinds of exposures, achieve "brilliant victories" inspired by clear "principles of justice," and remain healthy while doing so.[63]

The problem of finding such admirable physical specimens required the participation of a physician or surgeon on a recruiting board, because an officer without medical training or experience might be – and regularly was, is seemed – fooled by what Mann called "false and insidious marks of health." When most of the first soldiers were enlisted, he explained, "a large proportion ... were not ... fit for soldiers." They were "incapable of enduring the fatigues and hardships incident to war," because they were "habitually intemperate, with constitutions broken down by inebriation and its consequent diseases." These infirm "dead weights" and "decrepid [sic] men" ended up in the lines, however, because recruiting officers mistook the "bloated countenances" and ruddy cheeks of a drunkards as signs of health.[64] It would not be enough to warn recruiters of this danger either. As Cutbush noted, while there was an understandable tendency to pick men with a naturally rubicund complexion (pale faces were signs of potential debility and weakness), not only could this colour have signalled habitual drinking but it may well have been inspired by personal vanity: some men were apparently wont to fasten their neck-stocks a little too tightly, to achieve a fashionable glow in their cheeks.[65] If medical professionals were engaged in the recruitment process, however – in other words, if they had this crucially significant role, this expanded authority, to decide who would make up the nation's fighting force – mistakes like these could be eliminated.

Administrative authority of this nature, however desirable, was perhaps not as desirable as expanded authority within the active, fighting, man-euvering, and mobile army. The nature of this particular claim to power is interesting as, under Mann's blunt and forthright pen, it implicated acting (and occasionally named) members of the officer corps in the high mortality rates experienced on the Northern Frontier.[66] In April 1814, for example, in a letter to Brigadier General Smith, Mann excoriated an officer who had sent several men to his hospital (then at Burlington) in a "deplorable" and "moribund" condition. They also arrived "in an irregular manner" (meaning the correct paperwork had not been sent with them, a common complaint), and it appeared they had received no medical atten-tion whatsoever within their regiment. Mann noted that the regimental surgeon was technically responsible for providing this sort of care, but suggested that perhaps there was no surgeon (another common problem). In such a case, "it becomes the duty of the immediate commanding officer of the company."[67]

This was not the only time Mann called out officers for neglect. Indeed, he argued that those who would claim that disease-related deaths were the fault of a surgeon's "neglect of duty" were those who, in ignorance, misunderstood the real nature of disease and the possibilities of modern medical practice. Rather, it was the officers who neglected their duty. Mann was not averse to chastising sloppy and unprofessional regimental surgeons when he believed they warranted it. They were, however, as a whole unjustly turned into "scape-goats, on whom are heaped a multitude of sins" by those who ignored the fact that the root causes of disease were things "over which they have no control." What officers could but failed to control were the things that could actually help soldiers withstand the pestilential nature and harsh climates of their local environment. They failed to provide adequate discipline, to ensure that men were clean and neat in appearance or that they prepared their food in a "suitable manner"; they failed to enforce temperate habits, to restrict drunkenness, or to ensure that the men consumed their damaging spirit rations in as wholesome a way as possible (i.e., by not "obliging them to drink the whole at once"). They also, with alarming consequences, were wont to leave hospitals seriously under-manned, privileging the need to wage battle over the health of the men. As a result, officers were "no less, perhaps more greatly deserving of blame" for a soldier's death by disease.[68]

This heavy weight of responsibility lay with officers, Mann argued, because the health of the fighting man was supposed to be every officer's first concern. This was not a novel argument. The most well-used American training manuals of the war described an officer's primary responsibility as the maintenance and protection of soldiers' health: without healthy soldiers, there could be no fighting, let alone victory. For example, Friedrich Wilhelm von Steuben, author of a field manual used by American forces from the Revolution to at least 1814, insisted that preserving the health of the men was the first means of creating a successful fighting force. It not only preserved men for battle and improved their drilling, marching, and shooting capabilities but "gain[ed] an officer the love of his soldiers." In caring for them during sickness, the officer had "the power of exerting his humanity," and thus increasing their loyalty to his cause.[69] Essentially, health maintained by rigorous attention to temperate behaviour generated the loyalty necessary to inspire men to kill. (Ironically, so did alcohol: men were, on a few notable occasions, made "fighting drunk" before engaging the enemy.)[70]

The somewhat bombastic Brigadier General Alexander Smyth, a prominent player during 1812, channelled (or, less generously, plagiarized) von Steuben, listing the "preservation of the health of the soldiers" as the first and "greatest" care to be looked after by the officer corps. This required maintaining a watchful eye over "their cleanliness and manner of living," which implied everything from establishing camps in the best way, to daily assessments of health and the regular inspection of backpacks (a practice that had the added bonus of ensuring men weren't smuggling extra rations or contraband liquor). Reflecting the broad vision of bodily temperance that motivated men like Mann, Smyth also advised that officers ensure their men were dressed "neatly" and with a "soldier-like air," that they were relatively clean, regularly exercised by drilling, and sober enough to carry out their duties.[71]

Not surprisingly, many of these regulations were ones that Mann (and others) claimed were best conducted (or at least assisted) by medical personnel. The choice of where to camp, for example, was best left to the surgeon and his assistants rather than the demands of strategy; the surveillance and purchase of rations should also be left to medical staff, as should the purchase of clothing. During daily inspections, as Cutbush maintained, the decision about whether a man was truly sick instead of suffering a hangover from the previous night's debauch should rightly be the decision of someone with medical training – officers were apparently incapable of making the distinction. If men on a march felt the sudden onset of illness, moreover, either from drinking bad water or consuming spoiled rations, they should have a quick dram of whisky and "lose no time in sending for the surgeon," rather than reporting to a commanding officer.[72]

Advice as to what surgeons should do to protect soldiers' (and thus the nation's) health and how they should assert their authority are peppered throughout Mann's *Sketches*. So too are hints at why Mann and his colleagues were incapable of enforcing these kinds of regulations, or ensuring that conditions in camps and on marches were at least marginally adequate: they lacked any sort of command authority. At times, they could not even assert their power within the confines of their own hospitals. Only two pages into his "preliminary observations," in fact, Mann alludes to "disagreeable interferences" from officers who, "tenacious of authority, assume as much as may be implied by rules and regulations." He later details numerous instances of interference, where even "commissioned officers, of inferior grades" intruded into hospital grounds and "assum[ed] authority to order their men in and out of it *ad libitum*," without consulting the attending surgeons. When "detected in such unmilitary conduct, [they] justified themselves by claims of superior rank." Even long-serving officers were "guilty of similar misdemeanours."[73] In one case, Mann was forced to argue that it was inappropriate for an officer to charge two of his patients for desertion because they were convalescing under his care.[74]

While Mann was able – by approaching the commanding general – to prohibit at least some officers from discharging their men without medical authority, it appears to have been a cumbersome process. Such actions not only threatened the health of his patients (perhaps even more than some of the treatments they were undergoing) but also served as a constant reminder of his powerlessness. As he complained to Brigadier General Smith, "of what use can it be to send a dying man to the hospital, except to give the hospital department the credit of *killing,* and trouble of *burying* him?"[75] Instead, again tying the power of his profession to the nation's well-being, he admonished:

> The good of service requires that the medical staff of an army be not only well appointed, but respected by the officers of the line. Without due respect, advice, given by surgeons however correct, will not be regarded ... Invested as they are with authority, [officers] often affect to despise counsel offered by surgeons; who, under the present establishment, have no rank nor command in the army. The medical department will never command that degree of confidence and respectability from officers of the line, necessary to promote its greatest usefulness, until it is more immediately protected by government.[76]

Without this confidence and respect, the *Sketches* make clear, Mann and his like-minded colleagues would never achieve the insurmountable yet lifesaving duty of sobering (and cleaning) up the US Army. They would also, as Freeman's exploration of early American masculinity reveals, find it difficult to claim honour for themselves as gentlemen. Despite their expertise or their personal sense of integrity, men who were not openly and publicly esteemed might not be considered men of honour: "signs of disrespect were dangerous."[77]

While Mann thus sought to establish the medical department on an official footing, to claim and retain both respect and authority through the state, his colleague and superior, James Tilton, similarly suggested establishing a clearer rank for medical personnel within the army. Physicians "should be considered as the fourth character in a regiment; or next in consequence to the field officers," he argued, with the ability to override, without any sort of formal permission, the orders of officers whose rank was lower than their own.[78] Mann claimed independent authority was necessary in *all* cases, almost without regard to rank, within the purview of an army hospital. He softened the claim, likely aware that it might ruffle feathers, by stating that surgeons weren't demanding authority outside of the hospital: "they wish only to be respected in their own department." Naturally, improving pay and promotions was also a recommendation, and all of these changes would, he assured his readers, make the service more attractive to talented young surgeons who would otherwise only serve for a short time, perhaps to satisfy their curiosity, before moving on to more fertile and rewarding practice.[79]

That the doctors lacked authority and status in the army is reflective of the wider social and political status of the profession as a whole. With few exceptions, eighteenth- and early nineteenth-century American medical practitioners did *not* command the respect and deference they would later acquire. This was at least partly a result of the fact that many aspects of medical practice were rather terrifying and occasionally bordered on the blasphemous. In the regular course of their training, and sometimes in practice, physicians dissected, and thus "delved into unholy and forbidden things."[80] The American public was not averse to rioting at the news that medical men were opening up the bodies of the recently departed. Whatever their progressive motives, this kind behaviour trod too heavily over broad cultural anxieties about death, and about bodies opened up for the scrutiny of the living.[81] Indeed, according to army surgeon Stephen Chambers Henry, General William Hull, the "most execrable coward," surrendered Fort Detroit to General Brock in 1812 because he had been completely overwhelmed by the sight of bodies "torn almost to pieces," and by witnessing Chambers amputating the leg of an officer, all of whom were hit by Brock's first volley.[82]

Equally prejudicial to medical practitioners' claims for status was the piecemeal organization, uncertain hierarchy, and theoretical divisions of the profession. All of this generated professional rivalries and disputes. Disagreements over the course of a particular treatment, intensifying in the early nineteenth century as growing numbers of practitioners decried the "heroic" procedures of men like James Mann (an ardent defender of extreme bloodletting, for example), became "a common cause of public distrust."[83] During the war, the fact that many regimental and hospital surgeons in the US Army had less than admirable reputations was not particularly helpful either. Overall, in fact, there is a clear sense that patients did not always trust or agree with their physicians' prescriptions – what

Charles Rosenberg called the "conspiracy to believe" broke down.[84] *Medical Sketches,* for example, reveals that soldiers regularly resisted medical advice, refusing painful and disfiguring surgeries (i.e., amputations) or demanding familiar treatments that their surgeons considered ill-advised. The refusal of amputation, what James Tilton implied was an "obstinate" folly, may have been inspired by fears of what physical disfigurement meant to people at this time.[85] As the above-listed characteristics from Cutbush imply, wholeness, straightness of limb, and trimness of figure were defining features of manliness; to lose them was to lose more than flesh and bone.[86]

Resistance to medical authority also arose when folk cures or commonly available remedies, long-established as effective, were more pleasant than those prescribed by a medical practitioner (which, given the items on an apothecary's shelf, was not difficult to achieve).[87] This certainly may explain why Mann so often found himself reiterating that spirits were *not* an appropriate remedy or prophylactic for cold weather illness (he struggled against at least some medical opinion in this respect as well: see note 70). Understandably, for the average patient – whether soldier or housewife – taking a dram of whisky, rum, or brandy was far more pleasant than taking a dose of purgatives or emetics.

In late 1813 and into the winter of 1814, Mann encountered a case that drew all of these tensions and disputes (of patient resistance, of popular versus professional opinion, of the challenges arising from dissenting practitioners, and his unyielding belief in the dangers of distilled spirits) into sharp relief. The case centred on a Major Beebe, who, in November 1813, suffered a severe case of diarrhea. He was treated (incorrectly) by his regimental surgeon, and was eventually admitted to the General Hospital in Burlington after developing abdominal pain, nausea, vomiting, and constipation. His main attending physician was Dr. Henry Hunt, who, in a meticulously detailed report reprinted by Mann, outlined the various steps he took to diagnose and cure Beebe. Unfortunately for the patient, after many months of extraordinary suffering (at least some of it the result of attempts to cure him), he "expired without a struggle" on September 13, 1814.[88]

When Beebe first arrived at the hospital in Burlington, however, before Hunt took over his care, Mann attended him. Given Hunt's detailed report on Beebe's death, Mann decided that the case – at least his involvement with it – "requires a more full exposition" (perhaps particularly so, as Hunt claimed that Beebe's death was the result of *previous* medical treatments). According to Mann, Beebe arrived in relatively poor (but not irredeemable) condition, and most of his complaints could be explained not only by his pre-existing condition but also by the length of his journey to Burlington (ninety miles), and the fact that he had "indulged himself" with large amounts of alcohol "to resist the inclemency of the weather." To reverse these problems, Mann most likely cut off Beebe's liquor supply, then variously prescribed doses of cathartics, antimonials, and bloodletting, along with blistering, calomel ("until his mouth became sore"), ipecacuanha (in a preparation known as Dover's Powder, which also contained opium), as well as occasional warm baths to "remove general wandering pains." The major continued to decline, however, suffering serious abscesses on his legs (which Mann lanced), widespread edema, and a host of other physical discomforts.

Despite Mann's assurance that he was improving, Beebe was "very impatient under his circumstances," and was clearly demanding a change in medical regimen. According to Mann, Beebe consulted his friends, who "advised him to invite a physician to consult upon his case."

> Upon an interview my plan was opposed. The bark, wine, spirits, and opium were proposed in large quantities. To these I objected [because of] ... the constipated state of the bowels and rigidity of the sphincter ani. The patient had his choice. He preferred the stimulating process, as being more congenial to his own sentiments, that they were necessary to give strength, as they were more agreeable to his propensities. In consequence of some indecorous language of the consulting physician who was a citizen, I refused to visit the Major again, in the character of a physician.

Mann then reported (and one imagines he took great pleasure in doing so) that Beebe eventually "dismissed" the "stimulating prescriber" when his condition did not improve. It could not possibly have done, Mann declared, as "these medicines had the effect to place his stomach and bowels in an irremediable state, in which Doctor Hunt found them."[89]

That it was disrespectful language from a civilian practitioner that was the final straw for Mann's interaction with Major Beebe is instructive. It suggests that a wound to his reputation, his personal dignity, inflicted by "indecorous language" was more insulting, more dangerous to his status, than a disagreement about diagnosis or treatment of a dying man. I am also struck by his pointed identification of his rival as a *citizen* (meaning civilian, in this context). While he may not have meant anything derogatory by it, the effect is nonetheless powerful; military surgeons are presented as more highly skilled practitioners, while their active service to a higher cause demanded higher respect and deference. Indeed, Mann described his fellow regimental surgeons as possessing as much "cool bravery" as the army's best warriors: "equally exposed to danger as officers of the line," he wrote, they nevertheless executed their duties to the nation "with fidelity and assiduity."[90] However, it was equally true that Mann and his cohort could not always claim this bravery unequivocally, or the status and respect for their manliness that came with it. Instead, he had to defend it repeatedly, during and after the war.

This defence was particularly acute when it was made through the body of the drunken warrior. At their best, warriors were loyal, strong, and committed to sacrifice for the nation. They possessed the "high toned courage" and "superior valour" that expressed the core of America itself – "liberty and independence ... principles [these heroes had] imbibed from infancy."[91] Yet – as Mann expressed with all the rhetorical power of his office – such high-flown manliness could not survive if other, impure and highly destructive substances were imbibed. The soldier's body was a site for the display of national virtue, but it could not be so if it was inebriated or broken down by intemperance. Alcohol, unless taken with the careful, medically mediated intention of preserving the body, would destroy a man's physical form, leading to a lack of discipline, decorum, and courage. Significantly, Mann's book ties the sad stories of such ruined, sickly bodies to a message of how the nation might, quite simply, prevent such decay: prophylactic enhancement of a surgeon's authority. It is clear, however, if only from the continued and increasing rates of consumption in the United States, that this message was indeed, for Mann's time, a "heresy."[92] The social conviviality and manliness associated with drinking surely stymied his efforts. So, too, did the pervasive belief that spirits were sources of strength and health – a belief expounded by his contemporaries, and ironically confirmed by his own practice.

Notes

1 Edward Cutbush, *Observations on the Means of Preserving the Health of Soldiers and Sailors and on the Duties of the Medical Department of the Army and Navy: With Remarks on Hospitals and Their Internal Arrangement* (Philadelphia: printed for Thomas Dobson, 1808), 250. Cutbush also supplied instructions for soldiers on how to produce easy "home-brew," whether they were on a march, in an encampment, or settled in barracks (29–30). On Cutbush's life and career, see Frank Pleadwell, "Edward Cutbush, M.D.: The Nestor of the Medical Corps of the Navy," *Annals of Medical History* 5 (1923); Edgar F. Smith, *James Cutbush: An American Chemist, 1788–1823* (Philadelphia: J.B. Lippincott, 1919).

2 For the broad medicinal application of spirits and wine, see Jonathan Reinarz and Rebecca Winter, "The Spirit of Medicine: The Use of Alcohol in Nineteenth Century Medical Practice," in *Drink in the Eighteenth and Nineteenth Centuries,* ed. S. Schmid and B. Schmidt-Haberkamp (London: Pickering and Chatto, 2014), 127–39. Specific applications are also detailed throughout James Lind, *A Treatise of the Scurvy, in Three Parts, Containing an Inquiry into the Nature, Causes, and Cure, of That Disease* (London: A. Millar, 1757) and John Pringle, *Observations on the Diseases of the Army* (1753; 1st American ed., Philadelphia: Edward Earle, 1810). See also Benjamin Rush, *Observations on the Cause and Cure of the Tetanus* (Philadelphia, 1787), 461–62; James Tilton, *Economical Observations on Military Hospitals; and the Prevention and Cure of Diseases Incident to an Army* (Wilmington, DE: J. Wilson, 1813), esp. 59–60 (typhus fever).

3 J.B. Whitridge, "Report of a Case of Amputation," in *Medical Sketches of the Campaigns of 1812, 13, 14. To Which Are Added Surgical Cases; Observations on Military Hospitals; and Flying Hospitals Attached to a Moving Army,* by James Mann (Dedham, MA: H. Mann and Co., 1816), 218–20.

4 Mann, *Medical Sketches,* 37.

5 Thomas Laqueur, "Bodies, Details, and the Humanitarian Narrative," in *The New Cultural History,* ed. Lynn Hunt (Berkeley: University of California Press, 1989), 176–204.

6 On the broad history of late eighteenth- and early nineteenth-century histories of masculinity congruent with Mann's thinking, see especially Michèle Cohen, "'Manners' Make the Man: Politeness, Chivalry, and the Construction of Masculinity, 1750–1830," *Journal of British Studies* 44 (April 2005): 312–29, and Jared Orsi, "Zebulon Pike and his 'Frozen Lads': Bodies, Nationalism, and the West in the Early Republic," *Western Historical Quarterly* 42, 1 (Spring 2011): 55–75. There is a vibrant literature on eighteenth-century masculinity, far too extensive to note here. On understandings of masculinity in the early nineteenth-century United States, however, see, for example, Joyce Appleby, *Inheriting the Revolution: The First Generation of Americans* (Cambridge, MA: Harvard University Press, 2000); Ruth Bloch, "The Gendered Meanings of Virtue in Revolutionary America," *Signs* 13 (1987): 37–77; Thomas Foster, *Sex and the Eighteenth Century Man: Massachusetts and the History*

of Sexuality in America (Boston: Beacon Press, 2006); Joanne Freeman, *Affairs of Honor: National Politics in the New Republic* (New Haven, CT: Yale University Press, 2001); Mark E. Kann, *A Republic of Men: The American Founders, Gendered Language, and Patriarchal Politics* (New York: NYU Press, 1998); John G. McCurdy, *Citizen Bachelors: Manhood and the Creation of the United States* (Ithaca, NY: Cornell University Press, 2009); Sarah J. Purcell, *Sealed with Blood: War, Sacrifice, and Memory in Revolutionary America* (Philadelphia: University of Pennsylvania Press, 2002); Carroll Smith-Rosenberg, "The Republican Gentleman: The Race to Rhetorical Stability in the New United States," in *Masculinities in Politics and War: Gendering Modern History,* ed. Stefan Dudink, Karen Hagemann, and John Tosh (Manchester and New York: Manchester University Press, 2004), 61–76.

7 Obviously, neither can I claim to present anything like an adequate history of the War of 1812. Thankfully, others have done so before me. Several excellent histories (all of which influence my thinking on the conflict and Mann's role in it) are Nicole Eustace, *1812: War and the Passions of Patriotism* (Philadelphia: University of Pennsylvania Press, 2012); Donald Hickey, *The War of 1812: A Forgotten Conflict,* 2nd ed. (Chicago: University of Chicago Press, 1995); Jon Latimer, *1812: War with America* (Cambridge, MA: Harvard University Press, 2007); C. Edward Skeen, *Citizen Soldiers in the War of 1812* (Lexington: University Press of Kentucky, 1998); and Alan Taylor, *The Civil War of 1812: American Citizens, British Subjects, Irish Rebels, and Indian Allies* (New York: Alfred A. Knopf, 2010).

8 See particularly his defences of the elderly, arguably inept commanding general of the Northeastern theatre, Henry Dearborn, and Brigadier General John Parker Boyd, who was blamed for bungled attacks against Crysler's Farm in 1813 and Lacolle Mill in 1814 (esp. v–vi, 59–60, 93).

9 On Danforth, see Walter Burrage, *A History of the Massachusetts Medical Society, with Brief Biographies of the Founders and Chief Officers, 1781–1922* (Harwood, MA: privately printed, 1923), 25–26.

10 On medical education in the United States, see Whitfield J. Bell, "Medical Practice in Colonial America," *Bulletin of the History of Medicine* 31 (January 1957): 442–53; Thomas N. Bonner, *Becoming a Physician: Medical Education in Britain, France, Germany, and the United States, 1750–1945* (Baltimore: Johns Hopkins University Press, 1995); Mary C. Gillett, *The Army Medical Department: 1775–1818* (Washington, DC: Center of Military History, United States Army, 2004), 18–21; William Frederick Norwood, *Medical Education in the United States before the Civil War* (Philadelphia: University of Pennsylvania Press, 1944); Whitfield Jenks Bell Jr., "Philadelphia Medical Students in Europe, 1750–1800," *Pennsylvania Magazine of History and Biography* 67, 1 (January 1943): 1–29; Robert G. Slawson, "Medical Training in the United States prior to the Civil War," *Journal of Evidence-Based Complementary and Alternative Medicine* 17, 1 (2012): 11–27; Paul Starr, *The Social Transformation of American Medicine,* 2nd ed. (New York: Basic Books, 2017), 30–47; B. Stocky, *A History of Colonial Medical Education* (Springfield, IL: Charles C. Thomas, 1962).

11   On the varied quality of these apprenticeships, see Fanny J. Anderson, "Medical Practices in Detroit during the War of 1812," *Bulletin of the History of Medicine* 16 (January 1944): 262; Gillett, *The Army Medical Department,* 19; Starr, *Social Transformation,* 39–40. Thomas Apel suggests that these two avenues of education (at least as revealed by the 1793 yellow fever epidemic in Philadelphia) resulted in two separate, though occasionally overlapping, approaches to disease causation: localists (those who were university-educated) and contagionists (those who received apprenticeships). While Mann had been apprenticed, both Danforth's influence and his subsequent work experience placed him more firmly in the camp of the localists. See below, and Apel's excellent study, *Feverish Bodies, Enlightened Minds: Science and the Yellow Fever Controversy in the Early American Republic* (Stanford, CA: Stanford University Press, 2016), 5–7.

12   Mann referred to himself, and was usually referred to by others, as a surgeon; however, at times he also referred to himself as a physician (see *Medical Sketches,* 138, for example). In the European system, university-trained medical practitioners claimed the title of "physician," and their education was highly theoretical. Surgeons, by virtue of their more hands-on, practical training (and historical links to barbers) were generally (though, by the middle of the eighteenth century, far less consistently) considered to be of lower status. This distinction, perhaps resulting from the generally less organized state of the medical profession as a whole, does not seem to have been made as rigorously in the United States. See above, notes 10–11.

13   Along with *Medical Sketches,* Mann published papers on obstetrical and gynecological medicine, diabetes, cholera in children, and dysentery, the latter two both winning the Boylston Prize from Harvard University in 1803 and 1806, respectively. See *A Dissertation upon the Cholera Infantum: To Which are Added, Rules and Regulations, as Preventive Means of the Autumnal Diseases of Children* (Boston: printed for Young and Minns, printers to the States, 1804). His paper on dysentery is printed as an appendix to *Medical Sketches,* 275–304. Several of his public addresses were also published. See *An Oration, Addressed to the Fraternity of Free Masons ... on the Tenth of October, in Wrentham* (Wrentham, MA: Nathaniel Heaton, 1798); *An Address, Delivered Dec. 18, 1799 before the Brethren of Montgomery Lodge; at their Masonic Hall in Franklin; upon the Evening of Their Anniversary, for the Election of Officers, for the Ensuing year (1800)* (Wrentham, MA: Nathaniel and Benjamin Heaton, 1800); and *An Oration, Pronounced July 4, 1801, at the Request of a Number of the Inhabitants of Wrentham: In Commemoration of the Anniversary of American Independence* (Wrentham, MA: Nathaniel Heaton, June 1801). Mann also prepared *Rules and Regulations for the Hospital Department of the U.S. Army* (Albany: J. Buel, 1813), though it does not appear to have been officially adopted or released.

14   Mann, *Medical Sketches,* 229. Later in the book, referring to the practice (unfortunately adopted by Americans) of writing prescriptions "in a dead language," Mann "justly ridiculed" the English physician for this habit. It had "originated at a period of general ignorance," he wrote, "when learning was confined to a few men, who wore large

gowns and full wigs." He believed the habit hampered practice, making it difficult for poorly trained hospital attendants to safely manage patient medications (244–45). See also Apel, *Feverish Bodies,* 17–21.

15 Edward G. Burrows, *Forgotten Patriots: The Untold Story of American Prisoners during the Revolutionary War* (New York: Basic Books, 2008); David Dzurec, "Prisoners of War and American Self-Image during the American Revolution," *War in History* 20, 4 (November 2013): 430–51; Holger Hoock, *Scars of Independence: America's Violent Birth* (New York: Crown, 2017), 182–206, 212–24.

16 Mann, *Medical Sketches,* 234–35.

17 On Lovell, see James M. Phalen, "Chiefs of the Medical Department, U.S. Army 1775–1940, Biographical Sketches," *Army Medical Bulletin,* 52 (April 1940): 27–32. Author Stephen Craig suggests that Mann was having some difficulty managing his position as surgeon's mate in the newly established medical corps. It isn't clear why he was passed over for command of this body as he was held in high regard and had ample experience. However, the decision itself was politically fraught, as were many decisions made by American doctors. A detailed discussion of these politics can be found throughout Gillet, *The Army Medical Department.* See also Stephen C. Craig, *"Some System of the Nature Here Proposed": Joseph Lovell's Remarks on the Sick Report, Northern Department, US Army, 1817 and the Rise of the Modern US Army Medical Department* (Fort Sam Houston, Texas: US Army Medical Department Center and School, 2015), 29; Harvey E. Brown, *The Medical Department of the U.S. Army from 1775–1873* (Washington, DC: Surgeon General's Office, 1873), 108.

18 The most detailed biography of Mann currently available was compiled by James Phalen for the *Army Medical Bulletin* 47 (January 1939), https://achh.army.mil/history/biography-mann. Neither Phalen nor his sources mention any family, wife, or children, though Mann's Masonic addresses suggest that he had clear ideas of what an ideal wife might look like: Mann, *An Oration* (1798), 10–11, 28–29. See also Eliza C. Anderson, Scott W. Cowan, and Charles J. Yeo, "James Mann, M.D. (1759–1832): Military Surgeon for the 'Second War of Independence,'" *American Surgeon* 82 (June 2016): E123–E125.

19 Orsi, "Zebulon Pike," 60. See also John Robert Adams, *Male Armor: The Soldier-Hero in Contemporary American Culture* (Charlottesville: University of Virginia Press, 2008); Leo Braudy, *From Chivalry to Terrorism: War and the Changing Nature of Masculinity* (New York: Alfred A. Knopf, 2003); Stefan Dudink and Karen Hagemann, "Masculinity in Politics and War in the Age of Democratic Revolutions, 1750–1850," in Dudink, Hagemann, and Tosh, *Masculinities in Politics and War,* 3–21; Sam Keen, *Fire in the Belly: On Being a Man* (New York: Bantam, 1991). On the character of the American Army during this war, see, for example, Ricardo A. Herrera, *For Liberty and the Republic: The American Citizen as Soldier, 1775–1861* (New York: NYU Press, 2015); Skeen, *Citizen Soldiers;* John C. Stagg, "Freedom and Subordination: Disciplinary Problems in the U.S. Army during the War of 1812," *Journal of Military History* 78, 2 (April 2014): 537–74, and "Enlisted Men in the United States Army, 1812–1815: A Preliminary Survey," *William and Mary Quarterly* 43, 4 (October 1986): 615–45.

20 These causal explanations for illness are reiterated throughout *Medical Sketches*. For his discussion of dirt (which absorbed and neutralized infectious agents) versus timber floors, see 240; for his obvious preference for the localist explanation of disease, see particularly 286–87, 312. On other physicians subscribing to this view, and greater detail on its epistemological foundations, see Apel, *Feverish Bodies*, esp. 3–10, 15–16, 107–16, 139–49; Roy Porter, *The Greatest Benefit to Mankind: A Medical History of Humanity* (New York: W.W. Norton, 1997), 245–71; Charles E. Rosenberg, "The Therapeutic Revolution: Medicine, Meaning, and Social Change in Nineteenth-Century America," *Perspectives in Biology and Medicine* 20, 4 (Summer 1977): 487–89.

Some of the more prominent medical treatises based upon this thinking include those written by Benjamin Rush, as well as William Cullen, *First Lines of the Practice of Physic* (first published in 1777; also in Edinburgh by C. Elliot, 1784); Cutbush, *Observations;* W.E. Horner, "Surgical Sketches [from the War of 1812]," *Medical Examiner and Record of Medical Science* 97 (January 1853): 1–85; Pringle, *Observations;* and Tilton, *Economical Observations.*

21 Unlike at least some of his contemporaries, Mann did *not* subscribe to explanations of disease that incorporated astrological suppositions. These he considered "inoffensive and pleasantly amusing" (*Medical Sketches*, 29–30). For a history of these explanations of illness, see Mark Harrison, "From Medical Astrology to Medical Astronomy: Sol-Lunar and Planetary Theories of Disease in British Medicine, c. 1700–1850," *British Journal for the History of Science* 33, 1 (March 2000): 26.

22 Mann, *Medical Sketches,* 38. This is also central advice in Cutbush's *Observations* and Benjamin Rush's *Directions for Preserving the Health of Soldiers, Addressed to the Officers of the Army* (Published by Order of the War Board, 1777). While not regularly cited by Mann, it is clear that Rush's ideas on disease and healing influenced his thinking in many respects, including on the dangers of consuming distilled alcohol and the need for vigorous bleeding in certain cases of disease.

23 Kathleen Brown, *Foul Bodies: Cleanliness in Early America* (New Haven, CT: Yale University Press, 2009), esp. 118–89; Freeman, *Affairs of Honor;* Orsi, "Zebulon Pike," 65.

24 Adulterated food was a particular concern for the US Army, as merchants hoping to inflate their profits, or bakers attempting to stretch meagre supplies, were apparently wont to add plaster of Paris or ash to their flour (or to draw their water downstream from an army encampment that used that water to flush its latrines). See Mann, *Medical Sketches,* 73; Taylor, *Civil War,* 331–32.

25 One of the clearest explications of this therapeutic system is found in Rosenberg, "The Therapeutic Revolution." See also Porter, *The Greatest Benefit,* 245–303.

26 Pringle, *Observations,* 18. Dysentery is caused by viral, bacterial, or parasitic pathogens that are usually spread by contact between flies, infected stools, and food or drink. It causes abdominal pain, cramping, diarrhea (often bloody), and fever. In this particular case, the infection was said to have been a "typhoid form," suggesting that the sufferer was delirious at the height of his fever and had a rash and/or other

symptoms associated with this "putrid" disease. Later scourges of this illness in the US Army are well detailed in Vincent J. Cirillo, "'More Fatal than Powder and Shot': Dysentery in the U.S. Army during the Mexican War, 1846–48," *Perspectives in Biology and Medicine* 52, 3 (August 2009): 400–13. See also Erica M. Charters, *Disease, War, and the Imperial State: The Welfare of the British Armed Forces during the Seven Years' War* (Chicago: University of Chicago Press, 2014).

27　Mann, *Medical Sketches*, 13–14. Mann may have learned this wine cure during the Revolutionary War. See John Beck, *An Historical Sketch of the State of Medicine in the American Colonies from their First Settlement to the Period of the Revolution*, 2nd ed. (Albany: Charles VanBenthuysen, 1850), 14; and Tilton, *Economical Observations*, 59–60.

28　Mann, *Medical Sketches*, 137. Adulterated drink was equally a concern during the Revolution, when in at least one case from 1775 two men were killed in Boston after drinking "Poisonous Liquor." See Paul E. Kopperman, "'The Cheapest Pay': Alcohol Abuse in the Eighteenth-Century British Army," *Journal of Military History* 60 (July 1996): 453.

29　Mann, *Medical Sketches*, 109 (emphasis added).

30　Cutbush, *Observations*, 25–30 (emphasis in original). For similar concerns over the drinking of "new" rum by British soldiers in the West Indies, see Kopperman, "'The Cheapest Pay,'" 450.

31　Cutbush, *Observations*, 87, 93.

32　Rush, *Directions for Preserving the Health of Soldiers*, 6–8.

33　Rush, *An Inquiry into the Effects of Spirituous Liquors on the Human Body and the Mind* (Boston: Thomas and Andrews, 1790) (see the "Moral and Physical Thermometer," printed overleaf of the title page).

34　See, for example, Joyce Appleby, "Personal Roots of the First American Temperance Movement," *Proceedings of the American Philosophical Society* 141, 2 (June 1997): 141–59; Kopperman, "'The Cheapest Pay'"; Renée N. Lafferty, "'The Vice of a Cold Climate': Drink and Soldiering on Niagara's Wartime Frontier (1812–14)," *Social History of Alcohol and Drugs* 27, 1 (Winter 2013): 5–36; Charles Ludington, "'Claret Is the Liquor for Boys; Port for Men': How Port Became the Englishman's Wine, 1750s to 1800," *Journal of British Studies* 48 (April 2009): 364–90; Roy Porter, "The Drinking Man's Disease: The 'Pre-History' of Alcoholism in Georgian Britain," *British Journal of Addiction* 80 (1985): 385–96; W.J. Rorabaugh, *The Alcoholic Republic: An American Tradition* (New York: Oxford University Press, 1979).

35　Mann, *Medical Sketches*, 175. See also Freeman, "Introduction," in *Affairs of Honor*; and Orsi, "Zebulon Pike," particularly on the tensions between the exciting promise of "unchained individualism" in the post-Revolutionary period and the "simultaneous threats of avarice, deceit, selfishness, and rebellion," 58–59.

36　"A Report of Hospital Surgeon Lovell of the State of Disease among the Troops on the Niagara Frontier, during the Campaign of 1814," in Mann, *Medical Sketches*, 160.

37　Cutbush, *Observations*, 27, 20 (emphasis in original).

38 Mann, *Medical Sketches*, 35. See also Rush's introductory sketch of John Pringle, in which he suggests that this physician's integrity and honesty were the result of his abstinence: Pringle, *Observations*, xxvii. That sobriety (i.e., complete abstinence) could define manhood in this period is also suggested in Orsi, "Zebulon Pike," 68, and Lafferty, "'The Vice of a Cold Climate,'" 16.

39 Tilton, *Economical Observations*, 38; Cutbush, *Observations*, 95. The wartime Order Book for Fort Niagara suggests that this happened regularly (see Library and Archives Canada, MG24, Fort Niagara Order Book 1812–13), but the practice was not confined to Americans. A similar problem was apparent among British troops of the late eighteenth century. See John Bell, *An Inquiry into the Causes Which Produce, and the Means of Preventing Diseases among British Officers, Soldiers, and Others in the West Indies* (London: printed for J. Murray, 1791), 66; Michael Snape, *The Redcoat and Religion: The Forgotten History of the British Soldier from the Age of Marlborough to the Eve of the First World War* (London: Routledge, 2005), 96.

40 Mann to LeBarron (Apothecary General), January 31, 1814, reprinted in *Medical Sketches*, 258–59.

41 Mann, *Medical Sketches*, 111.

42 For the discussion of this "imperfect hermaphrodite," see ibid., 254–55; Lafferty-Salhany, "'At Last He Said He Was Not a Man': Malingering, Manliness, and the Singular Case of an 1812 Hermaphrodite" (paper presented to the Humanities Research Institute Winter Symposium, Brock University, December 15, 2016).

43 On the cultural links between notions of civilization and disgust, see, for example, Karen Halttunen, "Humanitarianism and the Pornography of Pain in Anglo-American Culture," *American Historical Review* 100, 2 (April 1995): 303–34; William Ian Miller, *The Anatomy of Disgust* (Cambridge, MA: Harvard University Press, 1997), esp. x–xi, 5–8.

44 Mann, *Medical Sketches*, 111. Emphasis in the original.

45 See Apel, *Feverish Bodies*, 8–9, 94–116; William J. Gribbin, *The Churches Militant: The War of 1812 and American Religion* (New Haven, CT: Yale University Press, 1973); Mark Noll, *America's God: From Jonathan Edwards to Abraham Lincoln* (Oxford: Oxford University Press, 2005); Andrew Preston, *Sword of the Spirit, Shield of Faith: Religion in American War and Diplomacy* (New York: Alfred A. Knopf, 2002), esp. 71–101.

46 Laqueur, "Bodies, Details, and the Humanitarian Narrative," 188.

47 Mann, *Medical Sketches*, 37. On the British spirit ration and the trouble with intoxication in the British Army, see Richard Holmes, *Redcoat: The British Soldier in the Age of Horse and Musket* (London: Harper Perennial, 2001), esp. 145–46, 151–55, 405–6; Kopperman, "'The Cheapest Pay'"; Lafferty, "'The Vice of a Cold Climate'"; Snape, *The Redcoat and Religion*, esp. 81–82.

48 Laqueur, "Bodies, Details, and the Humanitarian Narrative," 178. As he writes, "Mountains of facts create the effect of reality in tales of suffering and invite remedial action" (194–95).

49   Mann, *Medical Sketches*, 231.

50   Quote from the "Report of Hospital Surgeon's Mate Purcell, Autumn of 1814," reprinted in Mann, *Medical Sketches*, 155. See also Cutbush, *Observations*, 147–48.

51   See, for example, Mann, *Medical Sketches*, 35–36, 40–41, 110, 137; Cutbush, *Observations*, 55–56. Their predecessor, Rush, agreed (see *Directions for Preserving the Health of Soldiers*, 6–7), but John Pringle, whose work was frequently cited as a foundational text in the field, appears to be have been *less* concerned with spirits than with providing men with waistcoats and firewood (see *Observations*, 77–78, 83–55).

52   Mann, *Medical Sketches*, 310, 35.

53   Ibid., 35–36, 74.

54   It is clear from *Medical Sketches* that Mann and his colleagues regularly conducted autopsies on soldiers who had died from epidemic (or puzzling) illnesses. See especially "Cases of Dissections Reported by Hospital Surgeon's Mate, March ...," in *Medical Sketches*, 186–93. Mann may also have been familiar with one of the first illustrations of the liver of a habitual drunkard, printed in Matthew Baillie, *The Morbid Anatomy of Some of the Most Important Parts of the Human Body* (London: Edward Limebeer, 1793), 116.

55   Mann, *Medical Sketches*, 35. This was not the only circumstance in which Mann declared massive blood loss a boon to the patient. In the case of some gunshot wounds, the more blood expended, the better – provided said wound extended only to the "membranous coverings of the viscera," and had not resulted in the serious laceration of the intestine or an important blood vessel. In such cases, blood loss "obviat[ed] high inflammation" and might save the patient (225).

56   Ibid., 35.

57   Ibid., 310–11. Emphasis in the original. On the supposed health benefits of wool and flannel, see also Rush, *Directions for Preserving the Health of Soldiers*, 4–5.

58   Mann, *Medical Sketches*, 36–38. Benjamin Rush also called for the elimination of the ration, and claimed that, historically, armies had drunk only water and vinegar. See *Directions for the Preserving the Health of Soldiers*, 6–8.

59   Mann, *Medical Sketches*, 15, 122.

60   Ibid., 36–37.

61   Cutbush, *Observations*, 5–6.

62   Mann, *Medical Sketches*, 175.

63   Ibid., 175–77.

64   Ibid., 122, 142–43. Mann's wartime colleague James Lovell reported to him that some of the recruits who joined him in 1814 were "the miserable refuse of society, who never had energy enough to demonstrate that they lived, and scarcely enough to prove that they existed." See "A Report of Hospital Surgeon Lovell ... during the Campaign of 1814," in *Medical Sketches*, 160.

65   Cutbush, *Observations*, 5–6, 13.

66   Battle casualty rates during the War of 1812 were significantly *lower* than those for illness and disease. While 2,260 American men were killed in combat, Stagg, in

"Freedom and Subordination," estimated that perhaps as many as 17,000 died from non-combat illnesses or accidents (624). However, Hickey, in *The War of 1812,* notes that this number should probably be "taken with a grain of salt" (see 305–6, 435n11).

67 Mann to Brigadier General Smith, April 28, 1814, reprinted in *Medical Sketches,* 266.

68 Mann, *Medical Sketches,* 36, 121, 123–24. At times, in defence of officers Mann admired (or to absolve the medical corps of blame for spikes in death rates), he also targeted the federal government for neglecting its financial responsibilities to support the soldiers, or the anti-war press for seeking to undermine the war effort (see 142, for example). The worst cases of understaffing he reported occurred after surgical assistants were ordered to accompany various regiments marching into action (orders that contradicted directions from the Physician and Surgeon General of the Army). At that point, Mann claims to have been left to care for 730 patients entirely on his own. It is extremely likely that he had nurses (or recruited convalescents), but he did not appear to think their efforts worthy of note. See 252–53.

69 Friedrich Wilhelm von Steuben, *Regulations for the Order and Discipline of the Troops of the United States* (Exeter, NH: Thomas and Andrews, 1794), 64.

70 See, for example, Lafferty, "'The Vice of a Cold Climate,'" 22.

71 Alexander Smyth, *Regulations for the Field Exercise, Manœvres, and Conduct of the Infantry of the United States; Drawn Up and Adapted to the Organization of the Militia and Regular Troops* (Philadelphia: Anthony Finley, 1812), 193–94. Smyth is certainly not the only author who borrowed rather generously from others in this period. Mann avoided the practice (normally making direct attributions for anything not written by his own hand), but Edward Cutbush borrowed liberally from several authors (including John Pringle and Thomas Trotter, among others) – although he did acknowledge, in his preface, that he was "indebted" to their work. See *Observations,* x. On the subject of assessing a charge of plagiarism on a long-dead author, see Mark Spencer, "Was David Hume, the Historian, a Plagiarist? A Submission from His *History of England,*" *CLIO: A Journal of Literature, History, and the Philosophy of History* 47, 1 (2019): 25–50.

72 Cutbush, *Observations,* 56–57, 150. Cutbush was certainly far less worried about the effects of ardent spirits than his army colleague. Curiously, however, his text (and, as far as I know, never Mann's) was reprinted by the Massachusetts Temperance Alliance in 1865. It is unclear (I have not been able to obtain a copy) whether this later edition excised or altered any of his "spirited" language.

73 Mann, *Medical Sketches,* vi, 236–37, 270–71.

74 Mann to Colonel Smith, 29th Regiment (Plattsburgh), April 21, 1814, reprinted in *Medical Sketches,* 265–66.

75 Mann to Brigadier General Smith, April 28, 1814, reprinted in *Medical Sketches,* 266–67. Emphasis in the original.

76 Mann, *Medical Sketches,* 236.

77 Freeman, *Affairs of Honor,* xvi

78 Tilton, *Economical Observations,* 16–17. Cutbush also craved this sort of power when it came to the cumbersome process of procuring stores. See, for example, *Observations,* 138–39.

79 Mann, *Medical Sketches,* 264, 270–71. On the low pay of physicians generally, see Anderson, "Medical Practices in Detroit," 263–64; Paul Cushman, "Naval Surgery in War of 1812," *New York State Journal of Medicine* (July 15, 1972): 1883–84.

80 Richard H. Shyrock, "Public Relations of the Medical Profession in Great Britain and the United States: 1600–1870," *Annals of Medical History* 2 (1930): 320.

81 On cultural anxiety about the dead and dissection, see Thomas Laqueur, *The Work of the Dead: A Cultural History of Mortal Remains* (Princeton, NJ: Princeton University Press, 2015); John McManners, *Death and the Enlightenment: Changing Attitudes to Death in Eighteenth-Century France* (Oxford: Oxford University Press, 1985); Michael Sappol, *A Traffic in Dead Bodies: Anatomy and Embodied Social Identity in Nineteenth Century America* (Princeton, NJ: Princeton University Press, 2002). In 1788 (Mann may have been settled in the city at this time), a riot occurred in New York when the public learned of (illegal) medical dissections being carried out on the bodies of former slaves and impoverished whites. See Caroline de Costa and Francesca Miller, "American Resurrection and the 1788 New York Doctors' Riot," *Lancet* 377 (2011): 292–93; Robert J. Swan, "Prelude and Aftermath of the Doctor's Riot of 1788: A Religious Interpretation of White and Black Reaction to Grave Robbing," *New York History* 81, 4 (October 2000): 417–56.

82 It was "dreadful indeed, but no reason to surrender our Fort to a handful of men." Stephen Chambers Henry, "Letter of Surgeon Stephen Chambers Henry, Detroit, 1813, Addressed to His Mother, the Wife of Judge Joseph Henry," *Pennsylvania Magazine of History and Biography* 21, 1 (1897): 123–24.

83 Shyrock, "Public Relations," 314. See also Rosenberg, "The Therapeutic Revolution," 489–90, 496–504.

84 Rosenberg, "The Therapeutic Revolution," 489. See also Gillett, *The Army Medical Department,* 153.

85 Tilton, *Economical Observations,* 60. Ironically, Tilton notes that by refusing amputation, many revolutionary-era soldiers inspired surgeons to attempt new means of *saving* limbs. While, to my knowledge, there are no extant studies of the lives of disabled soldiers of 1812, the growing field of disability studies offers many insights into how we might understand their views, and the views others had, of their bodies. See, for example, Laurel Dean, "Revolutionary War Invalid Pensions and the Bureaucratic Language of Disability in the Early Republic," *Early American Literature* 52, 1 (2017): 141–67; Teresa Michaels, "Invisible Amputation and Heroic Masculinity," *Studies in Eighteenth Century Culture* 44 (2015): 17–39; Chris Mounsey, ed., *The Idea of Disability in the Eighteenth Century* (Lewisburg, PA: Bucknell University Press, 2014). Those interested in James Mann's vision of how the government might assist the "honorable" invalids of 1812, who had "become decrepit in the service of their country," might review his petition to Vice President Elbridge Gerry, reprinted in

Medical Sketches, 272–74. On amputations during the 1812 conflict, see Charles G. Roland, "War Amputations in Upper Canada," *Archivaria* 10 (Summer 1980): 73–84.

86 I do not wish to overstate this case, however. While there are clear indications that some men refused amputations and other "heroic" interventions on their bodies (see *Medical Sketches,* 211, for example), there are equally clear indications that others *demanded* them, revealing powerful faith in the army surgeon's ability to relieve pain – or, at the least, faith in familiar medical practices. See, for example, *Medical Sketches,* 26–27, and William Beaumont's account of treating the wounded at York in 1813 in Genevieve Miller, ed., *William Beaumont's Formative Years: Two Early Notebooks* (New York: Henry Schuman, 1946), 49; and Mann, *Medical Sketches,* 26–27.

87 Anderson, "Medical Practices in Detroit," 266; Porter, *The Greatest Benefit,* 283–87. One of the most popular texts offering medicinal recipes and nostrums to the reading public of the United States (into the twentieth century) was William Buchan, *Domestic Medicine: Or, a Treatise of the Prevention and Cure of Diseases by Regimen and Simple Medicines* (London, 1769).

88 Report of Henry Hunt, Hospital Surgeon, US Army, September 15, 1814, in *Medical Sketches,* 132–36 (quote on p. 136). Hunt's efforts, dramatically heroic, were doomed to failure, his report suggests, because the regimental surgeon had given the patient a supply of tablets containing acetate of lead. Either the damage from these pills (effective for some illnesses, but not this one) had already been done, or Beebe continued to take them without informing anyone. On Hunt's medical experience and reflections, see also Henry Hunt, "An Abstract Account of the Diseases Which Prevailed among the Soldiers, Received into the General Hospital, at Burlington, Vermont, during the Summer and Autumn of 1814," *American Medical Recorder* 1 (1818): 176–79.

89 Mann, *Medical Sketches,* 137–38.

90 Ibid., 271.

91 Ibid., 177.

92 W.J. Rorabaugh, in *The Alcoholic Republic,* 7–9, suggests that average consumption in the United States exceeded five gallons per capita between 1810 and 1830, peaking in the late 1820s, when the average man may have consumed as much as a half a pint per day of spirits alone. Mark Edward Lender and James Kirby, in *Drinking in America: A History* (New York: Simon and Schuster, 1897), 46, suggest an even higher per capita rate (seven gallons) for the same period.

Medicinal Purposes 6

Pharmacists, Professionalism, and Liquor Laws in Victorian Ontario

Dan Malleck

With the rise of the temperance movement in the nineteenth century, the ease by which people could access alcohol as a medicine became increasingly scrutinized. Alcohol had been used as medicine for millennia, and the social movement to constrain or even eliminate the trade in liquor did not reduce its utility, or popularity, as a medicine. Easily accessible and with demonstrable effects, alcoholic beverages remained fundamental to the *materia medica*.[1] Different alcoholic beverages had different medicinal purposes: some types of beer (especially porter and stout) were nutritive and could add weight to emaciated bodies; distilled spirits were stimulants, warming the body after shock or hypothermia; while wine had numerous therapeutic applications.[2] Since many prescriptions were sold in powder form, and since many drugs were not water-soluble, medicines were often diluted in spirits as a solvent. Nevertheless, with the problematization of drunkenness and concerns over the apparent damage "King Alcohol" wrought in the home, its status as *l'eau de vie* became suspect. As the temperance movement sought legislation to reduce or eliminate the trade in alcoholic beverages, the prescription and availability of medicinal alcohol became a matter of concern.

In the province of Ontario, the limits to alcohol were especially problematic to the expanding profession of pharmacy. Whereas earlier physicians would themselves compound and dispense medicines to their patients, by the last part of the century, patients and doctors increasingly looked to pharmacists to skillfully keep, prepare, and dispense remedies.[3] Since pharmacists' professional status was based upon their skill at compounding and their reputation as responsible and respectable vendors of dangerous drugs, including opium, strychnine, arsenic and other medicines that were legally labelled "poisons," they were ideally placed to properly manage socially contentious substances such as medicinal alcohol. However, as the temperance movement's pressure on governments intensified and lawmakers increased restrictions on the sale of alcoholic beverages, pharmacists found that their professional status could not shield them from the challenges of increasingly restrictive laws. Attempts to constrain access to alcoholic beverages resulted in a series of laws and amendments that pharmacists, trained in chemistry and biology rather than law and political science, had to interpret, negotiate, and even oppose. It was not simply a matter of lobbying the government for change. The pharmacy leadership had to contend with many of their pharmaceutical brethren who, drawing their incomes from the trade in a variety of products, often saw their special status as vendors of liquor to be a way of boosting revenues rather than simply tending to the health of the people. While the pharmacy leadership sought to present their profession as respectable, honourable, and worthy of the trust embodied in the legislation that gave them exclusive rights over the sale of certain remedies, some of their own colleagues, intoxicated by the influence of liquor revenues, were undermining their actions.

The challenges to pharmacy's authority over the dispensing of medicines came from all levels of government. Dominion laws permitting communities to vote to end the retail sale of liquor, known as local option laws, placed restrictions on the sale of medicinal liquor. In 1878, the pre-Confederation Dunkin Act, which allowed electors in municipalities of any size to vote themselves "dry," was replaced by the Canada Temperance Act (also called the Scott Act after Senator Richard Scott, who authored the law), under which local option votes could take place only at the level of county or city. In a Scott Act community, vendors had to apply and pay for a special permit to sell medicinal liquor. At the provincial level, license laws designed to limit the number of places in which people could purchase alcoholic beverages also placed restrictions on the amount of medicinal liquor that could be sold, and the reasons that people could purchase it. The 1876 Tavern and Shop Licenses Act, more commonly called the Crooks Act after its author, Provincial Secretary Adam Crooks, centralized the administration of license laws, creating boards of license commissioners to dole out licenses to taverns, saloons, and shops in each license district (roughly following the lines of electoral districts) and empowering provincially appointed inspectors to enforce the law and prosecute transgressors. Municipalities could impose further restrictions within the scope of these various laws. Changes through the rest of the century at both the provincial and Dominion levels further complicated the pharmacist's attempt to sell medicinal liquor. Finally, in the application of both these laws, the influence of municipal governments should not be underestimated. In places where councillors were more or less sympathetic towards temperance views, the law could be applied with more or less vigour.

Such complications were of particular concern to pharmacists because they directly challenged their professional status. The Ontario Pharmacy Act of 1871 was hard-won legislation for which many leaders in the profession had lobbied for many years.[4] Its advocates justified the law with two main arguments. First, pharmacists and physicians contended that the existence of well-trained and appropriately licensed pharmacists who understood the chemical properties of medicines, who could compound often complicated prescriptions, and who were able to assess the viability and potency of the many raw medicines that they stocked was essential to the treatment of the public. Second, stories of people being poisoned, either intentionally or accidentally, with medicines such as strychnine, arsenic, and opium, fuelled arguments that a poorly regulated drug retailing system threatened the health of the people.[5] These drugs were "poisons" in that they could cause death when taken in excess, but were "medicines" when part of a properly constituted prescription. Hence, pharmacy acts normally included a "poison schedule" listing the drugs that needed to be dispensed only by a pharmacist, and often only upon a physician's prescription.

As vendors, compounders, and keepers of a variety of medicines whose work often placed them between the learned physicians and the general public, pharmacists in Ontario as elsewhere throughout the Anglo-American world, blended the traditions of three traditional occupations: chemist, druggist, and apothecary. Chemists were manipulators of chemicals, not necessarily for medicinal use, whose skills involved the ability to distill essences and accurately combine chemicals of varying potencies and properties. Druggists were traders in medicines, and could be involved in transcontinental trade networks to facilitate access to remedies from far afield.[6] Apothecaries were traditional healers, trained by apprenticeship rather than the classical education of physicians, thus occupying the less elite role of trade rather than profession. They were considered such a significant threat to the physicians' practice that in the United Kingdom the medical profession pushed to constrain their ability to treat patients. As a result of legislation in the early eighteenth century, apothecaries were not allowed to charge for medical treatment, but they were allowed to charge for dispensing drugs.[7] This community-based sensibility helped pharmacists of the middle of the nineteenth century to argue against the machinations of physicians who wanted control over licensure of the pharmacists. Pharmacists argued, or at least implied, that physicians were elite and out of touch, whereas the pharmacists were attentive to the interests of everyday people. In an era when monopoly was considered anathema, and where many people, including legislators, saw the medical profession as an elitist group that was trying to claim complete control over the medical system, such arguments had some power.[8] Still, pharmacists and physicians agreed that the pharmacists' skill was important to the effective treatment of the people, and often described the pharmacist as "helpmeet" to the physician (alluding, interestingly, to the Biblical description of Eve). The relationship between doctors and pharmacists was therefore more than a little tense.

These varying social roles of the pharmacist – the competent compounder of medicines, protector of the health of the public, everyday retailer, and necessary helpmeet of the medical profession – came into conflict when the restrictions on alcohol as medicine began to affect the ability of pharmacists to do their work. Pharmacists argued that they were respectable and responsible professionals (even though they often intermingled the term "pharmacist" with the pre-professional term "druggists") who would judiciously dispense medicinal alcohol, and thus did not need to be subject to restrictions designed to clamp down on drunkenness. Yet many pharmacists who were "grandfathered" in under the Pharmacy Act, and who may have been more interested in profit than in professional acumen, were found to be selling liquor contrary to the law.

Pharmacists could also be seen as less than responsible when, in their role as helpmeet to the medical profession, they filled prescriptions that appeared designed to provide alcoholic beverages for recreational rather than therapeutic purposes. While attempting to constrain such activities as unbecoming of a learned profession, the pharmacy leadership had to deal with the effects of decidedly unprofessional behaviour by both their pharmacist confreres and physicians.

Such concerns intensified with the advent of the Crooks Act. Prior to the 1876 legislation, the licensing law had exempted licensed pharmacists from its provisions. Initially the Crooks Act placed only moderate restrictions upon the activities of pharmacists with respect to selling alcohol for medicinal purposes. It permitted a pharmacist to sell twelve ounces of liquor to individuals without a prescription, requiring only that the customer attest that the liquor was needed for medicinal purposes. Customers could purchase larger volumes of liquor only with the prescription of a physician.[9] All liquor purchases were to be recorded in a ledger that the customer had to sign, a process not unfamiliar to pharmacists since it was how they had to record the sale of poisons.[10] Generally, the leading voices of the pharmacy profession saw these restrictions as not terribly problematic. E.B. Shuttleworth, the editor of the *Canadian Pharmaceutical Journal*, called the law "perhaps a little irksome, and doubtless in many cases altogether unnecessary," but he admitted it was well-meant legislation and "every right-minded druggist will cheerfully comply with the new regulations."[11] When concerned pharmacists sent him questions about the specific parameters of the law, Shuttleworth consulted Premier Oliver Mowat, who explained that the law should not prevent duly registered pharmacists from doing their work so long as they sold liquor in packages of twelve ounces or less. Shuttleworth also spoke to a license commissioner – one of those whose job it was to grant liquor licenses – who had been told by Adam Crooks that such pharmacists would be immune from prosecution so long as their fees were fully paid-up.[12]

In his confidence in the professionalism of pharmacists, Shuttleworth seems to have ignored the fact that the nascent profession was made up of a range of vendors, many of whom may not have shared his idealization of pharmacy as a profession. Problems emerged within the first year of the Crooks Act's coming into force. In 1877, the provincial secretary (whose office administered the license law) sent questionnaires to the boards of license commissioners to evaluate the operation of the act and seek recommendations for changes to the law. The responses provide a remarkably rich, varied, and detailed discussion of the drinking practices of Ontarians, and included the complaint that some pharmacists were not following the law. In Ontario South, for example, the commissioners reported that druggists "now sell to anyone in quantities under 12 oz upon the person merely saying he wants it for medicinal purposes." More problematic was the fact that Saturday night, when all barrooms were supposed to close at 7 p.m., "the druggist does what the inn-keeper is prevented from doing, he sells in small quantities to all who apply."[13] Commissioners from Lanark North and Oxford South reported that some pharmacists who also held a medical license seemed to be especially notorious in violating the law.[14] The Oxford South commissioners cited the case of Dr. G. Lount, who was both a druggist and a physician. (Under the Pharmacy Act, physicians were permitted to sell drugs without further licensure from the Ontario College of Pharmacy.) Lount had been accused of selling liquor without a license when he refilled a prescription for brandy that another doctor had prescribed as a stimulant to a Mr. Gamble. The prosecution argued that brandy "was a customary and usual drink with Gamble," and that Lount had therefore been selling for beverage, not medicinal, purposes. Lount was acquitted owing to the fact that, as a registered medical practitioner and a pharmacist, he was legally allowed both to prescribe and sell liquor.[15] The Oxford South commissioners suggested that the law be changed so that "druggist *shall not* be allowed to sell any spirituous liquor whatever without a *certificate* from a *disinterested* licensed medical practitioner, produced by the *person* requiring said liquor."[16] Even though the main transgressors seemed to be physicians who ran pharmacies, the profession of pharmacy was painted with a deviant brush.

Such cases were of concern to the pharmacy leadership, since they undermined the authority and respectability of the profession. The year after the Crooks Act was passed, the *Canadian Pharmaceutical Journal* published testimony taken from trials of druggists for violating the license law. In almost all cases, the pharmacist was fined for selling illegally. One case, involving M.B. Mallory in Napanee, suggested that the drugstore had become a popular place for residents to buy liquor. Several customers who had purchased whisky there explained that they were asked whether the liquor was to be used for medicinal purposes and they said yes. They also signed the liquor register, although some did not remember signing it or what happened to the whisky. Some had returned later that day with an empty bottle and had had it refilled with few questions asked. Many of the witnesses said that they needed the whisky to "put on camphor," creating a remedy likely intended as a palliative for nausea and aches. Camphor was not a controlled substance under the Pharmacy Act, and it is not water-soluble, so needing liquor to dissolve camphor was not an unremarkable practice. Moreover, as the drug clerk (an assistant to the pharmacist) told the court, "whisky on camphor makes a tincture which I know would be dangerous to drink," so he did not consider such sales to be for beverage purposes.[17] Nevertheless, with a parade of people entering the drugstore claiming they needed twelve ounces of whisky to put on camphor, and stumbling off happily, the naïveté of the pharmacist was suspect.

As well as providing cautionary tales about not scrutinizing customers closely, such trials highlighted the importance of following the law precisely. In almost all cases it was clear that simply having the customer confirm that the liquor was needed for medicinal purposes was not adequate to assess the customer's motives. Moreover, filling in the liquor register properly was not sufficient to avoid prosecution (indeed, it was by calculating the seemingly disproportionate number of sales as listed in the register that the inspector could identify pharmacists' problematic selling behaviour). Instead, these stories made it clear to the readers of the *Journal* that the learned pharmacists' judgment was on trial, and in many cases that judgement was lacking.

This was not a minor issue: the authority of pharmacy hinged upon the respectable comportment, judicious decision making, and technical competence of the College's licentiates. This respectability was at the heart of arguments for a Pharmacy Act, and it was that idea of the pharmacist as a responsible gatekeeper for dangerous drugs that advanced pharmacists' professional aspirations. As learned, respectable, and licensed professionals, pharmacists were expected to be far more trustworthy than merchants who were simply interested in making money from the sale of drugs.[18] So when pharmacists were found to be violating the law for the sake of profit, it belied the claims of professional distance from the competitive market, and appeared to validate the concerns expressed by opponents of the Pharmacy Act that the law would simply create a trade monopoly. More vocal members of the profession often reacted harshly to such cases of professional misbehaviour. Indeed, contemplating the "medicinal purposes" clause of the Crooks Act, Shuttleworth reiterated the ideal of a responsible pharmacist making judicious decisions by referring to cases where pharmacists were convicted of violations of the act. The respectable pharmacist needed to use his own good judgment in undertaking the essential role of keeper and dispenser of medicine: "He should have no doubt as to the good faith of the [customer's] application [for medicinal liquor], and from decisions that have been rendered we conclude that frequent sales, at short intervals, to the same party, place the druggist on questionable and dangerous grounds."[19] The pharmacist needed to use his informed decision making to protect himself and the reputation of his profession.

Pharmacists' concerns grew as the law was made more restrictive. An 1881 amendment to the Crooks Act reduced from twelve ounces to six the amount of liquor a pharmacist could sell without a prescription. Shuttleworth was nonplussed, noting, probably naively, that "the dispensing of liquors is quite safe in the hands of our druggists" and that "the druggists of this city [Toronto] and country are, as a class, above taking advantage of any such illegal practices."[20] Two years later, he reassured his colleagues that pharmacists had nothing to fear from the law, but alluded to the fact that there may be a more strict reading of the law than would be ideal for pharmacists. When asked whether "more than six ounces of alcohol or liquor [could] be dispensed with roots, etc., as in filling various recipes containing so much buchu, hops, and the like, to a quart of spirit," he replied that this was "another point in which custom and common sense are greatly at variance with a rigid rendering of the law." If a pharmacist wanted to sell liquor as a proprietary remedy, he would need a compounder's (wholesale) license, but a compound tincture could be sold on an individual basis "provided it can be shown that it is for bona vide medicinal purposes."[21] In 1885, Shuttleworth fielded additional questions about tinctures, and again he relied on the professional acumen of pharmacists: "Whether any particular tincture or spirituous medicinal compound, can be so classed is not a question of law but a matter of fact, to be determined in each particular case."[22] It was the pharmacists' judicious evaluation of the uses of the substance that should determine that fact. Yet such pharmaceutical judiciousness remained elusive. A correspondent condemned his fellow pharmacists who were not being suitably scrutinized by local liquor detectives. He complained that whereas he dutifully sold only six ounces of liquor at a time, "I find myself suffering from the competition of others who make no limits in their sales ... Druggists should uphold the law ... or all must look on the quantity limit as a dead letter."[23]

Such violations of the license law (selling twelve ounces rather than six, dispensing tinctures as beverages, and so on) became more significant and caused greater concern in Scott Act communities. Pharmacists were well aware that strict liquor laws could turn their less scrupulous colleagues into ersatz tavern keepers. In 1881, an editorial note in the *Canadian Pharmaceutical Journal* told of a sudden increase in country drugstores in the state of Georgia after a new law abolished the barroom but permitted "druggists and physicians to sell liquor for medicinal purposes."[24] Closer to home, the situation created in Halton County after the implementation of the Scott Act there became an object lesson in the intricacies of the law. Halton was the first county in the province to support the Scott Act's local option provisions, and what took place there coloured perceptions of the law elsewhere. Under the Scott Act, liquor could not be sold in small quantities, only in amounts of at least a pint.[25] This was intended to prevent drugstores from becoming "tippling places" where people would stay to drink. Yet such quantities could invite some considerable scrutiny. In 1883, the Toronto *Globe*, a temperance-supporting newspaper, reminded readers of the "scandalous record" of "the fraud ... perpetrated by certain of the doctors and druggists in the Halton County under the guise of medical prescriptions," suggesting that the amount of liquor sold medicinally by three pharmacists came to over 6,000 quart bottles in a seven- to eight-month period. The *Acton Free Press,* a Halton County newspaper, did not dispute these numbers, but argued that the liquor sales amounted to ten to twelve barrels of liquor for a community of 10,000–15,000 people, which it considered an entirely reasonable proportion of medicinal liquor. It concluded that rather than shame, "our county has a great and just cause for congratulations."[26] Nevertheless, the *Globe* saw this case as a scandal of no small proportions and cast the net of blame wide. Physicians were prescribing the liquor, and pharmacists were filling the orders. The *Globe* was especially critical of the physicians, noting that they violated the spirit of the trust placed in them by the legislators who enacted the Scott Act, and who "surely [had] a right to expect that our doctors were, as a body, honest men, if not all gentlemen." The violations seemed remarkably bold, and the *Globe* editorial listed the types of unorthodox prescriptions revealed by an audit of pharmacy books:

> "A small quantity of whiskey"; another, "some brandy"; another, "some whiskey"; another, "one quart or more whiskey"; another, "various amounts"; still another, the best of all, "what he requires"!! What is to be said of for this for a prescription? "A lot of brandy"!! Curious also how the diseases about Georgetown always required about the same quantity, viz, a quart!![27]

Although pharmacists might justify such sales as simply the results of doing their job of following doctors' prescriptions, and assert that they were entirely within both their rights and the law to sell such amounts, trust in the pharmacists' learned and judicious decision making was strained. After all, considering pharmacists' claim of ignorance, how could something so important be entrusted to someone who seemed so naive?

To the pharmacy leadership, the respectability of their profession should have been a sufficient control on the distribution of liquor, but evidence to the contrary led to additional restrictions in locations where the Scott Act was in place. As noted earlier, the provisions of this act allowed medicinal liquor to be sold in dry communities only by vendors duly approved to do so under the Scott Act itself. The restrictions were significant, allowing only "one person in each township, two in each incorporated town, and, in cities, one to each four thousand population ... [to be] privileged to sell liquor for any purpose whatever."[28] According to pharmacists, such restrictions were highly problematic for several reasons. First, they meant that pharmacists, already legally licensed as professionals to sell restricted medicines (and, some would argue, substances that were much more dangerous than alcohol, including arsenic and opium), would have to pay a second fee for the license to sell medicinal liquor. Second, the act did not require the approved vendor of medicinal liquor to be a pharmacist at all, so pharmacists would have to compete with other retailers for the "privilege" of selling medicinal liquor. Third, such restrictions in the number of vendors could place the public in danger. As Shuttleworth illustrated in the *Canadian Pharmaceutical Journal*, these restrictions could negatively affect access to medicine:

> Take, for example, the village of Wyoming, in East Lambton. The residents of this thriving and populous district must either go to Petrolia, six miles south; Forest, seventeen miles north; Watford, twelve miles east; or Sarnia, sixteen miles west, before a drop of liquor can be obtained, no matter what the emergency may be.[29]

So, well beyond simply causing some confusion and risk of run-ins with the law, pharmacists argued that the restrictions on medicinal alcohol under the Scott Act could endanger the health of the people. Finally, and, for many pharmacists, most egregiously, the limited number of licenses would put respectable pharmacists in competition with each other. As Henry Watson, a pharmacist in the town of Milton (in dry Halton County) argued, "the Dominion government is greatly to blame for allowing men to prey upon each other as they are doing here. It is more akin to feudal times than our advanced civilization ... there is no virtue in Scott Act men in any way you take them, that should allow them this privilege." He closed by urging the College of Pharmacy to "get the profession ... out of tyranny."[30]

The college tried. In May 1884, soon after the situation in Halton gained attention, it sent a committee to the provincial government to seek modifications to the law that would benefit pharmacists. The committee's goal to have a clause inserted in the law to allow "druggists to sell alcohol without restriction" was not achieved. The best it could manage, which might have been cold comfort to their pharmacist colleagues, was a change to make physicians more clearly responsible in cases where a pharmacist filled a spurious prescription for medicinal alcohol. The committee observed that there would normally be no need for such a clause, but acknowledged the situation in Scott Act counties like Halton, where "abuses exist which this clause is intended to remedy."[31] Quoting the *Hamilton Spectator* (a temperance-supporting newspaper), the *Canadian Pharmaceutical Journal* noted that in one village in Halton, "the people are suffering from an epidemic, the prevalence of which may be judged from the fact that prescriptions calling for a specified quantity of the same potent stimulant were dispensed four hundred and fifty times during one month." The *Journal* reminded its readers that, in this case, "the physicians, not the druggists, are to blame."[32] The pharmacists needed legislation to protect them, in their role as helpmeet, from physicians' apparent greed and violation of the law.

Nevertheless, the restrictions on the sale of medicinal liquor in Scott Act communities remained in place and caused Ontario pharmacists considerable confusion, concern, and anger. In the pages of the *Journal*, many complained about the tricky situation they faced under the law. In 1882, a correspondent noted that he had been "almost forced into the liquor trade" when his municipality stopped granting liquor licenses to grocers because his was the only retail option for liquor of any kind. Then when the Scott Act came into force in his district, he was unable to get a liquor license and was stuck with a large stock of liquor that he was not allowed to sell.[33] In 1884, a pharmacist in Orillia reported that he had to deny whisky to a lady who refused to sign the liquor register, because she equated that procedure to being labelled a drinker. Although the pharmacist believed it was genuinely a medical purchase, he knew that not keeping a proper register could lead to a fine, since any druggist "who disregards it becomes an illicit dealer in liquors, subject to all the penalties and odium attaching to that class." Shuttleworth noted that it was not surprising that "respectable druggists decline to place themselves in such a position."[34] In 1885, Milton's Henry Watson, who had earlier begged the college to save pharmacists from the tyranny of the law, encouraged all pharmacists in Scott Act communities to avoid selling liquor altogether, for the sake of their business and the profession. "Don't let us be in a position when drunken men are seen in the streets (as drunken men will be seen in the streets) to have it said they must have been at the druggist ... No respectable druggist should allow his store to be made a refuge for the drunkard."[35] Six months later, the *Journal* published a series of comments from pharmacists in Scott Act areas, calling the law "a dead letter," "a failure," a "fraud," "a curse to the county," and "worse than useless."[36]

Along with virulent griping, many pharmacists continued to seek advice on how best to navigate the complexities of both the licensing and local option laws. The *Canadian Pharmaceutical Journal*, and later a competing journal, the *Canadian Druggist*, offered interpretations of the legislation and responded to readers' questions on the specifics of the act. Regarding the Scott Act's provision that a limited number of retailers would be licensed to sell intoxicating liquor in Scott Act districts, the *Journal* opined that this all hinged upon what the law meant by "intoxicating liquor." The editor argued that the term applied only to beverages normally used for non-medicinal applications, such as "beer, wine spirits and the like that are sold in taverns," but also some drinks that sat on the margins: "certain 'bitters' cordials, and the like, but [it] would certainly not embrace such articles as the pharmacopoeial tinctures, wines, liniments, etc. These are not beverages, but medicines."[37] Moreover, according to this interpretation, both druggists licensed to sell liquor under the act and those who did not hold a liquor license should be able to sell such remedies in which "there is sufficient of the medicinal ingredient to prevent them from being used as beverages."[38] Such assurances were put to the test when pharmacists were taken to court. Consequently, the college returned to Ottawa seeking amendments to the Scott Act to clarify what a pharmacist could and could not sell.

In 1885, when the Dominion government introduced legislation amending the act, the college's Committee on By-laws and Legislation offered language specifying which activities should be exempt from the law in Scott Act communities.[39] It was intended to deal with what the committee called "interference" in pharmacists' ability to carry out their work in service to the public. The committee requested that the legislation not impede the work of pharmacists in five specific areas of commerce:

- dispensing official preparations based on the pharmacopoeias sold for medicinal purposes
- filling physicians' prescriptions that included liquor as long as they were not more than eight ounces in volume
- selling patent medicines unless they were known to be used as intoxicating beverages
- vending perfume, lotions, or other alcohol-containing preparations not normally intended as beverages
- handling alcohol or methylated spirits used for industrial or chemical purposes.[40]

This proposal became integrated into a lengthy bill amending the Scott Act that was presented in the House of Commons in March 1885 and which faced significant modification in the Senate. The Senate debates were extensive and heated, and although there was less heat generated by the issue of medical liquor than other proposed amendments, members on both sides had a lot to say about liquor being sold as medicine. Sentiment in both houses seemed to be more suspicious of the actions of physicians in prescribing excessive amounts of liquor as a beverage than of pharmacists in dispensing it. Nevertheless, the content of the debates illustrates the perception of medicinal liquor, the tendency to see its use as generally non-therapeutic, how physicians' authority was challenged, and how pharmacists were vulnerable precisely due to their purported role as helpmeet to physicians.

One of the main changes proposed in the amendments of 1885 would have eliminated the quantity restriction on liquor sales in Scott Act communities, allowing physicians to prescribe in whatever volume they saw fit. During debates, senators presented contrasting images of physicians as respectable or dishonourable. Some argued that that most physicians would never manipulate the liquor laws for personal gain, conceding that there were, of course, a few exceptions, while others were not so forgiving. In the often impassioned debates, Senator Richard Scott, the eponymous author of the original act, presented examples of pharmacists and physicians who seemed to be flouting the law and selling amounts far above what the act permitted. He argued that many otherwise respectable physicians and pharmacists seemed to be keeping within the letter of the law but violating its moderationist spirit. He read reports from Scott Act counties "where I find the quantity dispensed, is practically unlimited." He listed a physician's prescription for "four gallons of brandy ... 27 pints of ale and beer, and ... ten quarts of whiskey." Scott concluded that "medical men have at the present moment as much license as we should give them in this respect," reiterating his concern with a wry observation about one prescription where a physician gave "an order for 70 pints of ale ... I suppose the person proposed to have a porter or ale bath."[41] To a teetotaller like Scott, such prescriptions seemed to be far out of line with appropriate medical treatment.

Scott's evidence appeared most damning when he presented the records of a single pharmacy in Prince County, Prince Edward Island. PEI was a dry province, since all three of its counties and the capital of Charlottetown had passed the Scott Act.[42] Evidence from this single pharmacy suggested that, although dry by statute, the province was far from dry in practice. All that a patient needed was a compliant physician and obedient pharmacists. "One drug shop, on a single day," recorded the following sales:

> Brad Black, 12 pints of whiskey;
> Mrs. James Read, 9 pints of whiskey;
> Howard Farrow, 8 pints of whiskey;
> Wm.S. Green, 10 pints of whiskey;
> Charles Clark, 8 pints of whiskey;
> T.H. Robble, 80 pints of ale and porter
> Brad Black, 18 pints of whiskey;
> Brad Black, 28 pints of whiskey;
> H.E. Wright, 16 pints of whiskey:
> D. Hunt, 24 pints of whiskey;
> Mr. Kirk, 20 pints of whiskey.[43]

New Brunswick senator James Dever shared Scott's concern about medical liquor, although he did not see it as just an issue with physicians; rather, he saw it as an illustration of how such a law should be thrown out because it privileged pharmacists and doctors to the disadvantage of other vendors. For Dever, pharmacists were not exempt from criticism "The druggist can bring in any quantity of alcohol and can sell it ... If druggists and doctors, and clergymen and priests, have the privilege of using alcohol as they please, the regular dealers, who have been employed in the business all their lives, should not be restricted."[44] Here anti-monopoly sentiments converged with temperance restrictions.

Yet such temperance sentiments belied the challenges of geography and medical treatment where alcohol remained an important multi-purpose remedy. Many of the senators who responded to Scott's charges noted that, whatever he thought of the physicians manipulating the system to provide alcohol as a recreational beverage for their patients, the current system was designed to enable physicians and pharmacists to play their crucial role of treating the public. PEI senator Robert Haythorne argued that the physicians he knew in his province "are about as upright and honourable men as can be found anywhere," and tried to give some context to Scott's claims. He suggested that such apparent transgressions of the law avoided the worst problems of prohibition:

> If the parties who had thus obtained liquor in undue quantities through the assistance of medical men had not obtained it in that manner they would have obtained it in some way perhaps more objectionable. At least they have had this advantage, that the liquor they obtained in the druggist shop was generally of a fair genuine quality, whereas if they had been driven to obtain it in other ways it might have been some vile compound which would have been attended with injurious effects.[45]

Senator William Almon, a physician from Sarnia, Ontario, clarified the variety of uses of repeated doses of alcohol, sometimes despite the patient's dislike of booze. In "cases of consumption, the medical man ... would say, in the first instance, take a tablespoonful of cod liver oil and a glass of liquor, three times a day, until the symptoms cease. The man may not care for the liquor any more than for the cod liver oil, but he takes it because the doctor orders it." Almon reminded the senators that the patient could not simply continue to go to a pharmacist or a doctor for every dose, and that as a result, patients might need to purchase larger quantities of liquor for their medicinal use.[46] At the same time, the law had to be shaped in such a way that it would not lead respectable vendors to commit a crime in order to meet their customers' medical needs. Conservative MP and physician Thomas Sproule, who supported the Scott Act in general, did not support increased restrictions on alcohol for medicinal purposes: "If the law is framed so that an ordinary business cannot be carried on without violating it, it would only make the vendors disregard the law and druggists would dispense [alcoholic medicines] whether they violated the law or not when they believed such articles were essential to the health of the people."[47] Responding to Sproule, George Casey, MP for Elgin West, contended that there was no such problem since the "general consensus of opinion among legal gentlemen" was that the Scott Act did not restrain "the liberty given to druggists to sell medicinal preparations and dispense perscriptions [sic] containing alcohol."[48] In these arguments, both doctors and pharmacists were considered to be looking out for the best interests of their patients and customers.

The legislation did not pass that year, mostly due to attempts to undermine the Scott Act by allowing beer and cider to be sold in dry counties, so when the College of Pharmacy returned to Ottawa the following April, it reiterated its role as responsible vendors of viable medicines. In 1886, when the college's Committee on By-laws and Legislation reported on its lack of progress on the issue of liquor licenses in Scott Act communities, it made a general assertion about the reluctance of pharmacists to be liquor vendors. Although "druggists generally do not desire to have placed in their hands the liquor business," the committee observed, "if this matter is to be entrusted to them, equal privileges should be granted to all."[49] This emphasis upon equality was also a fundamental aspect of the professional code: competition was anathema to the proper functioning of a respectable profession. Back in Ottawa, another amending bill, titled "An act relating to druggists," was presented, debated vigorously in the Senate, and passed with few amendments.[50] It, too, died in the House of Commons, however.[51]

The amendment finally passed in 1888, and it was a significant improvement on the previous arrangement. Under this law, pharmacists could sell any medicine containing liquor that was included in official pharmacopoeias, any patent medicine that was not known to be used as a beverage, any tinctures that were not intended as beverages, and up to ten ounces of spirits intended for medicinal purposes and ordered under a physician's prescription.[52] It was a notable change and addressed nearly all the issues the college's committee had presented to the government. As the celebratory front-page editorial in the *Journal* noted, "this uncertain and disagreeable state of affairs has, happily, been brought to a close, and ... a point has been gained by the recognition of the rights of the trade to class legislation of the nature indicated."[53] In many ways, the Scott Act amendments had become marginal by 1888, when most of the counties that had enacted the legislation in the middle of the decade were beginning to repeal it. Before the end of the decade, there would be no Scott Act counties left in Ontario. The remaining dry areas were holdovers from the pre-Confederation Dunkin Act.

Despite this setback for temperance, the movement continued undeterred, and the next decade saw a Royal Commission on the Liquor

Traffic in Canada, provincial and national plebiscites on prohibition, and additional constraints on the distribution of alcohol as a medicine.[54] Again, the rights and responsibility of the profession as a protector of the health of the community and a helpmeet to medicine became key issues. In 1897, the Ontario government passed an amendment to the Crooks Act that forbade pharmacists to sell any mixtures containing liquor unless by prescription, expanding the restriction that had previously placed limits only on the sale of liquor that could be used as beverages. In effect, the Crooks Act made pharmacists' work as restricted as if they were working under the Scott Act. Even then, the mixture could not be more than six ounces. It was a challenge to both professions, and the *Canadian Druggist* saw the legislation, titled "An Act to Further Improve the License Laws" as risible: "It would be very difficult ... for anyone of ordinary intelligence to discover the 'improvement' in the clauses related to the sale of liquor by druggists." The problem was simply that alcohol was far too ubiquitous for such constraints to be possible: "Alcohol, which is obtainable only from druggists, is put to almost innumerable uses in the household, in the arts, etc., and why should anyone requiring this spirit be compelled to procure a prescription for it?"[55] Moreover, the editor of the *Canadian Druggist* noted, in a gesture of solidarity with medicine, that it was especially an affront to the authority of the medical profession: "The doctor may name the medicine, but the legislature fixes the dose."[56] Arguing that the new law could be interpreted in such a way that the sale of proprietary medicines containing liquors could get a pharmacist in trouble, the college leadership spoke to the attorney general, who insisted that this had not been the intention of the amendment.[57] Nevertheless, J.E. Morrison, Shuttleworth's successor as editor of the *Canadian Pharmaceutical Journal,* explained that the new law exposed pharmacists to the same sorts of predatory inspection they had seen in the past. The law permitted anyone who brought a conviction against a pharmacist to receive half the fine. As a result, private detectives, who were often seen as disreputable characters who exploited the law for personal gain, could bring charges against pharmacists for breach of the law. "What is to prevent some of the numerous shysters or ex-jail birds ... from laying an information, induced by the money there is in it for them?"[58]

The challenges were practical and philosophical. Constraining pharmacists' ability to sell medicinal liquor limited customers' choices, placed pharmacists in danger of predatory prosecution for profit, and undermined the authority of pharmacists as professionals . Even though, as the *Journal* had noted in 1886, "black sheep are to be found in every fold," this did not seem to justify restricting all pharmacists' ability to carry out their professional duties and exercise their rights to practice.[59] Moreover, troublesome physicians such as those in Halton County responsible for thousands of quarts of liquor sold through three drugstores, were just as responsible for breaking the laws. So why should they, not the pharmacists, continue to be able to exercise their learned assessment and judicious reasoning? Even though the 1897 amendment "fixed the dose" of a physician's prescription, it was the power of the prescription that continued to empower the physicians.

This rhetoric reappeared a year later when the College of Pharmacy petitioned the legislature for changes to the Crooks Act so that pharmacists would not be unnecessarily restricted in doing their work. The text of the petition made a clear argument about the respectability of the pharmacists and the impracticality of the law. Positioning the profession as respectable citizens, the petition noted that pharmacists "welcome any legislation which will tend to prevent the disgraceful practice of the sale of liquor as a beverage by any of their number," but in the same sentence protested "the unfair restrictions" in the previous amendment, thereby asserting their professional autonomy. The petition outlined specific problems that highlighted not only the pharmacy profession's role in addressing the health of the people but also how the law inconvenienced everyday members of a community. Pharmacists would be guilty of violating the law "if they were to prepare a simple domestic mixture for colds in winter, or other complaints in summer, and these remedies require, as they nearly all do, to be made up with a certain amount of spirits." Under the current law, the petitioners argued, a druggist would have to "tell the unfortunate customer that he must first go to a doctor, and pay him to write out a prescription." Tying the pharmacist's work too closely to the physician's prescription was not in anyone's best interest, most especially, the petitioners argued, the customer. The doctor's fee was the crux of the issue. The petition's final point was that the sale of liquor in medical mixtures "can do no injury to the temperance cause, and will be a boon to the large number of people who cannot afford to pay a medical fee for every trifling

remedy."[60] The pharmacists tied their arguments yet again to the authority
of the physicians, ending their plea with the observation that "the medical
profession themselves do not express a desire to levy an involuntary tax of
this kind upon the community."[61] The college sent a copy of the petition to
every licensed pharmacist in the province, encouraging them to have their
patrons sign it and then forward it to their local member of the legislative
assembly. Dozens of druggists did so.

The license legislation was the topic of intense scrutiny in the next
sitting of the legislature. The pharmacists' petitions were part of a flood
of petitions related to the license law that the legislature received upon
opening in December 1897.[62] By early January, over 755 petitions had
been received from temperance advocates alone.[63] The *Canadian Druggist*
explained to its readers in a remarkable understatement that the lobbying
"tended to complicate matters." Along with the retail drug trade seeking to
be "relieved of the very unfair and unwarrantable wording of the amendments of 1897," and manufacturers asking for "concessions in reference
to the use of alcohol in manufacturing," temperance advocates asked for
"radical changes" and liquor dealers also "had suggestions and objections."[64]
The pharmacists joined both temperance advocates and liquor interests
in demanding changes to the law, a rare moment when Drys, Wets, and
moderates agreed on something.

When the pharmacists' deputation met with the government on December 23, they reiterated their perspective that the previous amendments were
problematic not only to druggists but also to the public. J.H. Mackenzie,
one of the college's representatives, called the existing law "an injustice
upon [the pharmacists] and an increased hardship upon the people who
have been in the habit of using simple remedies." He noted the "many cases,
such as measles, in which people require stimulants in combination with
saffron and other drugs, and they do not want to be under the necessity
of getting medical certificates." Mackenzie assured the legislators that "he
did not deny that there was a percentage of druggists who broke the law,
but the same might be said of every profession with the difference that the
percentage of druggists who did so was perhaps smaller." When one legisla-
tor noted that the problem was that some druggists were taking advantage
of the law, and that the government wanted to avoid drugstores becoming
"tippling places," Mackenzie agreed, and "expressed the readiness and

desire of the profession as a body to act with the Government to prevent abuse."[65] Yet again, combining the issue of the convenience of the public with the authority of pharmacists as a profession and the judicious decision making of most individual pharmacists, the deputation reiterated the idea that liquor, properly dispensed and mixed with useful and non-dangerous drugs, should not be considered a beverage or something threatening to the sobriety of the public.

The legislation amending the previous year's law had a unique epilogue. On the final day the legislature sat, when the lieutenant governor would normally proclaim the laws passed by the legislature, the premier observed that the amendments to the liquor act as they stood were too ambiguous and might open the trade of alcohol containing patent medicines to general merchants instead of keeping them in the responsible hands of pharmacists. He proposed that the legislation already passed be killed, and presented a new set of amendments that were quickly accepted by the opposition. This last-minute legislation, "An Act respecting the sale of Patent and other Medicine, and of Alcohol for the purposes of the Arts and Manufacturers," removed restrictions on the sale of most forms of medical liquor from the Crooks Act and allowed pharmacists to dispense simple remedies (like the aforementioned saffron and whisky) to customers without the need for a physician's prescription. The legislation, the editor of the *Canadian Druggist* noted, "should be satisfactory to the drug trade as well as being a safeguard against abuses which might creep in."[66]

By the turn of the century, Ontario's pharmacists had enjoyed the protection of a pharmacy act for a generation, and for nearly as long they needed to remain concerned about the legal intricacies constraining the sale of liquor. Notwithstanding the druggists who flouted the law and undermined the professional assertions the pharmacy leadership, the College of Pharmacy continued to argue that its trained, examined, and duly licensed members could ensure that medicinal liquor would be controlled and distributed appropriately. By reiterating that overly stringent licensing laws were an inconvenience and even a danger to the health of the public, pharmacists strengthened their position as respectable professionals. At the same time, the complicated professional relationship between pharmacists and physicians meant that their reputation could be either weakened or strengthened depending upon how that relationship was managed. The authority of physicians could be useful to pharmacists, who benefitted from physicians supporting pharmacists' claims to autonomy, but that relationship could also be problematic when physicians who appeared to use their prescribing power to undermine licensing laws drew pharmacists into a disreputable collaboration. Although pharmacists continued to situate themselves in a symbiotic relationship with physicians, they simultaneously argued that their professional skills and respectable character were qualities that enabled them to assert their autonomy and not see it repeatedly undermined by the need to be subject to a physician's decisions. Positioning themselves as representing the interests of everyday customers, pharmacists upheld simultaneously their profession's authority and the people's right to make decisions on what was best for their own health.

Notes

1 For an excellent overview of alcohol's combined use, see David T. Courtwright, *The Age of Addiction: How Bad Habits Became Big Business* (Cambridge, MA: Belknap Press of Harvard University Press, 2019).

2 Harry Paul, *Bacchic Medicine: Wine and Alcohol Therapies from Napoleon to the French Paradox* Clio Medica: Studies in the History of Medicine and Health Series (Amsterdam: Brill Rodopi, 2001); C. Anne Wilson, *Liquid Nourishment: Potable Foods and Stimulating Drinks* (Edinburgh: Edinburgh University Press, 1993).

3 The exception was proprietary remedies, available in pre-packaged forms which were unregulated and could come in varying degrees of quality and credibility. See Joseph M. Spillane, *Medical Monopoly: Intellectual Property Rights and the Origins of the Modern Pharmaceutical Industry* (University of Chicago Press, 2014).

4 Dan Malleck, "Professionalism and the Boundaries of Control: Pharmacists, Physicians, and Dangerous Substances in Canada 1840–1908," *Medical History* 48 (2004): 175–98; R.J. Clarke, "Professional Aspirations and the Limits of Occupational Autonomy: The Case of Pharmacy in Nineteenth-Century Ontario," *Canadian Bulletin of Medical History* 8 (1991): 43–63.

5 See Malleck, "Professionalism and the Boundaries of Control"; Clarke, "Professional Aspirations"; Peter Bartrip, "A 'Pennurth of Arsenic for Rat Poison': The Arsenic Act, 1851 and the Prevention of Secret Poisoning," *Medical History* 36 (1992): 53–69.

6 See Roy Porter, "The Rise of the English Drug Industry: The Role of Thomas Corbyn," *Medical History* 33 (1989): 277–95. Into the twentieth century, pharmacists often referred to themselves as "druggists" and sometimes, although less frequently, as apothecaries. In this paper I intermingle the terms, mostly for variety and alliteration but also when the quotations themselves are referring to "druggists." In my observation and reading, there was no difference in the eyes of the pharmacists by this time,

notwithstanding the fact that, historically, druggists were traders not learned professionals.

7 S.W.F. Holloway, "The Apothecaries Act 1815: A Reinterpretation, Part I: The Origins of the Act," *Medical History* 10 (1966): 107–29; Irving Loudon, *Medical Care and the General Practitioner: 1750–1850* (Oxford: Oxford University Press, 1986), esp. chs. 6–8. See also Stuart Anderson, *Pharmacy and Professionalization in the British Empire, 1780–1970* (Switzerland: Springer International, 2021).

8 Jeffrey L. Berlant, *Profession and Monopoly: A Study of Medicine in the United States and Great Britain* (Berkeley and London: University of California Press, 1975). More broadly, economic theory tended to follow Adam Smith, and well-known political economists, including John Stuart Mill, argued against monopolies. See Mill, *Principles of Political Economy,* People's Ed. (London: Longmans, Green, 1881), bk. V, chs. 10 and 11. Thanks to Shirley Tillotson for reminding me of this essential reading.

9 "Ontario Pharmacy Act 1871," s. 3, reproduced in *Canadian Pharmaceutical Journal (CPJ),* 4 (March 1871): 27–29.

10 "The Law Respecting the Sale of Liquor by Druggists," *CPJ* 10 (April 1877): 329.

11 Ibid., 328.

12 "The Law Respecting the Sale of Wines and Liquor by Druggists," *CPJ* 9 (July 1876): 437.

13 Ontario, Legislative Assembly *Sessional Papers* (1877) Paper No. 42, "License Report" (hereafter License Report 1877), response from Ontario South, 61–62.

14 License Report 1877, response from Lanark North, 55; Oxford South, 62.

15 "Important Liquor Case," *Acton Free Press,* November 30, 1876.

16 License Report 1877, response from Oxford South, 62 (emphasis in original).

17 "Prosecutions for Sale of Liquor by Druggists," *CPJ* 10 (June 1877): 411–13.

18 Dan Malleck, "Canada's First Drug Laws," in *When Good Drugs Go Bad* (Vancouver: UBC Press, 2015), 53–83. Register of sales is in Canada Temperance Act, pt. II, s. 99(4). See *Canada Temperance Act and Amendments* (Toronto: Rose Publishing, ca. 1884).

19 "Sale of Liquor by Druggists," *CPJ* 17 (March 1884): 112–13.

20 "Scott Act as Affecting Druggists," *CPJ* 14 (June 1881): 355.

21 Untitled editorial, *CPJ* 17 (August 1883): 3.

22 "Sale of Liquor by Druggists," *CPJ* 19 (November 1885): 46.

23 "Druggist," "Breaches of Liquor Laws" [Letter to the editor] *CPJ* 19 (November 1885): 58.

24 "Editorial Summary," *CPJ* 14 (April 1881): 320.

25 "An Act respecting the Traffic in Intoxicating Liquors" *Acts of the Parliament of the Dominion of Canada* 3rd Leg 4th Sess. (1878) 41 Vict, c 16, pt II, s 99(4).

26 "Physicians' Certificates for Liquor" [editorial], *Acton Free Press,* April 10, 1884.

27 "Liquor Sold Medicinally in Halton," *Toronto Globe,* April 18, 1884.

28 "Scott Act as Affecting Druggists," *CPJ* 14 (June 1881): 353.

29 Ibid.

30 "The Scott Act as Affecting Druggists," [Letter to the editor] *CPJ* 16 (September 1882): 55–56.

31 "The Amendments to the License Act," *CPJ* 17 (May 1884): 148–49; An Act to Improve the Liquor License Laws" *Statutes of the Province of Ontario* 5th Leg, 1st Sess (1884), 47 Vict. c. 34. s 12.

32 "The Amendments to the License Act," 149.

33 "The Scott Act as Affecting Druggists," *CPJ* 15 (June 1882): 354.

34 "News Items," *CPJ* 17 (June 1884): 165.

35 Henry Watson, "The Scott Act," [Letter to the editor] *CPJ* 19 (November 1885): 58.

36 "Sale of Liquor by Druggists," *CPJ* 19 (March 1886): 112–13.

37 "Scott Act as Affecting Druggists," *CPJ* 14 (June 1881): 354.

38 Ibid.

39 "Ontario College of Pharmacy – Minutes of the Semi-Annual Meeting of the Council – Report of the Committee on By-Laws and Legislation," *CPJ* 19 (September 1885): 24. These provisions were reported to the council well after they had moved through the two houses. As noted below, those discussions took place in May. The committee also reported on the failure of the legislation.

40 Ibid.

41 *Senate Debates* 5th Leg, 3rd Sess. (May 6, 1885) at 860 (Hon. R. Scott).

42 See Canada, Parliament, *Sessional Papers, 1895* (Vol 11) Paper No 21, "Report of the Royal Commission on the Liquor Traffic in Canada, with full Index to the Report and to the Evidence," 116.

43 *Senate Debates* 5th Leg, 3rd Sess. (May 6, 1885) at 862–63 (Hon. R. Scott).

44 Ibid., 861.

45 *Senate Debates* 5th Leg, 3rd Sess. (May 6, 1885) at 865–66 (Hon. R. Haythorne).

46 Ibid., 866.

47 *House of Commons Debates* 5th Parl, 3rd Sess, Vol 19 (June 18, 1885) at 2648 (Mr. T. Sproule). Sproule also observed that in areas where there was no physician, it would be impossible to get medicine, as repeated in *CPJ*. See *House of Commons Debates* 5th Parl, 3rd Sess, Vol 18 (April 13, 1885) at 1048 (Mr. T. Sproule).

48 *House of Commons Debates,* 5th Parl, 3rd Sess, Vol 19 (June 18, 1885) at 2648 (Mr. G. Casey).

49 "Ontario College of Pharmacy – Minutes of the Semi-Annual Council Meeting – Report of the Committee on By-laws and Legislation," *CPJ* 19 (March 1886): 119.

50 "The Druggist's Bill in the Senate," *CPJ* 19 (May 1886): 150.

51 "The Druggist's Bill," *CPJ* 19 (June 1886): 166. The bill was connected to a bill to open up sales of light wine and beer, which, according to the pharmacists, did not have the support of the Commons.

52 "Act in amendment of 'The Canada Temperance Act,'" *Acts of the Parliament of the Dominion of Canada* 6th Leg, 2nd Sess, (1889) 51 Vict, c. 35.

53 "The Scott Act Amendments," *CPJ* 21 (June 1888): 167–68.

54 For details of these developments see Dan Malleck, *Liquor and the Liberal State: Drink and Order before Prohibition* (Vancouver: UBC Press, 2022).

55 "An Act Further to Improve the License Laws," *Canadian Druggist* 9 (September 1897): 194.

56 Ibid.

57 "The Ontario License Act," *Canadian Druggist* 9 (July 1897): 146.

58 "Liquor in the Drug Store," *CPJ* 20 (July 1897): 515. For a discussion on liquor detectives, see Malleck, *Liquor and the Liberal State,* 100–3.

59 "Sale of Liquor by Druggists," *CPJ* 19 (March 1886): 112–13.

60 "Legislation Asked for," *Canadian Druggist* 9 (November 1897): 273.

61 Petition to Legislative Assembly of Ontario (undated, 1898), Registrar's Correspondence, 1898; F4616-2-2-1898, box B848119, Ontario College of Pharmacy fonds, Archives of Ontario. Also see text in "Legislation Asked For."

62 "Ontario Legislature," *Toronto Globe,* December 4, 1897. Petitions were presented in the first few weeks of the legislature's sitting. See Ontario, Legislative Assembly, *Journals of the Legislative Assembly* 8th Leg, 4th Sess. Vol 31 (1897–98), various pages.

63 "License Amendments," Toronto *Globe,* January 6, 1898.

64 "Amendments to the Amended Act," *Canadian Druggist* 10 (February 1898): 26.

65 "Legislature Takes a Vacation – Liquor Selling by Druggists," *Toronto Globe,* December 24, 1897.

66 "License Law Legislation," *Canadian Druggist* 10 (January 1898): 2–3.

A New Perspective on Harm Reduction 7

George Peters and the Chicago
LSD Rescue Service

Chris Elcock

Although no consensus definition exists, harm reduction can be described as a medical approach designed to mitigate the risks of harm that arise when a person takes a drug, particularly to protect the drug user from interactions with the drug-using environment. It is typically associated with opiate abuse:[1] many of those deemed to be addicted to heroin are given methadone and buprenorphine as substitutes because those substances are legal medicines that undergo quality control. Street drugs, by contrast, have varying levels of purity and are therefore more hazardous. Others continue to inject heroin but with clean needles, instead of recycling old ones and passing them around to other users. In the 1980s, harm reduction was seen as a way of checking the spread of HIV/AIDS among heroin addicts using infected needles.

The argument in favour of harm reduction can be roughly summed up as follows: "Drug users will take drugs regardless of the law and social stigma, so let us assist them to prevent further unnecessary damage." This contrasts with the zero tolerance approach of the war on drugs, which seeks to end drug abuse regardless of the many problems surrounding addiction. Instead, harm reduction looks beyond the simple termination of illicit and dangerous drug use and acknowledges it without passing any moral judgments on users.

Histories of harm reduction are scarce and tend to offer brief overviews rather than thorough examinations. Some begin in the Netherlands in the 1970s,[2] others in the 1980s in conjunction with HIV/AIDS in the Liverpool area,[3] and some scholars see the notion of "responsible use" that appeared in the United States in the 1970s as a precursor.[4] Even fewer studies have been written by historians, with the notable exception of Gemma Blok. Blok has looked at the rise of harm reduction policies in the Netherlands. With the surge in heroin consumption in Amsterdam in the early 1970s, this new approach supported users by giving them clean needles, even if they could or were willing to put an end to their consumption. As well, users received medical attention, counselling, and assistance to find decent housing and legal help.[5] There have been comparatively more histories of methadone and buprenorphine maintenance.[6] Harm reduction may also have precedents in the early debates about whether addicts should be legally provided with their doses of heroin or morphine. In New York, medical doctor Ernest Bishop contended that maintaining addicts indefinitely was both rational and humane.[7] Discussions revolving around the nature and causes of addiction climaxed in 1919 and 1920, but the US Supreme Court ultimately ruled that maintenance of addiction, for whatever reasons, was illegal.[8]

This chapter focuses on one of the hitherto undocumented aspects of the history of harm reduction by connecting this notion with the American psychedelic culture of the 1960s that had developed its own ethics of care towards drug users.[9] In 1965, George Peters founded the LSD Rescue Service in Chicago after he became concerned about the rising number of people taking lysergic acid diethylamide (LSD) in unsafe circumstances. He believed that hospitals and medical doctors did not know enough about the psychedelic experience to effectively treat them and return them to the community. Peters and his volunteers, on the other hand, had insider knowledge, which they put to use to benefit psychedelic drug users. The service provided medical assistance to those undergoing difficult experiences with the drug and later expanded its activities beyond psychedelic harm reduction to ensure that users were returned to the community to lead productive lives.

The evidence gathered in the writing of this chapter suggests that their efforts yielded positive results, even though Peters was not a qualified physician. Given the acclaim he received from several medical authorities, it appears that the LSD Rescue Service did help many drug consumers in the Chicago area. Peters also collaborated with the University of Chicago in a study of LSD users, which indicates that at least some academics were taking him seriously, and in 1969 he testified before the House of Representatives' Committee on Education and Labor to share information about patterns of illicit drug use and the work he was doing with his organization.[10]

Notwithstanding Peters's expertise, this was a controversial service that treated illicit drug users by prescribing and administering drugs without a licence. Without medical credentials, Peters studied psychedelic drugs thoroughly and self-experimented in order to understand their effects and thereby minimize the chance of adverse reactions.[11] He set up group therapies and counselling to help drug users, and carefully monitored them to create a kind of sociological profiling.

In studying Peters and his group, I examine a tension between legitimate and illegitimate medical knowledge. Where several historians have argued that the psychedelic experience could often blur dualistic points of reference – such as good/bad, subject/object, or inside/outside[12] – this chapter points to another dichotomy that was eroded by LSD. By focusing on lay knowledge[13] and illegitimate medicine, it builds on the scholarship that has examined how orthodox medicine, with its emphasis on objective measurement and scientific efficacy, has struggled to accommodate psychedelic psychotherapy, which was largely based on the subjective understanding of the patient.[14] Here, Peters's controversial organization operated on the fringe of legality, but, just like psychedelic psychiatry, which ultimately became frustrated by the efficacious requirements of medical sciences, it gathered important data and claimed positive results for its treatments of subjects.

Ultimately, this chapter argues in favour of a broad definition of harm reduction that should not focus solely on opiate abuse but also include psychedelic drug use, and hopes to spur further discussion on the topic.[15] Faced with the inherent complexity of the psychedelic experience and its potential for disquieting moments, hospitals sometimes struggled to treat LSD casualties (those who suffered from adverse LSD reactions). This led to the inception of the LSD Rescue Service, which lacked the legitimacy of the medical establishment but – precisely because it was not deemed a legitimate medical enterprise – was able to tackle problems that orthodox medicine could not.

The Making of the LSD Rescue Service

George Peters (born ca. 1937) may have encountered LSD in the US Navy as an unwitting covert test subject for the CIA's MK-Ultra project.[16] He was a frequent LSD user and had realized that the experience could lead to disquieting moments and sometimes episodes of terror and panic. Medical doctors conducting research into the therapeutic potential of LSD and psychedelics had also observed this issue. In the 1950s, they underscored the importance of taking the drug in a safe and supportive environment to minimize the chances of panic or even psychotic reactions.[17] By the same token, they were aware that the experience had several ups and downs and was rarely ever just good or bad. Most clinicians investigating the use of psychedelics as adjuncts in psychotherapy agreed, however, that problems could occur with individuals taking strong doses or with pre-existing psychological problems.[18] Average street dosage could be anything in the region of 100–300 micrograms. Age and past experiences with drugs may also have played an important part. Adolescents, whose personalities and egos were still under construction, were likelier to experience difficult moments and subsequent psychic damage than their older peers.

Peters, by contrast, was in his late twenties and had a great deal of experience with these substances. He estimated that between 3,000 and 5,000 doses of LSD were taken each week in the Chicago area in September 1965,[19] and noticed that several users suffered from adverse reactions, probably for the above reasons. "I became concerned upon learning that some had very distressing experiences (trips), and accordingly, tried to find some medicine that would cut short a bad trip,"[20] Peters wrote a few years later. He felt that doctors had not done enough to understand the mechanisms behind these difficult moments, and even less to prevent them. By the early 1960s, scores of publications underscored the potential for LSD and similar drugs to curb mental illness and alcoholism,[21] but this knowledge was by and large confined to academia and private practitioners. In any event, emergency services lacked Peters's practical knowledge of psychedelic trips.

A key event occurred that same year. One day, Peters learned that one of his friends was having a bad reaction after ingesting 300 micrograms of LSD – a strong dose by most standards. She believed her heart had stopped beating and landed in a hospital emergency room. There, she was asked to sign the admitting form but she got it into her head that the medical authorities were making her acknowledge her own demise by signing her death certificate. Peters went to the hospital to help out, and found "three policemen and 15 hospital employees listening to the girl's fantasies, but doing nothing to help her."[22] He realized that the staff did not know how to cope with the situation. He spoke with a bewildered ER doctor, who told him that he had heard of the drug but that it was the first time he was dealing with a case of LSD intoxication and he had no idea how he should treat it. Peters, on the other hand, had first-hand experience, and he suggested that the doctor administer Frenquel (azacyclonol), a tranquillizing substance known to suppress unwanted visions in people undergoing a psychotic experience. After twenty minutes, Peters and his friend left the hospital.[23] He decided that something had to be done to prevent these types of situations from occurring.

In the aftermath of this episode, Peters set up Naturalism, Inc. as a tax-exempt religious institution and created the LSD Rescue Service, also known as "LSD Rescue Group" and "LSD Line." The headquarters were decorated with posters, oriental rugs, and flashing lights to create a soothing atmosphere for those who turned up looking for assistance.[24] But the main purpose of the organization was to answer the many phone calls coming from people suffering from adverse reactions. Volunteers then travelled to the location where the subject was in need, and tried to help with "crisis-oriented psychotherapy which often includes de-sensitization processing." For acute cases, they administered drugs. Anonymity was guaranteed so that the user would not have to worry about legal issues.[25]

The Rescue Service was run by 20 part-time staff members and 130 volunteers.[26] It charged a $5 fee, but only if the user could afford it. Peters claimed to have financed the organization thanks to his full-time job as a television repairman,[27] and as a general rule, volunteers who worked full-time contributed four-fifths of their income to cover the expenses of the organization, which included renting resident apartments for volunteers where they could offer group therapy, help individuals solve their problems, and train others to become counsellors.[28]

In a letter likely written in 1966, staff member Ann Gillie explained that they helped anyone suffering from a difficult LSD experience, "in the form of a hand to hold, a shoulder to cry on – somebody who understands, and knows what to do." She estimated that about 10,000 people were taking the drug on a weekly basis, with around 100 trying it for the first time every day. This inexperience often led to discomforting moments:

> Fear – abject fear – is the most frequent cause of calls. People think they are going to die; they think their skin is disintegrating; they think they are crawling with maggots. They think their bodies have disappeared. They think they are Superman, and try to fly. They think they are Jesus Christ, and they walk the streets preaching. Very often they realize some traumatic experience they have spent their whole lives forgetting.[29]

The calls usually came from the 100 new trippers, who were ill-prepared for the powerful psychedelic experience or who had taken a strong dose. The service had probably "saved a few lives, and a few minds." The group hoped that others would follow its lead: "We have taken on the job for a simple reason. Nobody else is interested. Perhaps the responsible authorities will take an interest eventually, when this reaches epidemic proportions, but until then it's up to us. So we do our best."[30] Peters concurred: many of those who called had been turned down by all the other municipal social services. As LSD use increased, Peters began to notice a growing chasm between young drug users and medical practitioners, who looked down upon their consumption.[31]

Although Peters and his associates had experimented with LSD and similar drugs and sympathized with part of the psychedelic counterculture, they made it clear that they did not wish to encourage psychedelic drug consumption. By the same token, they refused to condemn LSD use in a war-on-drugs fashion. Instead, they wanted "to be of aid to the target populations in a more basic way – to assist them in self-understanding, understanding others, and in the understanding of them by others."[32] This very likely had to do with the nature of LSD and of the psychedelic experience. Whereas classic harm reduction for opiate abuse would focus on minimizing health hazards by distributing clean needles, the use of psychedelics could lead to life-changing experiences and to a great deal of ontological uncertainty. Accordingly, the Rescue Service paid critical attention to the meanings associated with psychedelics and how the drugs could affect users' lives. Because LSD is not dangerous to the body, they needed to concentrate on the mind.

To better understand the mechanisms behind adverse reactions, Peters experimented with LSD and like substances to trigger uncomfortable experiences, and gathered substantial data, which he then shared with "an underground net-work [sic] of dealers, adepts, and practitioners." According to him, his dissemination of information led to a sharp decline in phone calls requesting medical assistance or counselling. Some dealers even started giving free niacinamide to LSD purchasers, so that they could terminate the trip if they needed to. In practice, the antidotes were rarely used, but their mere presence in the general setting tended to reassure LSD users, who knew they could take it anytime the experience turned sour. This in turn reduced the likelihood of undergoing a difficult experience.[33] "Because this is a common vitamin that anyone may keep in their home, the actual number of emergency calls is decreasing," claimed Gillie.[34]

During the summer of 1967, the drug STP (2,5-dimethoxy-4-methyl-amphetamine) entered the drug arena. This extremely powerful and long-lasting psychedelic caused countless psychotic episodes among psychedelic drug users who thought they were taking LSD. Reports suggested it was an overwhelming experience. "You feel like your body is a conductor for tens of thousands of volts," according to one user.[35] Another tried it once and saw the walls crawling with insects.[36] Worse still, the Thorazine (chlorpromazine) treatment that was often used to counter the effects of LSD not only was ineffective but actually amplified the STP experience. Peters and one of his assistants conducted a bioassay over the course of several weeks to determine precisely the effects of the drug and how the experience could be interrupted. They concluded that the administration of Dilantin (phenytoin) during the peak of the experience was effective.[37]

From a scientific perspective, the data gathered on LSD and STP fell in a grey area. By conducting research into illicit substances, Peters attempted to bridge orthodox medicine and the drug underworld. As an insider privy to emerging underground drug trends, he could tackle a problem that orthodox medicine could not. "Research into these new drugs, while vitally necessary, is not being carried on by authorized hospitals or laboratories because of a serious lack of communication with clandestine drug users, dealers, distributors or manufacturers." The LSD Rescue Service, by contrast, was able to gather accurate information about these substances because it did not discriminate between legitimate and illegitimate knowledge.[38]

Yet, the data gathered did not remain confined to the underground. In 1967, suggestions that LSD could lead to permanent chromosome damage (which turned out to be inaccurate) were a source of concern for psychedelic drug users and the LSD Rescue Service.[39] Hence, Peters's group cooperated with the University of Chicago Department of Psychiatry in a preliminary study. They provided volunteers who had taken over 300 micrograms of LSD before or at the time of the blood tests. In turn, the research team promised Peters that the results of the study would not be kept inside the ivory tower and that they would inform the underground community of any long-term dangers.[40]

Peters's knowledge of drugs and their effects was not based solely on first-hand empirical experience. He was also influenced by orthodox medicine, such as the work conducted by Saskatchewan doctors Abram Hoffer and Humphry Osmond, who were seminal figures in the development of psychedelic therapy.[41] He used the Hoffer-Osmond Diagnostic Test in order to study drug users' perceptions of themselves, of other people, and of the objects surrounding them.[42] Hoffer and Osmond had also stressed the importance of providing patients with a supportive setting, and Peters paid critical attention to this principle to help LSD users manage their trips.

When the situation was desperate, psychopharmacology could be used for acute reactions. Peters preferred niacinamide, a derivative of vitamin B3, which was effective within the hour and had no side effects. Niacin, on the other hand could lead to flushing, itching, and shortness of breath. Thorazine, commonly used in hospitals to terminate LSD trips, was available by prescription only, and prolonged use could lead to effects similar to those of prefrontal lobotomy. Frenquel (by prescription) was an interesting drug because it did not block perception and allowed users to find positive meaning in their bad trip days after the experience: "Whatever hang-ups were responsible for the panic reaction in the first place usually pop into consciousness again within a few days of the trip in hallucinatory, more immediately recognizable forms."[43] In cases of outright violent reactions, the fast-acting barbiturate Carbrital (pentobarbital + carbromal) was deemed effective, and when no drugs were available, eight ounces of sugar or honey raised the blood sugar level, which was effective in sedating the patient and interrupting most perceptual changes.[44]

Peters's desire to protect drug users was sometimes in keeping with classic harm reduction. In the same way that methadone can be substituted for heroin, a more delicate substitute for amphetamines was found to prevent drug users from turning to Methedrine (methamphetamine hydrochloride), which helped enhance their mental processes and alleviated the feeling of physical lethargy that could be associated with the LSD experience. The vitamin thiamine hydrochloride (available without prescription) had a stimulant power equal to amphetamines, but "without the debilitating side-effects of the latter." However, Peters cautioned against overuse because it produced an imbalance in the organism's vitamin structure, even though it could be compensated to some extent with daily intake of food rich in vitamin B. Using this technique, the Rescue Service claimed to have treated nine cases of addiction.[45]

That Peters had no medical credentials did not stop him from conducting rigorous medical investigations in accordance with the scientific paradigms of the time and guided by ethics. To measure how the effects of LSD could be countered with Frenquel, he and his colleagues ran a double-blind controlled test, with subjects given Frenquel or saline solutions intravenously. This appeared to confirm the efficacy of Frenquel, but they stopped the study after ten cases when they realized that the investigations were unethical because they were carried out during emergency situations. After September 1966, they ceased to give the drug intravenously in favour of oral administration, probably because of the risks involved with needles during rescue missions.[46]

The Rescue Service also gathered substantial amounts of data on illicit drug users in the Chicago area and produced broad estimates on their numbers and profiles in 1968. Users were broken down into age brackets, with information about yearly incomes, socio-economic backgrounds, and the motivations behind drug use (escapism, recreation, and so on). An estimated 25,000 doses of illicit LSD were distributed every week. A map of the metropolitan area showed where LSD and cannabis users could be found congregating in certain parts of the city.[47]

Religion appeared to play a part in the healing process. Peters had been influenced by eastern spirituality: he had a statue of the Buddha in his bedroom and played "Zen music" to participants in the sessions he organized in his apartment. The attorney who assisted him with legal matters and other observers thought that "he was some kind of saint."[48] Like many LSD users with spiritual inclinations, Peters resented the top-down religions that framed God as a higher supernatural being ruling over His people. Instead, God should be found within the individual.[49] So one exercise he liked to prescribe was to sit in front of a mirror and repeat "I am the Lord thy God" over and over. In doing so, LSD casualties found a form of empowerment that gradually increased their level of self-confidence.[50]

This was part of a broader strategy to help LSD users struggling with its after-effects. Indeed, the Rescue Service did more than just assist people undergoing difficult LSD experiences; it also provided counselling to help them get over the long-term effects of the psychedelic experience. If the user had trouble identifying problems or was too anxious to speak during therapy, Librium (chlordiazepoxide) and Ritalin (methylphenidate) could be used to facilitate discussions.[51] Some drug users suffered from flashbacks months later and struggled to live with them. For example, a nineteen-year-old experimenter called the service and reported that "he was feeling the individuality woven fibers in his sheets as if his skin could see them. He said he couldn't sleep and felt as if his nerves were about to crumble." Peters managed to calm him down over the phone and eased his anxiety. The tranquillizers he had taken had not helped, so he took niacin for several months and the symptoms waned.[52]

Peters placed great emphasis on choosing the right words and frames of reference for the right audience, and conversely of listening to the caller and expressing empathy. Distraught parents looking for help for their children would have a frantic and fast-paced tone, while teenagers under the influence might struggle to verbalize the psychedelic effects and express their pain and discomfort. "When a person gets like that, one minute on the clock would seem like 50 years in his head. He begins to feel nobody can talk with him, that he's the only person on earth." But because Peters had first-hand experience of the drug, he could at least attempt to calm them down by using the same language of trips and relating to the users' feelings.[53]

LSD and psychedelics have the power to radically shake up ontological certainties, and under the influence of these mind-altering substances, users came to realize the consensual nature of reality and struggled to return to whatever role they might have had in society. Many had dropped out of school, quit their jobs, and generally become devoid of energy and inspiration. Hence, the Rescue Service offered a form of psychotherapy that was geared towards returning LSD users to a productive role in society. To achieve this, counsellors paid attention to their wishes and worked with them to find a long-term occupation. The Rescue Service set up workshops where they could take the time to express themselves through crafts and art; later, users found new careers in carpentry, leatherworking, or electronics.[54] One unhappy man came to Peters looking for help. When asked what he really wanted to do, he answered that he longed to be a successful businessman. He found liberation through counselling and achieved some success, but still wasn't happy so he came back looking for more answers. Peters told him to spread out the contents of his wallet on the table and burn the money ($3,500). He walked away allegedly cured from materialism, and went on to become a famous psychologist.[55]

A recurrent problem Peters encountered was young drug users' feeling of alienation from American society. "These young people say that they feel accomplishment within our American system is constraining and does not allow for self-expression, has inhibited them and made them more withdrawn."[56] Many had turned to drugs hoping to find "self-balance or adjustment," often because of their family environment, where "either one or both parents were alcoholic, schizophrenic, epileptic or eccentric." Still others had been brought up too rigidly or too permissively, and they struggled to lead a balanced life. They typically came from middle- and upper-class families and were between fifteen and twenty-two years of age.[57]

Peters and his associates felt it was necessary to actively promote their work by favouring community outreach. The Rescue Service advertised its services in newspapers and also gave presentations in schools to inform children about LSD and psychedelics. In March 1968, for example, staff gave 176 talks on drugs in elementary and secondary schools. Former users shared their experiences with students replacing the mysterious aspect of illicit substances with credible information.[58] Parents became interested in the service because they wanted to protect their children from drug use, and Peters set up family counselling sessions "since it is the anxiety within the family environment which tends to encourage drug abuse."[59] In doing so, he also tackled the problem of runaway children and tried to reconcile them with their parents.[60]

Looking at Peters and the LSD Rescue Service blurs the lines between the counterculture and the so-called mainstream society it criticized.[61] Rather than retreat into drug hedonism and withdraw from social and political causes, part of the counterculture was actively engaged in society instead of rejecting it outright. Peters, a Doctor of Divinity, seemed to have found inspiration in the psychedelic experience and was moved to help his fellow human beings as a result. Likewise, religious scholar Morgan Shipley has documented how a group of Tennessee mystics led by Stephen Gaskin travelled to New York City to set up a relief program in the South Bronx in the 1980s. They "interpreted the oneness of mystical consciousness as a catalyst for local and global engaged activism."[62] Such an involvement with the community thus found itself at the crossroads of politics and spirituality, and further illustrates how psychedelics could blur the lines between these spheres "through real-world projects of social justice."[63]

The LSD Rescue Service often dealt with young people who were deeply dissatisfied with postwar American society and turned to drugs to withdraw from it. Instead of helping them retreat into countercultural enclaves and condoning their rejection of society, however, the volunteers of the Rescue Service ensured that they were returned to the community with productive roles. Peters himself is a good example of this synthesis. He remained actively involved in the psychedelic counterculture by organizing movie screenings seminars, and rock concerts all revolving around psychedelics,[64] and he also tried to set up a head shop on the South Side of Chicago where enthusiasts could acquire the artwork, jewels, and clothing produced in the rehabilitation program.[65] However, these activities did not stop him from taking on a serious public health problem in a major US city.

A Controversial Service?

With all the work and the seemingly positive results, the media soon took note of the LSD Rescue Service. In 1966, one reporter compared Peters's organization to Alcoholics Anonymous. "A call to Peters's pad would bring him or a volunteer worker rushing to offer aid and comfort."[66] When asked about his motivations, Peters simply answered that no one else was doing it. In spite of the LSD Rescue Service's goodwill, however, one journalist published some disturbing facts about the functioning of the association: "There have been occasions when the only person available at Acid Rescue has himself been too spaced-out to be able to help a bum-tripper, and it has been said that LSD Rescue has given as many as twelve seconals (a powerful barbiturate) to bring them down from acid – and you never give anyone that many seconals, it can kill them." Even more disturbing were rumours that the association was collaborating with the Gang Intelligence Unit of the Chicago Police Department to harass a neighbouring Young Lords chapter in exchange for protection.[67]

The local police was also leery. When Peters called the head of the police narcotics unit and tried to explain his approach, the latter was not receptive and warned him that handling illegal drugs would make him subject to arrest like everyone else. As a result, Peters began to suspect that he was under police surveillance. On October 26, his apartment was raided and one policeman reported that he had found a cannabis cigarette. The raid was conducted after someone claimed to have purchased five joints from Peters for the sum of $5 in his apartment. Peters dismissed the price as ridiculous and contended that he barely ever was in his own apartment.[68]

These hostile reactions are not surprising, given the broader context of increasing drug use and the negative publicity surrounding psychedelics at the time. In 1965, former Harvard University professor Timothy Leary and bestselling novelist Ken Kesey, arguably the two most vocal figures to promote LSD, were arrested for possession of cannabis.[69] One year later, two events made the headlines and provided ample ammunition for opponents of LSD and psychedelics. A five-year-old girl accidentally ingested a sugar cube saturated with LSD and was taken to hospital,[70] and a brutal murder was also attributed to the drug.[71] Swiss firm Sandoz, the patent holder of LSD, withdrew it from distribution in 1966 because of the growing controversy surrounding the drug. This in turn created new black market opportunities, but without the quality and purity of licit LSD. Adverse reactions with poor-quality materials are very likely to have increased as a consequence, along with charges of manufacturing, distributing, and using an illicit substance.

The political climate of the time did not help either. In 1966, California and New York became the first states to ban non-medical LSD. The drug was federally prohibited in 1968, and the 1970 Comprehensive Drug Abuse Prevention and Control Act turned it into a Schedule I drug, deemed highly dangerous to health and of no medical value. Further, opiate use had increased throughout the 1960s and peaked in 1970, creating a nationwide sense of a drug epidemic. By contrast, the Dutch politics of harm reduction of the 1970s were helped by a more favourable context, "in which liberalism dominated the ideological terrain and anti-authoritarian sentiment was widespread in society at large."[72] As well, these liberal attitudes towards drug users can be traced back to the local counterculture in Amsterdam, which was much less political than its American or French counterparts, and attracted much wider support and sympathy.[73] This was simply not the case in the United States, where law-and-order candidates such as Richard Nixon and Ronald Reagan secured major political victories by blaming many of the country's social ills on the counterculture. The former branded Leary "the most dangerous man in America"[74] after he escaped from prison, and the latter claimed that a hippie was someone who "dresses like Tarzan, has hair like Jane, and smells like Cheetah."[75]

In this context, and from a legal perspective, Peters's enterprise was certainly a bold one and contrasted with a similar service on the other side of the Atlantic that was culturally sanctioned and officially funded. Indeed, Amsterdam also had its LSD rescue service in the form of the *Laurier* (Laurel), which offered assistance to people undergoing difficult experiences with the drug in a special room. As in San Francisco's Haight-Ashbury Free Clinic, Amsterdamers benefited from health care facilities for the local drug scene and drug tourism. Unlike its California counterpart, however, this was liberally funded by the city, rather than being the initiative of a few who realized that something had to be done to fight the squalor of the Summer of Love, or of those like Peters who felt that hospitals were ill-equipped to tackle the problem of adverse LSD reactions.[76]

Unlike the Chicago police, several medical doctors thought Peters was well-intentioned, even if they found him a bit strange and eccentric. Although the local chapter of the American Medical Association treated him with suspicion, the Cook County Board of Health gradually came to appreciate his work.[77] The city's health commissioner, Samuel Adelman, and nationally syndicated medical columnist Walter Alvarez, whose support Peters had been courting, felt that he was raising important issues. Alvarez, in particular, was receptive: "He's done some good work, even though he doesn't have the credentials for it, and he's tackled a problem that no one else was interested in ... If any man will go out at night and help people badly poisoned by a drug, I'm for him."[78]

Abram Hoffer, for one, did more than just laud the social benefits of Peters's group, and endorsed his research into psychedelic drug users and into ways of helping minimize the risk of bad trips. In an introduction to an article written by Peters in the journal *Schizophrenia,* Hoffer defended his choice to let Peters discuss his findings despite his lack of medical credentials, and then praised him for helping so many LSD users:

> George Peters and his group have between them helped more drug users than any other single group I know about and have taken an interest in these unfortunate and sick people rarely equaled by professionals. His observations and experience deserve to be recorded. The non-medical use of drugs has expanded beyond the ability of physicians and hospitals to deal with it. Perhaps the solution is being pioneered by groups like The LSD Rescue Group, using simple, safe and effective counter-acting chemicals.[79]

Alvarez, who was also a medical doctor and gastroenterologist eventually teamed up with Peters. He had a reputation for caring for the young and sympathized with those who did not like being bossed around by grown-ups, so it was no surprise that he left his gastroenterology practice and began tackling the problem of drug use among youth. He was impressed by Peters, whom he had met when the latter repaired his TV set, and by Peters's knowledge of drugs. He ultimately supported him by writing prescriptions and helping him purchase medication when the organization was low on funds.[80]

It is easy to see why medical doctors like Alvarez and Hoffer were so supportive and enthusiastic. By October 1966, Peters's methods were a success in the Chicago area. The number of LSD casualties plummeted from fifty to sixty a week to one or two a month,[81] leading to "an average of one known bad trip in 25,000."[82] Over the next three years, Peters declared that they had treated more than 7,600 drug users and that the Chicago office received approximately 200 calls a day seeking assistance, such as ways of ending an adverse reaction to a drug, with the Rescue Service then offering psychotherapy and counselling.[83] The group also claimed to have helped fifty-nine people suffering from lethargy and energy loss by providing them with daily intakes of thiamine hydrochloride (vitamin B1). These people "subsequently became active and effective individuals."[84]

Examining public health problems associated with LSD in other major US cities can be useful in measuring the impact of the Rescue Service and in placing its achievements in perspective. In New York City, fears of an epidemic led to a high-profile campaign to ban the drug. William Frosch of Bellevue Hospital, for one, noticed a sharp increase in LSD-related admissions in the psychiatric hospital from 1965 onward. For him, these were correlated with the increasing availability of the drug on the black market. During the 1966 US Senate narcotics hearings to discuss the utility and dangers of LSD, Frosch voiced his concerns about the many hospitalizations. Among the extreme forms of panic reactions, some people attempted to cut their wrists or jumped out of a window. A twenty-three-year-old man was also admitted after nearly stabbing a friend in the back and hearing "God's voice" following an LSD experience.[85] Two other New York medical doctors, Donald Louria and Robert Baird also testified before the Senate, pointing to the increase in LSD casualties in the city and arguing in favour of stricter measures against the drug.[86]

A year later, the situation was even worse in San Francisco, during the infamous Summer of Love. With so many teenagers travelling to the Haight-Ashbury district and hoping to become part of this countercultural Mecca came drug abuse, urban squalor, and sexual violence. Arthur Carfoni, who headed the Impact Plan at San Francisco General Hospital, was alarmed by the growing number of psychotic episodes:

> To date, our business ... has shot up to a terrific amount. For instance yesterday, approximately 14 people were brought into the hospital for

adverse reactions ... directly attributable to drugs ... It's a very – rather mixed thing. For some it's the beginning of a long-term psychotic process. For others it's one more adverse reaction which possibly will terminate within 48 hours, but certainly any type of psychotic reaction is something that's going to leave scars in the person's development.

What makes this statement even more troubling is that San Francisco had its own LSD Rescue Mission headed by Allan Cohen and Hank Harrison. Cohen was a clinical psychologist at the University of California at Berkeley; Harrison had been the manager of the Grateful Dead before their hour of glory, but he is best known for being the father of pop star Courtney Love. They had taken LSD over 150 times between them and ultimately concluded that the drug was dangerous, particularly for teenagers looking for chemical enlightenment or for something better than the comfort of American suburbia.[87] While it is difficult to assess the impact of the Rescue Mission due to lack of sources, it is worth noting that Harrison and Peters were collaborating – Harrison was invited to Chicago for a seminar and to show his educational movie *LSD-25*.[88]

Peters's enterprise now had connections across the country and abroad, and was praised for its brave medical relief. Yet its impact extended far beyond medical assistance and offered a kind of social rehabilitation program "to return drug users to a useful position in society." Peters stated that "in the past four years, LSD Rescue has returned more than 900 drop-outs to jobs or schools"; it also trained around 500 in carpentry and electronics as part of this program. Many former patients joined the staff and volunteers and helped defray most of the operating expenses by returning a percentage of their incomes to the program.[89]

According to a report, Naturalism, Inc. had created another 525 similar services patterned after the Chicago model by 1970: "We chose Chicago, Illinois as the starting point because of the Midwest morality, feeling that if it could be successfully run there that the rest of the country could go easily." More importantly, the organization began to shift away from drug issues and turned to mainstream social relief. In 1968, it set up the "lonely line" telephone service so elderly people could have someone to talk to when they wanted. In 1970, it put up an emergency shelter in Los Angeles for those needing food and housing, and in 1974, it ran a Samaritan service to help prostitutes through a form of counselling, particularly those who feared they might be institutionalized or jailed.[90]

Peters's LSD Rescue Service was interested not only in social relief but also in other, more radical missions that added an extra layer of complexity to the eclectic organization. In May 1967, it was poised to offer bond and lawyers for people arrested on drug charges. "It will be run like insurance with a $5 membership fee and $10/year dues," Peters wrote.[91] During the infamous 1968 Democratic Party convention that resulted in mass arrests and widespread police brutality,[92] he and several volunteers set up a booth in Lincoln Park for activists camping there, even if the latter were uninterested and local authorities ultimately saw it as just another problem. In Springfield, Illinois, they lobbied for more progressive cannabis laws[93] and against a bill designed to make psychedelics illegal.[94]

This particular form of pro-drug activism occurred at a time when the legalize marijuana movement (LeMar) was well underway and gaining momentum. In October 1969, clergyman David Brandenburger of Madison, Wisconsin, wrote to LeMar head Mike Aldrich seeking more information about his work. Crucially, Brandenburger also told Aldrich about his intention to found a Drug Rescue Center to curb drug abuse, which he explicitly defined as bad, addictive drugs, and made it clear that he was "in favour of using drugs to expand one's consciousness."[95] In response, Aldrich directed Brandenburger to Peters for further information and told him that Peters's LSD Rescue Service "had a pretty good bum trip service going on for several years."[96] Perhaps this centre – if it ever came into existence – was one of the many spinoffs patterned after Peters's organization. In any event, such a letter further suggests that Peters had become a well-respected figure.

However, examining the history of the LSD Rescue Service begs the question of whether the group's facts and figures are reliable. Although many of his supporters publicly endorsed his work and achievements, which seems to show that the data were indeed reliable, the latter part of Peters's life is cause for caution and further illustrates how this fascinating figure defies easy classification.

Parapsychologist Stanley Krippner had met Peters courtesy of Virginia Glenn, who is often dubbed the "midwife of the human potential movement" and who had a keen interest in alternative spirituality and altered states of consciousness. Krippner had joined the advisory board of the LSD

Rescue Service and was pleased with the initial results. But after Peters set up a branch in Los Angeles, the funding dried up. According to Krippner, the contributions coming from the volunteers were just one aspect of the finances and Peters had hitherto been able to count on wealthy supporters. Peters now began dealing cocaine and convinced his female volunteers to become prostitutes in order to make up for the loss of funds.[97]

By the late 1970s Peters's Church of Naturalism in Los Angeles had turned into a cult. Adherents were required to undergo a forty-day sensory deprivation exercise to gain membership, but more to the point, the church had become a front for cocaine trafficking.[98] Peters lived an eccentric lifestyle on his Laurel Canyon estate, far removed from the humanitarian ideals he had espoused in the 1960s. The estate hosted several rock bands and had its own security. Peters ate only the finest food and engaged in promiscuous sex. He was raided several times, with the police finding cocaine, Quaaludes (methaqualone), cannabis, hashish, and cash, but the drug charges never stuck. In November 1982, a one-time church secretary and a cocaine delivery man brutally murdered Peters and the church's treasurer on the estate.[99] According to Krippner, the two were expecting to find vast amounts of profits from the cocaine scheme, but they found nothing.[100]

Conclusion

How and why such a transformation occurred is open to speculation. Perhaps it was the turn to cocaine and the shift away from psychedelics that caused George Peters to shun his earlier role of drug reformer and to embrace unethical profits. This dark twist makes the whole story even more intriguing.

Nevertheless, this should not diminish Peters's achievements. In many ways, he pioneered the "event medicine" of psychedelic rave festivals today, with entire areas dedicated to attendees suffering from adverse reactions, where they can count on knowledgeable volunteers similar to those in the LSD Rescue Service (see in particular Zendo, a self-described "psychedelic harm reduction" non-profit organization[101]). Moreover, Peters was a highly idiosyncratic character. He was not afraid to self-experiment to gain insider knowledge, and, convinced that someone had to do the job, he practised medicine without a license in order to help LSD casualties. Perhaps his most significant quality was his capacity to build so many bridges to others around him. He was prepared to work with drug users, social outcasts, the counterculture, medical doctors, and the police, and did not see all these categories as irreconcilable. Unlike Timothy Leary, who has often been blamed for promoting reckless drug hedonism, Peters was active in the broad psychedelic culture while simultaneously ensuring that no one got hurt by overindulging.

When viewed as part of the broader history of harm reduction, the LSD Rescue Service appears even more remarkable. If we agree that "classic" harm reduction focusing on opiate addiction came about in the 1960s and 1970s, or in the 1980s in response to the HIV/AIDS crisis, then this was almost a century after the first cases of morphine addiction. LSD, on the other hand, which was discovered in 1938 and first tested on a human subject in 1943,[102] had reached only a relatively small number of Americans by the late 1950s and became a popular street drug essentially just a few years before the inception of the Rescue Service. As this chapter has suggested, this can be explained by both the complex nature of the psychedelic experience and the ethics of the psychedelic counterculture, which led certain individuals like Peters to take care of drug users.

Further studies would be useful to find out about the legacy of the LSD Rescue Service and whether medical facilities across the country incorporated the knowledge and data gathered throughout Peters's research. In a recent survey of the literature on psychedelic research and the risks associated with psychedelic drug use, Matthew Johnson, William Richards, and Rolland Griffiths cite benzodiazepine anxiolytics as the best pharmacological intervention; diazepam as the quickest antidote; and risperidone and olanzapine as the best drugs to use in case the psychotic reaction reaches an unmanageable stage. They also make it clear that chemical antidotes should be the last resort if a user is undergoing a severe adverse reaction.[103] At no point, however, are the findings of the LSD Rescue Service mentioned, which suggests that Peters's story and work have remained confined to the memory of a few.

By contrast, more recent stories point to the assimilation of lay knowledge into orthodox medicine. In 2006, a research group published a study that suggested that LSD and psilocybin could be used to treat cluster headaches (an excruciating condition).[104] What had led them to conduct this research was anecdotal evidence of people suffering from cluster headaches who had self-administered psychedelics hoping to alleviate their condition. One of them was Bob Wold, who started the ClusterBusters website (https://clusterbusters.org/) to gather information about the potential treatment of cluster headaches with psychedelics. For him, taking a single minimal dose every six months was enough to help end the attacks.

Future studies could also explore in greater detail the role of the psychedelic counterculture in the development of harm reduction. In particular, the story of Howard Lotsof and his research into ibogaine reveals an overlap with the first needle-exchange programs in New York City, ACT UP, and the movement to decriminalize marijuana.[105] That history, along with the one discussed in this chapter, points to a far more complex relationship between science, knowledge, and the psychedelic counterculture than has previously been assumed.[106]

Notes

1 Ingo Ilja Michels, Heino Stöver, and Ralf Gerlach, "Substitution Treatment for Opioid Addicts in Germany," *Harm Reduction Journal* 4 (2007); Maja Meise, Xi Wang, Marie-Luise Sauter, Yan-ping Bao, Jie Shi, Zhi-min Liu, and Lin Lu, "Harm Reduction for Injecting Opiate Users: An Update and Implications in China," *Acta Pharmacologica Sinica* 30, 5 (2009): 513–21; Victoria Smye, Annette J. Brown, Colleen Varcoe, and Viviane Josewski, "Harm Reduction, Methadone Maintenance Treatment and the Root Causes of Health and Social Inequities: An Intersectional Lens in the Canadian Context," *Harm Reduction Journal* 8, 17 (2011).

2 Gordon Roe, "Harm Reduction as Paradigm: Is Better than Bad Good Enough? The Origins of Harm Reduction," *Critical Public Health* 15, 3 (2005): 244; Gemma Blok, "Pampering 'Needle Freaks' or Caring for Chronic Addicts? Early Debates on Harm Reduction in Amsterdam, 1972–82," *Social History of Alcohol and Drugs* 22, 2 (2008): 243–61.

3 Diane Riley and Pat O'Hare, "Harm Reduction: History, Definition, and Practice," in *Harm Reduction: National and International Perspectives,* ed. James A. Inciardi and Lana D. Harrison (Thousand Oaks, CA: 1999), 2; Pat O'Hare, "Merseyside, the First Harm Reduction Conferences, and the Early History of Harm Reduction," *International Journal of Drug Policy* 18, 2 (2007): 141–44.

4 Peter Stoker, "History of Harm Reduction – Provenance and Politics, Part 1," *Journal of Global Drug Policy and Practice* 1, 2 (Summer 2007).

5 Blok, "Pampering 'Needle Freaks.'"

6 David T. Courtwright, "The Prepared Mind: Marie Nyswander, Methadone Maintenance, and the Metabolic Theory of Addiction," *Addiction* 92, 3 (1997): 257–65; Nancy

D. Campbell and Anne M. Lovell, "The History of the Development of Buprenorphine as an Addiction Therapeutic," *Annals of the New York Academy of Sciences* 1248, 1 (2012): 124–39; Claire Clark, "'Chemistry Is the New Hope': Therapeutic Communities and Methadone Maintenance, 1965–71," *Social History of Alcohol and Drugs* 26, 2 (2012): 192–216.

7   David F. Musto, *The American Disease: Origins of Narcotic Control* (New York: Oxford University Press, 1999), 76.

8   Ibid., 83.

9   For some discussions on the history of psychedelics, see Martin A. Lee and Bruce Shlain, *Acid Dreams: The Complete Social History of LSD: The CIA, the Sixties, and Beyond* (New York: Grove Weidenfeld, 1985); Jay Stevens, *Storming Heaven: LSD and the American Dream* (New York: Perennial Library, 1988); David Farber, "The Intoxicated/Illegal Nation: Drugs in the Sixties Counterculture," in *Imagine Nation: The American Counterculture of the 1960s and '70s,* ed. Peter Braunstein and Michael William Doyle (New York: Routledge, 2002), 17–40; Jesse Jarnow, *Heads: A Biography of Psychedelic America* (Philadelphia: Da Capo Press, 2016).

10   "Statement of George Peters, Director of Naturalism Inc., Chicago, Ill.," in *Hearings before the Select Subcommittee on Education of the Committee on Education and Labor, House of Representatives, 91st Congress, Hearings Held in Washington, DC, July 9, 10, 11, 14, and 21, 1969; New York, NY, July 25, 1969* (Washington, DC: US Government Printing Office, 1970), 864–78.

11   For more on the history of self-experimentation in medicine, see Lawrence K. Altman, *Who Goes First? The Story of Self-Experimentation in Medicine,* reprint ed. (Berkeley: University of California Press, 1998). Though part of this chapter examines efforts to curtail "bad trips" in Chicago, recent scholarship has called into question this notion and pointed to far more ambivalent interpretations of these difficult moments. See Erika Dyck and Chris Elcock, "Reframing Bummer Trips: Scientific and Cultural Explanations to Adverse Reactions to Psychedelic Drug Use," *Social History of Alcohol and Drugs* 34, 2 (2020): 271–96.

12   Erika Dyck, *Psychedelic Psychiatry: LSD from Clinic to Campus* (Baltimore: Johns Hopkins University Press, 2008); Chris Elcock, "From Acid Revolution to Entheogenic Evolution: Psychedelic Philosophy in the Sixties and Beyond," *Journal of American Culture* 36, 4 (2013): 296–311; Sarah Shortall, "Psychedelic Drugs and the Problem of Experience," *Past and Present* 222, suppl. 9 (2014): 187–206; Morgan Shipley, *Psychedelic Mysticism: Transforming Consciousness, Religious Experiences, and Voluntary Peasants in Postwar America* (Lanham, MD: Lexington Books, 2015).

13   I elaborate on this concept used by Suzanne L. Taylor in "Evidence-Based Policy? The Re-Medicalization of Cannabis and the Role of Expert Committees in the UK, 1972–1982," *International Journal of Drug Policy* 37 (2016): 129–35.

14   Matthew Oram, "Efficacy and Enlightenment: LSD Psychotherapy and the Drug Amendments of 1962," *Journal of the History of Medicine and Allied Sciences* 69, 2 (2012): 221–50.

15 Psychedelic harm reduction has been briefly touched upon in relation to the use of ayahuasca. See Kenneth W. Tupper, "The Globalization of Ayahuasca: Harm Reduction or Benefit Maximization?" *International Journal of Drug Policy* 19, 4 (2008): 297–303.

16 For more on the CIA's covert involvement with LSD, see John Marks, "Intelligence or 'Witches' Potion,'" in *The Search for the "Manchurian Candidate": The CIA and Mind Control: The Secret Story of Behavioral Sciences* (New York: W.W. Norton, 1988), 54–130.

17 Duncan Blewett and Nick Chwelos, *Handbook for the Therapeutic Use of Lysergic Acid Deithylamide-25: Individual and Group Procedures* (1959), ch. 6, http://www.maps.org/research-archive/ritesofpassage/lsdhandbook.pdf. For a similar and popular guide, see Timothy Leary, Ralph Metzner, and Richard Alpert, *The Psychedelic Experience: A Manual Based on the Tibetan Book of the Dead* (New York: Citadel Press, 1995).

18 Sidney Cohen, "Lysergic Acid Diethylamide: Side Effects and Complications," *Journal of Nervous and Mental Disease* 130, 1 (1960): 30–40.

19 "Naturalism, Inc.," 1968, 2, Kent State University, Special Collections and Archives, Virginia Glenn Papers (Glenn Papers), box 8, folder 57.

20 George Peters, "A Study of Psychedelic Drug Users," *Schizophrenia* 2 (1970): 103.

21 Torsten Passie, *Psycholytic and Psychedelic Therapy Research, 1931–1995: A Complete International Bibliography* (Hannover: Laurentius Publishers, 1997).

22 Peters, "A Study of Psychedelic Drug Users," 103.

23 Ann Gillie, undated letter, Columbia University, Rare Book and Manuscript Library, Peter Stafford Papers (Stafford Papers), box 2, folder "Bad Trips."

24 Robert Ross, "Chicago's Improbable Rescue Team," *Chicago Tribune,* September 21, 1969.

25 "Naturalism, Inc.," 2.

26 "Drug Center Chief Fights City on License," n.d., Stanford University Libraries, Department of Special Collections, R. Buckminster Fuller Papers (Fuller Papers), M1090, box 201, folder 4, series 2 Dymaxion Chronofile, subseries 1.

27 William Braden, "George: Acidhead or Saint?" *Chicago Sun-Times,* November 28, 1966, 4, Stafford Papers, box 11, folder "Peters, George."

28 Peters, "A Study of Psychedelic Drug Users," 105.

29 Ann Gillie, undated letter, Stafford Papers, box 2, folder "Bad Trips."

30 Ibid.

31 Ross, "Chicago's Improbable Rescue Team."

32 "Naturalism, Inc.," 2.

33 Lynn House, "The Editor Game," *Innerspace* no. 3, 1966, folder "Innerspace," box 21, Stafford Papers.

34 Ann Gillie, undated letter, Stafford Papers, box 2, folder "Bad Trips."

35 Don McNeill, "Is Acid Obsolete? The New Letters Are STP," *Village Voice,* April 12, 1967, Stafford Papers, box 13, folder "STP."

36 Amelie Edwards (real name obscured upon request), interview by the author, midtown apartment, New York City, March 22, 2013.

37 Peters, "A Study of Psychedelic Drug Users," 107.

38 "Naturalism, Inc.," 4.

39 Maimon. M. Cohen, Michelle J. Marinello, and Nathan Back, "Chromosomal Damage in Human Leukocytes Induced by Lysergic Acid Diethylamide," *Science* 155, 3768 (1967): 1417–19.

40 "Naturalism, Inc.," 4. Other than this source, I could not locate any evidence to illustrate this collaboration, so further research on this would be useful.

41 Dyck, *Psychedelic Psychiatry.*

42 Peters, "A Study of Psychedelic Drug Users," 105.

43 House, "The Editor Game."

44 Peters, "A Study of Psychedelic Drug Users," 106.

45 House, "The Editor Game."

46 Peters, "A Study of Psychedelic Drug Users," 105.

47 "Naturalism, Inc.," 11–14.

48 Braden, "George: Acidhead or Saint?" 4.

49 For more on this, see Robert C. Fuller, *Stairways to Heaven: Drugs in American Religious History* (Boulder, CO: Westview Press, 2000); Elcock, "From Acid Revolution."

50 Stephanie Harrington, "Bad Trip on LSD Line? The Return Fare is $5," *Village Voice* 7 (January 12–18, 1967).

51 Peters, "A Study of Psychedelic Drug Users," 106.

52 Ibid., 104–5.

53 Ross, "Chicago's Improbable Rescue Team."

54 Peters, "A Study of Psychedelic Drug Users," 104.

55 Harrington, "Bad Trip on LSD Line?"

56 Peters, "A Study of Psychedelic Drug Users," 104.

57 Ibid., 105.

58 Ibid., 104.

59 Ibid.

60 Ross, "Chicago's Improbable Rescue Team." For a history of runaway children in the 1960s, see Karen M. Staller, *Runaways: How the Sixties Counterculture Shaped Today's Practices and Policies* (New York: Columbia University Press, 2006).

61 Thomas Frank, *The Conquest of Cool: Business Culture, Counterculture, and the Rise of Hip Consumerism,* 1st ed. (Chicago: University Of Chicago Press, 1998); Arthur Marwick, *The Sixties: Cultural Revolution in Britain, France, Italy, and the United States, c.1958–c.1974* (Oxford and New York: Oxford University Press, 1998), 13; David Farber, "Building the Counterculture, Creating Right Livelihoods: The Counterculture at Work," *The Sixties* 6, 1 (2013): 1–24; Joshua Clark Davis, "The Business of Getting High: Head Shops, Countercultural Capitalism, and the Marijuana Legalization Movement," *The Sixties* 8, 1 (2015): 27–49.

62 Morgan Shipley, "'This Season's People': Stephen Gaskin, Psychedelic Religion, and a Community of Social Justice," *Journal for the Study of Radicalism* 9, 2 (2015): 42.

63 Ibid., 44–45.

64 George Peters to Virginia Glenn, May 4, 1967, Glenn Papers, box 3, folder 114.

65 George Peters to Virginia Glenn, early June 1967, Glenn Papers, box 3, folder 128. Joshua Davis has recently argued that head shops in the 1960s were not just a form of hip commercialism; rather, they were places around which the counterculture could rally and helped it stay afloat well into the 1970s. Here, the LSD Rescue Service offered a variant of this empowerment by helping drug users find a meaningful purpose in society. This further blurred the line between the counterculture and mainstream society. See Davis, "The Business of Getting High."

66 Braden, "George: Acidhead or Saint?" 4.

67 John Indian, "Bum Trip at Acid Rescue," *Chicago Seed*, n.d., Stafford Papers, box 17, folder "Seed." A bum trip or bummer is an adverse reaction to a psychedelic drug.

68 Braden, "George: Acidhead or Saint?"

69 For biographies of Leary and Kesey, see, respectively, John Higgs, *I Have America Surrounded: The Life of Timothy Leary* (Fort Lee, NJ: Barricade Books, 2006); Rick Dodgson, *It's All a Kind of Magic: The Young Ken Kesey* (Madison: University of Wisconsin Press, 2013).

70 Alfred Friendly Jr., "Police Fear Child Swallowed LSD," *New York Times*, April 7, 1966.

71 "NY Man 'Flying on LSD' Kills Mother-in-Law," *Daily Republic*, April 12, 1966.

72 Blok, "Pampering 'Needle Freaks,'" 244.

73 Ibid., 246.

74 Quoted in Higgs, *I Have America Surrounded*, 3.

75 Quoted in Peter Braunstein and Michael William Doyle, "Introduction," in Braunstein and Doyle, *Imagine Nation*, 6.

76 Blok, "Pampering 'Needle Freaks,'" 247.

77 House, "The Editor Game."

78 Braden, "George: Acidhead or Saint?"

79 Peters, "A Study of Psychedelic Drug Users," 103.

80 Ross, "Chicago's Improbable Rescue Team."

81 Peters, "A Study of Psychedelic Drug Users," 104.

82 "Naturalism, Inc.," 3.

83 Frank Giles, "'We Help Anyone, Anytime – As Long as It Hurts No Other,'" n.d., Fuller Papers, box 201, folder 4, series 2 Dymaxion Chronofile, subseries 1.

84 Peters, "A Study of Psychedelic Drug Users," 107.

85 William A. Frosch, "Statement of Dr. William A. Frosch, Psychiatrist, Bellevue Hospital, New York, N.Y.," in *The Narcotic Rehabilitation Act of 1966: Hearings before a Special Subcommittee of the Committee on the Judiciary, United States Senate, 89th Congress, 2nd Session, January 25–27, May 12, 13, 19, 23 and 25, June 14 and 15, July 19, 1966* (Washington, DC: US Government Printing Office, 1966), 302–5.

86 Donald B. Louria, "Statement of Dr. Donald Louria, Representing the Hon. Nelson A. Rockefeller, Governor of New York," in *The Narcotic Rehabilitation Act of 1966*, 154–72; Robert Baird, "Statement of Dr. Robert Baird, Director, Harlem Haven Clinic," in *The Narcotic Rehabilitation Act of 1966*, 385–99.

87 Dick Williams, *The Maze: Etched in Acid*, documentary, KPIX-TV, 1967, https://diva.sfsu.edu/collections/sfbatv/bundles/189388.

88 George Peters to Virginia Glenn, May 4, 1967, Glenn Papers, box 3, folder 114.

89 Giles, "'We Help Anyone, Anytime.'"

90 "Grow," n.d., 2, New York Public Library, Manuscripts and Archives Division, Timothy Leary Papers (Leary Papers), box 275, folder 9.

91 George Peters to Virginia Glenn, May 4, 1967, Glenn Papers, box 3, folder 114.

92 Frank Kusch, *Battleground Chicago: The Police and the 1968 Democratic National Convention* (Chicago: University of Chicago Press, 2008).

93 Ross, "Chicago's Improbable Rescue Team."

94 Harrington, "Bad Trip on LSD Line?"

95 David J. Brandenburger to Mike Aldrich, October 27, 1969, Leary Papers, box 73, folder 5.

96 Mike Aldrich to David J. Brandenburger, October 28, 1969, Leary Papers, box 73, folder 5.

97 Stanley Krippner, email to author, July 24, 2017.

98 "If This Was a Church, the God Was Cocaine," United Press International, December 1, 1983.

99 Lionel Rolfe, *Fat Man on the Left: Four Decades in the Underground* (Los Angeles: California Classics, 1998), 83–84.

100 Stanley Krippner, email to author, July 24, 2017.

101 http://www.zendoproject.org.

102 Albert Hofmann, *LSD, My Problem Child: Reflections on Sacred Drugs, Mysticism and Science* (New York: McGraw Hill, 1980).

103 Matthew W. Johnson, William A. Richards, and Roland R. Griffiths, "Human Hallucinogen Research: Guidelines for Safety," *Journal of Psychopharmacology* 22, 6 (2008): 603–20.

104 R. Andrew Sewell, John H. Halpern, and Harrison G. Pope, "Response of Cluster Headache to Psilocybin and LSD," *Neurology* 66, 12 (2006): 1920–22. See also Matthias Karst, John H. Halpern, and Michael Bernateck, "The Non-Hallucinogen 2-Bromo-Lysergic Acid Diethylamide as Preventative Treatment for Cluster Headache: An Open, Non-Randomized Case Series," *Cephalalgia* 30, 9 (2010): 1140–44.

105 Paul De Rienzo, Dana Beal, and Staten Island Project, *The Ibogaine Story: Report on the Staten Island Project* (Brooklyn: Autonomedia, 1997), http://ibogaine.mindvox.com/articles/ibogaine-story-staten-island-project/.

106 David Kaiser and Patrick McCray, eds., *Groovy Science: Knowledge, Innovation, and American Counterculture* (Chicago: University of Chicago Press, 2016).

PART 3

The Business of Pleasure and Panic

Flogging a Dead Horse? Adulteration and Brewing in Nineteenth-Century England   8

Jonathan Reinarz

In 1886, Warwickshire publican Frederick James Hunt, owner of the Turk's Head Inn, a public house in Alcester, circulated a statement accusing Flower and Sons brewery of adulteration, in an attempt to bring disrepute to his former employer. Rather than accuse the county's largest brewer of employing harmful chemicals or cheap and inferior barley substitutes when brewing, Hunt claimed that he had been informed by a well-placed informant that the Stratford brewers "had put horse flesh in their Beer."[1] The potential advantage of exploring this episode from a qualitative perspective, rather than adding it to the heap of cases counted by public health officers in the nineteenth century, is underlined by even the briefest examination of food adulteration in the contemporary British press.

The issue of horseflesh, for example, came to light on January 15, 2013, when it was reported that horse DNA had been discovered in frozen beef burgers sold in British supermarkets. Within days, horsemeat was found in numerous other food products advertised as beef. By March of that year, the Food Standards Agency in Britain had already conducted 5,430 tests, with 44 showing the presence of horsemeat in seventeen different products.[2] These included primarily burgers and lasagna, all labelled as beef and sold in a range of commercial outlets, some owned by Whitbread, once the world's largest brewery, now a multinational hotel, coffee shop, and restaurant company. While the specific adulterant in this case does not pose a direct threat to health, this peculiarly British scandal nevertheless revealed a complete breakdown in the reliability of the commercial food chain. Naturally, it also left open the possibility that food products might contain some harmful ingredients. As important, however, is the fact that the contaminating agent was horsemeat, which, although regularly consumed in continental Europe, remains taboo in countries such as the United Kingdom and Ireland. As significant is that the supply chain was traced to abattoirs in Romania, which, in line with joining the European Union in 2007, was required by law to reduce the number of horse-drawn carts on its urban streets, leaving countless numbers of stray horses abandoned. Many are thought to have ended up in the country's thirty-five plants licensed to process horsemeat.[3] Any future examination of this episode would therefore be missing an important and meaningful component were it to ignore the wider context of the case. Moreover, while food historian John Burnett, among other social and economic historians, revealed the prevalence of adulteration between the French Revolutionary Wars and the First World War, very few cases of adulteration, real and assumed, have been examined on a detailed cultural level by historians. This chapter will therefore consider a particular claim of adulteration at a single Victorian brewery in provincial England in the hope of demonstrating that such tales contain important lessons and rich meanings that food and drink historians have yet to fully unpack, appreciate, and incorporate into the existing literature.

The history of food and drink adulteration is extensive. At the heart of the European literature are stories of food fraud involving not only bread, tea, and milk but also beer. Extending back more than half a century to John Burnett's pioneering work on the day-to-day lives of working-class Britons, this story and its rehearsal as it relates to the brewing trade might appear akin to flogging a dead horse. In fact, *Plenty and Want,* Burnett's social history of food in England from 1815 to the present day (or 1966, when it was first published), originated with his doctoral research, a groundbreaking thesis examining the prevalence of adulteration in three products central to the English diet (or even identity): bread, tea, and beer, "the universal Cordial of the populace."[4] At the time his dissertation appeared, the "standard of living" debate among social and economic historians was in full swing, and Burnett felt that many important issues were being obscured by the flurry of scenarios and statistics put forth by the field's most influential figures in British history, beginning with Arnold Toynbee, J.H. Clapham, and T.S. Ashton, and maintaining momentum in the postwar era thanks to Eric Hobsbawm (who set out the "pessimistic" view), W.H. Chaloner, and R.M. Hartwell. Burnett reminded those willing to listen (both in a dissertation and in a subsequent book) that any "realistic discussion" regarding standard diets required qualitative as well as quantitative evidence.[5] Even if scholars (largely economists) could prove that salaries and food consumption were rising in the 1840s, the foods central to these debates were not necessarily "constant and stable factors."[6] The historical study of beer, moreover, was only just commencing at the time, with economic historian Peter Mathias's pioneering and monumental study appearing a year after Burnett defended his dissertation. From a modern vantage point, the social history of food is no longer "scanty,"[7] the historiography of drink having since surged from a trickle to a torrent. The first half of this chapter attempts to summarize some of the relevant literature that has appeared since Burnett began to shape this field, but alternative studies of adulteration remain both possible and necessary to advance the discussion beyond its present state.[8] The chapter's second half will therefore return to James Hunt's accusation and situate his claims in the context of wider changes impacting the brewing industry in the late nineteenth century.

A Gallop through the History of Adulteration

According to economic historians, the golden age of food adulteration in Britain lasted from approximately the end of the Napoleonic Wars to the 1860s.[9] The prevalence of trickery, substitution, and dishonesty in food production undoubtedly existed in primitive and medieval agrarian societies, but has been regarded by historians as an urban phenomenon, fettered as it was to the shift away from self-sufficiency and familiarity with rural production techniques.[10] As important, it was also tied to the earliest forms of government regulation of commercial enterprise, and has therefore generated considerable statistics and left traces in historical archives, even if quantitative data far outstrip qualitative sources.[11] A prerequisite to the development of trust in commercial activity in England was a uniform system of weights and measures, and the need for an early uniform measure of wine and ale was already spelled out in Magna Carta (1215).[12] This was supplemented in 1301 by English legislation that remained in place until 1824, when it was replaced by the imperial system.

In 1800, British brewers produced more than 10 million barrels of beer and per capita consumption of the amber nectar reached thirty-three gallons.[13] Whereas measures took a long time to change, tastes in beer had fluctuated regularly. Although much early legislation prohibited brewers from employing anything but malt, hops, and water, and bound public brewers to brew only at certain standard strengths, flavourings of all kinds had regularly enriched English ales. In the seventeenth century, the newly introduced lighter and brisker hopped beer was initially met with distrust by those used to the older, heavier ales, but tastes soon changed. With domestic brewing (which accounted for at least a third of beer production, possibly a half) in decline and the London brewers' guild in decay,[14] new measures were also required to detect fraudulent drinks as well as substitutes for beer's newest ingredients, including hops. Around 1720, London brewers introduced a novel drink named "porter," supposedly suitable for porters and other working people but rapidly gaining popularity outside its traditional constituency.[15] Although beer consumption may have varied with harvests and economics, brewers tried to keep prices stable given the proliferation of alternative drinks, such as coffee and tea. It is not surprising, therefore, that the widespread use of drugs and other adulterants to impart a fictitious strength or quality to beer dates from this period.

The enforcement of food trading laws in England generally remained under local control. Their implementation remained a concern until full-time inspectors were appointed in 1795. Well before this, a series of publications relying on simple chemical tests led to the proliferation of pamphlets on food adulteration, although many were regarded as "prejudiced and exaggerated."[16] Peter Mathias set forth his own reasons for the deterioration in food standards from the mid-eighteenth century: "low money wages translated against high costs in the distributive system and a failure of the distributive trades to advance as fast as urban populations."[17] Mathias knew all about the brewing trade and claimed in a subsequent work that the nuisance of adulteration did not disappear with the arrival of better economic conditions; it remained a "perennial complaint until 1830" (the end date of his study of the British brewing industry), if not much longer.[18] According to T.R. Gourvish and R.G. Wilson, who extended

Mathias's study to 1980, beer adulteration in London before the 1880s was a universal practice. And while nothing was ever proved against the big London brewers (apart from one infamous conviction involving Meux's brewery), "the charges laid against the publicans were formidable."[19] Those who engaged in the practice of adulteration quickly realized that beer, wine, and spirits were among the most profitable areas for food fraud.[20] And while punishments for such activities could be harsh, Mathias, among other scholars, appears to have placed some of the blame on the customers, who expected "the constant pot," demanding that the price of beer remain stable at three pence a serving even in times of political upheaval or famine. With brewers as keen to maintain retail prices, publicans, it has been said, "were virtually forced to adulterate."[21] Not surprisingly, the practice soon got out of control.

The most common form of adulteration in the drinks trade was watering down. This was also the least harmful example of food fraud; other additives were far more dangerous and were frequently added to alcoholic beverages in order to disguise dilution with water. In 1701, the list of prohibited ingredients in beer already included "foreign grains, Guinea Pepper, essentia bina (sugar boiled until thick, dark and bitter) and *Cocculus indicus*," a curare-like poison containing picrotoxin, which increased the bitterness and intoxicating effect of the drink. The fact that *Cocculus indicus* rapidly became the chief adulterant was closely tied to the fact that it allowed five bushels of malt to do duty as eight. By 1710, interdictions extended to include broom and wormwood and other bitter ingredients that were being employed to avoid the hop duty but only incurred the penalty of a £20 fine.[22] Copprice, or green vitriol (salt of steel), was also commonly added to give beer and porter a frothing head, for flat beer was publicly regarded as adulterated beer.[23]

In the nineteenth century, with rises in the tax on malt and hops, and abnormally high grain prices, beer was more regularly adulterated and the public began to complain routinely about the drink's "inferior quality."[24] As pale malts proved less expensive yet yielded greater extract, agents previously added to diluted beers were again introduced to darken hues; wine was laced with coal tar dyes, as few common adulterants could yet be detected by chemical analysis. In 1811, the government legalized the use of "colouring," but only those derived from burnt sugar. Rapidly losing control of the situation, the government reverted to its earlier policy in 1816, when the use of colouring agents and flavouring became a criminal offence; all ingredients other than malt and hops were forbidden. Any chemist or druggist convicted of supplying unlawful materials would incur a £500 penalty. While social reformers believed that beer consumption should be encouraged at the expense of gin and spirits, government investigations identified monopoly as another national threat and one of the major causes of adulteration.[25] The drop in beer consumption eventually gave proponents of free trade a powerful argument in favour of abolishing the beer duty and throwing open the retail trade to producers who purchased a two-guinea excise licence. Soon after, legislation was regarded to have had a deleterious impact on drink quality. The Beerhouse Act 1830, among other things, led to the proliferation of retail outlets (commonly known as "Jerry" shops) and consequently rendered it more difficult for inspectors to control the composition of beer. By fostering competition, the act undoubtedly accentuated the problem of adulteration, for the new beer shops, of which there were 24,342 six months after the act's passage,[26] quickly became notorious for the poor quality of their beer.[27] The belief that free competition would rid the market of inferior goods was thoroughly tried and tested in these years. Detection of adulteration had been left to the consumer, and few consumers were able to find good beer.

While generally acknowledged, the scandal of food adulteration in England was first exposed by the German-born chemist Friedrich Accum in his notorious *Treatise on Adulterations of Food, and Culinary Poisons* (1820). Described as the "quintessential public chemist of the early nineteenth century," Accum was originally employed as an analytical chemist in the Brande Pharmacy, who advertised themselves as the King's apothecaries.[28] He also served as assistant to Humphry Davy at the Royal Institution before setting up shop on his own, and in 1798 drafted a string of articles on the purity of drugs and medicine for the *Journal of Natural Philosophy*. From the purity of drugs, he gradually switched his focus to "Culinary Chemistry" and gained both a reputation for his private scientific training and unrivalled access to the public ear, becoming London's "pet chemist."[29] Appreciating the publicity value of books, he finally published his lurid and sensational *Treatise,* which provoked popular alarm.

Claiming to have drawn on two decades of research, Accum revealed the extensive use of adulteration in the food trades. Most worryingly, he found it impossible "to mention a single article of food which is not met with in an adulterated state."[30] Indeed, he regarded some substances as "scarcely ever to be procured genuine." Many adulterants were harmless, damaging only to the purse, but others were judged to be extremely unhealthy, even deadly. To this class belonged "the adulterations of beer, wine, spirituous liquors."[31] In the year 1819, he counted nearly a hundred convictions of brewers for using cheap and dangerous substitutes for malt or hops; he peppered the pages of his lurid account with the names of the convicted. Samples of porter said to leave the largest London breweries with an alcoholic strength of 5.25 percent were reduced to 4.5 percent when they were sold to the public.[32] The "hard, old beers" favoured by drinkers at this time were being "matured" through the addition of sulfuric acid, while sour beers were recovered by adding preparations of ground oyster shells.[33] While Accum's text, which went through four editions in two years, caught the attention of the public, not least due to a frontispiece that sported an arresting skull-and-crossbones emblem, it also seized the attention of those targeted by his criticisms, including the powerful manufacturers, druggists, and publicans. As a result, Accum soon found himself attacked as vehemently, and not only for his inaccuracies. Charged with defacing books belonging to the library of the Royal Institution, where he had once been employed, he chose to return to his native Germany rather than face public trial and possible disgrace.

Although Accum was rarely mentioned by name again, his text opened up the subject of adulteration to public debate, and spawned further investigations and texts on the subject. In 1845, Friedrich Engels pointed a finger at "Dealers and manufacturers [who] adulterate all kinds of provisions in an atrocious manner, and without the slightest regard for the health of the consumers."[34] Rising incomes in the "'thirsty' forties,"[35] on the other hand, has led historians to suggest that food fraud probably peaked in the 1850s.[36] As influential as Accum's work in documenting this latter period of corruption were the medical and scientific investigations carried out in the capital by physician and microscopist Dr. Arthur Hassall of the Royal Free Hospital and Dr. Henry Lethaby, who was consulted in all cases involving tobacco, snuff, and opium.[37] Purchasing "all the principal articles of consumption," usually in London's poorest neighbourhoods at night, Hassall's team examined "upwards of 2,500 samples" and, in the process, demonstrated "the exactness and power of the microscope in detecting many admixtures and adulterations."[38] Their findings were published in the *Lancet* between 1851 and 1854 and later compiled into a 648-page report, which led to the establishment of the first parliamentary inquiry on food adulteration in 1855–56. A subsequent survey of provincial towns published in the *Lancet* prompted the passage of An Act for Preventing the Adulteration of Food and Drink (1860), championed by Birmingham MP William Scholefield. The act empowered certain local authorities to appoint public analysts to investigate public complaints. Successful prosecution depended on individuals' being able to prove not only that the foods were adulterated but also that vendors were aware of this at the time of sale. Despite such limitations, these measures would influence food regulation in Britain's colonies and further afield.

Not surprisingly, Birmingham was one of the few provincial towns that appointed an analyst following the passage of the 1860 act. Although adulteration in the mid-Victorian period was said to be most rife in the south and Midlands, and far less than in Lancashire, Birmingham's first public analyst, Alfred Hill, reported few cases of adulteration by the 1870s. The tide had generally begun to turn in 1872 with the passage of the Adulteration of Food, Drink and Drugs Act, which empowered all borough councils to employ public analysts, who were tasked with monitoring the sale of drink. Despite the challenges these public servants faced, the proportion of adulterated samples fell gradually. While it is highly likely that this change was not entirely due to legislation, adulteration nevertheless declined from nearly 20 percent in 1877 to 11.2 percent in 1895 and 8.2 percent in 1913.[39] The appointment of public analysts became compulsory only with the introduction of the Sale of Food and Drugs Act in 1875, the year in which total expenditure on drink and tobacco surpassed £60 million.[40] However, not everyone was aware, or even convinced, of this decline.

Standard histories of adulteration tend to depict the improvement in food quality in the later Victorian period as primarily a scientific achievement, owing much to the work of Accum and Hassall, and the application of chemical and microbiological knowledge and analytical techniques to the practical problems of identification and measurement within a regulatory framework. That said, these new techniques were also tied to the introduction of new ways of doctoring alcoholic beverages. Burnett himself notes that "in exposing the techniques of fraud Accum instructed others in the very art he wishes to suppress."[41] In his study of science and brewing in the nineteenth century, James Sumner also draws attention to the multiple readings and uses of early chemical texts.[42] Brewing guides, while advising on the value of different waters for brewing purposes, also invariably rehearsed the long list of known adulterants and their attributes, thereby suggesting to some segments of the drinking public that the application of chemistry to brewing might as easily be employed for fraudulent purposes. The "brewers' druggist," who had begun to appear in the eighteenth century, was therefore more often regarded as part of, rather than the solution to, the problem. Indeed, many such druggists peddled banned items to any brewer who was prepared to listen, and the trade could not have been so organized and lucrative unless some were prepared to buy their illicit wares.[43] In 1798, the Board of Excise had been concerned about the emergence of "beer doctors," for though they did not brew, some produced upwards of 400 barrels in a single day, and paid no duty. Although this loophole was closed in 1802, 28 druggists and grocers were convicted between 1812 and 1818 for supplying brewers with banned articles, including *Cocculus indicus,* colouring, Spanish liquorice, and molasses. At the time, 34 brewers were convicted for using unlawful ingredients, and political cartoons began hinting at the complete replacement of good, honest English ale. In 1829 and 1830 alone, another 200 brewers were convicted.[44]

After 1830, however, adulteration appeared to move down the social scale, while the large brewers appeared to benefit more through their association with scientifically trained men. By the 1860s, discoveries around fermentation led to changes in beer production, with some brewers purchasing chemical apparatus, establishing laboratories, and even appointing their own in-house chemists. Primarily the result of work carried out by Louis Pasteur at the École Normale Supérieure in Paris and Emile Hansen at the Carlsberg Research Laboratory in Denmark, brewers learned to control the brewing process due to a greater understanding of yeast and the importance of cleanliness to production. Thermometers, hydrometers (which enabled individuals to gauge the density of a liquid), and microscopes all gave brewers greater control over fermentation and facilitated communication among those interested in the trade. Consequently, brewing textbooks not only became more numerous but also provided easy-to-follow instructions. Trade journals continued to disseminate the results of the latest research, and eventually technical education was improved due to the efforts of trade organizations, such as the Institute of Brewing, the newly appointed staff of England's first School of Brewing and Malting at the University of Birmingham, and consultant chemists who provided private tuition in London and Burton-on-Trent, among other brewing centres. By the turn of the century, brewers no longer heated their vats "as hot as their hands could bear," for the thermometer, together with a certain degree of scientific training, made such subjective language obsolete.

Although undertaken with more precision, brewing was still described as an art, occasionally a dark art. Horace T. Brown, who entered the service of Worthington's in 1865, recalled objections to setting up a small room for experimental purposes, for the apparatus might suggest to customers who visited the brewery that "the beer was being 'doctored.'"[45] Initially interested in the process of fermentation and the actions of yeasts, brewers' chemists soon turned their attention to the wider field of malt and hop substitutes. In 1847, sugar had been added to the list of permitted ingredients in beer and experiments were being done on the yields of other starches by chemists appointed at the largest Burton-on-Trent breweries. The Revenue Act of 1862 allowed brewers to use any safe substitute for hops, the price of which was subject to violent fluctuations. The hop duty itself was abolished the following year. Soon more controversial legislation would throw open the doors to experimentation, which was often undertaken at great expense and in secrecy. Discussing adulteration from any angle could still be a risky business.[46] Neither did the introduction of science at breweries allay any lingering fears that may have persisted about consuming bad beer.

While most foods were found to be relatively free of additives by the end of the nineteenth century, the brewing trade was subject to additional investigation at the point of production. Following the introduction of the Inland Revenue Act 1880, which saw the return of the beer duty that had been abolished in 1830, brewers were granted the use of any fermentable material, or the "free mash-tun," and began to brew lighter, more sparkling ales, which could be produced only with the use of additional sugar.

English farmers were particularly conscious of the increased reliance on grains from North and South America, and, together with their political allies, commenced a long campaign calling for the tighter control of beer ingredients.[47] The fact that this campaign, which sought to limit the use of sugar, rice, maize, and other barley and hops "substitutes," was introduced to Parliament as the Pure Beer Bill could only have raised further suspicions of adulteration among the drinking public, who were unlikely to see through the consumer-protection arguments of the farming lobby. The new definition of beer set out in the Customs and Inland Revenue Act, 1885 only highlighted how ambiguous the product had become: "A liquor which is made or sold as a description of beer, or as a substitute for beer, and which on analysis of a sample thereof shall be found to contain more than 2% of proof spirit."[48] To brewers, the commercial pressures to employ preservatives became only more compelling, given that shorter brewing times and lower specific gravities had reduced the keeping quality of beer. Salicylic acid and bisulfate of lime, along with boric acid, were therefore commonly added to beer before a grist consisting of malt and invert sugar, or of malt and some unmalted grain, allowed brewers to produce a more brilliant and stable beer at century's end. Lower-strength wines also witnessed the introduction of benzoic acid, while fluoride compounds were detected in dairy products. The production process, however, was now overseen by chemists, so what could go wrong?

Although the industry benefited from representation by eighteen brewer MPs in Parliament, the Pure Beer campaign gained impetus in the first year of the twentieth century. Beer duties still brought the Treasury £11.8 million in 1900.[49] Government action was therefore required when an epidemic of arsenic poisoning claimed at least seventy lives and created panic among beer drinkers, who were on average consuming thirty gallons per capita annually. The episode, which affected an estimated 6,000 persons with symptoms of peripheral neuritis,[50] was quickly traced to the consumption of beer from certain breweries that used sugar and glucose, two of the most common substitutes for barley; these had been contaminated with sulfuric acid containing abnormally large quantities of arsenous acid.[51] Bostock, the sugar manufacturer of Garston, near Liverpool, quickly recalled its glucose and invert sugar, which was found to have been made using sulfuric acid supplied by the Leeds firm of Nicholson and Son. A

Royal Commission was subsequently set up in February 1901 to examine the causes of the contamination and to advise on future preventive measures. When blame was placed on the two auxiliary firms rather than on any individual brewing companies, the brewers naturally felt exonerated. Nevertheless, the use of arsenic was prohibited in 1903 (boric acid, copper salts, and other metallic compounds were not banned until the mid-1920s), and it was subsequently discovered that arsenic contamination had been endemic previously due to the use of arsenic-containing coke to dry malt. Despite the fact that the nation's beer was probably purer than it had ever been, the Pure Beer lobby stepped up its activity between 1903 and 1914, and introduced another ten parliamentary bills to limit barley substitutes. The brewing press continued to fight back, and condemned the proliferation of anti-industry rhetoric in the popular press that sought "to blacken and defame the honourable trade."[52] In its defence, the industry claimed to employ chemists who would monitor both production and quality control of products more carefully. Although the Royal Commission downplayed the need for further statutory controls of brewing ingredients, not everyone was convinced of the trade's innocence, and the fact remained that one-quarter of the beer produced in 1914 was being brewed from materials other than malt and hops.[53]

A Charge of Adulteration

Like their smaller competitors, the Stratford brewery of Flower and Sons was not immune to accusations of adulteration, as Frederick James Hunt's allegation in 1886 made very clear. While the form of the slanderous charge outlined at the opening of this chapter may appear unique, its timing was of considerable importance. The date is crucial, for this particular allegation of adulteration came only six years after Prime Minister William Gladstone had granted England's 2,500 commercial brewers what has come to be known as the "free mash-tun." And while unusual, there is some evidence that knackers and butchers had been "pressed into the service of adulteration," as uncovered by John Burnett.[54] In his *Treatise on the Falsification of Food* (1848), John Mitchell, one of many Victorian writer-analysts inspired by Accum, also claimed to have detected a substance in samples of coffee that he identified as baked horses' liver. Peter Atkins's work on milk adulteration also contains references to the peculiar practice of adding livestock to liquid libations, in this case calves' brains to milk in order to generate an attractive and appetizing froth.[55]

Such precedents aside, the horse was also ubiquitous in Victorian society, and brewers in particular had unrivalled access to a not inconsiderable supply of equine material if they so desired. Moreover, the English rejection of hippophagy was already in evidence at this time. English civility, as cultural historians have argued, was partially defined and firmly privileged by an aversion to horseflesh.[56] Long free from the fear of dearth or famine, the average Englishman saw no need to consume this noble animal alongside which he worked. The sale of horseflesh for human consumption in other countries was on the increase, however, and would come to differentiate British subjects from their European confreres. The French government, perhaps most notably, had authorized the sale of horseflesh for food in 1856, and the ungulate rapidly came to comprise 5 percent of the meat consumed in Paris.[57] In the German capital, approximately 7,000 horses were slaughtered yearly. While there was nothing illegal about selling horseflesh as human food in England, it was often traded surreptitiously, primarily as pet food, and a bill to better regulate the sale of horsemeat had not yet been introduced in Parliament at the time the directors of Flower and Sons were faced with Hunt's accusation. An anxious English public would have to wait until 1889 for the Sale of Horseflesh, &c. Regulation Act to come into effect. That said, other changes would have fuelled public anxieties concerning activities in the brewhouse.

Scientific innovations that would enable individuals to detect adulteration had also recently brought changes to the production of beer. As with most scientific advances, however, the theories promoted by scientists during the nineteenth century were not introduced to the English brewing industry overnight. Some techniques and technologies were accepted more slowly than others. Many were actively resisted, and not just by the public. As Mathias has pointed out in his comprehensive study of the industry, this led to an intermediary stage "between the empiricism of the seventeenth century, and the beginning of fundamental scientific analysis in the mid-nineteenth century."[58] While the acceptance of a theory, such as Pasteur's on fermentation, suggested "a commitment to the same rules and standards for scientific practice,"[59] it also implied the rejection of many previously held views and conventions. Conversion proved especially difficult among those committed to established world views, or a traditional way of brewing. For example, in Germany at this time, as in England, a group of individuals attacked the brewing industry and claimed chemistry had "got into the beer."[60] Brewers whose businesses were still organized along craft lines believed their forefathers, who knew nothing of chemistry, had produced a better product. As a result, many brewers for a time dared not engage a person who was "guilty of the unpardonable sin of learning chemistry."[61] As already noted, the scientific method was resisted at some firms because the necessary instruments introduced by staff suggested to customers that beer was being "doctored."[62] Other critics felt that chemistry in general was being used to discover substitutes for "honest malt and hops," especially after 1880, when brewers were permitted to utilize materials more freely.

Brewing in Stratford-upon-Avon was beginning to be transformed by scientific and technological developments in the field of zymotechnology (the science of fermentation) during the last quarter of the nineteenth century. Flower's purchasing ledgers reveal the decision in 1878 to acquire a Watson and Son microscope, an investment that appeared symbolically to mark the firm's break with an unscientific past.[63] Production had begun to change much earlier, however, when the firm began relying on the services of a local "brewer's druggist," or brewers' chemist, as the firm of Kendall and Son preferred to identify itself. Settling in Stratford in 1836, Frederic Kendall had set himself apart from other provincial chemists when, in 1841, he became a founding member of the Pharmaceutical Society of Great Britain.[64] In subsequent years, the firm's growth very closely paralleled events in the brewing industry. By 1866, Kendall was supplying brewers like Flower and Sons with cleaning products and bisulfite of lime in order to improve the cleanliness of the brewing environment. The firm also regularly assisted the brewery in ascertaining the purity of water and other brewing products. Flower and Sons equally benefited from membership in trade associations, such as the Institute of Brewing and the County Brewers' Association. In October 1885, Charles Flower even chaired an event organized by the Institute of Brewing at which consultant chemist Bedo Hobbs spoke on "The Chemistry of Brewing." A copy of the lecture in the company archives contains notes made by Flower claiming that "I don't think we can do without the Chemist." Shortly afterwards, he engaged the services of Horace T. Brown, formerly of Worthington's, who had set up a laboratory and office in London and visited the brewery on four occasions. In the 1880s, as government control over brewing ingredients was relaxed, other articles, notably flaked malt, caramels and other black sugars, and, later, non-fermentable copper sugars and primings, were added to the list of materials Kendall and Son supplied the brewery – besides some more dubious products. For example, in 1887, the *Brewers' Journal* advertised Kendall and Son's Permanent Heading Powder, which, besides allowing brewers to retain a head on their ales, was claimed to restore sour beers.[65] Mechanical innovations faced far less opposition from the public, and refrigeration technology in particular promised to revolutionize brewing by freeing it from seasonality. Although quick to experiment with cooling machinery, however, Flower and Sons would not overcome the challenges of summer brewing until the 1890s. As a result, given the difficulties the Stratford brewers faced in the brewhouse, not to mention the expense associated with employing consultants, this period was characterized by increased secrecy. The covert way in which brewers discussed production would only have fuelled rumours of illicit tampering.

By the time the brewery faced Hunt's charge, Flower and Sons had become the largest employer in Stratford-upon-Avon. Founded by Edward Flower (1805–83) just after the introduction of the Beerhouse Act 1830, the brewery was a traditional family firm and the second generation, comprising two of Edward's three sons, Charles and Edgar, had just taken over as brewery managers. Although Stratford was an agricultural market town in the heart of rural Warwickshire, it had also changed, although not as dramatically as the brewery built by Edward in 1831. When he joined the firm in 1845, Charles found the business to be "in a small way," with sales in 1847 amounting to only £10,220. With the opening of rail lines to Birmingham in 1860 and greater demand for the firm's pale ales, sales grew to £40,000 in 1857 and reached £100,000 in 1866. Convinced that the business was in good hands, Edward eventually retired to London, where he resided with his wife, Selina, at 35 Hyde Park Gardens. Much of the profit was invested in improving the business. In 1870, the family completed its new fifty-quarter brewery, and production, along with the staff of 130 men, moved outside the town centre, next to Stratford's new rail lines.

Although the brewery was reorganized to take advantage of rail technology, traditional forms of transport continued to play an important role in the life of the firm and of the Flower family. Retired and relocated in London, Edward Flower now concerned himself less with the welfare of his workers than that of horses. For example, in his *Bits and Bearing Reins* (1875), Flower called for the abolition of a particularly fashionable nine-teenth-century apparatus used to restrict the movement of horses' heads. According to him, the bearing rein had survived as long as it had because ladies in particular liked "to see horses with their heads stuck up in the air and their legs prancing."[66] In reality, the rein restrained an animal's head in an "unnatural and fixed position, strain[ed] the windpipe and respiratory organs," and, consequently, induced "roaring and other maladies."[67] Flower called for its abolition and for the more humane treatment of animals in general. Besides delivering numerous lectures and corresponding with the editors of Victorian periodicals on the subject, Flower pursued his humanitarian mission by transforming a room in his home into a "chamber of torture" in which he displayed "the dreadful bits" and reins.[68] Despite his eccentricities, his efforts met with some success; according to various contemporary reports, he was able to convince Queen Victoria, after a brief confrontation in Hyde Park, to remove gag bearing reins from all horses in her service.[69] Following this triumph, Flower, assisted by Selina, wrote *The Stones of London* (1880), a tract imploring local government leaders to improve methods of road construction in order to ease the burden of the lowly cart horse. His efforts eventually earned him the title "The Mission-ary of Horses," as well as an entire chapter in Samuel Smiles's *Duty* (1880), one of the social reformer's many industrial biographies. In a better-known article, the editors of *Punch* referred to the Stratford brewer as "the most genial and practical of unpretentious philanthropists and hippophiles."[70]

While Edward Flower appears to have encountered the worst cases of equine abuse in the streets of the nation's capital (and his very political tracts were composed during a retirement spent in Hyde Park), it was in Stratford, as the managing director of a brewery, that he first seriously con-sidered the care and treatment of horses. Besides being members of what F.M.L. Thompson has described as a "horse-drawn society,"[71] a Victorian brewery required fifty horses for every 100,000 barrels it sold.[72] Numbers could of course vary depending on the size of a brewery's local trade and the amount of total sales contracted to private carriers. Soon after found-ing his business in 1831, Flower naturally required the services of several heavy horses to pull his drays throughout the town and greater Shakespeare country. Moreover, in addition to a number of Shire horses that hauled the firm's heaviest drays, the brewery, like many of its rivals, acquired several nags to carry Edward, his sons Charles (1830–92) and Edgar (1833–1903), and several travellers (salesmen) to customers who resided in the town, or even several miles outside of it. While canals conveyed supplies to the brewery, and ale to more distant customers as well as an export office in London, horses were the primary form of carriage for the firm, which had always largely depended on a loyal, locally based clientele.

Only in the area of production had horse power been entirely replaced by this time. Steam engines had been introduced to even the smallest breweries by the beginning of the nineteenth century. In previous centuries, horses had driven the mills used to crush malt,[73] one of the brewery's key ingredients, along with water, yeast, and hops. Used primarily for transporting goods over short distances, horses did not decline in number as a result of a growth in rail transport during the middle of the nineteenth century; instead, railways appear to have increased their use.[74] Canal transport, on the other hand, began its slow and steady decline only a few years after these waterways reached Stratford in 1816.[75] When Flower and Sons eventually rebuilt its brewery in 1870, the new premises were constructed at some distance from Stratford's canals. In the late nineteenth century, the firm appears to have engaged approximately thirty horses, though many were based at agencies in other provincial towns, such as Birmingham and Cheltenham, and in London. The majority were purchased from local breeders of heavy horses, such as Alfred Horne of Stratford and Thomas Hodges of not-so-distant Long Marston.[76] The average horse acquired by the brewery was either five or six years of age and cost between thirty and sixty pounds.[77] Most remained in the brewery's service for approximately ten years or until they became infirm, and were then either shot or sold to Mr. Gibbs, a local butcher, whose meat was eventually shipped to the Continent and later sold for consumption. At least, that is what the records implied.

Over the average ten-year career of a brewer's dray horse, the cost of maintaining each animal matched a drayman's wages; among the brewery's highest-paid manual labourers, draymen often earned up to twenty-five shillings a week in the second half of the nineteenth century. The expense of keeping horses increased even in the last years of the nineteenth century as the management of horses generally improved and became more "scientific." These developments, like other innovations during this period, appear to have been introduced rather haphazardly at breweries and generally depended on the particular knowledge a proprietor was able to acquire on his own or with the help of trade journals and employers' organizations. Nevertheless, because they attracted considerable attention when away from their stables, brewers' horses were regarded by their owners as mobile advertisements and therefore worth additional investment. Many also competed in annual horse shows when not otherwise employed with deliveries. Launched in 1885, the London Cart Horse Parade grew to be one of the largest of its kind. In 1900, more than 700 horses entered the competition to compete for cash prizes, one of which was awarded to Flower and Sons, whose horses were found to be in particularly good condition.[78] Surprisingly, the first trade paper relating to the care and management of horses was presented before the Institute of Brewers by C. Sheather in 1912, the same year in which many breweries were beginning to replace equine energy with motor vehicles.[79]

Though Sheather's article surely did not represent the practices of all brewers, it more than likely applied to Flower and Sons, whose proprietors had always taken a heightened interest in stable management. Edward Flower's presence certainly ensured that all horses were humanely treated during their years of brewery service. His third son, William Henry (1831–99), was considered an even greater authority on the horse than his father. William complemented his father's emotional pleas for the more humane treatment of horses with scientific evidence derived during his term as director at the Museum of Natural History in South Kensington.[80] In fact, the horse was one of the mammals (in addition to whales) of which Flower made a special study, and his famous treatise on equine anatomy even contains a section on bearing reins.[81] Besides conveying his detailed knowledge to the firm's staff through regular lectures,[82] William saw many of his own horses eventually join the firm's stables. One of the animals the brewery acquired in the 1880s was affectionately and quite appropriately named "Professor." At some of the largest London breweries, one might easily encounter 150–200 similar colossal specimens, each with its name over its manger.[83]

Although Flower and Sons did not come close to the size of London's brewing giants, the brewery had attained a degree of regional dominance by the 1880s. It had agencies throughout the Midlands, situated in Leamington, Birmingham, Wolverhampton, Cheltenham, and Oxford, and also opened and expanded offices in Liverpool, Manchester, Dublin, and London. By the time it established other regional outlets in Belfast, Bristol, and Kidderminster (1879), the consumption of beer in Britain appeared to have peaked. Any additional gains would therefore require capturing greater market share. Like many other breweries, Flower and Sons would aim to create guaranteed markets for its product by purchasing public houses or tying them to the firm through a system of loans. While this had been done as early as 1836, when Edward Flower "tied" the Union Tavern in Stratford to the brewery through a loan, the practice grew after the Wine and Beerhouse Act 1869 restricted licences and made such properties more valuable. By the 1879–80 brewing season, Flower and Sons had already acquired some two dozen houses, including the Nelson Inn in nearby Alcester, a neighbour and competitor of Hunt, who managed a smaller licensed property, the Turk's Head. With the arrival of limited liability in 1888, Flower and Sons' portfolio would only expand more rapidly, with sixteen new acquisitions in that year alone. Other acquisitions included the Shakespeare Inn, located at Harvington; the Stratford-based brewers rarely missed an opportunity to purchase licensed premises associated with the bard.

By this time, Flower and Sons had tied itself ever more closely to the Shakespeare name, which the brewery actively advertised. Not only had the firm used the playwright's celebrity to promote its pale ales soon after the business was founded by Edward Flower in 1831,[84] but the Patent Office at Chancery Lane in London had granted it exclusive use of Shakespeare's name and image in 1875.[85] Thereafter, the bard appeared on the brewery's buildings, its correspondence, and especially its labels, which were affixed to its bottles as well as casks. Furthermore, an early inventory of the firm suggests that one of the largest vats belonging to the firm was named "As You Like It,"[86] though Hunt's accusations likely convinced the public that "Comedy of Errors" was as appropriate a choice by the 1880s. Despite facing some difficulties in its attempts to brew a product worthy of Shakespeare's name, the family, in 1879, by which time the firm's ales were selling very well, paid great homage to him when Edward's son Charles donated to the town a site alongside the Avon where he constructed a theatre where Shakespeare's plays could be performed regularly. Openly associated with this significant local cultural venue, Charles epitomized the gentleman capitalist and soon after, like his father, withdrew from active participation in the management of the brewery. In time, another generation of brewery directors would build up a local cultural industry that attracted tourists in great numbers and ultimately outgrew and outlasted the town's previously dominant brewing industry.

While the Shakespeare Memorial Theatre was Flower and Sons' lasting tribute to Stratford's greatest writer, a far less significant testimonial is, for reasons that should now be obvious, more meaningful to the subject of this chapter. In 1887, almost a decade after the theatre was completed and a year before Flower and Sons became a limited liability company, Charles, the eldest of Edward's three sons, presented an original piece of scholarship to the town's Shakespeare Society in which he discussed the bard's knowledge of horses. Titled *Shakespeare on Horseback* (1887), the treatise catalogued the appearance of horses in Shakespeare's written texts and concluded that the author was indeed a hippophile, or, in Victorian parlance, a "horse fancier."[87] In an equally antiquarian work produced three years later, *Shakespeare No Dog Fancier,* Charles concluded that the bard was less fond of man's best friend. Although original, Charles's essays were never recognized as a significant contribution to the burgeoning field of nineteenth-century Shakespeare studies, and probably never will be. To begin with, his approach is not one deemed appropriate for assessing the playwright's work critically. Significantly, however, members of the public had only recently been called upon to employ a similar approach towards the Flower family when confronted with certain accusations against the local brewer that reflected on its own historical relationship with horses.

Conclusion

Like its competitors, the firm of Flower and Sons was not immune to accusations of adulteration. The form in which Frederick James Hunt's slanderous charge was made at the end of the nineteenth century, however, suggests that some firms overcame these attacks with greater ease than the most unfortunate businesses, whose sales might easily have declined dramatically with each accusation of adulteration. It also suggests that considerable meaning might lie at the heart of such allegations. While British dislike for horse meat needs little further elaboration, the charge clearly encapsulated the frustrations of a small player in a brewing world that was gradually coming to be dominated by regional and national giants. Few charges in this instance could have been more absurd, however. The chances of this particular accusation damaging Flower & Sons' reputation were slight, given the wide publicity that attended the proprietors' great efforts to improve the condition of horses, not only at the brewery but also on the nation's streets throughout the Victorian period. As a result, Hunt's accusation was almost immediately recognized as fictitious, and the publican quickly published an apology in the local press in order to avoid prosecution. Although standard practice at the time, Hunt's retraction was little more than a formality as most of the region's inhabitants had always been convinced of Flower and Sons' innocence. A modern audience need only briefly survey the literature relating to the brewery to reach a similar conclusion. Indeed, the Flowers, like Shakespeare, were horse fanciers.

Historians of food adulteration have been prolific, certainly since John Burnett completed his original doctoral dissertation. In the half-century since its appearance, the field of food fraud has grown, but so too has the historical literature relating to brewing. Most notably, the industry has been extensively mapped by Mathias and by Gourvish and Wilson, among others. Perhaps most relevant to this study, the history of science in the brewing trade has also grown substantially. Rather than constructing a progressive story of chemists unravelling the mysteries of brewing and helping firms take control of production, historians have revealed a more nuanced story of science being used, misused, and misunderstood, occasionally raising yields of wort but also occasionally fuelling the public's suspicions that brewers were consistently seeking new adulterants. Not surprisingly, the history of adulteration in the brewing industry shares similarities with food fraud in other sectors of the British economy from the eighteenth to the early twentieth century. The weight of public concern appears to have shifted at various stages of economic development and with legislation, from simple adulteration in the early part of this chronology to what E.J.T. Collins has described as "legalized adulteration" in the mature industrial economy.[88] There were many watershed moments, beginning with Accum's investigation in 1820 and the *Lancet*'s groundbreaking articles on the 1850s. By the end of the nineteenth century, adulteration had been rooted out by new methods, but it had "risen almost to the dignity of exact science" and "certain large companies" appeared to "trade almost entirely in 'faked' products."[89] It was also suggested that those without such talent at their disposal could as easily employ the brightest legal talent to drive the proverbial coach and horses through the Food and Drugs Act, and even influence parliamentary activity. Interestingly, while the reputations of the largest brewers have always been suspect, those of past heroes of this story have lately begun to shift, not least that of Friedrich Accum, who, even while blowing the whistle on an epidemic of food fraud, may have been motivated by the opportunity to generate some valuable self-publicity.

Meanwhile, the second part of this chapter, while offering a rare example of a single and highly specific charge of adulteration, once again concludes with the large producer looking squeaky clean. Many earlier studies have commented on the ability of big brewers to maintain a remarkably clean image compared with grocers, vintners, and certainly publicans.[90] The case of Flower and Sons demonstrates that they were never entirely immune to accusations of adulteration, especially after the Beerhouse Act 1830. It has not been my intention, however, to retry the Flower and Sons firm, but rather to question the way we continue to write the history of food fraud. Since Burnett's time, if not earlier, the public has never had to search hard to obtain statistics related to the brewing industry, let alone to adulteration. What remains in short supply are more qualitative studies of this phenomenon. It also bears reminding that this particular case played out in the local press, while others were fiercely contested in court and generated considerably larger archives. Uncovering more of these will take us beyond the numbers and shed much-needed light on how particular charges originated, how they both unfolded and concluded, and, most importantly, how they were situated in the culture of the time. Given a tendency among contemporary business historians to focus primarily on the growth of sales and productivity at the expense of an industry's social or cultural side, and the preoccupation of so many brewing historians with the extent of firms' tied estates, this study shows the need for new perspectives on England's industrial past. In terms of the history of alcohol, I hope I have shown that England's brewing heritage would look remarkably different were it viewed through horses' eyes.

Acknowledgment

The author is grateful to Peter Scholliers for his comments on an initial draft of this chapter.

Notes

1 *Alcester Chronicle,* February 13, 1886.

2 "Horsemeat Scandal: Withdrawn Products and Test Results," *BBC News,* March 22, 2013, http://www.bbc.co.uk/news/world-21412590.

3 Nadia Arumugam, "The Romanian Horse Cart Ban That's (Probably) behind Europe's Horse Meat Scandal," *Forbes,* February 14, 2013, http://www.forbes.com/sites/nadiaarumugam/2013/02/14/the-romanian-horse-cart-ban-thats-probably-behind-europes-horse-meat-scandal/#6a45ef4c5ee0. See also Megan Gibson, "Pony Burgers? Europe Gags on a Horsemeat Scandal," *TIME,* February 13, 2013, http://world.time.com/2013/02/13/pony-burgers-europe-gags-on-a-horsemeat-scandal/.

4 J. Burnett, *The History of Food Adulteration in Great Britain in the Nineteenth Century, with Special Reference to Bread, Tea and Beer* (PhD dissertation, University of London, 1958), 297.

5 J. Burnett, *Plenty and Want: A Social History of Food in England from 1815 to the Present Day* (London: Routledge, 1989), 86.

6 Burnett, *History of Food Adulteration,* 3.

7 Ibid., 293. Unable to draw on Peter Mathias's study, Burnett relied on F.A. King's *Beer Has a History* (London: Hutchinson's Scientific and Technical Publications, 1947) and A. Campbell's *The Book of Beer* (London: Dennis Dobson, 1956).

8 Interestingly, there is neither an article on "adulteration" nor an entry in the index in Jack S. Blocker, David M. Fahey, and Ian R. Tyrrell, eds., *Alcohol and Temperance in Modern History: An International Encyclopedia,* 2 vols. (Santa Barbara, CA: ABC-Clio, 2003).

9 E.J.T. Collins, "Food Adulteration and Food Safety in Britain in the 19th and Early 20th Centuries," *Food Policy* 18, 2 (1993): 95.

10 Burnett, *Plenty and Want,* 86; M. Bruegel, "How the French Learned to Eat Canned Food," in *Food Nations: Selling Taste in Consumer Society,* ed. W. Belasco and P. Scranton (New York: Routledge, 2002), 113–30.

11 Burnett, *History of Food Adulteration,* 292.

12 P.B. Hutt and P.B. Hutt II, "A History of Government Regulation of Adulteration and Misbranding of Food," *Food Drug Cosmetic Law Journal* 39 (1984): 11.

13 G.B. Wilson, *Alcohol and the Nation* (BA thesis, University of London, 1940), 57.

14 Burnett, *History of Food Adulteration*, 340.

15 Campbell, *Book of Beer*, 71–72.

16 Burnett, *Plenty and Want*, 87.

17 Peter Mathias, *Retailing Revolution: A History of Multiple Retailing in the Food Trades Based upon the Allied Suppliers Group of Companies* (London: Longman, 1967), x.

18 Peter Matthias, *The Brewing Industry in England 1700–1830* (Cambridge: Cambridge University Press, 1959), 112.

19 T.R. Gourvish and R.G. Wilson, *The British Brewing Industry 1830–1980* (Cambridge: Cambridge University Press, 1994), 138–39.

20 Collins, "Food Adulteration," 97.

21 Ibid., 114.

22 Burnett, *History of Food Adulteration*, 343.

23 Ibid., 381.

24 Ibid., 323.

25 Ibid.

26 Ibid., 365.

27 Brian Harrison, *Drink and the Victorians: The Temperance Question in England, 1815–1872* (London: Faber and Faber, 1971), 83.

28 James Sumner, *Brewing Science, Technology and Print, 1700–1880* (Pittsburgh: University of Pittsburgh, 2013), 128.

29 Ibid.

30 Fredrick Accum, *A Treatise on Adulterations of Food, and Culinary Poisons* (London: J. Mallet, 1820), 3.

31 Ibid., 4.

32 Burnett, *Plenty and Want*, 88–89; Accum, *Treatise on Adulterations*, 173–74.

33 Burnett, *Plenty and Want*, 89.

34 F. Engels, *The Condition of the Working Class in England* (Cambridge: Cambridge University Press, 2010), 69.

35 Burnett, *History of Food Adulteration*, 300.

36 Collins, "Food Adulteration," 96; Burnett, *Plenty and Want*, 91.

37 A.H. Hassall, *The Narrative of a Busy Life: An Autobiography* (London: Longmans, Green, 1893), 47.

38 Ibid., 45–46.

39 Collins, "Food Adulteration," 103.

40 The Scottish author and government reformer Samuel Smiles calculated that the total sums spent by the working classes on drink would have purchased 500 new cotton mills or 500,000 acres of land. See Burnett, *History of Food Adulteration*, 307. The expenditure on consumption of spirits tended to be half that of beer sales, and wine approximately an eighth of the expenditure on beer.

41 Burnett, *Plenty and Want*, 90.

42 Sumner, *Brewing Science, Technology, and Print*, 131.

43 Burnett, *History of Food Adulteration,* 393.

44 Ibid., 415.

45 H.T. Brown, "Reminiscences of Fifty Years' Experience of the Application of Scientific Method to Brewing Practice," *Journal of the Institute of Brewing* 22, 5 (1916): 272.

46 Sumner, *Brewing Science, Technology, and Print,* 131.

47 J. Phillips and M. French, "The Pure Beer Campaign and Arsenic Poisoning, 1896–1903," *Rural History* 9, 2 (1998): 195; and Michael French and Jim Phillips, *Cheated Not Poisoned? Food Regulation in the United Kingdom, 1875–1938* (Manchester: Manchester University Press, 2000), 12.

48 Burnett, *History of Food Adulteration,* 350.

49 Ibid., 203; French and Phillips, *Cheated Not poisoned?* 74.

50 The disease was generally regarded to result from chronic alcoholic poisoning and was characterized by paralysis of the muscles and loss of function in sensory nerves. See T.N. Kelynack and W. Kirkby, *Arsenical Poisoning in Beer Drinkers* (London: Baillière, Tindall and Cox, 1901).

51 Ibid., 199.

52 M. Copping, "Death in the Beer-Glass: The Manchester Arsenic-in-Beer Epidemic of 1900–1 and the Long-Term Poisoning of Beer," *Brewery History* 132 (2009): 44.

53 Burnett, *History of Food Adulteration,* 338.

54 Burnett, *Plenty and Want,* 92.

55 P.J. Atkins, "Sophistication Detected: Or, the Adulteration of the Milk Supply, 1850–1914," *Social History* 16, 3 (1991): 320.

56 K. De Ornellas, *The Horse in Early Modern Culture: Bridled, Curbed, and Tamed* (Lanham, MD: Fairleigh Dickinson University Press, 2014), 6.

57 "Horseflesh as Human Food," *British Medical Journal,* April 26, 1890.

58 Mathias, *The Brewing Industry in England,* 65.

59 T. Kuhn, *The Structure of Scientific Revolutions* (University of Chicago: 1970), 11.

60 *Country Brewers' Gazette,* June 6, 1883. "Brewing and Science."

61 Ibid.

62 E. Sigsworth, "Science and the Brewing Industry, 1850–1900," *Economic History Review* (1965): 538.

63 Shakespeare Birthplace Trust Records Office (SBTRO), DR 227/9.

64 P.J.T. Morris and C.A. Russell, *Archives of the British Chemical Industry* (Farington: British Society for the History of Science, 1988), 120–21.

65 *Brewers' Journal,* March 15, 1887.

66 S. Smiles, *Duty: With Illustrations of Courage, Patience and Endurance* (London: John Murray, 1936), 324.

67 Ibid.

68 Ibid., 309 and 324.

69 *Stratford Herald,* May 29, 1891.

70 Ibid., June 4, 1880.

71 F.M.L. Thompson, *Victorian England: The Horse-Drawn Society: An Inaugural Lecture* (London: Bedford College, 1970).

72 Gourvish and Wilson, *The British Brewing Industry*, 143.

73 J. Tann, "Horse Power, 1780–1880," in *Horses in European Economic History: A Preliminary Canter*, ed. F.M.L. Thompson (Reading: British Agricultural History Society, 1983), 23.

74 F.M.L. Thompson, "Nineteenth-Century Horse Sense," *Economic History Review* 29 (1976): 64.

75 C. Hadfield, *The Canals of the East Midlands* (Newton Abbot: David & Charles, 1966), 179–81.

76 Shakespeare Birthplace Trust Records Office (SBTRO), DR 227/47.

77 Ibid.

78 *Brewers' Journal*, June 15, 1900.

79 G. Lowcock, "Motor Vehicles for Brewers," *Journal of the Institute of Brewing* Vol. 18, Issue 1 (1912): 2–17.

80 C.J. Cornish, *Sir William Henry Flower* (London: Macmillan, 1904), 152–65.

81 Ibid., 215.

82 Ibid., 48.

83 Alphonse Esquiros, *The English at Home* (1863; repr., London: British Library, 2010), 259.

84 SBTRO, DR 227/121. A brief history of the firm can be found in L. Richmond and A. Turton, *The Brewing Industry: A Guide to Historical Records* (Manchester: Manchester University Press, 1990). A lengthier chronicle of the brewery's past is contained in J. Reinarz, *A Social History of Midland Business: Flower & Sons Brewery, 1870–1914* (PhD dissertation, University of Warwick, 1998).

85 SBTRO, DR 227/109.

86 SBTRO, DR 227/118.

87 C.E. Flower, *Shakespeare on Horseback* (Stratford-upon-Avon: No publisher indicated, 1887).

88 Collins, "Food Adulteration," 109.

89 W.H. Simmonds, *The Practical Grocer*, vol. 4 (London: Gresham, 1906), 222.

90 Burnett, *History of Food Adulteration*, 378.

Charlie Wing and the Alberta Liquor Control Board   9

The Story of the First Chinese-Canadian Hotel Licensee in Post-Prohibition Alberta

Sarah E. Hamill

In June 1921, a major fire destroyed most of the business district of Spirit River, Alberta. Undeterred, residents of the small village in northern Alberta opted to rebuild. Less than a year later, the *Edmonton Bulletin* reported that "Spirit River is better village being rebuilt."[1] The article painted a rosy picture, common to the booster rhetoric that had long been used to promote the "pioneer" regions of Canada.[2] The potential for oil development as well as gold mining came in for breathless discussion, accompanied by references to the new roads and routes to Spirit River. The article promised a "new era for the whole north country."[3]

Intriguingly, one of Spirit River's citizens was singled out for special praise: Charlie Wing, owner of the village's newly opened Dominion Hotel.[4] The hotel was doing a roaring trade and was "the finest hotel in the north country." The many miners, prospectors, and surveyors using Spirit River as their jumping-off point for the northern reaches of Alberta were apparently deeply appreciative. The article neglected to mention two other factors that would be relevant for both Wing and the Dominion Hotel's subsequent history: that there was another hotel in Spirit River, and that Wing was Chinese Canadian. These two factors would become particularly relevant once hotels like Wing's became eligible for hotel beer licences following the repeal of prohibition in 1924.[5]

Wing was not the only Chinese Canadian hotelier in Alberta during this period, but he was the only one to receive a hotel beer licence. Officially, the Alberta Liquor Control Board (ALCB) had no statutory impediment to licensing hotels run by Chinese Canadians. Unofficially, however, it adopted a policy against licensing such establishments.[6] The board's rationale was rooted in the racist assumptions about Chinese Canadians that were widespread in 1920s Canada. As ALCB chairman R.J. Dinning put it in 1924: "My experience in the past has shown conclusively that a Chinaman has little or no control over Whitemen and this would apply particularly in the beer room."[7] So how did Wing get the licence instead of the other hotel?

The story of how Wing obtained the hotel beer licence, which he held until he sold the Dominion Hotel in 1943, and of his subsequent relationship with the ALCB is as much about Wing as it is about attitudes, both racist and otherwise, towards Chinese Canadians. It is also just as much about small towns in Alberta as it is about post-prohibition attempts to actually *control* liquor sales. Crucially, Wing's experiences also highlight the devastating impact of Canada's and Canadians' racist attitudes and laws on individuals. In this chapter, I explore as far as possible the story of Charlie Wing and his relationship with the ALCB. I set out what is known of Wing's biography as well as his attempts to expand his business to include a second hotel in the neighbouring village of Fairview.

Charlie Wing before Spirit River

Little is known of Charlie Wing's early life. He appears to have been born in 1876 in China.[8] It is not clear when he came to Canada, but he became a naturalized citizen on October 7, 1907, in the County Court of Victoria, British Columbia.[9] According to the local history of Spirit River, the village where Wing later settled, he came to Canada in 1903.[10] This must be taken with a grain of salt – the local history is based largely on personal recollections and contains numerous errors; there is, for example, some confusion about the year in which half the village burned down.[11] Regardless of the exact date of his arrival in Canada or in Spirit River, it is likely that his early experiences in Canada were broadly similar to the experiences of other Chinese Canadians of this period.

Scholarly consensus exists concerning the history of late nineteenth- and early twentieth-century Chinese immigrants to Canada.[12] Chinese people, or more specifically Chinese men, began coming to Canada in large numbers during the second half of the nineteenth century. Many of these early immigrants helped build the transnational railway and, both during and after its completion, they also found jobs in the mines and mining camps of British Columbia.[13] At the turn of the twentieth century, most Chinese Canadians lived in British Columbia, and both Vancouver and Victoria had sizable Chinatowns. At the same time, Chinese immigrants had begun to move eastward, with Chinatowns beginning to appear in most major Prairie cities as well as the central Canadian cities.[14] In addition, particularly on the Prairies, there was usually at least one Chinese-run restaurant in each small town.[15]

As useful as Chinese Canadian labour was to the transnational railway, with its promise of national economic integration, Canadians did not consider Chinese people to be "desirable citizens."[16] Late nineteenth-century white Canadians, much like their American counterparts, were in the midst of a panic about racial purity. Concerns about moral and social decline led to a number of reform movements as well as significant racist backlash. For Chinese people, the backlash was manifested in a similar manner on both sides of the Canadian border. Both the United States and Canada imposed restrictions on Chinese immigration and limits on what Chinese people could do if and when they were admitted.[17] In Canada, several provinces, for example, passed legislation prohibiting Chinese men from employing white women,[18] while others passed legislation preventing even naturalized Chinese (and Japanese) men from voting.[19]

At the federal level, immigration restrictions on Chinese people expanded from a law that made it almost impossible for Chinese women to immigrate to one that banned any further Chinese immigration in 1923.[20] As such, many Chinese Canadian men, including Charlie Wing, had to leave their wives and children behind in China.[21] American and Canadian scholarship shows that in the Chinatowns of the major cities, Chinese men could and did form community groups, and through these groups found both social and legal support.[22] While smaller settlements, such as the many towns and villages on the Canadian Prairies did not have the large, formal social groups of major Chinatowns, many Chinese Canadians worked in partnership with each other.[23]

Although Chinese Canadian experiences have not tended to loom large in histories of prohibition in Canada, Chinese Canadians often found themselves accused of liquor law violations.[24] The records suggest that at least some Chinese Canadians in Alberta were convicted of such violations – though so too were ample numbers of white Canadians – but some of the accusations levelled at Chinese Canadians were motivated by little more than racist stereotypes about Chinese people. Anti-Chinese racism was not the driving force behind prohibition, but the concerns that animated anti-Chinese feeling were similar to those that drove the prohibitionists and other moral reformers of the period.[25]

During the first half of the twentieth century, Alberta had a relatively small Chinese Canadian community. According to the 1921 census, Chinese people made up less than three-quarters of a percent of Alberta's population.[26] Of this tiny proportion, the majority of Chinese Canadians were foreign-born, and the vast majority were not naturalized citizens.[27] In terms of his citizenship, then, Wing was something of a rarity in Alberta. What was more typical of Wing was his being in the hospitality business. Despite the small size of the Chinese Canadian population as a whole, Chinese Canadians ran a disproportionate number of cafes, restaurants, and the like.[28] This had the effect of making an otherwise small population highly visible.

The nature of the fears surrounding Chinese men in early twentieth-century Canada varied. Some of the concern was tied to the opium trade, which had become steadily demonized as the nineteenth century became the twentieth.[29] But some of the concern was little more than straightforward racism and a mistrust of people who were not Anglo-Canadians. Even though Anglo-Canadians tended to view Chinese men as a sexual threat to white women, they also tended to consider them as too effeminate to be real men.[30] The former fear was manifested in the so-called white women's labour laws, while the latter belief mattered when it came to licensing decisions once prohibition ended.[31]

Charlie Wing and the Dominion Hotel

As mentioned earlier, the exact date of Wing's arrival in Spirit River is unclear. What is more important, however, is what happened when he got there. Instead of being pushed to the margins of the nascent settlement, Wing somehow became an involved and admired citizen, and he continued to be warmly remembered decades after he died. He was a member of the local curling team, where he earned the nickname Charlie "Mac" Wing,[32] and he later played a key role in persuading a doctor to move to the town.[33] His hotel was among the finest anywhere in northern Alberta, and *Chepi Sepe,* the local history, contains many fond recollections about Wing and his hotel. People recalled him sharing Chinese tea and helping the curling team to a few wins, or remembered how their family stayed at his hotel until something more permanent came along.[34]

Yet, as warm as these local memories are, there is still a sense that he was somehow apart. It is also clear that, even as late as the 1980s, many of the white residents of Spirit River held stereotypical views about Chinese people. Some of the recollections have Wing or his relatives speaking in pidgin English and references to his Chineseness are never very far away. Whether or not his spoken English was fluent cannot be proven, but his written English, based on the letters he wrote to the ALCB, was no better or worse than other licensees of the period. (Of course, Wing could have had somebody else write his letters, and written language can be more fluent than spoken language.)

Nonetheless, Wing remained stereotyped. For example, in *Chepi Sepe,* one family recalled seeing Wing crying at their father's funeral and commented that "The Chinese are not supposed to be emotional."[35] As warmly remembered as he was, it is clear that some recollections still saw him as an other, as different, as not quite one of the community. Insofar as he foreshadowed the later "model minority" stereotype of Chinese Canadians and Chinese Americans,[36] he also foreshadowed the sense in which the "model minority" remains "immutably foreign."[37] Here Wing's experiences call to mind Yuko Kawai's argument about the dialectic of the model minority and the yellow peril. Kawai notes that these two stereotypes coexist and are inseparable;[38] no matter how good a citizen and how involved Wing was, he remained apart, even becoming a threat because of how successful he was. Granted, Wing's hotel and restaurant, particularly in Spirit River, were known as Wing's place or Wing's hotel,[39] rather than the "Chinese place," but this should not be taken as evidence that he never suffered racism while in Spirit River.

The version of the Dominion Hotel that was so praised by the *Edmonton Bulletin* in 1922 was built during Alberta's prohibition era.[40] Thus, the praise heaped on Wing by the *Bulletin* ought to be considered exceptional for three reasons. First, running such a high-quality hotel in a remote region of Alberta was incredibly difficult – hotels in Edmonton struggled to meet the standards Wing's hotel set. Second, Wing's Chinese origins render such praise unexpected given the racist attitudes of the time. Third, Wing had managed to build and run a successful hotel without the income from a bar. By the early 1920s, there were some mutterings that hotels really needed bars to be successful and that without such an income hotel accommodation was in terminal decline.[41] Here, hotelkeepers in favour of bars found common cause with those opposed to prohibition. As Spirit River was being rebuilt, a loose coalition who called themselves Moderationists or the Moderation League of Alberta[42] had already begun their attempts to repeal prohibition.[43]

In 1923, the activism of Alberta's Moderationists helped prompt a plebiscite over the future of prohibition. The result was firmly in favour of ending prohibition. The subsequent Liquor Control Act allowed for liquor stores and hotel beer parlours.[44] Almost immediately, hotelkeepers and other interested individuals began inquiring about the licensing system and making suggestions about who should be licensed.[45] Wing wrote the board in February 1924 to say that he intended to apply for a licence and that he was a "naturalized Canadian citizen."[46]

The newly formed ALCB had quite limited guidance about *who* would make a suitable licensee. Aside from the standard ineligibilities of those of poor character, recent convictions, and youth, neither the act nor the board's own regulations contained much in the way of additional qualifications or disqualifications. Federal legislation was also largely silent here, aside from the prohibition imposed on Status Indians.[47] Unlike British Columbia, Alberta never adopted explicitly racist limits, nor did it seem to require that all its licensees be naturalized citizens.[48]

What the ALCB did have were its own prejudices and preferences. In terms of the board's own staff, chairman and sole board member Dinning came out in favour of returned soldiers and, in his first annual report, boasted about the high numbers of such men among the board's staff.[49] With respect to potential hotel licensees, the board had to decide among those who applied. Upon receipt of an application for a licence and, in later years, renewal applications, the board would perform an inspection of the hotel.[50] The resulting report, typically a standard form filled out by one of the board's hotel inspectors, contained observations about the applicant and the applicant's hotel, as well as observations about how the hotel and applicant were viewed in the local community. Among the details recorded were the applicant's marital status and whether or not the applicant had any children. Another question concerned the prospective licensee's "nationality," which typically meant ethnicity or race rather than citizenship.

Despite the absence of any official policy on ethnicity and liquor licensing, the board *was* interested in knowing the ethnicity of those applying for licences, among other things. Using licensees' names as a rough proxy for ethnicity, it appears that 10 percent of licences were issued to those of non-British descent in the board's first year.[51] In the inspection reports, the inspectors were often inconsistent in how they described licensees; in Wing's case, they seemed uncertain of how to record his status.[52] At one stage, Wing was recorded as "Chinese (ex-Canadian)"; at another, he was listed as "Naturalized Canadian (Chinese)."[53] Here the inspector conflated questions of citizenship and race and offers an example of the fluidity of these concepts in the minds of the men tasked with recording them.[54] On paper, Wing was a Canadian citizen, but in practice white Canadians struggled to understand what that meant.

Such fluidity was not limited to Wing, however. Other applicants oscillated between "Scotch" and "Scotch Canadian" and even, on one occasion, between "English" and "French."[55] The purpose of the nationality section is not clear, but there is evidence that the board had ethnic preferences. One licence application from 1926 includes a letter from the applicants' lawyer, who noted that the two men, both of Ukrainian origin, had "excellent reputations amongst the Anglo-Saxon population with whom they may have come in contact."[56] Such a letter seems to be a precautionary measure that may speak to anti-Ukrainian bias more generally than any bias on the part of the board. Certainly the board did license a number of Ukrainian Canadian hoteliers, but when it came to Chinese Canadian hoteliers, only Wing was licensed.[57]

While at least some inhabitants of Spirit River may have been able to exempt Wing from some of the stereotypes commonly applied to Chinese Canadians, the ALCB initially seemed reluctant to do the same when hotel beer licences became an option. Wing was not the only Chinese Canadian hotelkeeper in Alberta in 1924, and he was not the only one to apply for such a licence, but the ALCB did not wish to grant licences to them. In fact, in May 1924, the board wrote to the reeve of Spirit River, to inform him that "the Board has notified the solicitors for several Chinese applicants that the Board is averse to the granting of licenses to Chinamen"[58] – an aversion they expressed several times as other people, including Wing's lawyers, wrote to the board to ask whether Wing would get the licence.

At this point, Spirit River had one other hotel: the Spirit Hotel. This hotel was operated by the Irish Canadian Bertha Lee. Lee had been convicted of illegal possession of liquor in 1922, making her a less desirable licensee.[59] Her hotel was really more of a rooming house and, according to the Alberta Provincial Police (APP), had developed a poor reputation since Lee began running it.[60] In theory, the ALCB could have opted not to grant a licence in Spirit River, but that would have left the village open to illicit alcohol. Given its out-of-the-way location and its small size, the only possible legal outlet in the village was either a licensed club, of which there seemed to be none, or a licensed hotel; it was far too small to support a liquor store.[61] Moreover, the populace *wanted* a hotel beer licence, and they wanted Charlie Wing to have it.

The praise heaped on Wing by the village is remarkable and goes beyond anything seen in other hotel files I have examined. Most importantly, the support for Wing continued for the months that it took for the ALCB to actually grant a licence. The board of trade said that Wing had a good character and a modern hotel, while one person noted a petition in his favour was circulated and "signed by practically every businessman, farmer, professional man, many Ladies, and even the local Minister."[62] The reference to the support of women is not accidental and, given that much of early twentieth-century anti-Chinese racism centred on the threat they posed to white women,[63] such a reference both reinforced this "threat" and sought to disassociate Wing from it. The reeve of the village replied to the board's refusal to grant licences to Chinese people with the fact that Wing's hotel was "modern ... electric-lighted," that he served food day or night, and that he "has always been a progressive citizen, always willing to help in the betterment of the District."[64] Both the ALCB's own hotel inspector and the local provincial police agreed that Wing was a proper candidate for a beer licence, though the hotel inspector's agreement was qualified with the comment "unless attitude of board in regards nationality."[65] As to that nationality, the inspector described Wing as "Chinaman naturalized in 1907."[66]

It is clear that for the ALCB the problem was Wing's ethnicity. On June 5, 1924, Chairman Dinning wrote to George F. Peek, the secretary of Spirit River's United Farmers of Alberta (UFA), to note the board's practice against licensing Chinese Canadians but that "you appear to have a Chinamen [sic] of an unusual type and we are prepared to give every consideration to the situation."[67] Still, the board did not agree to issue a licence. Even when Lee's hotel burned down in July, it continued to drag its heels, which, considering that by July most other licensed hotels were busy selling beer, highlights the significant delay in the board's decision.[68] A telegram from Dinning dated August 7 suggested that the board might issue a licence to Wing with a "definite decision in few days."[69] When no decision came, several citizens telegrammed Dinning on August 22 to ask whether Wing would get a licence.[70] As much as this speaks to the village's support for Wing, it can also be read as revealing something important about the white inhabitants of the village. It calls to mind Patricia Williams's observations (albeit in a very different context) about white entitlement[71] – the other residents of Spirit River wanted a licence and they were determined to get one. The residents did not counter the board's racism, except insofar as it would affect them. That is, they tacitly construed Wing as an exception rather than objecting to the racist assumptions underpinning the board's stance.

On August 23, 1924, Dinning wrote to J. Forster of the License Department to say that "we have no alternative but to issue a license to the Chinaman at this place [Spirit River], and if the requirements have all been met it will be in order for the license to be issued without further delay."[72] Licensing Wing was not a decision Dinning wanted to make, and he did so only because of the support Wing had from the local populace. Dinning's reluctance was likely rooted in his own assumptions about Chinese

Canadians as well as his concerns about how this would reflect on the newly created ALCB.

Once he had the licence, Wing proceeded to run one of the best hotels in Alberta. The local history claims that he received some kind of official acknowledgment as the best hotel in northern Alberta, but the archival records make no mention of such recognition.[73] Certainly, the hotel received almost continual praise and local opinion was always happy with Wing and his hotel. Ironically, such was Wing's reputation that when reports surfaced that Wing's hotel was not up to standard, ALCB staff expressed surprise that "Charlie Wing would allow his service to deteriorate to this extent."[74] As it turned out, the reports were unfounded.

There were, as was common with licensed hotels, a few issues here and there. In 1926, for example, Wing's beer room attendant served some beer to a minor. The ALCB's Enforcement Branch was of the opinion that the informant in the case had a grudge against the attendant for refusing him service;[75] nonetheless, a prosecution against Wing was laid on the grounds that he was responsible for the acts of his agent. The case was dismissed but Dinning warned Wing to be more careful in the future and said that had he been convicted, his licence would have been suspended.[76]

The following year, Wing had several months of trouble with his beer room and was blamed for several alleged instances of drunkenness in the town. The trouble with the beer room stemmed from Wing's difficulty in finding a suitable attendant. Somewhat unusually for a licensee, Wing did not actually work in the beer room himself, but instead hired white men to run it for him. Such a move was approved of by the ALCB and the APP. The local APP officer echoed Dinning's earlier comments about how Chinese men were unable to control drunk white men, while ALCB Preventive Officer A.W.A. Stewart-Irvine wrote that "I advised him [Wing] that, as the Licensee, he had every right to conduct his own premises, but that I thought it would be in his own interests to have a white man to assist him, as forceful measures used by him might rouse resentment."[77] Here the board sought to justify its request by claiming that *other people* might not like it. There is doubtless a kernel of truth in Stewart-Irvine's assertions but it must be read alongside the ways the board had used hotel licensees as a way of guaranteeing white-run establishments.[78] It would seem that despite the fact that the licensee was a Chinese Canadian, the board was still keen for the Dominion Hotel to *look* as though it were white-run.

Wing may have been happy to comply with the call for white staff, but he was unhappy with the allegations that his hotel caused drunkenness. He suggested that the drunken disturbances might have been caused by moonshine and not his beer parlour. He also defended his hotel's reputation, noting that "I am told by the travelling public that the Spirit River hostelry and beer parlour are conducted, not only on a par, but in much better shape that many in the province."[79] Wing's letter suggests some frustration with the ALCB's tendency to believe that *any* disturbance in the town was the fault of the local licensee. The problem for the board was that the local populace could not distinguish between drunkenness due to legal outlets and drunkenness due to illegal outlets of liquor. The board's critique of Wing was not motivated by any animosity towards Wing; rather, it was prompted by the board's concern for its own reputation. The board often displayed excessive concern about what the public thought, and would go to great lengths to protect its own reputation.[80]

Despite his frustration, Wing agreed to find another beer parlour attendant, while Dinning replied to Wing's allegations about moonshine with the comment that blaming "objectionable conditions" on moonshine was "an old, old excuse used by licensees when they are checked up."[81] Interestingly, in 1927, Preventive Officer Stewart-Irvine echoed Wing's opinion about the source of drunkenness in Spirit River. Stewart-Irvine had gone to the village to observe conditions during the Victoria Day holiday and blamed moonshine rather than Wing's hotel.[82] Although hotels did draw people towards legal outlets, illicit outlets remained despite the board's best efforts to stamp them out.

More important than these alleged infractions was Wing's tendency to hire white staff. Alberta had never had the white women's labour laws that were seen in Saskatchewan and Ontario. In Alberta, the only barrier to the hiring of white women by Chinese men was public opinion. In any case, Wing would have been precluded from hiring *any* woman to work in the beer parlour as the only woman allowed to work in licensed premises was the licensee or the wife of the licensee.[83] He remained free to hire whomever he wanted to take care of the other parts of the hotel. The ALCB seemed pleased that Wing had hired a white woman to look after the housekeeping issues.[84] The only recorded opposition to this dates from 1938, when the hotel inspector's report noted that one (unnamed) prominent citizen had doubts about "Orientals" hiring white girls "but could site [sic] no definite reason to support this opinion."[85] It is tempting to read the inspector's challenge as favouring Wing, but it could have equally been evidence that the inspector had his own racist suspicions about the moral character of Chinese men. Either way, the board had no qualms about Wing's hiring of white women, though in later years Wing's nephews took over some of this work.

Despite running one of the best hotels in northern Alberta, if not Alberta as a whole, Wing was not content to rest on his laurels. As early as 1925, he displayed an interest in expanding his business. In August that year, he wrote to the ALCB about securing a second licence in Waterhole, a neighbouring district. The board replied to say that it could not make any definite promises at that point in time.[86] Wing had bought a hotel in the region, however, and his struggle to get it licensed offers a stark contrast to his experiences in Spirit River.

The Empire Hotel, Fairview, Alberta

The Empire Hotel in Fairview seems to have initially been in the name of D.J. Wing, not Charlie Wing. It appears that the two men were either related or in business together, and, based on a letter from the secretary-treasurer of Fairview, they had been in Fairview for six years.[87] As with Spirit River, the service the Wings provided had made quite an impression, and they had "always maintained a clean and orderly house to which no-one need be ashamed to go with their wife or daughter and have many times supplied meals free to persons who had not the money to pay for them."[88] Again, the reference to "wife or daughter" both reinforced the racist fears about Chinese men and white women while seeking to dissociate the Wings from them. For some reason that was never explained, the board refused to issue a licence in Fairview, then known as the "Waterhole District," for "nearly five years."[89]

The ALCB's opinion on the suitability of a licence changed when the railway was extended west to Fairview in 1928.[90] In obvious anticipation of the railway's arrival, Charlie Wing appears to have completely rebuilt the Empire Hotel in the hope of getting a licence.[91] Wing was not the only one who thought that the arrival of the railway might change the board's mind with respect to a beer licence in Fairview. Two men, by the names of E.G. Norris and Matheson, bought the Fairview Hotel, dividing opinion over whether there should be a licence and, if so, who should get it. According to D.M. Kennedy, the MP for the region, who met with the ALCB supervisor of licences, "the only objection to Charlie Wing was the fact that he was a Chinamen [sic]."Kennedy noted Wing's connection to the territory and his "first-class accommodation," and the fact that Norris and Matheson were thought to have arrived in Fairview with the sole aim of securing a licence.[92] What potentially worked in Norris's favour was that he was a veteran of the First World War and had seen active service in France.[93]

As the board dithered over who should receive the licence, Fairview held a local option vote to determine whether *any* licence should be allowed. Tensions ran high in the run-up to the vote, and Dinning wrote to Stewart-Irvine that "it is necessary that we take every precaution to eliminate any possibility of the Board being accused of discrimination."[94] Dinning did not say towards whom he wished to avoid discriminating. It is likely that this is further evidence of the board's concern for its own reputation, more specifically that it be seen as neutral and even-handed.[95] As it turned out, on May 10, 1929, Fairview voted 255 to 217 against beer licences, rendering the question of who should receive the licence moot.[96]

In theory, the local option vote ought to have settled the matter. The Liquor Control Act stated that such votes could be held only every two years.[97] Fairview proved to be the exception, however, and the reason for this appeared to be the competition between potential licensees. When D.J. Wing had applied in 1924, a handful of people from the region had written to support this application,[98] but by the late 1920s the majority opinion appeared to have turned against the Wings. Days prior to the 1929 vote, Norris, the potential licensee of the Fairview Hotel, complained to the board days that people would vote dry just to keep the licence from going to a non-white person. Dinning replied that the board would be guided by the will of the majority and suggested an unofficial ballot alongside the local option vote with respect to the preferred licensee.[99] Once again, the board wished to be seen as merely following the will of the populace.

It is not clear when the unofficial ballot was held, but the board held one at some point between 1929 and August 27, 1930, when Fairview held a second local option vote. In the interval between the two votes, Dinning actually visited the Peace River district and saw both hotels. His opinion was that the Empire Hotel, which had reportedly cost Wing $40,000 and had hot and cold running water in all rooms, would do credit to any city, while the Fairview Hotel, which had reportedly cost only $10,000, was good but not good enough for a place like Fairview. Echoing Kennedy, Dinning wrote: "I cannot but think it was built solely for the purpose of obtaining a license." However, he also noted that the people in Fairview would rather have a "vendors' [liquor] store" than a hotel beer parlour.[100]

Three key points need to be unpacked from Dinning's commentary. The first concerns the relative standard of each hotel. Since its creation, the ALCB had assured the population of Alberta that it licensed only the *best* hotels.[101] The Empire Hotel was clearly the best hotel in northern Alberta, and had Wing been white it is difficult to see what objection the board could have had to granting him a second licence. The ALCB may also have boasted about all that it did for Canada's veterans but, again, had Wing been white, Norris's service would have been of little consequence. Regardless of how much sympathy the board might have had for former soldiers, the quality of hotel service to the public should have come first. Even though the ALCB knew that Wing was more than capable of running a licensed hotel, it refused to come out in his favour.

The second point has to do with Fairview's alleged preference for a liquor store rather than a beer parlour. Following the end of prohibition, Albertans could buy alcohol in a liquor store or through the mail in locations where there was no store, or buy beer in their local beer parlour, assuming their town or village had one. As the ALCB could not afford to open a physical store in every settlement in the province, these stores had a certain cachet. Liquor stores and their locations also spoke to efforts to push parts of the population towards certain *kinds* of liquor. For example, the ALCB refused to open a liquor store in Andrew, located in the central, eastern part of the province. The official reason was that Andrew was not big enough to justify a liquor store, but the unofficial reason probably had much to do with the large Ukrainian Canadian population in that area and fears about their likely drinking habits.[102] Thus, the existence of a liquor store suggested not only that a particular settlement was of a suitable size – which likely played to the pride of the boosters in developing regions such as Fairview – but also that the people of that settlement could be trusted to drink appropriately.

The third key point is that the ALCB itself seemed to want some form of legal outlet in Fairview. It is not clear that the purpose of Dinning's trip was solely to tour the hotels of the northern region. He was also involved in the development of the province's natural resources industry, and this may have played a part in his trip north.[103] Nonetheless, the ALCB did seem to be pushing for some form of legal outlet and began searching for a way around the two-year gap between local option votes. One potential solution centred on Fairview's shift from hamlet to village.

The government of Alberta referred the question of Fairview's local option to the Appellate Division of the Supreme Court of Alberta.[104] The reference procedure offered, and still offers, Canadian governments a way to obtain a judicial opinion on whether or not a certain course of action is legal. In the case of *Re Fairview,* the question posed to the court was "whether the Village of Fairview could be created a Local Option area prior to the expiration of two years after the taking of the local option plebiscite in the enlarged hamlet of Fairview, which plebiscite was taken on the 10th day of May, 1929."[105] The rather technical legal question turned on the fact that when Fairview had voted in 1929, it had done so as an "enlarged hamlet."

Initially, only municipalities or an electoral division could be a local option area. In 1927, the latter was "eliminated," but hamlets were also excluded from their overarching municipality, meaning that hamlets could not vote with the municipality and the municipality could not vote for its hamlets.[106] In 1928, the local option provisions were changed so that a hamlet could petition for a local option vote and then the lieutenant-governor-in-council could enlarge the hamlet by adding adjacent territory, even if that territory had not so petitioned for a vote. At the time of the 1929 vote, Fairview "had all the qualifications of a village" but was not made a village until March 28, 1929, three days after the enlarged hamlet of Fairview was made a local option area for the purposes of holding a local option vote.[107] Chief Justice of Alberta Horace Harvey, writing for the majority, noted that Fairview had never really exercised local option because of the addition of the contiguous territory,[108] the point being that he thought that the village of Fairview could have its desired local option vote.

When Fairview voted at the end of August 1930, the result was a tie: sixty-three in favour of beer licences, sixty-three against.[109] At the time, Wing appeared to be trying to find a way to circumvent the racism of Fairview's residents. He took the step he had suggested to the board in 1924 when he was trying to get a licence for the Dominion Hotel, and incorporated a limited company that he planned to use to apply for the beer licence.[110] The board replied that the majority wanted the licence to go to Norris, suggesting that they had already held their "unofficial" vote. The board advised Wing to let the matter stand, and that even though his hotel was better, they were bound by the wishes of the majority.[111] So much for licensing only the best hotels.

In terms of the unofficial vote, the results were 145 in favour of Wing and 158 in favour of Norris.[112] Given the result of the official local option vote, the ALCB declined to issue any licence in Fairview. Norris sold his hotel to E. McAdam, who would eventually receive a licence for the Fairview Hotel when Fairview definitively voted for beer sales in 1932.[113] Meanwhile, Wing's lawyers wrote to the board on November 14, 1930, asking for a refund of the licence and application fees as no licence had been issued. They also informed the board that the Empire Hotel had burned down.[114]

Charlie Wing's Life after the Empire Hotel

Despite Wing's failure to secure a licence for the Empire Hotel, he continued to run the Dominion Hotel in Spirit River and a restaurant or cafe in Fairview as well.[115] Both the local histories of Spirit River and Fairview comment on how Wing liked children and had a habit of handing out candy to them.[116] Even though Fairview failed to support Wing's attempt to obtain a beer licence, he still had a reputation for providing excellent service. In fact, his cafe would prove to be something of a bugbear for the eventual licensee of Fairview since McAdam could not compete with Wing's place, or the other Chinese Canadian–run establishments in Fairview.[117]

It is tempting to link Wing's fondness for children with the fact that his own children remained in China, no doubt a result of the immigration restrictions on Chinese people. With one exception, neither local history displays any awareness of these limits,[118] and neither do the ALCB's own records. In 1926, the ALCB hotel inspector noted that Wing's wife was in

China, while in 1935 the hotel inspector recorded that he had three children, all of whom were in China.[119] In 1934, there is a reference to Wing's working on the steamships between Vancouver and China, and perhaps he used this as a way to travel back to China to visit his wife and family.[120] The local history notes that Wing had "accepted a job from CPR steamships to establish boat runs from Vancouver to mainland China,"[121] so it may have been a business opportunity as well.

With respect to his family life, Wing's story was typical of many Chinese Canadians in the early twentieth century. Very few men were able to bring their families to Canada due to immigration restrictions placed on Chinese people for much of the first half of the century. Yet for all its similarities, Wing's story highlights the horrific consequences of this immigration policy. In February 1938, Wing left his hotel to travel to China once again. More specifically, he travelled to Nanking (Nanjing) and was "trying to locate his family."[122] The timing of his visit is significant, coming as it did just after the Nanking Massacre, a war crime during the Second Sino-Japanese War that saw Japanese soldiers committing mass murder and rape against the civilian population of city over a period of weeks at the end of 1937. There is no record of whether Wing found his family, or whether he lost any family members during the massacre, but he returned to Spirit River, where he seems to have died in 1944[123]. Even if he did find his family, the ban on Chinese immigration would have prevented him from bringing them to Canada. *Chepi Sepe* describes Wing as being survived by "his wife and one son in China."[124] While it is not clear whether his two other children died in the Nanking Massacre or at some other time, or even how many children he had,[125] what is clear is that, if not for the head tax and the ban on Chinese immigration, Wing's family would probably have been in Canada at the time of the Nanking Massacre.

In 1943, Wing sold the Dominion Hotel to Rupert Wady and Steve Kirstiuk. He informed the ALCB of the sale and thanked it for its "courteous treatment of me during the years I have operated the hotel."[126] As the 1930s gave way to the 1940s, Wing had been struggling to keep the Dominion up to standard. He was not alone – the Depression hit Alberta hard and all businesses, including hotels, were affected.[127] The board seemed sensitive to these difficulties and, while continuing to press for improvements, did not threaten punishment for non-compliance in the same way it would once have.[128]

Overall, the board's relationship with Wing is difficult to categorize. On the one hand, the ALCB did go from being deeply suspicious of any Chinese Canadian–run hotel to holding him in high esteem; on the other, the ALCB refused to support his efforts to secure the second licence, even though it knew his hotel to be better than the competition, not to mention his proven record of service. This is perhaps a reflection of the board's desire to allow the community to have the final say, given that they would have to deal with the consequences. Certainly, the reason Wing succeeded in Spirit River but failed in Fairview had much to do with the lobbying efforts of each village's populace and little to do with the board's own standards and policies, and, indeed, had little to do with Wing himself.

Anti-Chinese racism was still potent in Alberta in the 1920s and '30s, but given Wing's successful and apparently well-frequented cafe in Fairview, the nub of the opposition to him appears to have centred on his attempt to get a beer licence. This suggests that attitudes linking Chinese men with immorality still had traction in Alberta. No one who opposed Wing gave any explicit reasons why, other than making a reference to his race and the fact that it would be "outrageous" to give a licence to a Chinese Canadian.[129] At the time, hotel beer licences were something of a privilege and there were not enough for every hotel to be granted one. For some of the people of Fairview, such privileges were not to be bestowed on the basis of merit but on the basis of race. Then again, perhaps merit and race were synonymous in the minds of those in Fairview who opposed Wing. Wing may have been a naturalized citizen in a legal sense, but racism ensured that he was not an equal citizen.

Notes

1 "Spirit River Is Better Village Being Rebuilt," *Edmonton Bulletin,* March 2, 1922.
2 David C. Jones, *Empire of Dust: Settling and Abandoning the Prairie Dry Belt* (Calgary: University of Calgary Press, 2002), 20–33.
3 "Spirit River Is Better Village Being Rebuilt."
4 This was sometimes spelled "Charley Wing," but the more common spelling was "Charlie."
5 Prohibition was introduced by the Liquor Act, SA 1916, c 4, and repealed by Liquor Control Act, SA 1924, c 14.

6 R.J. Dinning to R.A. Harrington, May 17, 1924, Provincial Archives of Alberta (PAA), RG74.412, file 2387.

7 R.J. Dinning to Alex Bennett, Reeve of Waterhole, September 2, 1924, PAA, RG74.412, file 1307.

8 The year of birth is taken from what appears to be his gravestone in Spirit River's cemetery, a record of which is online: https://billiongraves.com/grave/Charlie-Wing/5666002#.

9 Charlie Wing to Robert J. Dinning, February 15, 1924; T.W. Lawlor to Premier Greenfield, May 1, 1924, PAA, RG74.412, file 2387.

10 Spirit River History Book Committee, *Chepi Sepe: Spirit River: The Land, The People* (Spirit River, AB: Spirit River History Book Committee, 1989), 919.

11 Ibid., 367 (note here the date is given as 1922).

12 Peter S. Li, *The Chinese in Canada*, 2nd ed. (Oxford: Oxford University Press, 1998); Patricia E. Roy, *The Triumph of Citizenship: The Japanese and Chinese in Canada, 1941–67* (Vancouver: UBC Press, 2007); Patricia E. Roy, *The Oriental Question: Consolidating a White Man's Province, 1914–1941* (Vancouver: UBC Press, 2003). See also Constance Backhouse, "Legal Discrimination against the Chinese in Canada: The Historical Framework," in *Calling Power to Account: Law, Reparations, and the Chinese Canadian Head Tax Case*, ed. David Dyzenhaus and Mayo Moran (Toronto: University of Toronto Press, 2005), 24; Constance Backhouse, "The White Women's Labor Laws: Anti-Chinese Racism in Early Twentieth-Century Canada," *Law and History Review* 14 (1996): 315; Peter S. Li, "Chinese Immigrants on the Canadian Prairie, 1910–47," *Canadian Review of Sociology and Anthropology* 19 (1982): 527; Anthony B. Chan, "Bachelor Workers," in *A Nation of Immigrants: Women, Workers, and Communities in Canadian History, 1840s–1960s*, ed. Franca Iacovetta, Paula Draper, and Robert Ventresca (Toronto: University of Toronto Press, 1998), 231. This list is not exhaustive.

13 Bruce Ryder, "Racism and the Constitution: The Constitutional Fate of British Columbia Anti-Asian Immigration Legislation, 1884–1909," *Osgoode Hall Law Journal* 29 (1991): 619, 642, 645; Chan, "Bachelor Workers," 238.

14 Li, "Chinese Immigrants," 530; Chan, "Bachelor Workers," 232.

15 Lily Cho, *Eating Chinese: Culture on the Menu in Small Town Canada* (Toronto: University of Toronto Press, 2010), 5–6.

16 Li, *Chinese in Canada*, 3, 17. For the railway's national importance, see Doug Owram, *The Promise of Eden: The Canadian Expansionist Movement and the Idea of the West* (Toronto: University of Toronto Press, 1992), 49, 101, 121–24.

17 Charles J. McClain, *In Search of Equality: The Chinese Struggle against Discrimination in Nineteenth-Century America* (Berkeley: University of California Press, 1994). Similar restrictions also existed in Mexico: Kif Augustine-Adams, "Making Mexico: Legal Nationality, Chinese Race and the 1930 Population Census," *Law and History Review* 27 (2009): 113.

18 Backhouse, "White Women's Labor Laws."

19 *Cunningham v Homma,* [1902] UKPC 60, [1903] 9 AC 151; Li, *Chinese in Canada,* 34. The same situation existed in the United States: John Hayakawa Torok, "Reconstruction and Racial Nativism: Chinese Immigrants and the Debates on the Thirteenth, Fourteenth, and Fifteenth Amendments and Civil Rights Laws," *Asian Law Journal* 3 (1996): 55, 69.

20 *Chinese Immigration Act,* SC 1885, c 71; *Chinese Immigration Act,* SC 1923, c 38; Li, *Chinese in Canada,* 63–66, 73–74.

21 Charlie Wing's family is discussed later in this chapter.

22 McClain, *In Search of Equality,* 14, 23, 47–48; Li, *Chinese in Canada,* 77.

23 Li, "Chinese Immigrants," 543–36.

24 See Sarah Elizabeth Mary Hamill, *From Prohibition to Administrative Regulation: The Battle for Liquor Control in Alberta, 1916 to 1939* (PhD dissertation, University of Alberta, 2014), 109–31.

25 For more on the reformers of this period, see Mariana Valverde, *The Age of Light, Soap and Water: Moral Reform in English Canada, 1885–1925* (Toronto: University of Toronto Press, 2008).

26 Dominion of Canada, Bureau of Statistics, *Origin, Birthplace, Nationality, and Language of the Canadian People (A Census Study Based on the Census of 1921 and Supplementary Data)* (Ottawa: F.A. Acland, King's Printer, 1929), 86.

27 Dominion of Canada, *Origin, Birthplace,* 95, 151.

28 Cho, *Eating Chinese,* 8 (she notes that the 1931 census shows Chinese people made up less than 1 percent of the population, but one out of every five restaurants, taverns, or cafes was run by a Chinese person).

29 See Dan Malleck, *When Good Drugs Go Bad: Opium, Medicine, and the Origins of Canada's Drug Laws* (Vancouver: UBC Press, 2015), 87–135.

30 Valverde, *Age of Light,* 57, 111.

31 This is further discussed below.

32 Spirit River History Book Committee, *Chepi Sepe,* 920.

33 Ibid., 920.

34 Ibid., 401, 568, 702, 747, , 844.

35 Ibid., 470.

36 Doobo Shim, "From Yellow Peril through Model Minority to Renewed Yellow Peril," *Journal of Communication Inquiry* 22, 4 (1998): 385–409.

37 Yuko Kawai, "Stereotyping Asian Americans: The Dialectic of the Model Minority and the Yellow Peril," *Howard Journal of Communications* 16, 2 (2005): 109, 117.

38 Kawai, "Stereotyping," 115; see also Shim, "From Yellow Peril."

39 Spirit River History Book Committee, *Chepi Sepe,* 367, 568, 702, 735, 747, 885.

40 I say version as it is unclear whether Wing ran a hotel or just a restaurant before the fire of 1921.

41 Sarah E. Hamill, "Liquor Laws, Legal Continuity, and Hotel Beer Parlours in Alberta, 1924 to c 1939," *Histoire Sociale/Social History* 49, 100 (2016): 581.

42 There are a few letters and so on from the Moderation League, but it does not appear to have left behind any records of its own.

43 For this story, see Sarah E. Hamill, "Prohibition Plebiscites on the Prairies: (Not-So) Direct Legislation and Liquor Control in Alberta, 1915 to 1932," *Law and History Review* 33, 2 (2015): 377–410.

44 Government Liquor Control Act of Alberta, SA 1924 (4th Sess), c 14.

45 See, e.g., Letter/petition from Rocky Mountain House, December 3, 1923, PAA, RG75.126, file 2565; R. Harris of Hotel Arlington, Pincher Creek, to Deputy Attorney General, October 18, 1923 (note that Harris actually wrote *before* the plebiscite had taken place); J.A. Livingstone to Deputy Attorney General, November 23, 1923, PAA, RG75.126, file 3728.

46 Wing to Robert J. Dinning, February 15, 1924, PAA, RG74.412, file 2387.

47 The prohibition was not repealed until after the Second World War: Craig Heron, *Booze: A Distilled History* (Toronto: Between the Lines, 2003), 319.

48 In British Columbia, licensees had to be citizens: Robert A. Campbell, *Sit Down and Drink Your Beer: Regulating Vancouver's Beer Parlours, 1925–1954* (Toronto: University of Toronto Press, 2001), 81.

49 *First Annual Report of the Alberta Liquor Control Board 1924,* in *Sessional Papers* (1925), 5 (roughly 75 percent of the board's staff consisted of returned men).

50 In cases of first-time applicants, the ALCB would also secure police reports and other references.

51 *First Annual Report.*

52 Cf. Augustine-Adams, "Making Mexico," 116.

53 Report of Inspector on Hotel Application, November 12, 1927; Report of Inspector on Hotel Application, December 14, 1924, PAA, RG74.412, file 2387.

54 Augustine-Adams, "Making Mexico," 117.

55 See, e.g., the descriptions of George McLean of Edmonton's Ritz Hotel and Bertha Hetu of the Queen's Hotel Edmonton, PAA, RG74.412, file 1199 and file 1191.

56 Friedmand and Lieberman, Barristers, to R.J. Dinning, December 28, 1926, PAA, RG74.412, file 1114.

57 Wing remained, as far as I can tell, the only Chinese Canadian licensee in Alberta until he sold his hotel in the 1940s.

58 ALCB to Reeve of Spirit River, May 8, 1924, PAA, RG74.412, file 2387. The reeve's name on this letter looks like "F.J. Hoelyn," but on a later telegram is transcribed as "F.J. Dodge." Based on the index of the local history, the correct name was likely James Freeman Dodge or Freeman James Dodge although his entries in the book makes no mention of his time as reeve: Spirit River History Book Committee, *Chepi Sepe,* 365–68.

59 The weight of prohibition-era convictions varied from province to province. In Alberta, particularly in the early days, it appears to have counted against becoming a licensee.

60 Report of Inspector on Hotel Application, May 21, 1924; A.P.P. Report, Spirit River Detachment, June 7, 1924; Lawlor of Lawlor and Sissons to Premier Greenfield, May 1, 1924, PAA, RG74.412, file 2387.
61 I will come back to this point later.
62 Secretary of Board of Trade to ALCB Commissioner, February 26, 1924; Lawlor of Lawlor and Sissons to Hughson Baker, Secretary of the Office of the Premier, May 7, 1924, PAA, RG74.412, file 2387.
63 Backhouse, "White Women's Labor Laws."
64 Reeve of Spirit River to ALCB, May 14, 1924, PAA, RG74.412, file 2387.
65 Report of Hotel Inspector on Hotel Application, May 25, 1924, PAA, RG74.412, file 2387.
66 Ibid.
67 Dinning to Peek, June 5, 1924, PAA, RG74.412, file 2387.
68 Lawlor and Sissons to Dinning, July 16, 1924, PAA, RG74.412, file 2387.
69 Telegram from Dinning to W.E. Davies, August 7, 1924.
70 Telegram from various citizens of Spirit River to Dinning, August 22, 1924, PAA, RG74.412, file 2387.
71 Patricia Williams, "Spirit-Murdering the Messenger: The Discourse of Fingerpointing as the Law's Response to Racism," *University of Miami Law Review* 42 (1987): 127, 147–50.
72 Memo from Dinning to Forster, August 23, 1924, PAA, RG74.412, file 2387.
73 Spirit River History Book Committee, *Chepi Sepe,* 110.
74 Supervisor of Licenses to ALCB Inspector A.T. Neale, July 31, 1930, PAA, RG74.412, file 2387.
75 ALCB Enforcement Branch, Liquor Report, Grande Prairie, October 14, 1926, PAA, RG74.412, file 2387.
76 Dinning to Wing, October 19, 1926, PAA, RG74.412, file 2387.
77 A.P.P. Report, Spirit River Detachment, April 25, 1927; Stewart-Irvine to Dinning, April 26, 1927, PAA, RG74.412, file 2387.
78 Hamill, "Liquor Laws," 581–602.
79 Wing to Dinning, April 1, 1927, PAA, RG74.412, file 2387.
80 Sarah E. Hamill, "The Alberta Liquor Control Board and the Question of Administrative Independence, 1924–1939," *Alberta Law Review* 55, 3 (2016): 766–67. Such a concern with reputation was by no means limited to the ALCB. Malleck shows that the Liquor Control Board of Ontario was just as concerned with its own reputation: Dan Malleck, *Try to Control Yourself: The Regulation of Public Drinking in Post-Prohibition Ontario, 1927–44* (Vancouver: UBC Press, 2012).
81 Dinning to Wing, April 4, 1927, PAA, RG74.412, file 2387.
82 Stewart-Irvine to A.H. Schurer, Supervisor of Enforcement, May 26, 1927, PAA, RG74.412, file 2387.
83 *ALCB Regulations,* Reg 13(h), found in C 604–24, *Alberta Gazette* (1924), 320–21.

84 Report of Inspector on Hotel Application, November 12, 1927, PAA, RG74.412, file 2387.

85 Report of Inspector on Hotel Application, September 26, 1938, PAA, RG74.412, file 2387.

86 Wing to Dinning, August 7, 1925; Dinning to Wing, August 11, 1925, PAA, RG74.412, file 2387.

87 Fairview's local history describes Wing has having one brother while *Chepi Sepe* lists him as having two: Hec MacLean, *Waterhole and the Land North of the Peace* (Fairview, AB: Waterhole Old Timers Association, 1970), 108; Spirit River History Book Committee, *Chepi Sepe,* 920. It is unclear whether the Wings lived in Spirit River or Fairview but it is clear that they worked in both.

88 Secretary-Treasurer to Dinning, July 25, 1924, PAA, RG74.412, file 1307.

89 Dinning to H.H. Hull, May 7, 1929, RG 69.289, file 98b. Based on the letter to Wing in 1925 a licence had been issued to the Home Hotel in Waterhole but it was under suspension at the time of the letter and seemed to have been for some time, Dinning to Wing, August 11, 1925, PAA, RG74.412, file 2387.

90 "Trains Operating Northern Extensions," *Lomond Press,* November 15, 1928.

91 See discussion of plans for a new hotel and then comments about the new hotel, Dinning to Messrs Phimester and Dundon, June 28, 1928; Memo from A.J. Mason to Dinning, December 1, 1928, PAA, RG74.412, file 1307.

92 Supervisor of Licenses to Dinning, December 13, 1928, PAA, RG74.412, file 1308.

93 Canadian Expeditionary Force Discharge Certificate, discharge date, August 23, 1919, PAA, RG74.412, file 1308.

94 Dinning to Stewart-Irvine, April 25, 1929, PAA, RG74.412, file 1308.

95 Hamill, "The Alberta Liquor Control Board," 766–71.

96 Hamlet of Fairview: Local Option Area, May 16, 1929, *Alberta Gazette* (1929), 372.

97 Liquor Control Act, s 71.

98 See, e.g., Mrs M Boyd to R.J. Dinning, June 11, 1924; Secretary-Treasurer of Fairview to Dinning, July 25, 1924, PAA, RG74.412, file 1307. Boyd was the President of the local Women's Institute.

99 Norris to Dinning, May 7, 1929; Dinning to Norris, May 9, 1929, PAA, RG74.412, file 1308.

100 Review of Commissioner during Trip to Peace River, June 8–11, 1929, PAA, RG74.412, file 1308; Review of Commissioner during Trip to Peace River, June 8–11, 1929; Commissioner to H.H. Hull, May 7, 1929; Memo from A.J. Mason to A.L.C.B Commissioner, December 1, 1928, PAA, RG74.412, file 1307.

101 *First Annual Report,* 9 (noting the board's preference for serving the public over beer sales).

102 Dinning to Premier Brownlee, August 5, 1932; Dinning to P.G. Thomson, November 9, 1932,PAA RG69.289, file 99a. For the opinion of British Canadians towards Ukrainians at this time see, Gregory Robinson, "Rougher Than Any Other Nationality?

Ukrainian Canadians and Crime in Alberta, 1915–1929," *Journal of Ukrainian Studies* 16 (1991): 147.

103 Dinning served as Alberta's representative on the Canadian coal committee, and in 1928 was appointed head of Alberta's Board of Standards for coal: "New Alberta Coal Board of Standards," *Wetaskiwin Times,* April 5, 1928.

104 *Re Fairview,* 24 Alta LR 603, 1930 CarswellAlta 28 (*Re Fairview* cited to CarswellAlta).

105 Gray to A.J. Mason, ALCB Secretary, June 23, 1930, PAA, RG74.412, file 1307.

106 *Re Fairview,* paras 3–4.

107 Ibid., paras 4–5, 1.

108 Ibid., paras 5, 11.

109 Village of Fairview: Local Option Area, September 5, 1930, *Alberta Gazette* (1930), 534.

110 Lawlor and Sissons to Dinning, August 25, 1930; PAA, RG74.412, file 2387; Lunney and Lannan to ALCB, May 8, 1924, PAA, RG74.412, file 1307.

111 Dinning to Lawlor and Sissons, August 26, 1930, PAA, RG74.412, file 1307.

112 Memo from Supervisor of Licenses to Dinning, September 3, 1930, PAA, RG74.412, file 1307.

113 The vote was held on October 13, 1932, and the results were seventy-nine in favour of licences and twenty-nine against: Local Option Area: Village of Fairview, October 14, 1932, *Alberta Gazette* (1932), 633; Acting ALCB Inspector to Dinning, July 4, 1932, PAA, RG74.412, file 1308.

114 Lawlor and Sissons to Dinning, November 14, 1930, PAA, RG74.412, file 1307. The local history of the region dates the fire to 1935: MacLean, *Waterhole,* 108.

115 MacLean, *Waterhole,* 108.

116 Ibid., 183; Spirit River History Book Committee, *Chepi Sepe,* 919.

117 Report of Inspector on Hotel Application, September 9, 1940, PAA, RG74.412, file 1309.

118 For the exception, see Spirit River History Book Committee, *Chepi Sepe,* 866.

119 Report of Inspector on Hotel Application, November 18, 1926, PAA, RG74.412, file 2387; Report of Inspector on Hotel Application, October 1, 1935, PAA, RG74.412, file 2388.

120 Report of Inspector on Hotel Application, October 10, 1934, PAA, RG74.412, file 2388.

121 Spirit River History Book Committee, *Chepi Sepe,* 110.

122 Dinning to Wing, February 25, 1938; Peter A. Wing to Dinning, February 26, 1938, PAA, RG74.412, file 2388.

123 Again this date is taken from his likely gravestone, a record of which is online: https:// billiongraves.com/grave/Charlie-Wing/5666002#.

124 Spirit River History Book Committee, *Chepi Sepe,* 920.

125 It is possible that Wing's children may have made it to Canada. Some recollections in *Chepi Sepe* refer to Wing's having nephews, while one or two others describe the

nephews as sons. Given the legal difficulty of Chinese immigration to Canada, it was not uncommon for younger Chinese men to claim a father in Canada, leading to the phenomenon of "paper sons," though this seemed to become an issue only after the Second World War: Li *Chinese in Canada,* 93. In my view, it is likely that the nephews really were nephews, as Pete Wing worked at the Dominion during the 1920s.

126 Indenture between Wing, Wady, and Kirstiuk, October 1, 1943; Wing to ALCB Chairman J.A. King, October 1, 1943, PAA, RG74.412, file 2388.

127 For a brief overview of the Depression in Alberta, see Howard Palmer and Tamara Palmer, *Alberta: A New History* (Edmonton: Hurtig Press, 1990), 244–80.

128 Actual licence suspensions and cancellations also decreased: Hamill, *From Prohibition to Administrative Regulation,* 348.

129 John H. Selkirk to Dinning, October 11, 1928, PAA, RG74.412, file 1307.

The Rise of the "Big Three" **10**

The Emergence of a Canadian Brewing Oligopoly, 1945–62

Matthew J. Bellamy

Towards the end of the Second World War, Edward Plunkett Taylor – the outspoken president of Canadian Breweries Limited (CBL) and the man who would later be dubbed "Excess Profits Taylor" by his critics – issued a statement that signalled that the business of brewing would soon be heading in a new direction: "There are too many breweries in all of the provinces, and there is a golden opportunity to sell our products in the entire country." In 1945, the Canadian brewing industry was made up of sixty-one breweries, and together they brewed 159 brands. Ontario and Quebec were home to the nation's largest breweries – CBL, Labatt, Molson, and National Breweries. This region was the heartland of the Canadian brewing industry, and the Canadian economy more generally, and its captains of industry had long looked to the "hinterland" for opportunities for growth.[1] Nevertheless, when Taylor made his statement in 1945 not a single Canadian brewery was truly national. The biggest breweries were regional concerns, catering almost exclusively to beer drinkers in their home provinces. But during the next two decades, the structure of the industry was transformed as production became concentrated in the hands of the "big three" – CBL, Labatt, and Molson.

By 1962, these three breweries were producing almost 95 percent of the beer sold in Canada. Nearly all of the sixty-one breweries operating in

1945 were still producing beer, but most of them were now owned by the big three. The big three had a physical presence in every region of Canada except for the Maritimes and Northern Ontario, and their brands dominated the marketplace.[2] The market structure of the Canadian brewing industry thus shifted during the postwar period from one made up of a relatively large group of regional brewers catering to local drinking preferences into a stable national oligopoly. This structural shift was accompanied by the homogenization of taste as the big three produced similar-tasting beers that were brewed to appeal to as many customers as possible. Operating within a regulatory regime that privileged their product over other recreational drugs, the big three saw their sales soar. At one level, therefore, this chapter examines the relationship of production and capitalism to the patterns of individual consumption.

On the surface, the transformation of Canadian brewing mirrored changes taking place in the industry elsewhere. The period 1945 to 1975 witnessed the consolidation of the brewing industry in the Netherlands, Belgium, France, Italy, West Germany, Australia, New Zealand, the United Kingdom, and the United States. To be sure, the degree of concentration varied from nation to nation.[3] It was relatively low in West Germany, moderate in the United Kingdom, and high in France, the Netherlands, Belgium, and the United States.[4] In Canada, the level of concentration was also high, but the postwar consolidation of the Canadian brewing industry began earlier and went further, faster than in any other country. One of the questions this chapter seeks to answer is, why?

The brewing industry has long been a focus for those interested in the causes of concentration. With its relatively simple production technology and its appeal to a mass consumer market, there were plenty of opportunities to achieve economies of scale.[5] The rise of national shipping brewers in the United States at the end of the nineteenth century provides case study support for Alfred Chandler's notion of "three-pronged investment" in production, managerial organization, and distribution and retailing networks. The concentration in Belgian brewing during the interwar years, on the other hand, has been attributed to technological change, economies of scale, and escalating endogenous sunk costs in advertising.[6] The same factors are widely credited with transforming the US brewing industry after the Second World War. An increase in minimum efficient scale due to technological innovation, combined with competition in advertising outlays, led to the emergence of a national brewing oligopoly.[7] After their triumph, the national brewers in the United States proved to be largely invulnerable to competition from new entrants because of their large "sunk" investments in television advertising. This was also the case in West Germany after 1990, where local brewers were dealt a fatal blow by national television advertisements promoting the brands of the nation's biggest brewers. As in the States, large national brewers bought exclusive network rights to major sporting events, and local spots entailed significant cost disadvantages in comparison with national advertisements.[8]

For those who have studied the British brewing industry from an "institutionalist" perspective, the practice of tying pubs to brewers, the legal restrictions on opening retail outlets, and the permissive policy on mergers were key drivers of postwar consolidation.[9] Institutional factors also played a critical role in the emergence of a brewing oligopoly in New Zealand and Australia.[10] Finally, there are those who stress the role of entrepreneurship in determining the extent, nature, and speed of consolidation in the brewing industry.[11] For instance, in his study of the British brewing industry after 1945, Tony Millns argues that one of the key factors in the emergence of the national brewing oligopoly was "the strategic vision and the influence of personality, best seen in the example of Eddie Taylor."[12] Having built a brewing giant in Canada, E.P. Taylor set his sights on changing the way the British brewing industry operated. "His pioneering vision had a profound impact both on the structure of the brewing industry and, with the rise of lager," Millns argues, "the nation's drinking habits."[13] Thus there is a great deal of debate regarding the causes of concentration in the brewing industry.

This chapter enters the debate by examining the factors that led to the creation of a brewing oligopoly in Canada. In the process, it answers the following questions: What role did institutional and entrepreneurial factors play in determining the postwar structure of the Canadian brewing industry? To what extent were advertising expenditures critical in sorting out the winners and losers in the competition for market share after the war? What barriers to entry prevented brewers from challenging the hegemony of the big three during the period under review?

I argue that the emergence of a national brewing oligopoly in Canada was a result of a mixture of entrepreneurial and institutional factors, and sunk costs in advertising. Having created a brewing powerhouse in Ontario, Taylor turned his attention to conquering the national marketplace. Institutional factors determined how he went about accomplishing his objective. Discriminatory markups on out-of-province beer, price controls, restrictions on alcohol advertising, and a permissive policy towards takeovers combined to make the acquisition of small and medium-sized firms the main route to market consolidation. With the price of beer fixed by the various provincial liquor authorities, competition took the form of advertising races. The big three managed to maintain their oligopoly in part because the distribution system worked to their advantage.

In what follows, I examine the strategic vision of E.P. Taylor and the institutional factors that caused him to expand by way of mergers and acquisitions; analyze the strategies and structure of two "fast followers" (Labatt and Molson); consider the promotion of popular brands and its effect on the nature of competition; and examine the barriers to entry that helped the big three maintain their oligopoly and reduce consumer choice.

First Mover

CBL was the first brewer to become truly national in Canada. Since 1930, Taylor had been acquiring breweries in Ontario and rationalizing their operations. Smaller plants were shut down without regard to their brands, but the brands of larger breweries, such as O'Keefe and Carling, which had appreciable market share, were maintained even after the plants associated with their names had been shut down. This "merger for monopoly" strategy met with mixed results prior to the war. Although Taylor succeeded in reducing the level of competition and gaining a 30 percent share of the Ontario market, his plants were often burdened by excess capacity. Writing to National Breweries president Norman Dawes, Taylor characterized the position of his brewery in 1939 as being at a competitive disadvantage vis-à-vis Labatt – a large, family-owned, regional brewer that had been making beer in London, Ontario, since 1847. Taylor described Labatt as "embarrassingly profitable and engaged in lavish expenditures on its customers."[14] In the years that followed, however, CBL profited from both the wartime demand for beer and rising prices, and Taylor began talking about a geographic expansion.

Taylor was bullish on the industry's postwar prospects. He had witnessed the remarkable speed with which Canadian industry had converted to war production. As the end of the war drew near, he became increasingly convinced that Canadian industry would show equal speed at converting back to peacetime production. In Taylor's optimistic opinion, the postwar period would not witness the same type of economic slump that had followed the First World War; rather, the economy would take off into a period of rapid growth fuelled by unprecedented consumption. The good economic times would increase the demand for beer, soaking up CBL's excess capacity.

Taylor was prescient. The immediate postwar period saw a huge increase in the demand for beer. For the first time in Canadian history, a large majority of the population had the disposable income necessary to participate in life's consumer pleasures. Across the nation, Canadians drank more beer than ever before. Between 1944 and 1952, per capita consumption grew from 8.99 to 13.72 gallons per annum. In subsequent years, it remained stable at approximately 13.50 gallons per annum.[15] Ontarians and Quebecers continued to be the heaviest beer drinkers, but western Canadians were catching up by 1950. Taylor's positive perception of things to come, combined with his proclivity for risk taking, sent him searching for existing breweries that would help him expand production to meet the postwar demand.

In the final months of the war, CBL assumed control of the Bixel Brewing and Malting Company of Brantford and the historic Walkerville Brewery in Windsor, Ontario. It also acquired Capital Breweries in Ottawa. This final acquisition was the most significant of the three because it solidified CBL's position in Eastern Ontario and helped accelerate the firm's push into Quebec. CBL's acquisitions at the end of the war thus strengthened its overall position relative to others in the Canadian brewing industry (see Table 10.1).[16]

Having accomplished his goal of creating a regional brewing giant, Taylor set his sights on conquering the national marketplace. "Having been successful in Ontario," he stated, "we have now raised our sights and plan to repeat the process ... so that we can become a truly national concern."[17] To that end, he purchased the Frontenac Brewery in Quebec

Table 10.1 Market position of breweries selling in Ontario, 1944–62

Year	Labatt (%)	CBL (%)	Molson (%)	National (%)	Others (%)
1944	30.6	31.0	7.2	15.8	15.4
1945	25.3	40.7	5.9	16.5	11.6
1946	24.7	41.9	5.5	16.2	11.7
1947	23.1	46.8	5.3	14.0	10.8
1948	20.6	50.0	6.0	12.8	10.6
1949	18.9	55.6	6.7	10.3	8.5
1950	18.4	56.9	7.6	9.3	7.8
1951	21.6	55.3	7.6	8.3	7.2
1952	23.1	54.2	7.9	7.6	7.2
1953	22.3	51.5	8.7	10.2	7.3
1954	22.3	56.9	8.5	5.9	6.4
1955	22.4	64.4	8.9	-	4.3
1956	22.0	63.4	10.1	-	4.5
1957	20.9	63.1	11.6	-	4.4
1958	20.7	60.9	13.7	-	4.7
1959	21.8	n/a	n/a	-	n/a
1960	23.3	56.6	15.0	-	5.1
1961	23.1	56.6	15.1	-	5.1
1962	23.5	55.3	16.5	-	4.7

Source: John Labatt Limited, *Report to the Directors* (1962); J.C.H. Jones, *Competition in the Canadian Brewing Industry* (PhD dissertation, Queen's University, 1966), 129.

in 1951. The following year, he took control of National Breweries, the company that had been the source of his initial inspiration. The Quebec-based brewer had been losing market share since the end of the war. Between 1947 and 1951, National Breweries' share of the Quebec market declined from 50.3 percent to 39.8 percent, and production fell from 1.5 million to 1 million barrels per annum. In large part, the decline was due to management's failure to recognize the shift that was taking place in consumer tastes. Beer drinkers in Quebec were moving away from such heavy and hoppy ales as National's principal brand, Dawes Black Horse. With too many plants and too many brands, the company had to bear the unrelenting costs of overcapacity. Once a vibrant presence in Quebec, National Breweries was suddenly vulnerable. After Norman Dawes rejected his merger offer, Taylor purchased enough stock to gain control of the company, and CBL became Canada's largest brewer in terms of capacity and sales. Taylor subsequently renamed the firm Dow Brewery Limited after the company's bestselling brand. Dow joined O'Keefe and Carling as brands that CBL would produce, market, and distribute in key markets across the nation in the years that followed.

After acquiring National Breweries, Taylor turned his attention to gaining a foothold in the west. The western economy was booming, especially after the discovery of oil beneath the wheat fields of Leduc, Alberta. And although combined sales in Manitoba, Saskatchewan, Alberta, and British Columbia amounted to only a quarter of the domestic beer market, Taylor was convinced that the west would soon experience "a growing population" and with it an increasing appetite for beer.[18]

In theory, Taylor could have produced his brands in Central Canada and shipped them westward, as had been done south of the border. The American "shipping brewers" had gained a national presence at the end of the nineteenth century by utilizing the railroads, refrigeration, advertising, and, above all, economies of scale.[19] But such an approach was practically impossible in Canada for two reasons. First, as Taylor noted in a confidential memo, "the immense distance in Canada means it is not practical for breweries in the east to ship to the west and compete with western breweries."[20] Ontario-based brewers had been attempting to gain a share of the western beer market since the late 1800s. But as Labatt and Carling had discovered, western Canadians were generally unwilling to pay the premium for their beer. As in the United States at the end of the nineteenth century, smaller brewers were able to outperform their larger counterparts based on price and taste, especially given the consumers' preferences for draft beer.[21] Second, the sale of beer was controlled by provincial governments, which set up the equivalent of tariff barriers against imports from other provinces.[22] As demonstrated in Chapter 9, provincial liquor authorities regulated the alcoholic beverage industry to meet local demands and needs. The provincial tariffs were substantial. In Manitoba and Alberta, for example, a charge of five cents per bottle was imposed on out-of-province beer. For those large central Canadian brewers, such as CBL, Molson, and Labatt, who were seeking to expand their market share after the Second World War, this increased the price of their brands by approximately 30 percent above the price of local brands.[23] In Saskatchewan and British Columbia, imported brands were priced at a premium and were exclusively available in government-owned and controlled liquor stores.[24]

Thus, Taylor determined that the wisest strategy was "to purchase two or three prosperous western concerns."[25] "It is our plan," he boldly stated, "to build up in the four western provinces a strong and robust brewing consolidation in the same manner that Canadian Breweries Limited was put together and developed in eastern Canada."[26] To that end, in 1953 CBL acquired Western Canada Breweries Limited, a regional holding company that owned Vancouver Breweries and Drewry's breweries in Manitoba and Saskatchewan. The following year, CBL purchased Grant's Brewery in Manitoba, and the year after that it acquired the Red Deer Brewing Company in Alberta.

CBL's aggressive external growth strategy was made possible by the federal government's relatively permissive policy towards mergers. Generally speaking, Canadians have been sympathetic to the concentration of corporate power. And while laws have been passed to prevent combines and promote competition, the courts have more often than not interpreted these laws in favour of big business.[27] In 1952, Canada's antitrust legislation was seemingly strengthened when the federal government revised the Combines Investigation Act. The act gave the courts the first real possibility of discouraging any merger that "operated, or is likely to operate, to the detriment, or against, the interest of the public." At the time, no one knew how the act would be interpreted. It was not until the 1959 trial of CBL for contravening the merger section of the act that an answer emerged.

The government's charge was that over the course of thirty years CBL purchased or otherwise gained control of thirty-seven breweries in Ontario. These mergers, according to the prosecution, operated to "the detriment or against the interest of the public." Taylor's lawyers made the case that CBL was a respectable manufacturer of a moderate alcoholic beverage, the price of which was set by the provincial liquor authorities. As such, the corporation was not operating to the detriment of the public. The court agreed. In his ruling, Justice McRuer of the Supreme Court of Ontario stated that there was no evidence to show that the public interest had been "detrimentally affected" by the activities of CBL. Furthermore, in the judge's opinion, it was not an offence "for one corporation to acquire the business of another because it wishes to extinguish a competitor." Following the ruling, the

Globe and Mail reported that it was "No Crime to be Big."[28] The court's decision gave a green light to CBL and the rest of the big three, and the postwar acquisitions continued unabated.

After the trial, CBL picked up where it had left off. In 1961, it acquired three more breweries in Alberta, increasing its manufacturing capacity by more than 500,000 barrels a year (see Table 10.2). In 1962, CBL acquired the Bennett Brewing Company in St. John's, Newfoundland. Thus, by the end of the period under review, CBL controlled breweries stretching from the Atlantic to the Pacific. The postwar economic boom and a regulatory environment that privileged the production and consumption of beer led to unprecedented production at CBL. As the other chapters in this book show, governments in liberal democracies have been reluctant to permit the use of most drugs for pleasure. For example, when public drinking returned to Canada after prohibition, provincial governments allowed the consumption of beer and light wine only. Other recreational drug use – weed, cocaine, LSD, speed – was strictly prohibited.

Table 10.2 Breweries acquired in western Canada, 1953–61

Year	Brewery	Province	Capacity in 1961 (barrels)	Acquiring company
1953	Shea's Winnipeg Brewery	Manitoba	200,000	Labatt
1953	Drewry's Ltd.	Manitoba	200,000	CBL
1953	Drewry's Regina Ltd.	Saskatchewan	85,000	CBL
1953	Drewry's Ltd. (Saskatoon)	Saskatchewan	90,000	CBL
1953	Kiewel Brewing Company	Manitoba	60,000	Labatt-CBL
1953	Pelissier's Brewery Ltd.	Manitoba	40,000	Labatt-CBL
1953	Vancouver Breweries Ltd.	British Columbia	390,000	CBL
1954	Grant's Brewery Ltd.	Manitoba	50,000	CBL
1955	Red Deer Brewing Co. Ltd.	Alberta	100,000	CBL

Year	Brewery	Province	Capacity in 1961 (barrels)	Acquiring company
1958	Sick's Prince Albert Brewery	Saskatchewan	175,000	Molson
1958	Sick's Regina Brewery Ltd.	Saskatchewan	150,000	Molson
1958	Sick's Lethbridge Brewery	Alberta	225,000	Molson
1958	Sick's Edmonton Brewery	Alberta	140,000	Molson
1958	Sick's Capilano Brewery	British Columbia	150,000	Molson
1958	Lucky Lager Brewing (New Westminster)	British Columbia	230,000	Labatt
1958	Lucky Lager Brewing (Victoria)	British Columbia	100,000	Labatt
1960	Fort Garry Brewery Ltd.	Manitoba	60,000	Molson
1960	Saskatoon Brewing Company	Saskatchewan	100,000	Labatt
1961	Calgary Brewing and Malting	Alberta	250,000	CBL
1961	Big Horn Brewery Co. Ltd.	Alberta	50,000	CBL
1961	Bohemian Maid Co. Ltd.	Alberta	110,000	CBL

Source: Frank Roseman, *The Canadian Brewing Industry: The Effect of Mergers and Provincial Regulation on Economic Conduct and Performance* (PhD dissertation, Northwestern University, 1968), 233.

Fast Followers

While CBL was the first Canadian brewer to go national, the innovative corporation soon had competition. At Labatt there was a sense that it needed to copy CBL's strategy or perish. As early as 1945, Labatt executives began to reflect on what was needed to succeed in the postwar world. They concluded that in order to survive, the brewery would have to expand its capacity to meet the demand for its products, and the quickest way to do this was to acquire a number of existing breweries. This strategy would require access to a larger pool of capital, so in June 1945 Labatt – which had been family-owned since 1847 – joined CBL and Molson as publicly traded companies.[29]

In 1952, Labatt followed CBL westward by purchasing one of western Canada's largest independent brewers. Shea's Winnipeg Brewery's origins lay in the Old Winnipeg Brewery, which was built in the brothel district of Colony Creek by Celestin Thomas in 1873, before Winnipeg obtained its city charter. A change in the company's capital structure in 1926 placed a percentage of voting stock in public hands, and by 1946 over 50 percent of the shares were owned by two Winnipeg hospitals. In 1952, the hospital boards indicated their intention to sell their shares in the brewery to raise funds for their health care facilities.

The story of Labatt's takeover of Shea's is significant because it provides further insights into the institutional barriers that Canadian brewers faced when going national. The first barrier related to distribution. In the west, brewers were allowed to own hotels, which gave them an exclusive channel for funnelling their beer to consumers. For example, in Manitoba virtually all the hotels were tied to either Shea's or CBL. Almost 90 percent of draft beer and approximately 57 percent of bottled beer were sold in hotels owned by Shea's and CBL. Various western provincial governments enacted laws in the 1950s requiring brewers to sell their hotel holdings, but the brewers often found ways around these laws. For example, when Taylor heard about the government's plans to cut the ties between the brewers and the hotels, he decided to sell the company that held CBL's hotels, Reliance Securities Limited, to a friendly buyer. "If we have to get out of the hotel business," he said, "we must have Reliance in friendly hands in order to retain the gallonage of these hotels." With that goal in mind, Reliance was sold to Alex Campbell, the former vice president of finance and treasurer of Taylor's Western Breweries Limited. Campbell agreed not transfer his shares in the company to anyone deemed by Taylor to be "unfriendly."[30] The move allowed CBL to sidestep the legislation and maintain its market share in Manitoba. Thus in 1953, when Labatt was seeking to enter the Manitoba market, CBL and Shea controlled one of the principal modes of distribution. If Labatt wanted to get its beer into the hands of consumers, it would have to purchase Shea's.

The other benefit of so doing was the fact that the Ontario-based brewer would automatically gain a significant slice of the western market. This was due to the system of sales quotas that existed in Manitoba and other western provinces. Following prohibition, which came to an end in each of the western provinces at various points in the 1920s, production became concentrated in the hands of a few relatively large western breweries (such as Sick's, Lucky Lager, Drewry's, and Shea's). Having cornered their respective regional markets, the large brewers agreed not to compete with one another for market share. In Manitoba, such an agreement split the market more or less down the middle, with 60 percent of sales going to Shea's and the other 40 percent allocated to Drewry's. The quota agreements were attached to the firm. Thus, when CBL acquired Drewry's in 1953, it instantly gained 40 percent of the Manitoba market. Later that year, when Labatt purchased Shea's Winnipeg Brewery for $9 million, it immediately acquired the other 60 percent.[31]

By the summer of 1956, Labatt had plants operating in Ontario, Manitoba, and Quebec, and centralized management from London was becoming increasingly difficult. Labatt – again following the lead of CBL – began decentralizing its operations. Like E.P. Taylor, Jake Moore, who became the first non-family president of Labatt in 1958, was of the opinion that national breweries should be operated on "as decentralized a basis as possible so that decisions can be made at the level closest to the scene of action."[32] The move made strategic sense, given the different provincial liquor regulations. Separate operating divisions were created for each of the provinces where the company had a physical presence. Each operating division was given responsibility for all company activities in its area. At the same time, a head office was set up in London to serve in an advisory capacity to the heads of the operating divisions. Relieved of the detailed supervision of day-to-day activities in the three operating divisions, executives in London could concentrate all of their efforts on directing the overall operations and planning.[33]

Before the decade was out, Labatt had purchased Lucky Lager Brewing in British Columbia as well as the Saskatoon Brewing Company in Saskatchewan (see Table 10.2). When Labatt purchased the Bavarian Brewery Limited in St. John's, Newfoundland, in 1962, it, like CBL, could claim to be a "truly national concern." As Moore stated in October that year: "The acquisition gives the Company production facilities from the Atlantic to the Pacific and puts us in a position to compete in the total Canadian market."[34]

Always a "fast follower," Molson soon undertook its own national expansion. Like Labatt, it employed both a brown-field and green-field approach, acquiring existing breweries as well as building new ones. Molson's first move came in 1955: the oldest continuously operating brewery in Canada (established in 1787) struck back at the Ontario brewers that had invaded its home territory of Quebec by building a 300,000-barrel brewery on Fleet Street, Toronto right in CBL's backyard. In 1958, Molson went west, purchasing the Prairie powerhouse Sick's Brewery, the maker of such popular Prairie brands as Bohemian and Old Style Pilsner. Molson continued to manufacture these brands alongside a few of its own flagship brands. In 1962, it again quickly followed the actions of CBL and Labatt by purchasing Newfoundland Brewery Limited, an established brewery in St. John's.

By 1962, therefore, three breweries were national in scope. Indeed, only two areas in Canada were without a plant that was manufacturing the national brands of the big three: Northern Ontario, which was dominated by six small local brewers, and the Maritimes, which was controlled by S. Oland and Sons and Moosehead (see Table 10.3). With only a few exceptions, therefore, the main route to geographic expansion and market consolidation in Canada after the Second World War was through the acquisition of smaller and medium-sized firms.

Table 10.3 Percentage sales by province of the leading breweries in Canada, 1958

Firm	NS	NB	QC	ON	MB	SK	AB	BC	Canada
CBL	14.9	5.7	51.8	60.9	41.0	34.2	7.9	36.0	48.2
Molson	6.2	3.7	43.3	13.7	0.4	50.9	40.6	16.3	25.3
Labatt	6.5	1.3	4.7	20.7	50.2	0.4	0.3	35.1	15.9
CB&M[1]	–	–	–	–	–	3.0	51.2	5.3	4.1
Oland[2]	67.7	15.2	0.2	–	–	–	–	–	1.8
Moose-head	4.7	74.1	–	–	–	–	–	–	1.2
Others	–	–	–	4.7	8.4	11.5	–	7.1	3.5
Total	100.0	100.0	100.0	100.0	100.0	100.0	100.0	100.0	100.0

Notes:

1 Calgary Brewing and Malting Company.

2 S. Oland and Sons (now Oland Brewery).

Source: J.C.H. Jones, *Competition in the Canadian Brewing Industry,* 116.

The Nature of Competition

One of the defining features of the Canadian brewing industry after the Second World War was the virtual absence of price competition. This was because the price of beer was fixed by the various provincial liquor control boards. To be sure, the liquor authorities often acted on the brewers' advice when it came to setting price – raising the spectre of "regulatory capture."[35] For example, in Nova Scotia, New Brunswick, and British Columbia, the liquor authorities arrived at their retail price merely by adding a markup after the beer was purchased from the brewers. In Quebec, the Quebec Brewers' Association, the Tavern Keepers' Association, and the Licensed Grocers' Section of the Retail Merchants' Association jointly fixed the price at which beer was sold within province. The Liquor Control Board of Ontario (LCBO) fixed the price of beer in government stores and licensed drinking places in that province. Until 1956, Manitoba fixed prices in a manner similar to Nova Scotia, New Brunswick, and British Columbia. Thereafter, however, the government set the prices after negotiating with local brewers.

With the price of beer fixed, competition took the form of advertising races to promote a handful of "flagship brands." As business historian Teresa da Silva Lopes notes, owning popular brands is essential to success in the brewing industry.[36] Popular brands create a constant revenue stream for firms due to consumers' propensity for long-term brand loyalty.[37] As one Canadian brewing executive put it in the early 1960s: "The ideal accomplishment [of marketing] is to so influence them [i.e., beer drinkers] that they will ask for our brands not just once or occasionally but *always* – which is the difference between making a sale and winning a loyal customer."[38]

In developing their flagship brands, the big three aimed to satisfy as many beer drinkers as possible. "It takes no great brain," Labatt's director of marketing, Paul Henderson, proclaimed in 1963, "to conclude that if we give the consumer what he in fact wants in a product, then our chances of bankrupting our enemies will be vastly improved."[39] Years of research had shown a trend in Canada towards "milder," "smoother," and "mellower" tasting beers. When Canadians were asked to describe a "poor" beer, more often than not they stated that it was "bitter," "sharp," or "hard to take."[40] As a result, the big three began making blander beers that tasted more or less the same.

"In brewing today all brands of any one type are fairly close," stated Labatt's quality control manager, John Compton, in 1963, "and it is the finer points we are working on."[41] To determine those "finer points," the big three employed professional taste testers. The taste tests revealed that there was little inside the bottle to distinguish the brands of the big three from one another. For example, one test revealed that Molson's Laurentide, which was introduced in 1962 to tap into the rising tide of French nationalism in Quebec during the Quiet Revolution, was "a copy of Labatt's 50."[42] Public opinion surveys further confirmed the extent of the homogenization. In 1964, 80 percent of Canadians polled stated that "the mass of brands are much alike."[43]

To make these lighter-tasting beers, the big three diluted the mash with non-malt cereal. The tradition of adulterating beer, which Jonathan Reinarz writes about in Chapter 8, was not restricted to the nineteenth century. During the last half of the twentieth century, the big Canadian brewers added corn grits during the brewing process. The quantity of corn grits added to the brews of the big three represented about 40 percent of the mash recipe. Like their Victorian counterparts, these companies were motived by the cost savings realized from adulteration. Besides making the beer appear clearer and taste lighter, corn grits were about a third of the price of barley malt.[44]

Prior to the 1970s, truly national beer brands did not exist in Canada.[45] This was due to two fundamental reasons. First, the diverse nature of Canada worked against the ability of companies to easily create brand identities that resonated with people from coast to coast.[46] Second, there were regional differences in the *type* of beer preferred by Canadians. Those living in Ontario, Quebec, and the Maritimes, for example, were far more likely to drink ale. In Newfoundland, Saskatchewan, Alberta, and British Columbia, on the other hand, there was a marked preference for lager. As a result, executives at the big three decided to promote a flagship ale and a flagship lager in those regions where a preference for each type of beer existed. When Labatt's senior executives met at Oakwood, Ontario, in 1959 to discuss the subject of flagship brands, they decided to promote Labatt 50 as the company's flagship ale and Labatt Pilsener as its flagship lager. They also decided to keep producing popular regional brands, such as Lucky Lager in British Columbia, and selling them alongside the company's flagship beers in local markets. Molson embraced a similar strategy, brewing such popular regional brands as Old Style Pilsener and selling them together with its flagship brands, Export Ale and Canadian Lager. Finally, CBL chose to promote Carling Red Cap and Dow Ale, as well as Carling Black Label and O'Keefe Old Vienna lager as its flagship brands.

With very little difference in terms of the substance of Canadian beer, the big three attempted to distinguish their brands with elaborate and expensive advertising campaigns, the goal of which was to increase market share and breed brand loyalty. When it came to promoting their brands, Canadian brewers faced a number of regulatory hurdles. In the post-prohibition period, provincial governments placed tight restrictions on liquor advertising in an attempt to curb alcohol consumption. There was no uniform national advertising code to which beer advertising had to adhere. Instead, all liquor advertisements had to conform to provincial liquor control board standards, which could range from controls on the size and content of the advertisement to outright bans.[47] After television appeared on the Canadian scene in the late 1940s, the federal government prohibited brewers from running television commercials as well. And even after these regulations were relaxed in 1955, commercials still could not feature a person drinking, or a beer bottle, or a glass of beer. The ad could, however, feature a beer's disembodied label, so long as it was entirely separate from the actions of the preceding commercial.

Despite the tight government restrictions on advertising, there were loopholes that the big three exploited. Because they were based in Central Canada, these firms promoted their brands in magazines like *Maclean's* and *Saturday Night* that were published in Quebec – where the restrictions on beer advertising were far more slack – but sold them across the country. This type of advertising, therefore, had a national impact, and Canadian consumers were aware of the brands of the big three before a truly national beer market existed. It was in part to capitalize on this brand awareness that the big three expanded outside Central Canada after the war. In addition, they had the financial resources necessary to run ads in the United States – where brewers had freer rein to advertise their products – knowing full well that these ads would be viewed by a large segment of the Canadian population. The actions of the big three frustrated regulatory bodies, which complained that they could control only the forms and context of advertising generated within particular provinces, whereas the newsstands and airwaves were full of material sent in from the United States.[48]

When it came to advertising on television stations in Canada after the regulations were relaxed in 1955 (and before 1963), the brewers were restricted to only twelve seconds of "hard-sell" advertising, during which time the product could be identified by brand name.[49] The other forty-eight seconds were filled with a "soft sell." The big three brewers spent thousands of dollars to craft commercials that put this time to effective use. For instance, in 1956, CBL spent over $800,000 on television commercials, while Labatt and Molson spent close to $300,000 each.[50] In contrast, brewers other than the big three did not spend a single dollar to promote their products on television that year.

The big three used the soft-sell time to associate their brands with the "good life." The ads constructed a "desirable lifestyle" in relation to contemporary social conditions, including shifts and tensions in the broader gender order.[51] Television commercials often showed fit, happy, handsome, heterosexual people engaged in a range of pleasurable pursuits. In addition, the big three sponsored sporting events on television. In 1957, for example, Molson began sponsoring *Hockey Night in Canada,* Canada's most popular televised sports program. Labatt, on the other hand, became the official sponsor of the Canadian Football League in 1960.

While these national forms of advertising excelled in promoting brand loyalty, they were also far more expensive than local or regional methods of promotion. The size of a firm's advertising budget was thus critical to postwar growth and survival. Jake Moore, a rising star at the Labatt brewery, commented in 1954 that "the heavier expenditures for sales promotions permit the larger brewery to gain increasing public acceptance at the expense of its lesser known rival."[52] The same point was put slightly differently in a 1955 agreement on advertising between the members of the big three. "The brewery with the largest advertising budget," the agreement succinctly stated, "will be the brewery to gain."[53] As a result, the big three firms began spending huge sums of money to advertise their products. In 1956, Molson spent just over $2 million on advertising, roughly a quarter of which was on television ads. That same year, Labatt spent just under $900,000, while CBL spent almost $4.5 million. CBL's total expenditure for everything from Christmas decorations for retail stores, to sponsorship of tournaments and sports teams, to magazine and television advertisements totalled over $13 million.[54]

The smaller brewers could not compete. Because the circulation of national media was much wider than their market, they found it impossible to use national advertising economically. When asked why his firm did not advertise in periodicals or other media that were circulated nationally, the vice president of Oland and Son – the brewer of the popular east coast beer Alexander Keith's India Pale Ale (IPA) – Victor Oland stated: "We did for a while ... for almost a year, but then we figured that only 8 per cent of the people lived in the Maritimes who were in a position to buy our beer, which meant that immediately 92 cents of the dollar was lost." Lacking the financial resources of the big three, Oland resorted to local advertising and promotion when he attempted to break into Quebec in 1957. Unfortunately for the company, its expenditure of $103,000 on advertising was minuscule compared with the amount being spent by the big three, and the east coast brewer gained just 0.3 percent of the Quebec market.

By 1962, the brands of the big three dominated the Canadian market. In every province outside Atlantic Canada, the bestselling brands were owned by CBL, Molson, and Labatt. In Quebec, Molson Export, Dow Ale, and Labatt 50 were the top-selling brands. In Ontario, Carling Black Label, O'Keefe Old Vienna, Molson Canadian, and Labatt Pilsener were the most popular with drinkers. In Manitoba and British Columbia, one in three beer drinkers drank Labatt Pilsener, making it the bestselling brand in those two provinces. In Saskatchewan, the bestselling brand was Molson's Old Style Pilsener and Bohemian, both of which were formerly Sick's Brewery products.[55] Thus, the production and promotion of a small number of flagship brands played a critical role in the rise of the big three and the demise of local brewers.

Barriers to Entry

Given the fact that there was little to distinguish the bland-tasting brands of the big three, one might hypothesize that there would have been an opportunity for a brewer to enter the Canadian market, and perhaps challenge the hegemony of the big three by introducing unique-tasting products. Only a few tried, however, and these gained at best only a thin slice of the Canadian beer market before being acquired by one of the big three. Why was this the case?

In part the answer lies in the fact that government's price fixing had the effect of putting greater emphasis on non-price competition, especially in advertising. As noted above, the smaller regional brewers did not have the financial wherewithal to compete. Thus, the enormous outlays necessary to market a few flagship brands constituted an important deterrent to potential entrants. South of the border, however, a number of firms had both the capital and the expertise to take on Canada's big three. Indeed, the biggest American brewers – Anheuser-Busch, Schlitz, Pabst, and Ballantine – were far larger than the biggest Canadian breweries in terms of production capacity, advertising expenditures, and sales. Furthermore, because Canadians often viewed American magazines and television commercials, an awareness of American brands existed in Canada. Yet these brewers were also unsuccessful in gaining a presence in Canada during the period under consideration. Why?

The short answer is after the Second World War, the nation's brewers – through their lobbying agency, the Brewers' Association of Canada – successfully pressured the federal and provincial governments to protect them from foreign competition. The federal government increased the tariff on imported beer to a minimum of 12.5 percent per gallon.[56] In addition to the federal tariff, foreign brewers seeking to sell their products in Canada had to hurdle three non-tariff barriers used by provincial authorities to discourage the domestic consumption of non-Canadian beer: listing practices, distribution requirements, and discriminatory markup policies. Each province had its own unique distribution system, with its own distinct policies and practices. These added to the foreign brewers' cost of doing business in Canada, further protecting domestic brewers from foreign competition. Liquor control boards routinely imposed conditions on the supply of imported beer. For example, sales quotas and performance standards had to be continuously met. Distribution systems often restricted the sale of imported beer to provincially run liquor board outlets, where foreign brewers were forced to pay extra fees and meet the additional requirements.[57]

In 1956, the Goebel Brewing Company of Detroit, Pabst Brewing Company of Milwaukee, P. Ballantine and Sons Brewing Company of New Jersey, Anheuser-Busch of St. Louis, and Joseph Schlitz Brewing Company of Milwaukee sought permission from the Liquor Control Board of Ontario to sell their beer in that province. The LCBO referred the American brewers to the Brewers Warehousing Company, which was effectively owned and operated by the big three. Brewers Warehousing agreed to distribute their products provided that the American brewers agreed that: (1) their beer would be marketed in standard Canadian "stubby" bottles; (2) they would use cartons of the standard Ontario size, shape, and type; (3) they would pay a service charge of $1.25 per case of twenty-four bottles; (4) a deposit of sixty cents per case of twenty-four bottles would apply. Eager to find a compromise, the American brewers proposed using their own standard long-neck bottles or cans, which would be non-refundable, and asked that this be taken into consideration when determining the price structure. Their request was rejected. Despite representations from the US Brewers Foundation and the United States Embassy, Brewers Warehousing remained firm in its stance that the American brewers would have to meet all of its requirements. Goebel proposed a further solution to the bottle problem by suggesting that the deposit could be charged when the bottles were purchased and refunded when they were returned, and that the store would discard the American bottles. Again, Brewers Warehousing was not willing to "depart from established standards."[58] The provincial distribution requirements and discriminatory markups on foreign beer, in addition to the federal tariff, made it uneconomical for American brewers to sell their beer north of the forty-ninth parallel.

During the period under consideration, only one Canadian firm attempted to challenge the hegemony of the big three in the Central Canadian market. In 1956, Oland still held 67.5 percent of the market share in Nova Scotia, although this was down from 73.3 percent three years earlier. Oland's losses had come at the hands of the big three, who by 1956 controlled 32.5 percent of the Nova Scotia market. With its share of the market declining at home, Oland decided to expand into Ontario and Quebec to take advantage of the large number of Maritimers working in the army and the civil service.[59] That year, it asked the Brewers Warehousing Company to distribute its products. Since Oland was a Canadian company, Brewers' Warehousing stated that it would be charged only seventy-five cents per case to cover the cost of handling its beer. While the fee was less than that charged the American brewers, it was over twice the amount being paid by the big three. When asked at the 1959 trial of CBL whether he thought Oland and Son had been treated fairly by Brewers' Warehousing, Victor Oland stated that he did not; in retaliation, he "went back to Nova Scotia and I was instrumental in having a further barrier against their goods [i.e., the brands of the big three] coming into the province."[60] Thus, contrary to what was taking place in Britain during the nineteenth century – where, as Reinarz notes in Chapter 8, brewers sought to undermine each other (on one occasion with rumours about adding horse meat to beer) – in Canada the big three brewers walked in lockstep with one another whenever external post-prohibition pressures threatened to reduce their profits.

Conclusion

If there is any consensus in the literature regarding the causes of consolidation in the brewing industry, it is that the factors are complex, often varying from time to time and place to place. In Canada, a combination of entrepreneurial and institutional factors determined the pace, direction, and form of consolidation. The fact that the postwar consolidation of the Canadian brewing industry began early and went further faster than in other developed economies was due to the entrepreneurship of E.P. Taylor. He was a disrupter, the source of what Austrian economist Joseph Schumpeter called "creative destruction."[61] His intuition and ambition, combined with the imperialist outlook of the Central Canadian commercial elite, led him to look to the "periphery" for opportunities for growth. His pioneering vision had a profound effect on the structure of the industry, ultimately transforming Canadian brewing into a stable oligopoly.

In terms of the form of consolidation, institutional factors played a decisive role. Due to the nature of the regulatory regime, the big three were forced to embrace a policy of external growth. Interprovincial trade barriers, provincial jurisdiction over the retail sale and distribution of alcoholic beverages, local sensitivities, as well as a permissive policy towards takeovers all combined to make the acquisition of small and medium-sized firms the main route towards market consolidation in Canada. In order to become truly national concerns, the big three had to have a physical presence in each of the regions. The end result was that the Canadian brewing industry took on a multi-plant form during the period under consideration.

These postwar acquisitions completely changed the market structure of the Canadian brewing industry so that competition took the form of advertising and sales promotion. At a time when the price of beer was fixed by the various liquor control boards, advertising became essential to a brewer's survival. The success of the big three was due to their ability to produce a small number of standard flagship brands that appealed to a large segment of the beer-drinking population, and to market them with sophisticated and expensive advertising campaigns. The result was the extinction of local styles of beer and the homogenization of the survivors into similar-tasting lagers and ales. The comparative advantage of the big three was thus directly related to the size of their promotional expenditures and their use of the national media, as well as their ability to control the channels of distribution.

Notes

1 Dominion Brewers' Association, *Facts on the Brewing Industry in Canada* (Montreal: Federated Press, 1948), 32, 38.

2 The Northern Ontario market was protected by a Wartime Prices and Trade Board order that prohibited brewers south of the forty-sixth parallel from selling their products in the north. See Ontario, Department of Provincial Secretary and Citizenship, *Report of the Inquiry into the Brewing Industry of Northern Ontario* (Toronto: The Carswell Company, 1972), 2–3. For more on the Northern Ontario beer market see, Daryl White. "Draught, Development, and Discourse: The Northern Ontario Draught Beer Monopoly, 1972–92," *Journal of Canadian Studies/Revue d'études canadiennes* 47, no. 2 (2013): 8.

3 S.R.H. Jones, "The New Zealand Brewing Industry, 1840–1995," in *The Dynamics of the International Brewing Industry since 1800*, ed. R.G. Wilson and T.R. Gourvish (London: Routledge, 1998), 247–65; David T. Merrett, "Stability and Change in the Australian Brewing Industry, 1930–94," in Wilson and Gourvish, ibid., 229–48; Tony Millns, "The British Brewing Industry, 1945–95," in Wilson and Gourvish, ibid., 142–59; T.R. Gourvish, "Economics of Brewing, Theory and Practice: Concentration and Technological Change in the USA, UK and West Germany since 1945," *Business and Economic History* 23, 1 (Fall 1994): 253–61.

4 Gourvish, "Economics of Brewing," 256.

5 I. Horowitz and A.R. Horowitz, "Firms in a Declining Market: The Brewing Case," *Journal of Industrial Economics* 13, 2 (1965): 129–53; M.T. Brouwer, "The European Beer industry; Concentration and Competition," in *The Structure of European Industry*, ed. H.W. de Jong (The Hague, Boston, London: Martinus Nikhoff, 1981): 39–57; F.M. Scherer, "The Determinants of Industrial Plant Sizes in Six Nations," *Review of Economics and Statistics* 55, 2 (May 1973): 135–45; Leonard Weiss, "Optimal Plant

Size and the Extent of the Sub-optimal Capacity," in *Essays in Industrial Organization in Honor of Joe S. Bain,* ed. Robert T. Masson and P.D. Qualls (Cambridge, MA: Ballinger Publishing Company, 1976), 126–34.

6   Peter Van Der Hallen, "Concentration in the Belgian Brewing Industry and the Breakthrough of Lager in the Interwar Years" (discussion paper, Katholieke Universiteit Leuven, 2007).

7   A.M. McGahan, "The Emergence of the National Brewing Oligopoly: Competition in the American Market, 1933–1958," *Business History Review* 65, 2 (Summer 1991): 229–84; D.F. Greer, "The Causes of Concentration in the U.S. Brewing Industry," *Quarterly Review of Economics and Business* 21, 4 (Winter 1981): 100; J. Sutton, *Sunk Costs and Market Structure: Price Competition, Advertising and the Evolution of Concentration* (Cambridge, MA: MIT Press, 1991), 287–95; Victor J. Tremblay and Carol Horton Tremblay, *The U.S. Brewing Industry: Data and Economic Analysis* (Cambridge, MA: MIT Press, 2005), 41–66.

8   Lisa M. George, "The Growth of Television and the Decline of Local Beer," in *The Economics of Beer,* ed. Johna Swinnen (Oxford: Oxford University Press, 2011), 213–27.

9   Silviano Esteve-Pérez, "Consolidation by Merger: the U.K. Beer Market," *Small Business Economics* 39, 1 (July 2012): 207–29. For a different perspective, see Millns, "The British Brewing Industry," 151–54.

10 S.R.H. Jones, "The New Zealand Brewing Industry," 257–60; Merrett, "Stability and Change," 237–43.

11 Gourvish, "Economics of Brewing," 260; Per Boje and Hans Christian Johansen, "The Danish Brewing Industry after 1880: Entrepreneurs, Market Structure and Technology," in Wilson and Gourvish, *Dynamics,* 59–74.

12 Millns, "The British Brewing Industry," 154.

13 Ibid.

14 Frank Roseman, *The Canadian Brewing Industry: The Effect of Mergers and Provincial Regulation on Economic Conduct and Performance* (PhD dissertation, Northwestern University, 1968), 159.

15 Brewers' Association of Canada, *Brewing in Canada* (Ottawa: Ronalds–Federated Limited, 1965), 118–19.

16 Albert Shea, *Vision in Action: The Story of Canadian Breweries Limited from 1930 to 1955* (Toronto: Canadian Breweries Ltd., 1955), 57–64.

17 Sneath, *Brewed in Canada: The Untold Story of Canada's 350-Year-Old Brewing Industry* (Toronto: Dundurn Group, 2001), 169.

18 "Finance at Large," *Globe and Mail,* November 17, 1953, 22.

19 Thomas C. Cochran, *The Pabst Brewing Company: History of an American Business* (1948; repr., Westport, CT: Greenwood Press, 1975), 72–78; McGahan, "Emergence of the National Brewing Oligopoly," 237–43.

20 E.P. Taylor, October 26, 1942, quoted in Sneath, *Brewed in Canada,* 169.

21 Martin Stack, "Local and Regional Breweries in America's Brewing Industry, 1865 to 1920," *Business History Review* 74, 3 (Autumn 2000): 435–63.

22 E.P. Taylor, October 26, 1942, quoted in Sneath, *Brewed in Canada,* 169.

23 Roseman, *The Canadian Brewing Industry,* 229.

24 Ibid., 230.

25 Ibid.

26 E.P. Taylor, quoted in Albert Tucker, "Labatt's: A History – From Immigrant Family to Canadian Corporation" (unpublished manuscript in the author's possession), 309.

27 See Michael Bliss, "Another Anti-Trust Tradition: Canadian Anti-Combines Policy, 1889–1910," *Business History Review* 47, 2 (Summer 1973): 180.

28 "No Crime to be Big," *Globe and Mail,* February 10, 1960, 6.

29 John Labatt Ltd., Board of Directors, Minutes, June 7, 1945, 149. Labatt Collection, vol. 8, 149.

30 J.C.H. Jones, *Competition in the Canadian Brewing Industry* (PhD dissertation, Queen's University, 1966), 72.

31 Roseman, *The Canadian Brewing Industry,* 227.

32 Jake Moore, "Speech to the Staff," May 10, 1967, Labatt Collection, Box A08-053-1126, File "Management Philosophy."

33 John Labatt Ltd., Board of Directors Minutes, March 5, 1956, Labatt Collection, vol. 9, 15.

34 Jake Moore, "Know Your Company," October 29, 1962, Labatt Collection, Box A08-053-1126, File "Management Philosophy," 5.

35 For the brewers' influence on provincial liquor authorities, see J.C.H. Jones, "Mergers and Competition: The Brewing Case," *Canadian Journal of Economics and Political Science* 33, 4 (November 1967): 557–59. For a discussion of "regulatory capture," see George Stigler, "The Theory of Economic Regulation," *Bell Journal of Economics and Management Science* 2 (Spring 1971): 3–21.

36 T. da Silva Lopes, *Global Brands: The Evolution of Multinationals in Alcoholic Beverages* (Cambridge: Cambridge University Press, 2007), 1–66, 129–79.

37 P. Barwise and T. Robertson, "Brand Portfolios," *European Management Journal* 10, 1 (1992): 277–85.

38 P.J. Henderson, "Labatt's Eight Beer Marketing Laws," February 5, 1963, Labatt Collection, Box A08-053-112.

39 Ibid.

40 "An Awareness and Attitude Study of Alberta Breweries and Brands," January/February 1964, 52, Labatt Collection, Box A08-05-594.

41 John Compton, "Quality Control," February 19, 1963, 10, Labatt Collection, Box LATXT0039.

42 Ibid., 9.

43 "An Awareness and Attitude Study of Alberta Breweries and Brands," 42.

44 F. Appleton, *Brewing Revolution: Pioneering the Craft Beer Movement* (Madeira Park, BC: Harbour Publishing, 2016), 8–10.

45 Matthew J. Bellamy, "The Making of Labatt 'Blue': The Quest for a National Lager Brand, 1959–1971," *Business History* 62, 1 (2017): 123–50, DOI: 10.1080/00076791.2017.1310195.

46 Ibid.

47 Cheryl Krasnick Warsh and Greg Marquis, "Gender, Spirits and Beer: Representing Female and Male Bodies in Canadian Alcohol Ads, 1930s–1970s," in *Contesting Bodies and Nation in Canadian History*, ed. Patrizia Gentile and Jane Nicholas (Toronto: University of Toronto Press, 2013), 204–8; Craig Heron, *Booze: A Distilled History* (Toronto: Between the Lines Press, 2003), 331–32.

48 J.C.H. Jones, *Competition in the Canadian Brewing Industry*, 146–55; Heron, *Booze*, 317–18.

49 "BBG Permits Beer and Wine Ads to Run to Longer, Mention Brands," *Globe and Mail*, September 11, 1963, 1.

50 J.C.H. Jones, *Competition in the Canadian Brewing Industry*, 148.

51 Warsh and Marquis, "Gender, Spirits and Beer," 203–25.

52 Jake Moore, "The Outlook for the Brewing Industry," Labatt Collection, Box A08-053-1077, file "Histories of John Labatt Limited."

53 J.C.H. Jones, *Competition in the Canadian Brewing Industry*, 142.

54 Ibid., 148 and 150.

55 "Remarks on Main Areas of Marketing Opportunity," October 17, 1962, Labatt Collection, Box A08-53-1022, file "Directors' Meetings."

56 Brewers' Association of Canada, *Brewing in Canada*, 97.

57 Ibid., 25.

58 J.C.H. Jones, *Competition in the Canadian Brewing Industry*, 208.

59 *Financial Post*, October 10, 1964, 33.

60 *R v Canadian Breweries Ltd*, [1960] OR 601, 5004.

61 Joseph A. Schumpeter, *Capitalism, Socialism and Democracy* (New York: Harper and Brothers, 1942), 83.

Contributors

Cynthia Belaskie is a doctoral candidate at York University and managing director of the Canadian Housing Evidence Collaborative at McMaster University. Her doctoral research looks at British women and their relationships with alcohol in the nineteenth century.

Matthew J. Bellamy is an associate professor of history at Carleton University. He specializes in Canadian business, and political and cultural history. He is the author of *Profiting the Crown: Canada's Polymer Corporation, 1942–1990* and *Brewed in the North: A History of Labatt*. He contends that no industry is more revealing about culture, history, and attitudes than brewing.

Chris Elcock is an independent historian of LSD and psychedelics. In 2013 he received the American Culture Association's William M. Jones Award for Outstanding Graduate Student Paper in American Culture for his work on the American psychedelic movement. He is currently finishing a monograph on the history of drugs in New York City and coediting a book on the international history of psychedelics.

Eric Fillion is a Buchanan Postdoctoral Fellow in the Department of History at Queen's University. His research explores the social and symbolic importance of music, within countercultures and in Canadian international relations. He is the founder of the Tenzier archival record label and the author of *JAZZ LIBRE et la révolution québécoise: musique-action, 1967–1975*.

Sarah E. Hamill is an assistant professor at the School of Law, Trinity College Dublin. Her main areas of research are property law and theory, and legal history. Her work has appeared in *Social & Legal Studies,* the *Law and History Review,* and the *Canadian Journal of Law and Society.*

Renée Lafferty-Salhany is an associate professor of history at Brock University. Her first book, *The Guardianship of Best Interests: Institutional Care for the Children of the Poor in Halifax, 1850–1960,* received the Canadian Historical Association's Clio prize for Atlantic Canada. Her research on drink during the War of 1812 era has led her deep into examining the fluids that went into, and came out of, soldiers' bodies. It's not gross at all.

Dan Malleck is a medical historian specializing in drug and alcohol policy, a professor in health sciences at Brock University, and the director of Brock's Centre for Canadian Studies. He is author of three monographs on drug and alcohol history in Canada. His book *Try to Control Yourself: The Regulation of Public Drinking in Post-Prohibition Ontario 1927–1944* received the Canadian Historical Association's Clio prize for Ontario. He is also the editor of a four-volume primary source collection *Drugs, Alcohol, and Addiction in the Long Nineteenth Century* published by Routledge right before the pandemic began. He doesn't think there is a causative connection between that book and pandemic drinking, but you never know.

Greg Marquis is a member of the Department of History and Politics at UNB Saint John where he teaches courses in Canadian and criminal justice history. His research interests include the history of crime and policing, alcohol and drugs, and popular culture.

Jonathan Reinarz is a professor of the history of medicine at the University of Birmingham. His current research focuses primarily on the history of hospitals, medical education, and accidents. He has published on apprenticeship, labour relations, advertising, and the role of brewers' chemists in the brewing industry. He continues to work on the subject of brewing and alcohol history and has been a member of the Editorial Board of Brewing History since 2006.

Cheryl Krasnick Warsh is a professor of history at Vancouver Island University. Dr. Warsh has published seven books on the history of asylums, women's health, children's health, consumerism, and substance use and abuse. Her biography of Dr. Frances Kelsey will be published by Oxford University Press in 2022. Her upcoming projects include biographical studies of abortion provider Dr. Garson Romalis and children's literature critic Josette Frank. Working at home during the COVID-19 pandemic has honed her skills of typing one-handed while patting an insistent Irish terrier. Dr. Warsh was elected a fellow of the Royal Society of Canada in 2017.

Index

Note: "(t)" after a page number indicates a table

Midgely, Clare, 66
military, 134, 135–36, 139, 145–46, 147
milk, 40, 138, 220, 230–31
Miller, Ralph, 119
Millns, Tony, 272
Mills, Sean, 97n8
mint juleps, 46
Misuse of Drugs Act (England), 112
Mitchell, John, 230
MK-Ultra project, 194
moderation, 6
Moderation League of Alberta, 249–50
Moderationists, 249–50
modernity, 3
Molson, 270, 279, 282, 284, 286, 287
monopolies, 188n8
Monterey International Pop Music
   Festival, 82
Montreal: attitudes toward vagrant
   women, 36; female drinking in,
   42–43; political activism in, 97n8;
   prostitution in, 41, 44; substance
   abuse at high schools, 92–93; youth
   alcohol consumption, 33. *See also*
   Manseau
Moore, Jake, 281
morality, 144
Morel, Bénédict Augustin, 37
morphine, 40, 192
Morrison, J.E., 183
Morrison, Jim, 117, 124
mothers, 34, 38, 52, 54
movie theatres, 42
Mowat, Oliver, 170
Munro, John, 119, 123, 124
music, 124
music festivals, 82, 86. *See also*
   Woodstock Pop Festival

Nanjing (Nanking), 261
Narcotic Control Act (1961), 81

Narcotic Control Act to the Food and
   Drugs Act, 90–91, 93
narcotics, 39
National Breweries, 270, 273, 275, 276
National Commission on Marihuana
   and Drug Abuse, 123, 128n58
National Council on Alcoholism (US), 47
national movements, 65
nationalism, 136
natural evil, 144
natural history, 133–34
Naturalism, Inc. (religious institution),
   195, 207–8, 209
Netherlands, 192, 204
New Brunswick, 283
New York City, 200, 206
New York State, 138, 192, 204
Newfoundland Brewery Limited, 282
niacinamide, 197
Nicholson and Son, 229
nicotine, 110
Niessen, Olwen, 64
Nilsson, Harry, 123
Nixon, Richard, 108, 114, 122, 123, 204
Norman, Philip, 108, 111, 112
Norris, E.G., 257, 260
Norris, Jill, 63
Nova Scotia, 283

Office de la prévention et du traitement
   de l'alcoolisme et des autres toxicom-
   anies (OPTAT), 78–79, 84, 92–96, 97n5
oil development, 209, 276
O'Keefe, 273
Oland, Victor, 287
Oland and Son, 287, 289, 290
olanzapine, 210
Old Style Pilsener, 285
Old Winnipeg Brewery, 280
Ono, Yoko, 106, 109, 110, 111, 112,
   114–15, 118–22, 127n41